LORD READING

The Life of Rufus Isaacs,
First Marquess of Reading

LORD READING AS LORD CHIEF JUSTICE IN 1914

From the portrait by Oswald Birley in the possession of the Corporation of Reading

H. Montgomery Hyde

LORD READING

The Life of Rufus Isaacs,
First Marquess of Reading

FARRAR, STRAUS AND GIROUX
NEW YORK

Library of Congress Catalog Card 68–11961

First American Edition

Printed in Great Britain

Contents

Contents

Illustrations

Acknowledgments

By gracious permission of Her Majesty the Queen I have been allowed to use certain correspondence and other papers in the Royal Archives relating to Lord Reading. I am grateful to Mr Robert Mackworth-Young, Librarian at Windsor Castle, for his help in making this possible.

Crown-copyright material in the India Office Library transcribed in this book appears by permission of the Secretary of State for Commonwealth Relations.

I wish to express my thanks to the following for permission to quote from material in which they control the copyright: the late Sir Maurice Bonham Carter (Asquith Papers), the Beaverbrook Foundation (Lloyd George Papers), the Earl of Birkenhead (Birkenhead Letters), the Hon. Godfrey Samuel (Samuel Papers), and the Trustees of the Houghton Library of Harvard University (W. H. Page Papers) and the Yale University Library (House Papers and Wiseman Papers).

My thanks are due to others who have assisted me in various ways, especially in putting manuscript material at my disposal and allowing quotations from published works. In particular, I would mention Colonel G. T. Baines, Miss Rosemary Brooks, Cassell & Co. Ltd, Mr D. H. Elletson, Miss Daphne Gifford, Victor Gollancz Ltd, Sir Geoffrey Harmsworth, George G. Harrap & Co. Ltd, William Heinemann Ltd, Professor R. F. V. Heuston, the Rt. Hon. Cledwyn Hughes, M.P., Hutchinson & Co. (Publishers) Ltd, Mr Robert Jackson, Sir Shane Leslie, Methuen & Co. Ltd, John Murray, (Publishers) Ltd Nicholson & Watson Ltd, the Oxford University Press, the Secretary of the Pilgrims, the Public Trustee, the Marquess of Reading, Eva Marchioness of Reading, Stella Marchioness of Reading, Viscount Rothermere, the Secretary of the Stock Exchange, Mr A. J. P. Taylor, Sir Derek Walker-Smith, M.P., Mrs Eirene White, M.P., Sir Arthur Willert, and the staffs of the Bodleian Library, the British Museum, the Houghton Library of Harvard

Acknowledgments

University, the House of Lords Record Office, the India Office Library, the London Library, the Public Record Office, and the Yale University Library.

I am likewise indebted to those who have permitted the reproduction of illustrations, particulars of which are shown in the text.

H.M.H.

Lamb House,
Rye.
July, 1967.

1

Junior Barrister

1

Marquess of Reading, Earl of Reading, Viscount Erleigh, Viscount Reading, Baron Reading, Privy Councillor, Knight Grand Cross of the Bath, Knight Grand Commander of the Star of India, Knight Grand Commander of the Indian Empire, Knight Grand Cross of the Royal Victorian Order, Grand Cordon of the Order of Leopold of Belgium, Constable of Dover Castle and Lord Warden of the Cinque Ports, Captain of Deal Castle, Secretary of State for Foreign Affairs, Viceroy and Governor-General of India, High Commissioner and Special Ambassador to the United States of America, Lord Chief Justice of England, Attorney-General, Solicitor-General, Member of Parliament, Bencher of the Middle Temple, Queen's Counsel . . .

Such were the principal titles and orders and offices to which Rufus Daniel Isaacs, former City clerk, ship's boy and stockjobber on the Stock Exchange who got 'hammered', the first Jew to become successively Attorney-General, Lord Chief Justice, Ambassador, Viceroy, and Foreign Secretary in Britain, and the first commoner to rise to the rank of Marquess since the Duke of Wellington, attained in seventy-four years of an adventurous and crowded life. At the time of his failure on the Stock Exchange his business debts amounted to £8,000; when he died half a century afterwards, having long since paid all his creditors in full, he was worth more than a quarter of a million pounds. Mrs Asquith, the wife of the Liberal Prime Minister, described him as the most ambitious man she had ever known. Yet his son and confidant, the second Lord Reading, who was probably closer to him than anyone else at the height of his career, did not believe that, with the possible exception of the Attorney-Generalship, he deliberately set out to attain any one of the great offices which he held. 'Indeed, their very diversity almost excluded design.'

It is worth while looking briefly at the family and social background

1

of the central figure in this remarkable and romantic tale of material success. Contrary to some popular belief, the family was by no means poor. Rufus's father Joseph Isaacs and his uncle Harry, later chosen Lord Mayor of London, ran a prosperous fruit import and ship-broking business in Spitalfields, M. Isaacs & Sons Ltd, which they had inherited from their father Michael Isaacs, who had founded it soon after the end of the Napoleonic Wars. This Michael was the son of Samuel Isaacs who was also in the fruit business, although in a more modest way than his two sons, apparently being content with a stall in the Aldgate fruit market in Duke's Place.

Samuel Isaacs was born when George II was still on the throne of England. He lived to see his great-grandson Rufus, who could just remember him by sight, since Rufus was five years old when this astonishing patriarch died at the age of one hundred and six.

To go back one more generation. Samuel's father, also called Michael, was the first of the family to settle in England. It is very probable that his forebears originated in Spain, whence like other Jews they were driven out by the Inquisition to seek refuge in the Low Countries, eventually crossing the North Sea to East Anglia to take advantage of the policy of toleration towards the Jews initiated by Oliver Cromwell and continued after the Restoration by Charles II and his successors. The first Michael Isaacs established himself in the Essex town of Chelmsford. It was in the latter part of the eighteenth century that his centenarian son Samuel moved to London.

Samuel's son Michael, the founder of the family fruit business, married a Spanish lady of the same faith named Sarah Mendoza, whose father Aaron Mendoza came from Madrid. Aaron's better known younger brother Daniel Mendoza was the celebrated boxer and prize-fighter, whose neatness and dexterity when pitted against strength and brute-force had revolutionized the 'noble art' by the turn of the century. Daniel Mendoza was a pioneer, and his amazing feats of pugilism -- he was virtually a world champion -- besides making him something of a national hero immensely raised the prestige of the Jews with the British public, showing as they did how Jews could fight and that it was no longer safe to insult a Jew unless he were an old man and alone. Although the two never met, since the boxer died in 1836, having retired from the ring to become the land-lord of a public house in Whitechapel, Rufus Isaacs grew up with a profound respect for his great-uncle, whose classic *Art of Boxing*, first published in 1789, gave Rufus many useful hints as a successful amateur.

Michael Isaacs and his wife began their married life in old Samuel's house at 19 Mitre Street, Aldgate, where their two sons were born, Henry, the future Lord Mayor of London, in 1830, and Joseph, Rufus's father, in 1832. Both brothers survived into the present century.

Although Jews had been permitted to settle freely in England by Cromwell, they were long debarred from holding public office. The process of emancipation did not begin until the year of Henry Isaacs's birth and was not completed until thirty years later when orthodox Jews were admitted to full parliamentary and political rights. The first Jewish Q.C., Francis Goldsmid, was appointed in 1858, but the first Jewish judge, Sir George Jessel, did not take his place on the Bench until 1873, and the first Jewish peer, Lord Rothschild, was not created until 1886. Henry Isaacs was quick to take advantage of the removal of Jewish disabilities, becoming a member of the Corporation of London in 1882 and in due course Alderman and Sheriff. He was knighted in 1887, the year of his shrievalty, which was also the year of Queen Victoria's Golden Jubilee. Two years later he was elected Lord Mayor of London.

Sir Henry Isaacs took a particular interest in public works, and the building of Tower Bridge is said to have owed much to his persistent initiative. The misfortune of having two daughters born deaf and dumb made him deeply interested in methods of teaching those thus afflicted and he became a recognized authority on the pure oral system of teaching deaf-mutes by means of lip-reading. He recorded his experiences in a little book which he wrote under the title *Sounds versus Signs*. He was also a keen freemason, eventually becoming Grand Warden of Grand Lodge, to which office he was appointed by the Prince of Wales, afterwards King Edward VII.

It was as a small boy at a dancing class that Joseph, the younger of the two Isaacs brothers, first met his future wife Sarah Davis. Sarah was the eldest of a family of thirteen children. She was twenty years of age when she married Joseph Isaacs, who was twenty-three, in 1855.

After their marriage, Joseph and Sarah Isaacs lived not far from Mitre Street in a house at 3 Bury Street, St Mary Axe, then a predominantly Jewish quarter, and it was there that their fourth child and second son Rufus Daniel Isaacs was born on October 10,

1860. He was called Rufus after the eldest of his mother's six brothers and Daniel after his grandfather Davis. His name was to prove an invaluable asset, for 'Rufus Isaacs' formed a distinctive nomenclature which was not easily forgotten.

2

As more children followed Rufus – there were nine altogether in the family – a larger house was needed, and soon after Rufus's birth his parents moved the household to Finsbury Square. Their new home was also in the City of London, since merchants still liked to live near if not directly above 'the shop', although the City was gradually becoming less residential with the easy access to the suburbs provided by the railway and the omnibus. A few years later, the family moved again, this time right away from the City and the orthodox Jewish community in which they had previously lived. This second migration, which took place largely at the instance of Rufus's mother, appears to have been prompted by the desire to escape from the City, which still had something of an air of the ghetto about it, to a less inhibited neighbourhood, where the orthodox and the less orthodox members of the Jewish faith could mix more readily with non-Jews, now that Jews were no longer subject to any civil disabilities. The household was accordingly established in Hampstead – at 21 Belsize Park – which was to remain the Isaacs family home for the next quarter of a century.

Parental discipline was far from being harsh, and Rufus and his brothers and sisters seem to have had a very happy and united home life, although Rufus in particular was always getting up to every kind of mischief. Joseph Isaacs was a kindly and indulgent father, though occasionally given to violent explosions of wrath on account of some prank on the part of his boys. He would pursue the delinquents round the garden, cracking a carriage whip as he did so, until their mother would intercede. '*Assez*, Joe,' she would say, for she prided herself on a fluent knowledge of the French language. Although the domestic régime could hardly be called severe, Joseph Isaacs nevertheless firmly believed in the Biblical precept about spoiling the child through sparing the rod, and he did not spare it; but the corporal punishment which he frequently administered to his erring offspring seems to have been fairly mild by comparison with the floggings which were the custom in many Victorian families and schools.

Unlike Joseph Isaacs, with his heavy black moustache and side-whiskers, which gave him an unmistakable Hebraic appearance, his wife, who had brown hair, grey eyes and a short straight nose, the latter feature inherited from her father, did not look much like a Jewess. She was supposed to be delicate and would regularly lie in bed all morning, running her establishment most efficiently from this retreat. However, the legend of her delicate health, which she was given to putting about herself, was somewhat belied by the fact that she bore her husband nine children and lived to the age of eighty-eight. According to her grandson, she was an undemonstrative woman who viewed her children with complete detachment, although she had a real and deep affection for them. 'She had no intellectual interests, read great quantities of worthless novels, adored a game of whist or nap, took no exercise and had no women friends, holding that women were not to be trusted and that it was a mistake to indulge in intimacy with such unstable creatures.'[1] With these views it is hardly surprising that she was more interested in her sons than her daughters. If she had a favourite among the boys, it was undoubtedly Rufus.

All except one of her brood, a son named Albert who died as the result of an accident at school, lived to maturity, and at least two besides Rufus achieved some distinction in their lives. One was the daughter Esther, who studied art, became a reputable painter, and married Alfred Sutro, the well-known playwright and translator of Maurice Maeterlinck. The other distinguished member of the family was the fourth son, Godfrey, who after a long spell in the family business eventually left it to become Managing Director of Guglielmo Marconi's Wireless Telegraph Co., Ltd, at the invitation of the celebrated Italian inventor. Godfrey Isaacs will figure later in these pages.

Rufus's scholastic education was somewhat desultory. Children were sent to boarding-schools early in those days, and at the tender age of four Rufus, together with his elder brother Harry, who was a year older, found himself packed off to a kindergarten kept by a Polish Jew named Barcynsky in Gravesend. After a year there the two boys were removed, as their mother was apparently dissatisfied with their progress in foreign languages, in which she was anxious that they should shine. Accordingly they were transferred to another boarding establishment, this time in Brussels, where the lessons under

[1] Lord Reading: *Rufus Isaacs* (1942), Vol. I, p. 12.

the dispensation of a certain Monsieur Kahn were conducted in French. Here Rufus gave signs of being something of an infant prodigy, if the following story can be believed. The whole school, which consisted of boys from the ages of six to eighteen, used to compete for a prize for the pupil who could recite by heart two pages of French prose with the greatest degree of accuracy, each boy being allowed ten minutes in which to memorize the text. It was just the kind of exercise which appealed to Rufus, who was already gifted with a remarkable visual memory. At all events he was the nearest to word perfect, and so to the intense surprise of masters and pupils alike he was awarded the prize, although he was the youngest boy in the school. He liked to repeat the story of this triumph in later life, when 'he would freely admit' as his son put it, that 'no subsequent success had been as easy or as sweet'.

The two Isaacs boys were such a trial to the Monsieur Kahn that the long-suffering master eventually wrote to their father saying that they were incorrigible together and that their father must remove one of them. Solitary confinement on a diet of bread and water was quite unavailing. On one occasion, when both boys were undergoing this punishment they threw all the furniture in the room out of the window into the courtyard below, so that when the master came to release them, he 'found them sitting cheerfully in an excellent imitation of a prison cell'.

In the event it was the elder boy who had to go, and Rufus was able to settle down to his lessons undistracted by the more mischievous Harry. During the next two years he spent in Brussels he picked up a good smattering of French without much effort. At the end of this period he returned home and was sent as a boarder to an Anglo-Jewish private school in Northwick Terrace, Regent's Park, which was under the charge of a Mr A. P. Mendes, and where Harry was already a pupil. Rufus was now rising nine, and becoming increasingly precocious. For instance, we learn that Mr Mendes had a daughter about the same age as Rufus, and it was soon apparent that he was violently attracted by her, although his passion was confined to the passing of notes and sweets in the classes at which she was also a pupil. Here too he began to learn Hebrew, and also German. No mention is made of Latin or Greek in the school curriculum, the classical subjects so popular in Christian schools at this time.

By all accounts Rufus was an engaging but extremely idle pupil. 'Isaacs secundus, you will go to the devil!' was the frequently uttered prophecy of his teachers. According to a schoolboy contemporary, who recalled some of his activities at the Mendes academy many years later, 'lessons he left unlearnt, class work he shirked, and mischief was his only devotion. Nor was he mischievous only in himself – he delighted in inspiring others in his "wicked ways" ... demoniacal young mischievous boy with sparkling eyes who was ever in disgrace or being caned, and yet withal was ever merry and deliciously humorous.' The same witness remembered one occasion when he was 'specially rebellious' and consequently 'brought down for corporal punishment', and Mr Mendes sat astride the culprit on a bench, all the while vigorously belabouring his posterior with the cane. 'Isaacs screamed and twisted about – well, to the complete satisfaction of the master. But those who could see the victim's face, which the headmaster could not, would have seen that young Isaacs was exercising his lungs only because he knew well that it was the shortest way of shortening the punishment. We who were watching the whole proceeding knew the contrary, for his screams notwithstanding, Isaacs was laughing all the time.'[1]

His formal education was completed at University College School, then situated in Gower Street, London, which he entered in September, 1873, and left in the following July, after a single academic year. The headmaster was the noted Latin scholar and mathematician Professor T. H. Key, a Fellow of the Royal Society and 'a teacher beloved by his pupils' who had ruled the school for the past forty years with humanity and understanding and had recently raised its numbers to six hundred, being one of the first English headmasters to include natural science in the ordinary school curriculum. He was also a pronounced Liberal in politics and he made no secret of his views in school. It is possible that Rufus Isaacs was influenced by them as a pupil. It is certain that in the comparatively short time he spent there, the boy greatly impressed Professor Key with his ability, since the headmaster begged the boy's father to allow him to stay on for three or four more years and then go to the University, after which he recommended that Rufus should read for the Bar.

But Joseph Isaacs was determined that Rufus should join his elder brother in the family business. The extension of his education to include a University degree seemed merely a postponement of the boy's earning power, and as for the Bar it was a precarious profession with a further period of waiting for rewards which were most

[1] Cited by Syed Sirdar Ali Khan in *The Earl of Reading* (1924), p. 3.

uncertain. Hence the decision that Rufus must become a fruit merchant. But first his father felt that he had better brush up his German,
and for this purpose he was dispatched for six months to stay
with a family in Hamburg with which the father had business
connections.

Early in 1875, fourteen-year-old Rufus Isaacs returned to London
and began work as an apprentice in the offices of his father's firm,
M. Isaacs & Sons, Ltd, fruit merchants and ship-brokers, then
established in Moscow House, Eastcheap. He was slightly consoled
by the fact that, since the firm now acted as shipping agents, there
might be opportunities for further foreign travel.

3

The youthful apprentice was destined to be disappointed. He was
soon intensely bored by the sight of his office stool, and although he
acquired some knowledge of the fruit business as well as the details
of general commercial practice, he found the routine of City life
thoroughly uncongenial. Furthermore, the chance of foreign travel
did not materialize, and the longer he stayed in his father's office
the more he longed to get away. Eventually his father came to the
conclusion that the best way of curing his second son's restlessness
was to let him have a spell of sailing before the mast. He accordingly
proposed that Rufus should join a vessel for whose owners his firm
acted as agents. The ship, the *Blair Athole*, was bound with a general
cargo for Rio de Janeiro. Rufus welcomed the suggestion and immediately went off to buy a sea chest. He was told that there was no
time to be lost, since the *Blair Athole* had already sailed from the
Port of London and would put in at Cardiff, where it was quickly
arranged that he should board her.

Years afterwards, when he had become rich and successful, the
story got about that Rufus Isaacs had run away from home as a
young man and gone to sea of his own choice. This was not true.
The idea of going to sea originated with his father; indeed Joseph
Isaacs accompanied his son to Cardiff and personally handed him
over to the charge of the ship's Master. Another fictitious tale which
gained credence was that young Rufus was engaged as a cabin boy.
This was a relatively luxurious form of employment compared with
that which in fact he undertook, namely ship's boy, the most lowly

of deck-hands, who was customarily given the dirtiest and most unpleasant of tasks to perform.

The *Blair Athole* was an iron-built, full-rigged vessel of some 1,777 gross tons, which had recently been launched in Glasgow and which was now under the command of Captain Alexander Taylor, an expert sailor but an extremely tough Scot from Stirling. The ship's complement consisted of a medley of nationalities. Besides the Master and four officers who were British, the crew included two Germans, two Swedes, two Portuguese, a Frenchman, an Italian, an Austrian and a Brazilian. By the time the *Blair Athole* reached Cardiff, two of the crew had had enough of her and they promptly deserted. More were to do so in the course of the voyage, since the boatswain was a bully who made liberal use of a rope's end or belaying pin to enforce his orders and was cordially detested by the other crew members.

The original proposal put forward by the *Blair Athole*'s Master and accepted by Joseph Isaacs was that his son should join as an apprentice. But when the formal agreement of apprenticeship was put before Rufus and he discovered that it would bind him to serve for two years, he flatly refused to sign the document on the ground that the prospective apprentice might well wish to be free from any such bond of service before the expiry of the two-year period. It was in vain for the Master to point out that there were already two other apprentices on board and they were both quite happy and well satisfied with the arrangement. His remarks were reinforced by Joseph Isaacs, who pointed out with obvious irritation that he had no intention of his journey to Cardiff being wasted and that Rufus must comply without further ado, as he did not want to have him at home any longer. At length, after some angry words had been exchanged, Rufus agreed to a compromise. He was quite ready to go to sea, he said, but he would not do so as an apprentice. Instead he would sign on as a member of the crew. This meant that he would be bound by the ship's articles which provided for the crew to be paid off on the vessel completing the voyage and returning to her home port. This he guessed would be well within two years of signing on. (In fact it turned out to be slightly less than a year.) Eventually the two others assented, and Rufus Isaacs signed the articles and agreed to serve as ship's boy at a wage of ten shillings a month. The date on which he made this dramatic decision was October 10, 1876, his sixteenth birthday.

It took the *Blair Athole* more than seven weeks under sail to make the coast of Brazil. Soon after leaving Cardiff she ran into bad weather, with the result that the ship's boy had to contend with violent sea-sickness in addition to his other difficulties, for he was still very much of a landlubber. Certainly if he had signed as an apprentice, his lot would have been considerably easier. Perhaps the most distasteful duty which he had to perform was cleaning out the pig sty, an operation which bearing in mind the Jewish ban on the eating of pork, he was to describe in an after-dinner speech many years later as 'one which in view of my origin I might well have been spared!'

If the *Blair Athole*'s Master was not exactly a Captain Bligh, he was a fairly strict disciplinarian, and he expected his orders to be understood and obeyed with the utmost speed. Almost at the outset of the voyage the ship's boy had a lucky escape from incurring his wrath. When a storm blew up, sail had to be taken in quickly and the crew were soon busily occupied in this duty. Happening to see the ship's boy unoccupied, Captain Taylor pointed aft and roared at him: 'Boy, up there and make fast that mizzen crojick clew-garnet!'

Rufus, who had never been in a sailing ship before, did not have the slightest idea of what this order meant, namely to secure the rope by which the clew or lower corner of the lower square sail on the aftermost of the *Blair Athole*'s masts was hauled up. However he jumped to it and by a stroke of luck the first loose end of rope which he could see and which he seized proved to be the right one. If his feat earned him no praise from the Captain, at least it saved him from a tongue-lashing or worse.

According to Board of Trade regulations, each member of the crew was entitled to a daily ration of one pound of bread, $1\frac{1}{2}$ lb of beef or $1\frac{1}{4}$ lb of pork, half a pound of flour or one eighth of a pint of peas, one eighth of an ounce of tea, half an ounce of coffee, two ounces of sugar and three quarts of water. But there was no means of enforcing these regulations at sea, and the actual fare was both less in quantity and poor in quality. Salt pork and biscuits formed the staple diet in practice. There were so many weevils in the biscuits that at last the crew held an indignation meeting among themselves and decided to send a representative to the Master to complain. Their choice fell on the ship's boy either as the junior member of the crew who could not disobey the others or else because of his obviously superior education, and so with some trepidation Rufus made his way aft to the Master's quarters.

It was Rufus's first essay in advocacy, and, as he later liked to recall, it proved unexpectedly effective. After he had heard what the lad had to say, Captain Taylor paused for a moment's reflection and then informed him that in future the biscuits should be baked.

Rufus returned to his comrades in the fo'c'sle feeling somehow that his mission had been a failure. To his surprise the other crew members shook him by the hand and warmly congratulated him on his achievement. It was then explained to him that, once the biscuits had been baked, they could be broken with a belaying pin and the weevils much more easily removed before the biscuits were eaten. The most spectacular victories are not always the most effective, as Rufus used to point out in later years citing this experience as an example, and it is often well worth while to score a local success even if one cannot win a decisive battle.[1]

As soon as the vessel had berthed in Rio harbour, the crew were given shore leave and went off to the less salubrious quarters of the town in search of drink and women. Rufus did not accompany them. He had had enough of the seafaring life and he decided to desert. With this object in view he wandered off on foot, making his way through one of the picturesque valleys between the Carioca Mountains to the south and the wooded heights of the Serra do Mar to the north. Eventually he found himself in the open country beyond the city limits, and here he hoped to hide until the *Blair Athole* had sailed for her next port of call. But he had no money and no food, and he realized he risked starvation if he remained more than a day or two in this condition. Indeed he was already faint with hunger when he encountered a stout Negress, who took pity on him and invited him into her cabin, where she fed him on bananas for two days. But this temporary relief quickly came to an end when she made it clear to her guest that she expected some return for her action. In fact, as he told his son long afterwards, 'his generously proportioned protectress began to make advances to him as unmistakable as they were unalluring'. He quickly realized that it was possible to pay too high a price for such hospitality as he had enjoyed, and he consequently chose the first convenient opportunity, when her attention was otherwise engaged, to make his escape.

He could see from this vantage point overlooking the bay of Rio that the *Blair Athole* was still in the harbour. The idea now occurred to him of joining another ship bound for a British port. So he made

[1] Reading, Vol. I, p. 23; Riddell, Vol. I, p. 195.

his way back to the dock area and took a bed in a seamen's lodging-
house. This move led to his undoing, although the precise mode of his
capture is uncertain. According to one account, he gave himself
away by saying he could do logarithms in reply to a query from a
visitor. Another version has it that his presence in the lodging-house
was reported to the harbour master, who interrogated him closely
as a suspected deserter. During the questioning the harbour
master's daughter is said to have come into the office and she was a
girl of such dazzling beauty that the sight of her quite unnerved
Rufus, who began to answer carelessly and eventually his identity was
discovered.

As a punishment he was set to shovelling coal from the dockside
into ships' bunkers, being the only white man in a gang of Negroes,
Indians and half-castes. This arduous labour lasted for a month, at
the end of which period the *Blair Athole* was ready to sail again, and
Rufus was returned ignominiously on board. He had certainly
learned his lesson: he made no further attempt to jump ship.

The next port of call was Calcutta, and on January 12, 1877, the
Blair Athole began the long voyage across the South Atlantic and
round the Cape to India. The boatswain, whose name was Isaac
Cribb, proceeded to take it out on Rufus for deserting and took
sadistic pleasure in inflicting every possible humiliation on the ship's
boy, cursing and cuffing him at every turn. Matters came to a head
one tropical night on deck, when Rufus, possibly in trying to escape
the blows of his tormentor, accidentally tripped him, so that the
boatswain fell down. Picking himself up he rushed in a fury at Rufus
with the intention of giving him the thrashing of his life. But the
ship's boy, remembering the precepts of Daniel Mendoza, quickly
sidestepped the attacker and parried his blows. They continued to
fight as the crew crowded round, forming an impromptu ring. Eventually Rufus landed a neat uppercut on the boatswain's chin and he
went down hard on the planks. When they saw that the hated boatswain had been completely knocked out, the sailors raised a great
cheer. It was the story of David and Goliath over again. His spectacular victory made him something of a hero with the crew, and he
was left strictly in peace by the bullying boatswain for the rest of the
voyage.

Fourteen weeks after leaving Rio, the coast of Bengal came in
sight, and on April 23, the *Blair Athole* dropped anchor at the mouth
of the river Hooghly. Here the pilot came on board, in a smart

uniform with well-polished brass buttons and wearing white gloves. Rufus was ordered into the pilot boat and told to carry the pilot's bag up the ship's gangway. He did so with marked eagerness, for (as he afterwards admitted) he considered it to be the proudest day in his life.

The *Blair Athole* remained in Calcutta for nearly a month. Rufus enjoyed his stay and his visits ashore, much of which he spent at a roller skating rink. At last the time came for the pilot to come aboard again and guide the ship down the river. As he watched enviously, Rufus wondered whether he could ever one day become as grand as that pilot in his brass-buttoned uniform and white gloves.

Many years later, near the end of his career, he recalled the day he left Calcutta:

> I have often wished that I could have seen ahead. I have often dreamed of that time when I stood at the capstan head and helped to heave my small weight at the capstan bar with the rest of the company on the forecastle, to get our ship into a proper position to be towed by the tug to take us down the Hooghly until we could sail. I remember, as we were drawn from the quay by hauling at the capstan, we sang as we paced the forecastle: 'Hooray, my boys, we're homeward bound!' and 'Goodbye, Calcutta!' I, in my dream said: 'Good-bye Calcutta, I shall return, but not on the forecastle's head.'[1]

It cannot have been within the wildest dreams of the barefooted ship's boy that the next occasion on which he would sail the Hooghly would be forty-four years later and in a much grander uniform than the glamorous river pilot's – that of His Imperial Britannic Majesty's Viceroy of India – to the accompaniment of a salute of thirty-one guns.

4

After an uneventful homeward voyage, the *Blair Athole* docked in the Port of London on September 15, 1877, just short of a year of when she first set sail. Without waiting for the vessel to be moored, Rufus leaped on to the quayside, leaving his sea chest behind in his eagerness to get ashore. His departure on this occasion was quite legitimate, as he had been properly discharged with the sum of £3 11s. in his pocket, the balance of the pay due to him as ship's boy. And however

[1] Speech at the Pilgrim's Dinner, London, April 28, 1926.

pleased he was to leave the vessel, he never regretted his sailing experience. Indeed it left him with an abiding love of the sea, which was to persist for the rest of his life.

Rufus reached his parents' home in Hampstead shortly before his seventeenth birthday. After a talk with his father, it was decided that he should resume his apprenticeship in the family business in the City. But he found it difficult to settle down and early in 1878 his father arranged with a German firm, Junker and Heynemann, with which the Isaacs firm did considerable business, for Rufus to spend a year in their offices in Magdeburg. Unfortunately his stay there came to an abrupt end after eight months. In the household of one of the partners where he lived was a young Dutchman, whose family also had connections with Junker and Heynemann and who like Rufus was learning the business. The two youths did not take to each other and their mutual antipathy reached its climax one night at dinner in a violent quarrel. Rufus was eventually provoked to seize hold of the soup tureen on the table and pour its contents over the infuriating Dutchman's head. Thereupon he was immediately dispatched home in disgrace.

Rufus returned to the office stool in Eastcheap with no fixed idea of his final vocation. But he felt with an ever increasing conviction that he was not cut out to be a fruit merchant and ship-broker. During the next few months he cast about for some more exciting occupation and consultations within the family led to another change. His eldest sister, Frances, was now married to a stockbroker named Albert Keyzer, of the firm of Keyzer and Frederici. She now proposed— more to get him away from the monotony of the fruit business than to fulfil any predilection he may have shown for the stock market —that Rufus should enter his brother-in-law's office in Copthall Court as a clerk, with a view to eventually becoming a fully fledged member of the Stock Exchange. He began his new work in the latter part of 1879.

A week or so after his nineteenth birthday Rufus Isaacs applied on the customary form to the Committee for General Purposes to be admitted a member. At that time the rules of the Stock Exchange required all candidates for membership to be over the age of twenty-one at the time of making application, and the form they were called upon to sign contained a printed statement to this effect. Candidates had also to find securities who would undertake to pay the creditors a liquidated sum if the Member should be declared a defaulter within four years; in the case of clerks, three sureties of £500 each were required. Rufus Isaacs's application was posted in the Exchange on November 3, 1879, and it was passed by the Committee a fortnight later.[1]

In declaring that he was 'of age', when in fact he was only nineteen, Rufus had knowingly made a false statement. Years later, at the time of the Marconi scandal, he explained to the then Prime Minister, Mr Asquith, the reasons which had prompted this action, after certain newspapers had discovered it and were using it against him.

> I acted in this matter upon private advice and was assured (quite wrongly) and I believed that this statement was only required as a matter of form to prevent the repudiation of obligations on the ground of infancy and that the effect of my signature was to make myself as responsible as a man of full age would be.[2]

Although he thus sought to justify his action, it was an unfortunate one which was likely to be found out sooner or later. In the event, as will be seen, it was nearly to cost him his promotion to the judicial bench.

As soon as he had become a member of the Stock Exchange, Rufus Isaacs entered into partnership with a certain Mr Gerald Phipps as jobbers in the foreign market with an office close by that of Keyser and Frederici in Copthall Court. If he had continued in partnership in his brother-in-law's firm, his career on the Stock Exchange would have been even shorter and more ignominious than it turned out to be. A few months later, the firm of Keyser and Frederici were unable to meet their obligations, and were duly declared defaulters. The failure had one result for Rufus; he had to find another security to sponsor his own membership of the Exchange, since his brother-in-law was naturally no longer acceptable. But he seems to have had no difficulty in obtaining a suitable substitute, so that the firm of Phipps and Isaacs could carry on. Eventually the partnership was dissolved by mutual consent at the end of three years, for what reasons is not known. Thereafter, for a short time, Rufus Isaacs continued to trade on his own account in foreign bonds and securities.

Although his career on the Stock Exchange was to terminate suddenly and disappointingly a few months later, his time there was not wasted. He learned a great deal about financial dealings, particularly in the foreign market, and the knowledge thus acquired

[1] MS Stock Exchange Admissions Book. (I am indebted to the Secretary of the Stock Exchange for the accompanying particulars.)
[2] Isaacs to Asquith, July 30, 1913: Asquith Papers.

was to prove of the greatest value to him when he eventually began to practise at the Bar.

Among his particular Stock Exchange friends was an endearing and popular character called Jack Angle. He was a noted amateur boxer of his day, and when he discovered that Rufus was a grand-nephew of the celebrated Daniel Mendoza and could himself put up quite a good showing with his fists, he suggested that he should improve his technique in the ring by taking lessons. Accordingly he introduced him to a well-known bruiser named Ned Donelly, who kept a school behind the Café Royal. On most afternoons, after the Stock Exchange had closed, Rufus would repair to Donelly's for a lesson or a practice round with Jack Angle. Here he improved considerably under Donelly's drastic tuition. On one occasion when Donelly was sparring with him, the bruiser told his pupil to hit him as hard as he could. Rufus responded with a series of punches which drew blood, with the result that Donelly, momentarily losing his temper, chased Rufus round the ring and retaliated with such force that he broke the bridge of his nose, which bore evidence of this blow for the rest of its owner's life. As a result of this encounter, Rufus's father forbade him to compete in the forthcoming amateur championship contest of his weight, much to Rufus's disappointment. Instead he had to content himself with exhibition bouts in working-men's clubs in the East End of London, where he would also act as timekeeper while Jack Angle refereed.

Although he weighed under eleven stone, Rufus was extremely quick on his feet and did not hesitate to take on much heavier if slower opponents. Once he knocked out a tough who had annoyed him outside a coffee stall in Trafalgar Square where he was having a cup of coffee late one night with his brother Harry. Harry kept an improvised ring, and at the conclusion of the contest the brothers only just managed to escape in a passing hansom cab before the arrival of the police on the scene. Such prowess naturally won him the admiration of his sisters' girl friends, who were similarly impressed by other spectacular feats, such as standing on his head in a box in the old Empire music-hall and applauding vigorously with his feet. In fact he was quite a young 'swell'. With his earnings on the Stock Exchange, he was able to buy a thoroughbred mare, on which he used to ride out proudly into the country beyond Hampstead on Sunday mornings, usually in the company of a cavalcade of other young people. To the girls indeed he was quite irresistible, although their mothers were on the whole disapproving. 'I know he's a very bad man,' one girl confided to his sister Florrie, 'but if he asked me to marry him tomorrow I could not possibly say no!'

On the face of things, it seemed that Rufus had at last settled himself in a useful and financially rewarding occupation and that he might look forward to a prosperous career on the Stock Exchange but within a relatively limited business and social world. Then, suddenly and unexpectedly, catastrophe struck. His working capital had been seriously depleted by the break-up of his partnership with Mr Phipps, and he was unprepared for the slump in the foreign market which developed in the spring of 1884. No doubt, too, advantage was taken of his inexperience and lack of caution to unload stocks on him which should have been considerably marked down in price. At all events he woke up one awful August morning to realize that he was insolvent. The Committee was duly informed and there could only be one result. On August 14, 1884, two of the waiters in the 'House' solemnly struck the rostrum in front of them with their hammers as a prelude to the dread announcement which followed. There was a deadly hush, as the members were informed that Mr Rufus D. Isaacs, jobber in the foreign market, was unable to meet his obligations.[1]

The immediate effect of the 'hammering' was that Rufus ceased to be a member of the Stock Exchange, in whose eyes he now became for all practical purposes a bankrupt, his business affairs being taken over by two Official Assignees. However, a defaulter is not a bankrupt in the legal sense, since by the Stock Exchange rules he has been debarred from carrying on any other business and he is consequently unlikely to have any significant liabilities outside the 'House'. The bulk of his creditors therefore are fellow members of the Exchange and they prefer to make their own arrangements for dealing with his estate, fixing the amount of the dividend payable from his existing assets, rather than employ the machinery of the ordinary Bankruptcy Court with its Receiving Order and Public Examination. Rufus Isaacs's liabilities amounted to £8,000. But his three sureties were not called upon to pay the amounts which they had individually guaranteed, since the debtor had been a member of the Stock Exchange for more than four years.

Gossip had it long afterwards that Rufus Isaacs owed his downfall on the Stock Exchange to the behaviour of a fellow Jew in the South

[1] *The Times*, August 15, 1884.

African diamond industry, the redoubtable J. B. ('Jack') Joel, who
had 'caused Isaacs's bankruptcy by some stockbroker's trick', and
that Isaacs had threatened to 'get even with him' one day and in fact
had done so.[1]

Whether there is any truth in this story cannot be substantiated.
What is beyond doubt, however, is that twenty-four years later Rufus
Isaacs was to worst Jack Joel in a dramatic criminal trial at the Old
Bailey.

5

After brooding over his failure, which he felt acutely, Rufus decided
that there was nothing for it but to make a completely fresh start,
preferably in some faraway part of the world. His choice fell on the
Central American state of Panama, where a French company (of
whose activities he knew something from his experience in the foreign
market) was planning the construction of the canal which was
eventually to link the Atlantic with the Pacific Ocean. Gold and other
metals were also being mined there, and it seemed about the most
likely place on the globe where he could quickly retrieve his shattered
fortunes and repay his Stock Exchange creditors. Somewhat reluctantly his father agreed, ignoring his mother's objections. A
passage was taken on a ship sailing from Liverpool, farewells were
said, and Rufus duly departed to catch the boat train at Euston
Station.

No sooner had the sound of the carriage wheels and the horse's
hooves died away outside the house in Belsize Park than Mrs Isaacs
went into a violent fit of hysterics. She had never forgotten the advice
of the headmaster of University College School that Rufus should go
to the Bar and she insisted that her favourite son should be given a
chance to do this. Although very doubtful of the wisdom of such an
uncertain and relatively costly step, in order to pacify his wife Joseph
Isaacs agreed to discuss the possibility. His eldest son Harry was
thereupon dispatched in a hansom and told to pay the driver the
double fare if he could reach the station before the train left.

The hansom clattered into the forecourt at Euston and Harry

---

[1] See the interesting letter from Walter Hines Page, U.S. Ambassador in
London, to President Wilson (January 16, 1918), cited by Lord Beaverbrook in
his *Men and Power* (1956), p. 96.

dashed on to the platform just as the guard was about to blow his whistle. In a matter of moments he had spotted his brother and pulled him and his bags out of the carriage. An hour later the astonished Rufus was back in Belsize Park, to the relief of the whole family, who had lingering thoughts that he might have refused to return.

His material future posed an immediately pressing question. His father had a friend named Algernon Sydney, who was a solicitor, and with the object of discovering whether Rufus had any aptitude for the law, it was arranged between them that Rufus should go into Mr Sydney's office at 46 Finsbury Circus, for six months. This gave him an opportunity of seeing how the preliminaries of litigation were conducted, how briefs were prepared and counsel instructed, and all the other paraphernalia peculiar to the solicitor's side of the legal profession. The experiment was an immediate success; Rufus showed the most lively interest in everything that went on in the office and in the courts which he attended with Mr Sydney; advocacy made a particular appeal to him and long before the six months were up he had acquired a fixed determination to become a barrister. The next step was to join one of the four Inns of Court, and in due course, on January 10, 1887, he was admitted a student of the Honourable Society of the Middle Temple.

There now began the three-year business of 'eating dinners', and being coached in the various subjects for the Bar examinations. These included Latin, of which he had learned practically nothing at school, but which was necessary in order to pass Roman Law; needless to add, he found it a great drudgery, but he persevered under the tuition of a well-known 'crammer' of the day called Hinde. Then in his final year he went as a pupil into the chambers of a busy junior, John Lawson Walton, destined like himself to become Attorney-General in a Liberal Government.

Rufus was fortunate in his choice of master. Although quite unlike his pupil in family background and upbringing – Lawson Walton was an ardent Wesleyan Methodist and inclined to be somewhat narrow-minded – he was nevertheless an excellent master with a born gift of advocacy and a deep respect for the law, from both of which qualities Rufus was to benefit. Another busy member of the same chambers at 2 Crown Office Row, was Harry Poland, who combined a big criminal practice – he had been a Treasury Counsel for over twenty years – with extensive common law work, particularly in rating and licensing cases. He took a fancy to Lawson Walton's new pupil, allowed him to read his briefs, and promised him some 'devilling' when he had been 'called'.

Poland, who was to live to congratulate the pupil on becoming Viceroy of India and eventually to die in his ninety-ninth year, gave Rufus a piece of advice at this time which the prospective barrister always remembered. 'Never come to the Temple later than ten o'clock in the morning and never leave it before six o'clock in the evening. What chance of success has a barrister who strolls into chambers about 11.0 a.m., with a great cigar in his mouth, lounges about till lunch-time, and then takes himself off to a club, or what he calls "home"?'

Rufus worked hard at his law books, and he passed in all the examination papers at the first sitting, including the hated Roman Law. As soon as the results had been announced and before he was formally called to the Bar, he moved into a set of chambers on his own, which he had taken at 1 Garden Court, round the corner from Crown Office Row. It was a bold step characteristic of his growing self-confidence, since most barristers at the outset of their careers were content to get a room or even the share of a room in established chambers. The next step was to be 'called'. For this it was necessary to find a Bencher of the Inn, who was prepared to certify that the candidate was a fit and proper person to be called to the Bar. Through the good offices of his uncle Henry, who was a City Alderman and had just been knighted in that year of Queen Victoria's Golden Jubilee, Sir Thomas Chambers, the Recorder of London, acted as the necessary sponsor. This formality completed, Rufus Isaacs put on his barrister's wig and gown for the first time on the evening of November 17, 1887. The ceremony was performed after dinner in the historic hall of the Middle Temple by the Deputy Treasurer, Mr (later Sir) Peter Edlin, on behalf of the Prince of Wales, whose year of office as Treasurer was just coming to an end.

Rufus then settled down in his new chambers to wait for briefs. As a rule a barrister's first brief comes either as the result of family influence or the influence of the barrister's clerk with a solicitor's clerk. The second and several subsequent briefs may find their way to his chambers for the same reason. Whether they will continue, reinforced by briefs from more solicitors, naturally depends upon how the young barrister shapes in these first few cases. The first brief which was delivered to Rufus Isaacs arrived two days after his 'call'. It came from a firm of commercial solicitors in the City, who had been instructed by the Isaacs family in a suit in which M. Isaacs & Sons, Ltd, was being sued for breach of contract over the supply of a consignment of fruit from Spain. Rufus was instructed to settle the defence, that is to draft the written pleadings in answer to the plaintiff's claim. The brief in the matter of *Young* v. *Isaacs* was marked two guineas, with a half-crown for the barrister's clerk, which was the customary fee.

A little over a fortnight later, a second set of papers arrived at 1 Garden Court concerning the same matter. This time the brief, which was to go out to Spain and take the evidence of the witnesses there on commission, was marked at 75 guineas. It so happened that the young barrister, had received advance news of this unexpected windfall and had taken advantage of it to do something which he had been contemplating for some time and which was to affect his personal happiness deeply. He was consequently not in his chambers when the precious brief was delivered to his clerk, since he had gone to the West London Synagogue to get married.

Junior Barrister
21

2

Queen's Counsel

1

The lady whom Rufus Isaacs had chosen to share his life was a
rather delicate looking girl of twenty-two with hazel eyes and fair
wavy hair called Alice Cohen. The Cohens were neighbours of the
Isaacs's in Hampstead, but whereas in Rufus's family it was his
mother who was the dominant personality, in Alice's family it was
her father. Albert Cohen was of German-Jewish origin, his father
having been a Hamburg merchant who dealt in cotton goods. As a
young man he had come to England, where he had built up a substantial import-export business, particularly in the British colonies.
Outside his business, his chief interest lay in reading books on
philosophy and science, and he had the reputation of being something
of a recluse, as well as a tyrant in the home. Indeed he was extremely
strict with his children in their upbringing, very different from the
easy-going Joseph Isaacs. On the other hand, he was devoted to
Alice, who was his third daughter, and when he learned that Rufus
Isaacs, whom he regarded as a wild young man, wished to marry her,
his immediate reaction was to refuse his consent to what he regarded
as a most unsuitable alliance and to forbid Alice to see or communicate with her suitor again.

Rufus and his future bride originally met in the same way as his
own parents had done, at a dancing class. But they had lost touch
during the period of Rufus's travels, and it was not until towards
the end of his ill-fated membership of the Stock Exchange that they
renewed their acquaintance, this time in the house of some mutual
friends. They were immediately attracted to each other and in due
course Rufus proposed and was accepted. Then followed the paternal
ban on the match, whereupon Alice went into the 'decline' which
usually followed when young love was blighted by a stern Victorian

22

parent, and she took to her bed. The family doctor quickly saw what was the matter, but preferred to avoid the responsibility of saying so by calling on the opinion of a second and more eminent physician than himself. This was a well-known doctor of the day, Sir William Gull, and he had no qualms about speaking quite frankly to the patient's father. 'Give her the young man and I promise you she will soon recover,' he said. 'Otherwise she will die.'

In the face of this alarming pronouncement, Albert Cohen surrendered and told Alice that she could marry her young man as soon as he had completed his legal studies. The necessary notice was given to the Rabbi of the West London Synagogue in Upper Berkeley Street; and there, on December 8, 1887, amid a large gathering of both families and their friends, Rufus Isaacs and Alice Cohen were declared man and wife according to the rites and ceremonies of the Jewish religion. Besides the respective fathers of the bridegroom and bride, the marriage register was signed by the bridegroom's uncle, the recently knighted Sir Henry Isaacs, who was Sheriff of London and Middlesex that year, and whose presence gave the occasion an added air of civic importance.

For their honeymoon the bridal couple went to Valencia, thereby combining pleasure with work, since it was in this Spanish Mediterranean town that the witnesses, whose evidence had to be taken on commission in the matter of *Young* v. *Isaacs*, resided. Also living in Valencia at this time were Rufus's elder brother Harry, who was the local representative of the Isaacs family fruit business, and another young man Albert Van Gruisen, representing a similar business in the North of England; he was later to marry Rufus's sister Florrie. While Rufus was busy with the witnesses, Harry and young Van Gruisen showed Alice the sights of Valencia. In the evenings they would all meet for a meal, where they would be joined by a young barrister on the other side, whose name was John Hamilton. Destined for the Bench, Hamilton's judgments, particularly in the House of Lords when he had become Lord Sumner, were to be greatly distinguished for their wit and literary expression and to be among the very few judicial utterances which have been considered worthy of inclusion in *The Oxford Book of English Prose*; but at the time of his visit to Valencia he had not succeeded in earning more than £100 in any of the five years in which he had been practising. He impressed Rufus on this occasion not with the elegance of his language nor the depth of his legal knowledge, but rather with the enormous helpings

B

of unfamiliar Spanish dishes of which he partook and which Rufus and his wife sampled very gingerly.

At the end of a fortnight, Rufus Isaacs and his wife returned to London and their new home which they had set up at No. 10 Broadhurst Gardens, Hampstead, a suburban villa of no particular distinction, near Finchley Road railway station. They had £200 a year of their own on which to start out on the adventure of married life, and they were supremely happy.

He began to practise, as every newly called barrister does, with small cases in the county courts, magistrates' courts and at the Quarter Sessions with pleas in mitigation of sentence and an occasional defence. His first professional appearance in wig and gown is said to have been in a London county court case in which he represented a fruit merchant who was being sued by a costermonger, and which he lost. The plaintiff, who alleged that some boxes of fruit he had purchased from the defendant were unfit for human consumption, grew annoyed at the line of Isaacs's cross-examination, which suggested that he was not telling the truth. 'Look 'ere, Guv'nor!' said the irate plaintiff. 'Some of those 'ere figs are in Court, and if you eat three of them and aren't ill in five minutes, I'll give up the bloomin' case!'

The judge thought that the defendant's counsel ought to submit to the experiment, but the resourceful young advocate suggested that it would be more fitting for his client to accept the challenge. Unfortunately he had misjudged his client's veracity.

'What will happen if I don't eat those figs?' the fruit merchant whispered to his counsel.

'Probably the judgment will go against you.'

'Very well, then, I'll lose the case,' was the unhesitating reply. And, as the result of the defendant's reluctant behaviour, the costermonger won his case.

The brief in this his first Court case was marked a guinea for counsel which with the clerk's fee was paid in cash and which included a golden sovereign. Rufus Isaacs had the sovereign set in a brooch for his wife, which he proudly presented to her. She was delighted, but her pleasure was not shared either by her own family or her husband's who both thought that the gift was an unnecessary extravagance and that the sovereign should have been put into the young barrister's bank account.

In the first two years in practice Rufus Isaacs did much better than his friend Hamilton, in spite of the latter's wide intellectual gifts and the fact that he had been to Oxford, an omission in his own education which Rufus always regretted. The fees for the first year amounted to £519 and for the second to £750, although in this latter figure £230 came from a single case. His part in this case was a relatively minor one – two other junior counsel of longer standing at the Bar were briefed with him as well as one of the best known leaders of the day – but it brought Rufus Isaacs into the public eye, since the matter at issue was of the most widespread interest, the plaintiff being a baronet and the defendant an earl, and both being well-known figures in society and on the turf. It also gave Rufus Isaacs an opportunity of studying a brief in a complicated field of which he had little or no previous knowledge and of familiarizing himself with the whole technique of racehorse training and riding and with all the nicer points of 'form'.

The case arose out of a speech which Lord Durham, a Steward of the Jockey Club and a prominent owner, made at the annual Gimcrack Dinner at York on December 13, 1887, in which without specifically mentioning any names he had cast strong aspersions upon 'a well-known and what the sporting Press calls a fashionable and aristocratic racing stable'. Those with any knowledge of racing had no difficulty in pinning down the allusion to Sir George Chetwynd, Bart., whose horses were trained by Mr Sherrard and ridden by Charles Wood. But to remove all doubts on the matter, Lord Durham issued the following statement: 'I now state that the substance of my speech at the Gimcrack Dinner at York was to the effect that the horses in Sherrard's stables have shown constant and inexplicable changes of form, and that Wood, the jockey, has been in the habit of pulling them. I also accuse Sir George Chetwynd of having connived at serious malpractices which are contrary to the rules of racing.'

Sir George Chetwynd issued a writ for libel against Lord Durham, claiming £20,000 damages. It was on the preliminary paper work in setting out the plaintiff's refutation of the serious charge made against him that Rufus Isaacs spent many long and anxious hours, incidentally running the whole gamut of racing practices and malpractices. As leader, in whose consultations with the lay client Rufus Isaacs naturally participated, the plaintiff's solicitors had instructed Sir Henry James, Q.C. (later Lord James of Hereford, the distinguished Law Lord). With him as one of the other junior counsel was A. T. Lawrence, who as Lord Trevethin was destined more than thirty

years later to succeed Rufus Isaacs, then Lord Reading, as Lord
Chief Justice of England. The leader on the other side was that great
Irish advocate Sir Charles Russell, Q.C. (later Lord Russell of
Killowen and another future Lord Chief Justice). With him as his
principal junior counsel was Charles Willie Mathews, afterwards
Director of Public Prosecutions. To be professionally associated in a
sensational case with such well-known and established members of
the Bar was a rare privilege for a junior barrister of barely eighteen
months' standing and still in his twenties.

Normally a libel action of this kind would have been tried in the
Queen's Bench Division of the High Court by a judge and special
jury. But on account of its exceptionally technical nature, the parties
agreed that it should be decided by a court of arbitration consisting
of the Jockey Club Stewards, who were at that time Mr James
Lowther, M.P. (afterwards Speaker of the House of Commons and
created Lord Ullswater), the Earl of March and Prince Solticoff. The
arbitrators opened their sittings in the Whitsun vacation on June 10,
1889, in a court-room set aside for them in the Law Courts, since
they could not sit in term time owing to the leaders being heavily
engaged before the Parnell Commission, James appearing for *The
Times* and Russell for Parnell. Nor could they sit in Ascot Week for
obvious reasons, so that the court adjourned for this period.

It is unnecessary to recapitulate the details of the court proceedings,
which lasted for twelve days, as handicappers, owners, trainers,
jockeys, stable lads and other racing figures followed each other into
the witness-box. Rufus Isaacs played no direct part in them, but he
sat behind his leader and listened with admiration to the ingenuity
with which he answered Sir Charles Russell, arguing with great
skill that the existence of the circumstances which might have led Sir
George Chetwynd to suspect certain malpractices such as 'pulling'
was not the same thing as proving that he actually did know them.
In the result the decision was on the face of it a draw, in which each
side was ordered to pay its own costs, the arbitrators finding for
Chetwynd on the more serious charge of 'pulling' his horses, but
finding against him in the matter of lesser malpractices, such as
running horses in certain races not to win but to secure good handi-
caps in future races. In effect, however, Chetwynd was the loser since
on the first count the arbitrators awarded him the contemptuous sum
of a farthing damages and on the second held that he was unfit to be
or remain a member of the Jockey Club or to associate with honour-

able men. This was enough to put an end to his career on the Turf and also to show that Lord Durham, although he did not succeed in substantiating the whole of his case, at least had reason to be dissatisfied with the state of affairs in the racing world and had some justification in taking the strong line he did in calling attention to it.

While briefs continued to be delivered at Garden Court in a slow but steady trickle, the demands on Rufus Isaacs's earning power increased. Besides a wife he now had a baby son to support – this was his only child, Gerald, born in 1889 – and he was now making an effort to pay off the more pressing of his Stock Exchange creditors. Fortunately he was gifted with a strong physical as well as mental constitution, and he could work very long hours, although he always found the paper work involved in settling written pleadings something of a drudgery. So as to gain more experience of court work, he joined a Bar circuit, choosing the Northern Circuit, largely because his sister Florrie had now married Albert Van Gruisen and was living in Birkenhead. But Rufus Isaacs never regularly 'travelled the circuit', usually only appearing at assizes in Liverpool or Manchester when he had a brief there. Also, except for the year when his uncle Henry was Lord Mayor of London and he was consequently invited to the mayoral banquets and other corporation functions, he practically gave up going out in the evenings while he was a junior barrister.

The story is told that the famous solicitor Sir George Lewis dropped into the High Court one day, and saw a young barrister arguing a point of law with energy and clarity, showing a comprehensive grasp of financial detail. 'Who's that young man?' the solicitor asked an acquaintance. 'He knows what he is talking about and I like his style.' 'That's young Rufus Isaacs' was the reply. The solicitor nodded and made a note of the name for future reference.

After his old master Lawson Walton had 'taken silk', in 1890, and joined the front row of barristers in court, Rufus Isaacs was frequently 'led' by him. Following one such case, in which Rufus Isaacs had Lawson as his leader and had been of outstanding help to him both in the preparation of the case and its presentation in court, the leader decided that the time had come to express his appreciation in a particular manner. Accordingly, on May 7, 1891, Lawson Walton wrote to his former pupil: 'I have taken great pleasure in observing your early and rapid rise in our profession and the promise which it gives of achievement in the future. As your old master in the art and mystery of the law, I should like to show my recognition of the position which you have achieved and my interest in your future career by offering for your acceptance a red bag. *Sic itur ad astra.*'

This stage in the career of every 'rising junior', at which he is presented with a red bag in which to carry his briefs and wig and gown into court in place of the original blue one with which he began to practise, had been reached by Rufus Isaacs within four years of his call to the Bar. It was indeed a most creditable achievement.

2

Lawson Walton used to say of Rufus Isaacs that he was the only man he knew 'who has not had to go through the grind of Quarter Sessions and the County Court like the rest of us'. If this remark was not strictly true, it did underline the fact that Rufus Isaacs succeeded in building up a practice in the High Court more rapidly than many of his contemporaries. In this he was greatly helped by the establishment of what was in effect a new division of the High Court for the trial of commercial cases. In the early 'nineties the business community in the City complained that the judges were frequently ignorant of commercial practice in the cases that came before them. In 1892 there was a loud outcry when an extremely technical case about general average came before Mr Justice Lawrence in the non-jury list, and this unlearned judge (one of the political promotions of Lord Halsbury) showed himself palpably unfit to try the case. There were also complaints that procedure in the trial of such cases was unnecessarily complicated and costly and that unnecessary delays and inconvenience resulted from doubt as to when the cases might come on. Hence the creation of the Commercial Court with a simplified procedure, including the fixing of a definite day for the trial and a reduction in expense through the admission of secondary evidence when strict proof would involve an exorbitant cost. A highly qualified judge in the person of Mr Justice Mathew, later Lord Justice of Appeal, was appointed to preside over the new tribunal, in the work of which Rufus Isaacs began to specialize from its inception. Here the technical knowledge which he had picked up during his years in the City, particularly in the foreign market of the Stock Exchange proved invaluable when grappling with such matters as charter parties and bills of lading.

Rufus Isaacs's growing High Court practice received an immense fillip from an action which, although it was to become a leading case in the law of torts or civil wrongs, had an extremely modest beginning. One afternoon a solicitor, who had not previously instructed him, called at Garden Court with a thin bundle of papers and asked the clerk whether Mr Isaacs would write an opinion for him. The clerk accepted the brief which was marked at one guinea. Looking back in after years, Rufus Isaacs used to cite this incident as an excellent example of the incalculable element of the luck of the Bar, since he might just as easily have written the opinion, received the guinea fee and heard no more about the matter. In fact from the purely legal point of view, the case was probably the most important in which he figured in the whole of his career, going as it did to the Court of Appeal and eventually receiving two hearings in the House of Lords, thereby making legal history in industrial relations under the title of *Allen* v. *Flood*.

Briefly the facts were these. Two shipwrights named Flood and Taylor were engaged by the Glengall Iron Co. to repair the woodwork of the good ship *Sam Weller* then lying in Regent's Dock. Some ironworkers, who were also employed on the ship, objected to the employment of Flood and Taylor who they knew had repaired iron-work on other ships. One of the ironworkers, who belonged to the Boilermakers' Union, sent for the Union's London delegate whose name was Allen and informed him that unless Flood and Taylor were discharged they would stop work. Allen accordingly approached the management and stated that unless the company discharged Flood and Taylor (as it quite lawfully could) the ironworkers would come out on strike. The two shipwrights were thereupon discharged, 'for peace and quietness', as the managing director put it, and with the financial help of their own union, they now proceeded to sue Allen, together with Knight, the Chairman, and Jackson, the General Secretary of the Boilermakers' Union, for maliciously inducing the company to break its contracts with them and also for intimidation and conspiracy.

The case was tried by Mr Justice Kennedy and a common jury in the Queen's Bench Division of the High Court in February, 1895, Rufus Isaacs being led by his old master Lawson Walton, Q.C., for the plaintiffs Flood and Taylor, while another future Attorney-General, William Robson, Q.C., appeared with other counsel for the defendants.

A foreman of the Glengall Company, John Edmunds, stated in evidence that he had told Allen that his action was 'very arbitrary'. A subsequent witness, who was a master mariner, employed more forthright nautical language, when he declared that he had told Allen that it would give him great pleasure to 'chuck him in the dock'. However, Allen had escaped this fate, since he appeared in the witness-box, where he caused some laughter by saying with a nice mixture of metaphor that 'while he came down with the olive-branch in his mouth, Mr Edmunds not only kindled a fire but poured oil upon it.' After hearing all the witnesses, the judge ruled that there was no evidence of conspiracy or intimidation or coercion. Nor had there been any breach of contract. He then left it to the jury to say whether Allen had maliciously induced the Company to discharge the plaintiffs. The jury found that he had and consequently awarded the plaintiffs £20 each by way of damages. This verdict was against Allen alone, since the jury also found that neither Jackson nor Knight had ever been consulted by Allen about the dispute and that they knew nothing about it. The question of whether Allen was liable in law the judge reserved for the legal argument of counsel.

Lawson Walton, who had the greatest confidence in his junior, shared the burden of argument with him and let him make the opening speech. In this Rufus Isaacs argued most persuasively that there was no material difference between inducement to break a contract and inducement not to enter into a contract, and that where the inducer was actuated by malice he was liable. In support of the latter contention he cited various cases earlier where it had been laid down that 'he that hinders another in his trade or livelihood is liable to an action for so hindering him'. Thus the two shipwrights had a lawful right to work on iron, and it was gross tyranny to prevent them from doing so. Lawson Walton followed on the same lines, claiming that there had been a wrongful interference with the plaintiffs' lawful rights and with their freedom of action. In the result Mr Justice Kennedy agreed with this view and gave judgment for Flood and Taylor with damages of £40.

Allen thereupon appealed to the Court of Appeal, and applied for a new trial on the ground of misdirection of the jury; there was also a cross-appeal against the trial judge's ruling in favour of Knight and Jackson. The appeals were heard on April 3, 1895, before the Master of the Rolls, Lord Esher, and Lords Justice Lopes and Rigby. In dismissing both the appeal and the cross-appeal, the Court unanimously found that the fact of Allen having acted 'maliciously' gave rise to a cause of action against him.

Allen now took his case to the House of Lords, and so it came about that Rufus Isaacs as a junior barrister of barely eight years' standing was given the opportunity of addressing the highest tribunal in the land. After some delay the appeal was heard by seven Law Lords, including the Lord Chancellor, Lord Halsbury, who presided, in December, 1895. It was initially inconclusive, since the Law Lords interrupted Lawson Walton's argument on the fourth day with the ruling that the point at issue, namely Allen's liability in law, was of such difficulty and importance that they desired to take the opinion of the judges of the High Court before making up their own minds. It was not until fifteen months later that the hearing was resumed before the original Law Lords reinforced by two more of their number as well as eight High Court judges, probably the most formidable and impressive array of legal learning which has ever sat to determine a cause.

When it came to the turn of Rufus Isaacs to address this unique assembly of judges, which he naturally did with some trepidation, his audience on that spring afternoon in 1897 appeared a mixture of boredom and somnolence. But gradually the Law Lords began to show interest, and next morning when Rufus Isaacs rose with an apology for taking up so much of their Lordships' time, the Lord Chancellor politely told him that he should not in any way curtail his argument; he was thus encouraged to remain on his feet until the luncheon adjournment. After Robson had replied for the appellant, the Lord Chancellor announced that he proposed to submit to the High Court judges the question of whether there was evidence of a cause of action fit to be left to the jury. The judges through the mouth of their senior member Mr Justice Hawkins, later Lord Brampton, said they would take time to consider their reply.

Two months later, the judges decided by a majority of six to two that there was evidence of a cause of action fit to be left to the jury, as Rufus Isaacs and his leader had contended. Indeed, in the view of the majority, there was an abundance of such evidence to the effect that, as Mr Justice Hawkins put it, 'without excuse or justification, and not in the exercise of any privilege or in defence of any right either of his own or the boilermakers, the defendant has wilfully, unlawfully, unjustly and tyrannically invaded and violated the plaintiffs' right by intimidating and coercing their employers to deprive them of their present and future employment to their injury; and the plaintiffs, therefore, are entitled to maintain their injury.'

The final act in this long drawn-out legal drama was played on December 15, 1897, when contrary to the opinion of the High Court judges the Law Lords decided by a majority of six to three that there was no evidence fit for the jury and that consequently no action lay against Allen. It is noteworthy that the Lord Chancellor gave judgment with the minority. The majority view which was expressed by Lord Watson now embodies a most important principle in English Law, namely that an otherwise legal act does not become illegal because it is inspired by a bad or 'malicious' motive. 'It is, in my opinion,' said Lord Watson, 'the absolute right of every workman to exercise his own option in regard to persons in whose society he will agree or continue to work.' Allen's action had been no more than the delegated exercise, so to speak, of this right on behalf of the boiler-makers, and for this he could not be made liable, no matter how malicious was his motive. 'The existence of a bad motive in the case of an act which is not in itself illegal will not convert that act into a civil wrong for which reparation is due.'

Although the ultimate decision went against his clients and the opinion which he had first given in the original guinea brief, Rufus Isaacs emerged from this legal marathon with immensely increased prestige at the junior Bar. He had been seen and heard by every important judge in the country from the Lord Chancellor downwards, a fact which had not gone unnoticed by solicitors. So that long before the final judgments in *Allen* v. *Flood* were enshrined in the Law Reports, the table at 1 Garden Court was piled high with briefs. His professional income for the years 1896 and 1897 averaged £7,000 a year, most of which (as he afterwards admitted) he spent. In the former year he had taken a young man just down from Oxford named Francis Oppenheimer as a pupil; as soon as the High Court judges delivered their opinion in the House of Lords – incidentally the last occasion on which they were ever to be summoned for this purpose – Rufus Isaacs hurried back to chambers with his pupil and immediately sent out for a bottle of champagne from which they drank to the health of Allen against Flood. The protracted dispute between these two celebrated litigants also encouraged Rufus Isaacs to leave the little villa in Hampstead for a commodious flat at Palace Court, Bayswater.

When his work first began to grow, Rufus Isaacs would bring his papers home and work on them after dinner. But he soon found that his tired brain responded slowly and besides that his preoccupation encroached on the few precious hours he could otherwise spend with his wife. So he decided to give up working in the evenings and, since he found that he never needed more than five hours' sleep, got up early in the mornings and worked on his briefs then. Accordingly he would rise at four o'clock and work until eight when he would have a bath and shave. He had no fire in the room, but he would dress warmly and every hour the devoted family servant, a chubby sandy-haired Devonian named Emma Squires, would bring him a cup of tea. Originally engaged as a nurse for his baby son, she was to remain in his service for upwards of forty years and to prove a wonderful help and confidante in all kinds of ways.

The legend of his industrious zeal long persisted in the Temple where it used to be said that Rufus Isaacs only went to bed during the Long Vacation. But magnificent as his constitution was, he could not maintain this severe regimen indefinitely with impunity. Shortly after moving into his new flat in Palace Court, he began to suffer from recurrent attacks of bleeding from the nose and eyes, a sure sign of overwork. He himself was inclined to make light of the trouble, but the doctor whom his wife persuaded him to see took a different view and foretold the most serious consequences if the patient would not reduce the volume of his paper work and take things more easily all round. There was only one practical solution and that was to ask the Lord Chancellor 'to be accorded the honour of a silk gown', in other words to be appointed one of Her Majesty's Counsel, which would ease the tension by relieving him in the drudgery of drafting pleadings and the other preliminaries of litigation. Of the wisdom of such a move Rufus Isaacs was extremely doubtful, since no junior of only ten years' standing had ever before been allowed to exchange his stuff gown for a silk one and so to take his place in the front row of barristers' seats in court. However he undertook to consult one of the leaders in the Commercial Court, J. C. Bigham, who had just become a judge.

When he duly called on him, the judge advised him to apply for silk immediately, 'Sit down and write the letter of application now,' said Mr Justice Bigham. But Rufus Isaacs was not wholly convinced and he answered that he would think it over.

He then called on the judge of the Commercial Court, Mr Justice

Mathew, who repeated Bigham's advice. 'I should take silk,' Mathew urged. 'Don't make the mistake I made of postponing your application until you are old and have lost your energy. If you do, you will never apply.'[1]

Although he was still doubtful, Rufus Isaacs decided to take his courage in his hands and write the letter to Lord Halsbury. Considerably to his surprise, his name was included in the next list of 'silks', for Halsbury had not forgotten his performance in *Allen* v. *Flood*, which had so much impressed the Law Lords at the time.

And so Rufus Isaacs, at the age of thirty-seven and of the unprecedented standing at the Bar of barely ten years, proudly took his place in the front row of Queen's Counsel.

3

Fortunately Rufus Isaacs had a great deal of work on hand at the time of his promotion to the front row, most of which his clients were willing that he should complete as a silk, taking in another junior with him. The gratifying result was that, not only did his new work continue to keep him busy in the courts, but he earned more fees in his first year as a silk than he had ever done when he wore a stuff gown, while the work was less onerous and more congenial. As he afterwards told his friend Lord Riddell, the newspaper magnate, 'had I not been a success as a Q.C., it would have been serious, as I had no other income. The change in work put me right.'[2]

For the next few years Rufus Isaacs's work continued to be largely in the Commercial Court where he consolidated his position as a leader, and he only gradually branched out into other and general fields. He always made a point of being pleasant and agreeable to everyone in court.

Meanwhile Rufus Isaacs had taken into his chambers as tenants two newly called barristers, who were to render immense help to him as 'devils'. One was Walter Schwabe (later Sir Walter Schwabe and Chief Justice of Madras); the other was George Branson, a future Junior Treasury Counsel – incidentally an appointment which Rufus

[1] Riddell, Vol. I, p. 107. Mathew never did apply for silk, being appointed straight from the junior Bar to the Bench at the age of fifty-one.

[2] Riddell, Vol. I, p. 108.

Isaacs was mainly instrumental in obtaining for him – and afterwards a High Court judge for eighteen years.

The first case of general interest in which Rufus Isaacs's name came prominently before the public was in October 1899, at the Old Bailey, where he defended a company promoter, undischarged bankrupt and former solicitor named Edward Beal for making and publishing a false prospectus and obtaining money by false pretences in connection with the flotation of the London and Scottish Banking and Discount Corporation, Limited. Known in the City as 'the Black Prince' from his magnificent coach drawn by four beautiful horses, Beal was charged along with three of his associates, Lambert, Singleton and Wain, before Mr Justice Channell. The company had been formed as a discount bank, especially for small tradesmen, but very little business had been done, Beal 'faking' the profits in order to declare dividends. The total amount obtained by way of subscriptions from the public was £20,000, not perhaps such a great sum compared with other fraudulent issues, but when the company was wound up, the assets amounted to only £336.

As soon as the prosecution had closed its case, which on account of its complexity took the Solicitor-General, Sir Robert Finlay and three junior counsel seven days to present, Rufus Isaacs put his client straight into the witness-box without first addressing the jury. This is common practice today, but at the time of this trial it was unusual, since it took place only a year after the passing of the Criminal Evidence Act which generally speaking permitted an accused person for the first time to testify on his or her behalf in court. It was at once a gesture of confidence and defiance, which impressed the jury. On the other hand the privilege in this instance was a two-edged sword, as Beal was naturally cross-examined by the prosecution, and the answers thus elicited put his guilt beyond question. It was in vain for Rufus Isaacs to plead that the company was bona fide and the reason for its failure lay in the hostility of more conservative and established banking institutions. Beal, who was described by the judge as 'the brains of the undertaking', was convicted and sentenced to four years' penal servitude. Singleton and Wain for their part as accessories received eighteen months and twelve months respectively in the second division, while Lambert, who was shown not to have been privy to or even aware of many of the company's transactions, was acquitted. Incidentally, Lambert was defended by a young Q.C., who had been made a silk at the same time as Rufus Isaacs and whose successful career as a leader was to run parallel with that of Rufus Isaacs during the next few years. He was a tall, good looking man with a commanding presence and a most melodious voice, which worked wonders with juries, particularly in criminal trials. His name was Edward Marshall Hall.

In those days, unlike the practice today, a seat in Parliament was an almost indispensable step to a seat on the judicial Bench. It so happened that both Rufus Isaacs and Marshall Hall were adopted as parliamentary candidates about this time, Rufus Isaacs as a Liberal in the London division of North Kensington and Marshall Hall as a Conservative in the Lancashire town of Southport. Both stood at the General Election in 1900, the so-called 'khaki election', which took place amid an immense wave of patriotic fervour engendered by the Boer War and resulted in a sweeping victory for the Conservatives. Marshall Hall was among those returned at the head of the poll and so gained the lead in the political stakes over Rufus who was defeated in North Kensington. It was natural for Rufus Isaacs to join the Liberals, since Liberalism was the normal party political faith of his race in England.

Although Rufus Isaacs supported the 'Liberal Imperialist' wing of the party under the leadership of Lord Rosebery in the House of Lords and Mr H. H. Asquith in the Commons, which believed the Boer War should be waged and won as against the anti-war wing led by Sir Henry Campbell-Bannerman, the prospect of winning North Kensington for the Liberals was a forlorn one. To start with, the Conservative and Unionist candidate, Mr Thompson Sharpe, was the sitting Member, who knew the division well, while the Liberal candidate was a complete newcomer. Nor were Mr Sharpe and his supporters anxious to inform the electors of the Liberal candidate's attitude to the War; on the contrary they campaigned with the slogan 'every vote given to the Liberals is a vote given to the Boers'. What is more the Conservative was defending a majority of 916, a relatively large one in those days of small electorates and marginal constituencies. Finally Joseph Chamberlain, the all powerful Unionist Colonial Secretary, sent a circular letter to every elector on the eve of the poll endorsing Mr Sharpe's candidacy.

Yet, in spite of all the big guns brought against him, Rufus Isaacs somewhat surprisingly succeeded in reducing the Conservative majority in North Kensington by 186 votes. The result, announced on October 5, 1900, was as follows:

W. E. T. Sharpe (C.) . . . 3,257
Rufus D. Isaacs (L.) . . . 2,527
                                   ———
Conservative majority . . .   730
                                   ———

Having thus won his spurs in party political battle, Rufus Isaacs might reasonably expect to be given a better constituency to fight at the next General Election or at least one with a better chance of a Liberal win. In the event he did not have to wait until the next General Election, as will be seen. Meanwhile he returned to rapidly increasing practice as a silk. The next two noteworthy cases in which he appeared arose out of the conduct of the Boer War.

The first of these was a libel action brought by Mr Arthur Chamberlain, the Colonial Secretary's brother, against *The Star*, the Liberal evening newspaper, as the result of articles alleging the use of political pressure in the securing of Government contracts for the supply of cordite for the armed forces. The whole question of such Government contracts had been raised by the Liberal Opposition in the House of Commons with such vehemence that the Government agreed to refer the matter to a Select Committee. The Committee duly reported in August, 1900, that it was fully satisfied with the allocation of contracts for cordite, among others; these included the contracts with the Midlands firm of Kynoch's, of which Mr Arthur Chamberlain was Chairman. It appeared that on several occasions this firm had put in a tender higher than its competitors, and was later given the opportunity of revising its tender to a figure acceptable to the War Office or Admiralty. This practice was justified by the Select Committee as being 'in the public interest'. Answering a parliamentary question in the same month as the Committee reported, the Colonial Secretary stated: 'I have no interest, direct or indirect, in Kynoch's or in any other firm manufacturing ammunition or war materials.'

Not content with these assurances, *The Star* proceeded to make some independent inquiries which revealed that Mr Joseph Chamberlain had shares in the Birmingham Trust Company, which in turn had invested 10 per cent of its capital in Kynoch's. The Minister, therefore, had an interest in Kynoch's, even if only indirectly, and Kynoch's had undoubtedly received preferential treatment in its contracts with the Government. *The Star* decided that such manifestations of a bad system must be attacked, and launched a series of articles to this effect. The attack was manifestly directed against the

Colonial Secretary, and to some extent also against his son Austen, then in his first ministerial post as Civil Lord of the Admiralty.

'Joe' Chamberlain and his son were both anxious to commence libel proceedings, but they were advised that an action would not lie. Consequently the plaintiff was the Colonial Secretary's brother Arthur, who claimed that the articles, alleging that he brought family influence to bear in obtaining Government contracts for cordite for Kynoch's on advantageous terms, were a libel upon himself. *The Star*'s defence was that, in so far as the remarks complained of were statements of fact, they were not defamatory; and in all other respects the articles were fair comment on matters of public interest. The trial came on before the Lord Chief Justice, Lord Alverstone, and a special jury in the King's Bench Division of the High Court on March 21, 1901, and lasted for five days. For the plaintiff, Sir Edward Clarke, K.C., a former Solicitor-General and probably the greatest living advocate, led Dr Blake Odgers, K.C., and Mr Whitmore Richards, while Mr Rufus Isaacs, K.C. and Mr Eldon Bankes, K.C., appeared for the defendant newspaper. The reason for the unusual spectacle of two King's Counsel conducting the defence in court without the assistance of junior counsel was that the written particulars of the defence and other preliminaries had all been prepared by Eldon Bankes, who was a junior at the time but had taken silk before the case came to trial.

Sir Edward Clarke in his opening speech presented his client as 'essentially a commercial man' of patent integrity whose character had been most unjustifiably attacked as Chairman of Kynoch's. He gave a convincing account of his activities in his examination-in-chief, and when his turn came to cross-examine Rufus Isaacs realized that it would be impossible to shake his evidence in any appreciable degree. However he did succeed in bringing out a few points, which must have made an impression upon the jury.

'In your opinion would it be legitimate to use political influence to get contracts for Kynoch's?' he asked.

'No,' replied Mr Chamberlain.

'Do you consider it would be legitimate to make use of the name of the Secretary of State for the Colonies to advance the interests of Kynoch's or any other company in which you are interested?'

'There are circumstances in which it would be perfectly legitimate.'

'Have you ever done it?'

'No.'

'Have any of your subordinates?'

'One did so without my knowledge,' said the witness. 'A gentleman of the name of Cullen has done so. He was the manager of the London office of Kynoch's until about six months ago.'

'How did he do it?' queried the defence counsel.

'By writing letters to the Agents-General of the Colonies.'

The plaintiff witness added that Mr Cullen had dictated a letter to the Foreign Office asking for introductions, and that this letter had been signed by the London director of Kynoch's. Among the introductions requested was one to the Prime Minister of New South Wales in which the Agent-General had been asked to mention in his letter that the chairman of the company was the Colonial Secretary's brother.

Pressed further on this matter, Mr Arthur Chamberlain said he had formed no opinion as to the object Mr Cullen had in mind when he wrote his letter.

'Is your mind a blank on the subject?' Rufus Isaacs asked him.

'Quite a blank,' was the bland reply.

Having made his point on this letter and on a similar one to the Agent-General for Queensland, Rufus Isaacs asked no further questions which might have spoiled their effect on the jury, but passed to other aspects of the case. One of these was the reduction of tenders.

'Do you say it would be wrong to describe it as a highly unusual process to be allowed to reduce your tender?' counsel went on.

'It is not highly unusual,' answered the witness.

'Is it unusual without the "highly"?'

'I cannot argue about that.'

'I suppose it is not a common thing?' the Lord Chief Justice interposed at this point.

'No, it is not common,' Mr Chamberlain admitted.

'Then it is unusual,' declared the judge.

Finally, in reply to the suggestion that the Colonial Secretary had forgotten about the Birmingham Trust Company's interest in Kynoch's when he gave his answer in the House of Commons, the witness asserted that this was impossible, as his brother had never known about it.

In his speech to the jury, Rufus Isaacs stressed that no imputation had been made on the plaintiff's private character, the articles being directed against his brother and nephew who were ministers of the Crown. The kernel of the matter was the Colonial Secretary's statement in the House of Commons, for it was a public statement inviting contradiction or refutation; and 'it is a thousand times to be regretted,' said Rufus Isaacs, his voice taking on an added note of sternness, 'for the sake of purity and honour of our national life that the statement which was made on August 8th was never contradicted.' He concluded by asking the jury to say that taking the broad aspects of the case, the defendants had been justified in making their comments. 'You must deal with the whole question broadly and in a public spirit,' he almost admonished them, 'and I look to you to vindicate the position the defendants have taken up in fearlessly commenting on matters of great public importance.'

The judge summed up in favour of the plaintiff, as indeed he was bound in the light of the evidence to do, for there could be little if any doubt that Mr Arthur Chamberlain had been libelled, and the jury returned a verdict accordingly. On the other hand, it said much for Rufus Isaacs's advocacy that when the jury were asked to consider the question of damages they should have awarded the plaintiff the relatively small sum of £200, which showed that they thought there was some moral justification for the articles but that the newspaper's zeal had outrun its discretion in publishing all of them. At all events *The Star* was jubilant about the result, and on the next day it ran a leader in which it paid a warm tribute to 'the vast skill and the perfect discretion with which the defence in the Chamberlain case was conducted by the counsel to whom it was confided in the face of even adverse circumstances and against such redoubtable opponents as Sir Edward Clarke – the unquestioned head of his profession – and Dr Blake Odgers, K.C. . . .'

The other case in which Rufus Isaacs figures arising out of the South African War, and more directly so than the Chamberlain case, was a criminal matter, which aroused considerable public interest at the time. It concerned a young South African, Dr Frederick Krause, who was charged on a number of counts with incitement to murder under the Offences Against the Person Act, 1861, and with attempted soliciting to commit murder. Krause came up at the Old Bailey on January 17, 1902, before the Lord Chief Justice, Lord Alverstone. The prosecution was led by the Solicitor-General, Sir Edward Carson, K.C., M.P., and the leading counsel for the defence was Rufus Isaacs. A curious feature of the case was that the prisoner, his intended victim and both the leading counsel were all members of the Middle Temple.

Krause, who had been employed in the Public Prosecutor's Office in Johannesburg, had temporarily lost his right to practise after the end of hostilities for declining to take the oath of allegiance to the British Crown like other Boers and had come to Europe on leave from his office. The legal adviser to the Military Governor of Johannesburg, Lord Roberts, was an English barrister named Forster practising in the town, and it was as the result of his advice that Krause and others like him were deprived of their advocates' certificates. Krause consequently conceived such a violent hatred towards Forster that he wrote two letters to a friend and former colleague in the Public Prosecutor's office in Johannesburg, one Cornelius Broeksma, urging that Forster should be 'shot dead in some lawful way, or otherwise put out of the way'. 'The sooner this was done,' wrote Krause, 'the better for our cause'. In fact, however, the letters never reached their addressee, since before they could do so, Broeksma was arrested on a charge of high treason, tried by court martial and executed. Eventually the letters were intercepted by the military censorship in Johannesburg, and it was on the strength of having written them (which he did not deny) that Krause was arrested and brought to trial.

In opening his defence of the prisoner, Rufus Isaacs argued a point of law with great skill. He submitted that, as there was no evidence that Broeksma had ever received the letters, there could be no offence, since it was necessary for the mind of the person solicited to be reached. From this view the Solicitor-General dissented, arguing that it was a question for the jury whether the accused had written the letters, whether they incited to murder and whether Krause intended their delivery to Broeksma.

Rufus Isaacs rejoined with the submission that mere intention was no offence under the law, nor were intention plus an act sufficient to convict when the person to be affected was not reached. After a night's reflection the Lord Chief Justice upheld this view, which is undoubtedly the correct one, with the result that Sir Edward Carson was obliged to drop this part of the indictment and concentrate on the lesser charge of attempting to solicit a person to commit murder.

The outcome was that Krause was found guilty of this lesser charge and received the maximum sentence of two years' imprisonment. But for the ingenious argument put forward by his leading counsel he might well have got a life sentence, as provided by the statute.

In this case Rufus Isaacs broke new ground in three respects. It was the first of his many forensic battles with the great Irish advocate, Sir

Edward Carson. It was also the first time that he was briefed by the well-known firm of solicitors, Lewis and Lewis, who were to give him much lucrative work during the succeeding years. Finally, his argument became the authority for the important proposition in law, established by the case of *Rex* v. *Krause* that, where an accused is charged with soliciting a person to murder another and the incitement is by letter, evidence of the receipt of the letter must be given if the charge is to stand.

4

For three years after their taking silk, Rufus Isaacs and Marshall Hall ran more or less neck and neck in the matter of professional income, although Marshall Hall was perhaps a little more widely known through his election to the House of Commons. Then disaster suddenly struck Marshall Hall. In a libel action against the *Daily Mail* at the end of 1901 in which the plaintiff, for whom Marshall Hall appeared, was an attractive young actress, Marshall Hall suggested that an adjournment had been obtained by the defendant newspaper for the purpose of finding out something detrimental to his client's character, and this suggestion undoubtedly inflamed the damages which the jury ultimately awarded against the newspaper. There was no foundation for this suggestion, and Marshall Hall's conduct was severely and somewhat unfairly criticized in the Court of Appeal, particularly by Lord Justice Mathew, who was known to dislike him. In its reports the Press was uniformly hostile, and as a result Marshall Hall's practice was nearly ruined. By the middle of the following year he was in financial difficulties, and Rufus Isaacs, when he heard this, wrote offering assistance. Marshall Hall did not at first refuse the offer, which was made with generosity and courtesy – 'I have a great desire to assist you,' Rufus Isaacs had told Marshall Hall, 'whilst placing you under the minimum sense of obligation possible under such circumstances'. Marshall Hall suggested that Rufus Isaacs should lend him £500 on the security of a valuable pearl pin, with an option to purchase the pin for this sum at the end of twelve months if the loan had not been repaid by that time, when he would be at liberty to resell the pin at a profit. But Rufus Isaacs replied that he had no wish either to purchase the pin to keep or to resell it, that he would buy it immediately for £500 on the understanding that Marshall

Hall would repurchase it within twelve months at that price. However, Marshall Hall felt too proud to accept the offer on these terms, and so the arrangement fell through, and Marshall Hall returned the cheque which Rufus Isaacs had sent him.

The courts were now about to rise for the Long Vacation, and Rufus Isaacs sent Marshall Hall the following characteristic letter:

> 1 Garden Court,
> Temple,
> London.
> August 12, 1902.

My dear Marshall Hall,

As you will not have the cheque, I have destroyed it, and now return your pearl. I understand your views and respect them deeply. At the same time I cannot forbear repeating to you that you can count on me in need, while I hope it will not happen. But, if it did, you and I are friends, and need not waste more words about it than these. I am ready when called upon.

Good-bye, my dear friend, for the present. Your dash and courage will stand you in good stead now, as always, in fighting the battle of life, and when we return to these haunts I hope you will be quite restored to health and spirits – professionally I am quite sure you have *had* your bad times.

> Yours very sincerely,
> Rufus D. Isaacs.

This gesture of Rufus Isaacs is a fine example of the chivalry and comradeship which are among the most distinctive features of the Bar. Marshall Hall, who was able to raise the money he needed from the sale of his collection of old silver, was always to remember it.

After writing to Marshall Hall in his attempt to help him in his misfortune, Rufus Isaacs went abroad for the Long Vacation. It was his first visit to the Continent for three years, since the English had been so unpopular during the Boer War that he preferred to stay at home for his annual holiday. He had previously spent two summers at Aix-les-Bains, partly for the sake of his wife's health and partly for his own, since he had developed a tendency to gout. Instead of returning to Aix, he decided to fall in with the suggestion of his old pupil Francis Oppenheimer, whose father was British Consul-General in Frankfurt, and try the waters at Homburg. This near-by spa had suddenly become fashionable through the patronage of King Edward VII, who had chosen it as a cure for gastronomic indulgence. Other members of the legal profession who frequented the spa included the

Lord Chancellor, Lord Halsbury, and Sir George Lewis, the well-known solicitor and senior partner in the firm of Lewis and Lewis, which had recently instructed Rufus Isaacs in the Krause case. It was Sir George who arranged for Rufus Isaacs to be presented to the King, a ceremony which took place in the Kurhaus and at which Rufus Isaacs had to exhibit some dexterity in dropping on one knee and kissing the royal hand while carrying a large glass of spa water. The King took an immediate liking to his subject and frequently invited Rufus Isaacs and his wife to meet him during his stay. Other members of the royal circle at Homburg with whom Rufus Isaacs was to become friendly with no disadvantage to himself were two newspaper proprietors, Sir Edward Lawson (later Lord Burnham) of the *Daily Telegraph* and Lord Glenesk of the *Morning Post*.

On his return to the Temple, Rufus Isaacs found himself briefed in two lucrative but widely dissimilar cases of note. The first was a society divorce suit which attracted much public attention on account of the titled people figuring in it. It is unnecessary to follow in detail this case, in which Sir Charles Hartopp, a gay, impecunious, racing baronet, filed a petition against his hunting wife on the ground of her adultery with Lord Cowley, while Lady Hartopp cross-petitioned for a decree by reason of her husband's adultery and cruelty, citing a certain Mrs Sands as intervener. Lady (Millicent) Hartopp, who had money of her own, was as well connected socially as her husband, being the eldest daughter of Mr Charles Wilson, M.P. (later Lord Nunburnholme), while her mother was a great-niece of the first Duke of Wellington. After a lengthy and expensive hearing, which lasted thirteen days and cost the parties the enormous sum of £15,000 – publication of evidence in divorce matters was permitted in those days and the evidence in this case was reported with considerable particularity and as eagerly lapped up by newspaper readers – both petitions were eventually dismissed after the public washing of a lot of dirty linen.

Rufus Isaacs appeared for Mrs Sands, who was described by Lady Hartopp's counsel Sir Edward Clarke as 'a very beautiful woman living apart from her husband, and who was known to be accessible to gentlemen who were prepared to pay somewhat heavily for her favours'. Although she had previously lapsed from virtue, Rufus Isaacs succeeded in convincing the jury that Mrs Sands had latterly been leading a chaste life and had not been guilty of any misconduct with Sir Charles Hartopp. 'A history and a past are great deterrents for keeping persons from the witness-box, because they fear the raking up,' he said. 'She has a history and a past, but it has not kept her from the box. Every effort was made to prevent her from going into the box, but she went, hard as it must have been for her, with the knowledge of the sins she has committed, and she has given her denial of her guilt with Sir Charles. The mere fact that she has for a time not been leading a proper life does not disentitle her to be believed in her denial that Sir Charles has committed adultery with her.' This speech created such an impression that applause broke out in court which was promptly suppressed by the judge. The evidence on which Sir Charles attempted to get a decree was as palpably flimsy, that the respondent and co-respondent called each other by their Christian names and occasionally dined alone together, that Lord Cowley helped Lady Hartopp to hang some pictures and even removed his coat and waistcoat in the process, and that they each had a private telephone installed in their respective country houses with which to carry on conversations with each other rather than use the public telephone in the village post office.

The other noteworthy case, very different from the Hartopp divorce, in which Rufus Isaacs appeared during the Michaelmas Term in 1902, proved to be a matter of immense importance to trade unions throughout the country. It arose from a strike of railwaymen against the Taff Vale Railway Company in South Wales, as a result of which the Company brought an action against the railwaymen's union, the Amalgamated Society of Railway Servants, seeking an injunction to restrain the Society from picketing the 'blackleg' labour with which the Company had replaced the strikers. The Society, relying on the prevalent belief that a trade union could not be sued in the courts, took out a summons, asking that they should be dismissed from the action. The issue of trade union immunity from legal process in these circumstances was decided against the union in the court of first instance, reversed on appeal by the Court of Appeal, and finally confirmed by the House of Lords who held that a trade union had the same duties as a private individual and its funds were subject to the same liabilities, thus taking the view that, although a trade union was not a corporation, it could nevertheless, under statute law, sue or be sued in its registered name. The question of legal principle having been determined in this sense, the Company's pending claim against the union for loss caused by the strike came before Mr Justice Wills in the King's Bench Division on December 2, 1902.

Rufus Isaacs, who led for the union, argued that one of the terms of the final settlement of the dispute had been that the Company should discontinue all legal proceedings, and that this action was consequently a breach of that agreement. Many of the railwaymen were members of the Society, and it was clearly impossible, he said, to sue the Society after an agreement had been made not to sue some of its members. It was an ingenious and persuasive argument – incidentally put forward immediately after the advocate had made his successful speech on behalf of Mrs Sands in the Divorce Court – but it had one fatal flaw. The agreement had been made with the men and not with the Society, and as the trade union was not a party to the agreement, it could not take advantage of it. This point was seized upon by Eldon Bankes for the Company, and eventually accepted by the judge after a discussion lasting four hours.

Rufus Isaacs fought on gamely, pleading that it was not right to saddle the union or its general secretary with responsibility for acts of violence committed by its pickets, whom they had not nominated, nor by persons who had acted without instructions and outside their authority. But the judge rejected this further argument, saying in his summing up that he considered the evidence of conspiracy to molest and injure the plaintiff company by unlawful means to be absolutely overwhelming. In the result the jury found for the Company on all counts, the question of damages being left to the judge to assess. This was eventually fixed by agreement between the parties at £23,000.

The judgment in the Taff Vale case filled trade unions throughout the country with consternation. The case had cost the Railway Servants' Society £50,000, and so long as the law remained unaltered no union could embark on a strike, no matter how amply justified, without fear of their funds being seriously depleted now that the unions could be sued for loss resulting from acts done in furtherance of industrial disputes.

The issue of trade union liability became a burning political issue and in the following General Election it was to occupy a prominent place in the Liberal Party programme as well as in that of the emerging Labour Party. It was not surprising, therefore, that one of the first pieces of legislation introduced by the new Liberal Government when it took office four years later was the Trade Disputes Act, 1906, which was designed to protect those engaged in industrial disputes from the operation of the law of conspiracy. By this time Rufus Isaacs was in Parliament and he had the satisfaction of voting for a measure which altered the law in the sense which he had so strongly advocated in the Taff Vale case. Meanwhile he had become quite a hero with the trade unions, and on his visits to Wales their more enthusiastic members were apt to drag him and his carriage in triumph about the country whenever he appeared to make a speech on a Liberal platform.

5

The case which finally established Rufus Isaacs in the public eye as one of the most outstanding, if not the most outstanding of the younger leaders at the Bar, was the trial of Whitaker Wright, a well-known company promoter and one time millionaire, on criminal charges of publishing false balance sheets of various concerns which he controlled. The trial, at which Rufus Isaacs led the prosecution, was of absorbing public interest, particularly in the City of London where Whitaker Wright had been regarded as a species of a financial genius until his biggest project collapsed in ruins bringing many others down with him. Moreover the trial involved its central figure in an immediate aftermath of tragedy which was to affect Rufus Isaacs deeply and which he could never forget as long as he lived.

Whitaker Wright was born in the north of England in 1845, the son of middle-class parents of extremely moderate means; he never lost his Northumbrian burr which gave the impression of confidence and solidity. As a youth of twenty-one, with some knowledge of geology and inorganic chemistry, he migrated to the United States where he started work as an assayer. With 500 dollars he had saved he bought a half share in a mine, which he sold on the mine turning out a big success. This provided him with enough working capital and was the foundation of his fortune, since he now invested in various mining companies, making and losing two fortunes in the great mining boom at Leadville. Ten years after landing in America he was a millionaire, and although he had lost much of his money before he decided to return to England in 1889, he still had enough to launch out on another spectacular and initially successful career in the City of London.

He began to form what are known as 'promoting companies', that is to say, companies with which the shareholders' money was used not to work properties but to acquire them. Such a concern was the West Australian Exploring and Finance Corporation, which he floated in 1894. Next came the London and Globe Finance Corporation, which he likewise used as a central company through which to promote other ventures. His profits from these two undertakings were £238,436, to which his expert knowledge of mining and plausible manners combined to contribute much in the pioneer and profitable task of opening up Western Australia. The most notable of the mining companies floated there by the London and Globe was Lake View Consols whose shares at one time rose to £29. In 1897 he was able to acquire the assets of the London and Globe, and of Western Australia, combining them to form a new company which he renamed the London and Globe Finance Corporation with a capital of £2 million in £1 shares, of which Whitaker Wright received £605,000. Having appointed himself managing director, he looked about for a titled chairman whose name would inspire confidence with the investing public. His choice fell on Lord Loch, a former Governor of Victoria, but after a few months Lord Loch retired from the chairmanship on the plea of other overriding commitments, although he remained a director. His Lordship recommended another retired pro-consul as his successor, the Marquess of Dufferin and Ava, a former Viceroy of India and Governor-General of Canada, who had just relinquished his last official post of Ambassador in Paris and 'loathed being idle'. Lord Dufferin accepted Mr Wright's handsome offer, and with the announcement of his appointment as chairman, the shares of London and Globe immediately rose to £2.

At first the promotion work of the new company was very profitable. For instance, it acquired the Ivanhoe mine at Kalgoorlie from a small colonial company with a capital of £50,000, and refloated it in London with a capital of £1,000,000 in £5 shares, the issue being a great success. In 1897, Whitaker Wright also launched the British America Corporation with a capital of £1½ million to acquire mining concessions in British Columbia and the Yukon. All these ventures were directly controlled by the financier from an office at 43 Lothbury, with a single staff of clerks. At this time he was dealing in millions of pounds and he certainly seemed to have the Midas touch. It is true there were occasional ugly rumours about the financial position of the London and Globe, but the Corporation continued to pay modest dividends and it was known to have made large profits from its holdings of Lake View Consols.

Whitaker Wright's private operations were on the same stupendous scale as his public ventures. His palatial town house, next to Londonderry House, in Park Lane, was filled with the most costly art treasures. At Lea Park, his country place near Godalming, he surrounded himself with the most extravagant luxuries such as a well-equipped observatory and a private theatre, and imported armies of workmen to level hills which obstructed his view and to dig artificial lakes. Underneath one of the lakes he had a billiard saloon constructed with a glass ceiling through which he and his guests could observe the fish above in the intervals between play, while the specially imported ancient carp silently watched the players below. In a near-by grotto illuminated by coloured lights, Italian boatmen would row the more romantically minded visitors. In the stables were fifty horses, each eating his head off in a separate cubicle. The owner had a mania for Italian marble fountains, and hordes of Italian sculptors and monumental masons were imported to construct them. He had one carved out of a solid block of marble weighing sixty tons, which was so heavy that it had to be dragged to Lea Park by traction engines. His guests at the height of his fame and fortune included prominent members of the aristocracy and nobility, and even royalty was known to patronize his entertainments. Farther afield in the Solent his famous yacht *Sybarita* defeated the German Emperor's *Meteor* in sight of the Royal Yacht Squadron.

If all had gone well with his business ventures, there is no reason why this multi-millionaire should not have ended up with a peer's coronet in addition to his other possessions. To be fair to him, none of his companies was bogus, and some of them, such as the Ivanhoe mine, paid large dividends. His decline really began when he directed his attention to the project of an underground railway in London, a field of which he had little or no technical knowledge, unlike his successful mining speculations. The London and Globe took over the construction and financing of the Baker Street and Waterloo Railway, afterwards known as the Bakerloo Tube, and locked up most of its ready money in it. Shortly afterwards the London and Globe had to step in to support the shares of Lake View Consols which dropped sharply after the rich find of ore which caused the rise was exhausted. The results were disastrous for Whitaker Wright and the company, which lost £782,000 in a single transaction in Lake Views. Yet on December 15, 1900, a balance sheet showed the parent company in a flourishing condition. Thirteen days later the London and Globe Finance Corporation announced its insolvency and went into liquidation. The disaster involved the failure of many members of the Stock

Exchange, the liquidation of several of the subsidiary companies, including the British America Corporation, and the ruin of many small investors. The reports of the Official Receiver, who examined Whitaker Wright, showed that the companies had long been on a false financial basis. It appeared that the accounts had been manipulated in such a way as to conceal deficits and the dividends paid by the London and Globe, not having been earned but having been provided by means of loans from the other companies, the balance sheet for the year 1899 showed a fictitious profit of £463,372, whereas there was a deficit in the region of £1,600,000.

In spite of the public outcry which followed the financier's public examination by the Official Receiver, and the raising of the matter in Parliament, the authorities refused to prosecute Whitaker Wright, although the Solicitor-General, Sir Edward Carson, openly expressed the view that a false balance sheet had been issued. The reason was a loophole in the Company Acts, which at that period penalized the publication of a false prospectus but made no provision for the institution of criminal proceedings where a false or misleading balance sheet had been published. Finally, one of the Corporation's creditors, a broker named John Flower, went to Mr Justice Buckley (afterwards Lord Wrenbury) in the Chancery Division and asked him to sanction a private prosecution, the costs to be paid out of the remaining assets of the London and Globe. The judge, who felt that on the facts a prosecution would lie under the Larceny Act, made the necessary order; but before any further step could be taken, the news broke in the City that Whitaker Wright had fled the country and was on his way by sea to America. Extradition proceedings were thereupon set in motion, and after a long delay, due to doubts about their validity owing to the financier's previous long residence in the United States, he was eventually brought back to England to stand his trial.

Whitaker Wright was tried, not at the Old Bailey, where the defence knew that he would stand little or no chance with a common jury, but at the Law Courts in the Strand before a special jury of householders. The formidable prosecuting team consisted of Rufus Isaacs, K.C., Horace Avory, K.C. (later Mr Justice Avory), Guy Stephenson, afterwards Assistant Director of Public Prosecutions and G. A. H. Branson, also afterwards a High Court Judge. Whitaker Wright was defended by Lawson Walton, later Attorney-General, Richard Muir, later Director of Public Prosecutions and Felix Cassel, afterwards Judge Advocate General. The presiding judge was

Mr Justice Bigham (afterwards Lord Mersey). The trial which, occupied twelve days, opened on December 11, 1904, and in spite of the extreme technical character of much of the evidence, the court-room was crowded throughout the hearing.

The detailed and prolix indictment contained twenty-six counts, the case against the financier being one, to quote Rufus Isaacs, 'of as great complexity as has perhaps ever been presented'. Briefly the issues involved the questions whether the balance sheets and reports of the London and Globe Corporation for the years 1899 and 1900 were false in material particulars; whether they were false to the knowledge of Whitaker Wright: and if so, whether these false accounts and reports were published for the purpose of deceiving shareholders or defrauding creditors or inducing other persons to become shareholders. When it was suggested that an abstract of the indictment should be put before the jury so that they could find a separate verdict on each count, Mr Justice Bigham remarked: 'I might as well give the jury Archbold's *Criminal Pleading* or the *Encyclopaedia Britannica.*'

It took Rufus Isaacs five hours to open the case for the prosecution. His speech was generally hailed as a masterpiece of conciseness and lucidity, although Mr Justice Bigham, great commercial judge though he was, was obliged to interrupt from time to time to say he found it difficult to thread his way through the financial maze which the prosecuting counsel was unfolding. Time and again Rufus Isaacs would quote figures running into millions of pounds without referring to a note, and once he raised a laugh in the solemn atmosphere of the court by saying that a mere item of £10,000 was not worth talking about. There was another ripple of mirth when he referred to the list as having been put in the 1900 balance sheet at £2,332,632 0s. 1d. – the penny, as Rufus Isaacs observed, 'being an artistic touch'. Indeed the financial jugglings in which Whitaker Wright had indulged were as amazing as some of his statements were palpably misleading. A particularly glaring example of the latter was Whitaker Wright's statement at the last shareholders' meeting of the London and Globe that over a million pounds had been written off during the past year from the value of the assets, whereas £960,000 represented not depreciation but dead loss.

On the seventh day of the trial, Whitaker Wright left his seat at the solicitors' table – the fact that the trial took place in the Law Courts spared him the humiliation of sitting in the dock – and went into the witness-box. With his goatee beard, gold pince-nez and black frock-coat, the defendant looked a thoroughly respectable business man, as he answered his own counsel's questions with a careless ease, telling how he had lent the London and Globe £400,000 of his own money, which he had intended settling on his children, and confidently asserting that there was nothing criminal in his arranging for his companies to lend money to each other as the occasion required. He looked less happy as Rufus Isaacs began his cross-examination by asking why he had gone to America when he knew that a prosecution was pending. It was a coincidence, he explained, as he had already booked passages for himself and his wife. But the men in the jury-box did not look at all favourably impressed by the coincidence, any more than they did by the defendant's explanation of the inter-company payments.

'You received all this money as chairman of one company from yourself as chairman of another?' Rufus Isaacs asked him.

'I do not like that way of putting it,' Whitaker Wright replied.

Then, after a moment's pause, he added amid some laughter, 'The money was paid by one company to the other.'

Pressed for details, the financier was forced to admit that he had made 'slips' on two occasions when he was anxious to conceal the true state of affairs. For instance, in a letter to Lord Dufferin he had said that the amount of profit shown was after allowing for a deduction of £500,000 from the market value of the shares, whereas he ought to have said 'cost or par value'. On the whole, Whitaker Wright kept his temper, but once, stung by Rufus Isaacs's quiet but persistent probing, he burst out that counsel would like him to be chairman, secretary and everything in the company. 'No,' answered Rufus Isaacs, amid laughter, 'I think *you* were quite enough.'

The Globe's balance sheet for 1899 had been bad enough, but the accounts for the following year were worse. The financier looked very worried and began to mop his brow, as Rufus Isaacs's relentless questioning continued about what he had told the shareholders at the last annual general meeting.

'You said over a million sterling had been written off for depreciation. That was untrue?'

'I do not admit it,' replied the witness. 'You must take the whole report together.'

'You said "over a million sterling"?'

'I should have said "for loss and depreciation".'

'Have you any doubt that this statement is absolutely untrue?'

'In its connection it is true. But I ought to have said "loss and depreciation",' the financier repeated. 'It was an extempore utterance.'

'That is,' said Rufus Isaacs with an air of finality, 'as it stands, the statement is untrue.'

Whitaker Wright left the witness-box a beaten man, with the verdict against him a foregone conclusion. Rufus Isaacs's closing speech for the Crown lasted a day and a half, but it really boiled down to a reiteration of the fact that the financier had convicted himself out of his own mouth when he admitted in cross-examination that he had published the 1900 balance sheet in order to conceal from the shareholders the true state of affairs. While the judge was summing up, strongly against him, the accused man was observed scribbling the Roman numeral VII on a piece of blotting paper in front of him. And seven years' penal servitude, the maximum under the statute, was the sentence which Mr Justice Bigham passed upon him. Beyond a slight twitching of the face, Whitaker Wright showed no signs of emotion, when he stood up to hear it. 'My lord,' he said, bowing to the Bench, 'all I have to say is that I am as innocent as any person in this court of any intention to deceive or defraud the shareholders.'

Accompanied by two court officials, he was taken to one of the consultation rooms near the court-room so that he could have a discussion with his advisers about the possibility of an appeal. Here he was joined by his leading counsel, Lawson Walton; his solicitor, Sir George Lewis; his accountant, and the surety who had gone bail for him. 'This is British justice,' the financier exclaimed when the door had closed. 'What have I done? I am amazed. I have done nothing wrong. I think it is disgraceful.' For a moment or two it looked as if he would give way to his feelings. But he recovered his composure and thanked them all for what they had done for him. 'Everything that could be done has been done.'

Sir George Lewis poured out some whisky, added some water, and handed the glass to his unfortunate client, together with a cigar which he took from his own case. After he had had a drink, the financier took out his gold watch and chain and gave them to his surety. 'I shall have no use for these where I am going,' he remarked with a bitter smile. 'Keep them for me until we meet again.'

He talked on for a quarter of an hour or so about an appeal and also about what should be done with his personal property. Then he excused himself and went to the door. The two court officials were waiting outside and he informed them that he wished to go to the lavatory. They raised no objection. Then, during the minute or two he was in the lavatory he swallowed a capsule of potassium cyanide, a deadly poison, which he had somehow managed to secrete under his tongue. On returning to the consultation room, he asked for a glass of water, which he drank, presumably to dissolve the poison more quickly. He then threw away the cigar he had nearly finished smoking and asked his accountant for another. As he lit it, his hand was seen to be shaking violently. A moment later he collapsed and fell back in his chair. The others rushed to his assistance and a doctor was immediately summoned. But Whitaker Wright was beyond human aid. He died just as the doctor arrived.

The news of the financier's sudden end spread quickly through the Law Courts. Rufus Isaacs was in consultation in another room with a solicitor and the lay client, an actress, when his clerk came in to tell him what had happened. At first Rufus Isaacs thought that the financier had died from natural causes and that he had helped to kill him. He was extremely upset in consequence and was unable to continue the consultation. Later, when he heard that Whitaker Wright had taken his own life, he felt considerably relieved. He was reassured too by the leading article which appeared in *The Times* next day and which paid tribute to 'the exemplary fairness' with which he had conducted the prosecution of the dead financier.

There were some, notably his defending counsel, who thought that Whitaker Wright deserved more pity than blame. Certainly he was no bogus company promoter, and all his ventures were basically sound. The trouble was that the public was slower to appreciate their value than he estimated. The Baker Street and Waterloo Railway, for instance, was a speculation, but it was the forerunner of the whole of the London underground system. And how many of the thousands who daily travel on the Bakerloo recall that this profitable line owed its beginning to a man who committed suicide rather than go to prison for seven years?

Solicitor-General

1

The Whitaker Wright case with its dramatic climax made the name of the dead financier's prosecutor known throughout the land. Not only did it bring a further flood of briefs to Garden Court, but it reminded the party chiefs at Liberal Headquarters that Rufus Isaacs deserved a better constituency than the forlorn hope of North Kensington which he had contested at the last General Election. Although the next Election was not expected for at least two years, Rufus and his Liberal friends considered that it would be desirable if he could find a seat where the Member would not be seeking re-election and the Liberal Committee was looking for a candidate to replace him. By a stroke of luck, the ideal seat for Rufus Isaacs suddenly became available at this time in the borough of Reading.

During the past twenty years, Reading had changed its allegiance several times, when it had returned Conservative and Liberal candidates alternately at four successive elections. The sitting Member, Mr George William Palmer, was a Liberal. He was also a man of strong local influence, both as a former Mayor of Reading and the head of the well-known firm of biscuit manufacturers, Huntley & Palmer. He suffered from increasing deafness which resulted in his decision not to go forward again. With his support, coupled with the fact that the tide was beginning to run against the Conservative Government in office, Rufus Isaacs felt he had a good chance of retaining the seat for his party. It was also a convenient seat both to 'nurse' and in the event to represent, since it was less than an hour's run by train from London, which meant that the prospective candidate or Member could always get back to town the same night after an evening meeting. Another consideration was that Reading was unlikely to make the same heavy demands upon his time and energies that might be expected of a London borough.

Rufus Isaacs accepted the Reading Liberal Committee's invitation to become the prospective Liberal candidate, feeling sure that he would have not less than two years to get to know the division and its electorate. However, within a few months, in July, 1904, Mr Palmer announced that his health made it necessary for him to retire immediately. And so Rufus Isaacs, who was looking forward to a leisurely Long Vacation as a relief from the burden of professional work, suddenly found himself plunged into a by-election fight in a constituency where he was still a comparative stranger.

In the 1900 Election, Mr Palmer's majority had only been 239 out of a total of 14,000 voters. Also the Conservative candidate, Mr Charles Keyser, was a well-known property owner in the neighbourhood, whose influence might be expected to counterbalance if not outweigh the retiring Member's support for the Liberal newcomer. Besides this, Mr Keyser, who had fought the seat twice, could rely on the help of other local industrial interests, notably from Suttons, the seed merchants, and Simmonds, the brewers. So by all appearances the by-election looked as if it would be a pretty close-run affair, as indeed it proved to be.

The Liberal candidate and his wife made their headquarters in the Lodge Hotel, a small temperance establishment near Huntley & Palmer's biscuit factory, since the larger hotels, which were licensed for the sale of alcoholic drinks, were all Tory strongholds. The Lodge was adorned with large banners and posters lettered in red proclaiming the slogan 'Rufus for Reading'. Indeed it appeared throughout the town; it caught the eye immediately and, as it turned out, prophetically.

Although he had the disadvantage of not being a local figure, nevertheless Rufus Isaacs was the candidate for a party which under the parliamentary leadership of Sir Henry Campbell-Bannerman at least had the semblance of unity. The Conservatives, on the other hand, were split on the issue of tariff reform, the dissident Protectionist wing being led by Mr Joseph Chamberlain, who had recently left the Government; while the Prime Minister, Mr Balfour, and his supporters were still largely committed to the general policy of free trade and were disinclined to go beyond a certain measure of 'reciprocity' in the matter of international trade and tariffs. Mr Keyser was understandably cautious in his election address and did his best to please both wings of his party. 'The question of Fiscal Reform has long had my careful attention,' he wrote, 'and I am of opinion that the state of Trade in the Empire necessitates a most careful inquiry into the whole matter, and that some measures should be adopted to preserve to this country the industries and manufactures that are now so seriously handicapped by unfair competition.'

The campaign was brief but hectic and covered the August Bank Holiday. Rufus Isaacs opened it with a speech in the Town Hall, pouring scorn on his opponent's political indecision.

> I can't help thinking that he must have been reading Mr Balfour's speech at Sheffield and out of the maze of it he must have penned this paragraph: 'The question of Fiscal Reform has long had my careful attention.' Mark that! Mr Keyser is not starting upon his initial study of Fiscal Reform, but it has long had his attention.
>
> 'I am of the opinion that the state of Trade in the Empire necessitates a most careful inquiry into the whole matter.' One would have imagined that he might have arrived at that conclusion without long and careful consideration.

After he had torn the luckless Mr Keyser's manifesto to shreds, the Liberal candidate let there be no doubt about where he himself stood politically. He was unreservedly for Free Trade, taxation of land values and reform in a wide field, particularly Army reorganization, licensing, education and the legal position of trade unions. His view on education was 'in favour of a great and comprehensive system of education, free and controlled by the people, so that the utmost advantages to be derived from study should be brought within the reach of the poorest of the community'. On the trade-union question he was already an expert, having appeared for the railwaymen's union in the celebrated Taff Vale case as described in the preceding chapter. Now he declared himself 'in favour of amending the laws affecting trade unions so as to afford adequate protection to the association of working men'.

During the following nine days before the poll, some distinguished and brilliant speakers came to Reading to support the Liberal candidate at his meetings. From the Front Opposition Bench in the House of Commons there was Mr Lloyd George, who bitterly attacked the Government's education policy. From the back benches there were Mr Herbert Samuel (later Viscount Samuel), Mr John Freeman-Thomas (later Marquess of Willingdon), and Mr Winston Churchill, who had originally been elected a Conservative but had recently crossed the floor of the House to sit with the Liberals. Another speaker on Isaacs's platform at this election was a brilliant youngster just down from Cambridge where he had been President of the Union; his name was Edwin Samuel Montagu and he was the son of Sir Samuel Montagu, first Lord Swaythling, the Jewish banker and philanthropist. All these men were later to be closely and, in the case of Lloyd George, intimately associated with Rufus Isaacs in politics and public life.

Polling took place on August 4, 1904. Immediately after the close the ballot boxes were brought to the Town Hall for the count. Shortly after ten o'clock the Returning Officer declared the result as follows:

Isaacs, Rufus D. (L.) . . .	4,770
Keyser, Charles E. (C.). . .	4,540
Liberal majority	230

The news was conveyed to the immense crowd waiting outside by the appearance of a placard bearing the inscription: 'Rufus D. Isaacs, K.C., M.P.' The victor immediately stepped out on the balcony, but so great was the volume of cheering from his Liberal supporters that he could not make himself heard and had to withdraw indoors where an improvised platform was hastily set up. In moving the customary vote of thanks to the Returning Officer, the new M.P. spoke with remarkable candour. After referring to the fact that both his opponent and his predecessor were local men, he said: 'I came of course as a stranger. I only wooed you as a politician. I never attempted to do anything else than to appeal to you as a politician.' Indeed this made the Liberal victory all the more remarkable on the occasion, when it is remembered that Rufus Isaacs polled only nine votes less than Mr Palmer had done at the previous Election.

On leaving the Town Hall, the successful candidate and his wife were dragged round Reading in their carriage before being brought back to their hotel. There he received another ovation, and after he had gone inside the crowd kept shouting for him to come out and speak to them. After hesitating for a minute or two behind a curtain, the victor finally appeared at the window where he made one of the shortest speeches in his career. 'Bravo, Reading,' he exclaimed. 'This is your victory, not mine.'

Four days later, shortly before Parliament rose for the summer recess, Rufus Isaacs was introduced and took his seat in the House of Commons. His sponsors on this occasion, which the custom of the House required, were Mr Herbert Gladstone (later Viscount Gladstone), the Liberal Chief Whip, and Mr (afterwards Sir) Alfred Rose, who lived near Reading and had been of immense help to the new Member during the election. Flanked on either side by these two gentlemen, he slowly advanced to the Table, to the accompaniment of loud cheers from the Opposition benches, duly took the oath, signed the Members' Roll and shook hands with the Speaker. At the age of forty-three, Rufus Isaacs was already in the first rank of his chosen profession; he was now about to begin a fresh career in Parliament.

Unlike the rising young junior on the Northern Circuit F. E. Smith, who was to ask his first parliamentary question and make a celebrated and controversial maiden speech within twelve days of his election, Rufus Isaacs spent many months in absorbing the peculiar atmosphere of the House of Commons before he made any attempt to 'catch the Speaker's eye' in a debate. It was not until nine months had passed that he put down his first question on the Order Paper and that was merely for a written answer. Hardly calculated to arouse deep nationwide feelings, it was to ask the President of the Local Government Board why the Reading Poor Law Guardians had not been allowed to provide tea in place of gruel to casuals entering the vagrancy wards at night, and whether the Board would not reconsider its decision. But the Minister was not prepared to make an exception to the general principle, particularly as the whole subject of vagrants was 'being investigated' by a departmental committee.

Two more months were to pass before Rufus Isaacs addressed the House for the first time. The occasion, which occurred during the passage of the Aliens Bill, was not perhaps the best he could have chosen. This measure, designed to regulate immigration, had come before a Committee of the whole House, but it was being discussed at such length, owing to the number of amendments put down by the Opposition, that Mr Balfour for the Government was obliged to move a 'guillotine' resolution, that is that further consideration of the Bill should be governed by a fixed time-table. It was in the debate on this strictly procedural motion that Rufus Isaacs rose to deliver his maiden speech.

It was on the whole an urbane and polished performance, but from the nature of the subject it lacked the fire and sparkle that another occasion might have offered. However, it did contain a criticism of House of Commons procedure which is still valid.

> Whatever charges have been levelled against Members of the Opposition [he began], I at least may be entitled to some credit for not having obstructed the proceedings of the House . . . The ordinary man in the street would have known that this Bill was impossible in the five days it has been before the House. I understand that only eleven days out of a total of seventy-three have been given to legislation. As a new Member of the House I have my lessons to learn, but I have been sitting and learning them for some time, and I should have thought, even without becoming a Minister and certainly without becoming a Prime Minister, that it was possible to remedy that position with the greatest ease . . . Judging from my short experience of the way in which Parliament's affairs are conducted, the House of Commons as a means of passing legislation is a very ineffective body indeed.

The speaker went on to discuss the merits of a particular clause in the Bill concerning political refugees and the right of asylum. In so doing, of course, he was strictly speaking out of order, but as it was a maiden speech he was allowed some latitude by the chair and was not pulled up as the ordinary Member might well have been. But it was noticeable that when Mr Balfour came to wind up the debate, he administered a mild rebuke to the new M.P. for Reading whom he charged with 'having made now the speech which he is afraid he will be excluded by this resolution from making at a later stage'. However, the Prime Minister did make a graceful reference to the maiden speaker 'who has a deservedly high reputation in other spheres of activity and whose intervention in our debates I am sure all of us welcome'. From the Front Opposition Bench Mr Lloyd George was more enthusiastic. He described the speech as 'admirable' and went on to endorse the newcomer's criticism of parliamentary procedure. 'What struck the honourable and learned Member most of all was that this was a futile place to come to do work in,' he said, 'and that is what strikes every business man.'

Rufus Isaacs was sufficiently encouraged by the reception of his maiden speech to intervene on the Report Stage of the Bill twelve days later when he moved an amendment to the clause designed to afford protection to refugees on account of religion. He wished to extend this asylum to those persecuted for their political opinions as well. However, the Attorney-General, Sir Robert Finlay, felt the

Government could not accept such a widely drawn amendment, and it was duly defeated on a division by 214 votes to 152.

It would be unfair to describe Rufus Isaacs as a failure in the House of Commons. He was a man who made friends easily and professional colleagues apart he cultivated some useful friendships in the House, such as that of Lloyd George. He enjoyed the company of the smoking-room on the relatively infrequent occasions that he joined it. If he was not in the chamber, he was usually to be found in the library working on the next day's briefs. When he did speak, he was always heard with attention. But he was never a House of Commons man in the sense that Lloyd George and Winston Churchill were. On legal and legislative questions his judgments were shrewd and sound as befitted the able lawyer that he was. But there always remained the feeling somehow that he was speaking to a brief or addressing a jury. And this was understandable, since he seldom reached the House before the evening having spent the greater part of the day in court or at consultations with clients in his chambers. As he himself once said, in recalling this period of his life, 'I was tired out when I got to the House.'

2

Although he could fulfil most of his constituency engagements and return to London on the same day owing to the excellent train service between Reading and Paddington, Rufus Isaacs decided to look round for a place in or near the division, which would also serve as a convenient refuge from London at week-ends and during the law vacations. For two months in the summer of 1903 he rented the Rectory Farm at Streatley, a pleasant spot on the edge of the Berkshire Downs. This was a good base for house hunting, and he and his wife made many excursions to inspect possible houses in the neighbourhood of Reading. Eventually their choice fell upon a rambling mansion with an attractive garden and a picturesque lake called Fox Hill on the outskirts of the town.

Fox Hill was the scene of many gay week-end gatherings during the dozen or so years that Rufus and Alice Isaacs lived there. From the political field the guests included Lloyd George, Augustine Birrell, Charles Masterman, Alec Murray (the Master of Elibank), while on the literary and theatrical side there were J. M. Barrie, A. E. W.

Mason, and Alfred Sutro and his wife Esther, who was a sister of Rufus Isaacs. Young Gerald Isaacs, who was now growing up and would soon be going to Oxford, was to recall these happy occasions, particularly his father's boisterousness at breakfast, when his 'heartiness of spirits and appetite were always a source of wonder to his less resilient family and friends'. Once when Augustine Birrell was staying in the house, the guest happened to wake early. It was a fine summer morning, his windows were wide open, and he heard someone singing in the garden. 'He looked out, and there was his host, in flannels, capering about on the lawn, and singing from the pure joy of being alive!' Birrell glanced at his watch; it was half-past four. Rufus Isaacs 'was having a little exercise in the garden before starting work at his briefs'.

He had long since given up riding, but there was a tennis court on the property and he tried to keep fit there. He had also become a keen golfer and would often go over to Walton Heath to play with Lloyd George and his friends, notably Alec Murray, Percy Illingworth, Charles Masterman and George Riddell. Besides these pastimes, he took up motoring. His first vehicle, an open 20–30 h.p. Renault with a yellow body, was quite sensational in its way, having side doors instead of the more usual entry from the back. But the dust and wind encountered in this vehicle, not to mention the paraphernalia of veils, gauntlets and goggles, proved too much for his wife. So a closed Delaunay-Belleville landaulette was acquired for her use. He also had a small Panhard on which he tried to learn to drive. But quickly realizing that he had no aptitude for this novel pastime, he gave it up and henceforth relied on chauffeurs, of whom he had two at this period. They can be seen in a photograph with Alice Isaacs and the Delaunay-Belleville taken outside the front door of Fox Hill in that comfortable Edwardian era when food and servants were both abundant and cheap.

By this time Rufus Isaacs had acquired a new town house in the then fashionable and opulent Park Lane. It was a small house in the attractive crescent of Georgian houses opposite Grosvenor Gate. It had a tiny study on the third floor next to his son Gerald's bedroom. When Gerald was down from Oxford during the vacations, he would often return to the house in the early hours of the morning to en-counter his father on his way to begin the day's work on his briefs. 'He always behaved perfectly on such occasions,' his son was later to recall, 'and after the exchange of a few impersonal remarks we withdrew to our respective sanctums. By common consent no reference was made at breakfast to our earlier meeting and his "Good morning" carried no hint of recollection or reproach.'

His changed social surroundings, reflected in Fox Hill and the house in Park Lane, were fully justified by his professional success. His earnings at the Bar for the year 1904 were more than £28,000, an enormous figure for those times. In one commercial action, in which he appeared for the defendants against Sir Edward Clarke, when Lake George Gold Mines Ltd. sued Gibbs, Bright & Co. for negligence and fradulent misrepresentation in connection with the sale of copper mines in Australia, his brief for the defence was marked at 2,000 guineas. This was probably an unprecedented fee; in his subsequent career it was only twice equalled and never exceeded. The brief, with the stupendous figure marked on it by the instructing solicitors, became a centre of interest in court and barristers' and solicitors' clerks would come and peep at it in awe as Rufus Isaacs's clerk kept jealous guard over the precious document.

Some years later, while Rufus Isaacs was playing golf with Lloyd George and George Riddell, chairman of the *News of the World*, the Press magnate asked him which of his law cases had impressed him most. Rufus Isaacs thought for a minute and then said: 'The defence of Sir Edward Russell, editor of the *Liverpool Post*, on a charge of criminal libel. Serious public issues were involved, in addition to which my client was a fine, striking personality.' The trial took place at Liverpool Assizes on the eve of the General Election in December, 1905.

Sir Edward Russell (later first Lord Russell of Liverpool) had been editor of the *Liverpool Daily Post and Mercury* for over thirty-five years and was a most respected public figure in the city where he had spent a lifetime in journalism. The newspaper, of which he was also the owner, was a Liberal organ, and Sir Edward, who had been a Liberal M.P. for a short time, reflected his party's policy in his editorial articles. It was one of these editorials, in which he criticized certain members of the Licensing Committee of the Liverpool justices, that led to criminal libel proceedings being taken against him.

In 1904, a Licensing Act had been passed by Parliament with the object of reducing the number of liquor licences granted to publicans in cases where there were complaints or it was felt that there were too many public houses in a district. The extinguished licence holders were to receive compensation, which was to be levied by the local

Licensing Committee of magistrates on the surviving licences. It was consequently in the interests of the liquor trade to have the compensation levied at the lowest possible rate laid down by the Act, which would mean that those who had their licenses renewed would have to pay a minimum amount of compensation, while a fewer number of licences would be extinguished than if compensation had been levied at a higher rate.

At the beginning of 1905, the whole body of Liverpool justices met to constitute a Licensing Committee. Sir Edward Russell proposed in the *Liverpool Post* that the Committee should consist of seven Conservatives and seven Liberals with Sir Thomas Hughes, an independent Conservative of progressive views, as chairman. But this suggestion did not commend itself to the Conservative majority of justices, and as a result the Committee was made up of ten Conservatives, including Sir Thomas Hughes, and six Liberals. On July 12, the Committee met to consider the rate of compensation to be levied in respect of twenty-nine public houses which had been reported to the Committee as being unfit to have their licences renewed. The Liberal minority proposed to levy the full rate, which would have amounted to £37,000. This was opposed by eight of the Conservatives, who wished for half the maximum rate, and although Sir Thomas Hughes tried to reach a compromise by proposing three-fifths, the Conservatives carried their motion for the half-rate, the voting being on strictly party lines.

Next day Sir Edward Russell attacked the eight Conservatives in an editorial which gave rise to the criminal proceedings. 'These gentlemen will hardly pretend that they were influenced in the course they took by a desire to diminish the number of licences in the city,' he wrote. He went on to state that what the Conservatives on the Committee really desired was 'to hamper and obstruct those who are striving to effect without "gross injustice and discontent" a sorely needed reduction. The effect of the Committee's decision will be to make the rate of reduction actually less than it was under the old order of things, a result which no doubt was shrewdly foreseen. We congratulate "the Trade" upon the ability and courage of their friends – we had almost said their representatives – on the Licensing Committee.'

The eight Conservatives who had been mentioned by name in the editorial decided to take immediate proceedings. Five days later, on their solicitors' instructions, Mr F. E. Smith successfully applied to a Divisional Court for a rule nisi for the issue of a criminal information against Sir Edward for libel. A further application to make the rule absolute was granted by Lord Alverstone, the Lord Chief Justice, after hearing arguments from counsel led by Mr H. H. Asquith, K.C., for the applicants. At the trial, which opened before Mr Justice Bray in St George's Hall, Liverpool, on December 7, 1905, Mr Asquith's place as leader for the defence was taken by Rufus Isaacs, while Sir Edward Clarke relinquished the lead for the prosecution to Mr W. F. Taylor, K.C., with Mr F. E. Smith as junior counsel. Sir Edward Russell pleaded 'Not Guilty' on the ground that the libel was true and published in the public interest, and that there was no imputation of corrupt or dishonest motives. As Rufus Isaacs defined the issue in his opening speech to the jury, it was 'substantially a question of whether or not Sir Edward was making a comment which he had a right to make on a public body. In view of the defence the whole matter was dominated by political considerations.'

The principal witness for the prosecution was Mr Isaac Morris, the Conservative Vice-Chairman of the Committee, a typical hard-headed, slow-moving northern business man. Rufus Isaacs cross-examined him with characteristic skill. He began by asking him about the advantage to the Conservative Party of having effective control of the Licensing Committee.

'I can assure you,' the witness declared, 'that politics were not introduced into the matter except in so far as forming the two parties or two sets of men.'

'Did not that give you a political advantage?' asked Rufus Isaacs.

'No.'

'Why was it done then?'

'To represent the two parties on the Bench.'

'And why should the two parties on the Bench be represented?' counsel persisted. 'Why should the Conservatives be anxious to have a majority if it was not to give the Conservatives a political advantage?'

The witness looked nonplussed for a few moments. Then the realization dawned on him that he had been led into a neatly laid trap. 'You put a very difficult question,' he replied at last, to the accompaniment of laughter in Court.

Rufus Isaacs quickly pressed home his advantage. In reply to further questions, Mr Morris was forced to admit that he had insisted on a proportionate as against an equal political representation, and that he had once gone to the local Conservative Club to 'invite' men to serve on the Committee. And, when divisions took place in the Committee, he had to admit that they were on party lines.

'You thought it was an advantage to have the Conservatives in a majority on the Bench?'

'Yes, on the Bench and everywhere else.'

'And, thinking that,' Rufus Isaacs went on to clinch the matter, 'you were desirous to get a majority on the Committee?'

'Yes,' answered Mr Morris, whose guard was now completely down. 'The facts are there. We can't dispute them.'

Mr Morris was followed into the witness-box by another of the eight aggrieved Conservatives, Sir Charles Petrie, a former Lord Mayor of Liverpool. From him Rufus Isaacs extracted the most valuable admission for the defence. When he had read the article, Sir Charles said, he had never thought that the writer had meant to make any imputation of corrupt or dishonest motives against himself. He regarded it as quite inconceivable that Sir Edward Russell should have done so.

After three more of the Conservative justices had given evidence, Mr Taylor for the prosecution announced that he did not propose to call the others as their evidence would be mere repetition. Answering Rufus Isaacs, the last of three witnesses, Mr Frodsham, in the words of the defence counsel, 'let the cat out of the bag' when he admitted that the liquor interest 'do support the Conservative Party and there is good reason why they should'. As Rufus Isaacs remarked when he came to address the jury, 'that observation of Mr Frodsham's is the answer to the whole of the case'.

In defence of his client, Rufus Isaacs had this to say:

> I don't hesitate to say in a public court that not only was Sir Edward Russell entitled to make the observations contained in this article upon the action of these licensing justices in Liverpool, the predominant political party on this committee, but that he was entitled to comment upon the action of a judge upon the Bench, and upon the action of all the magistrates in every court throughout the country. The days are not coming in this country when criticism of those holding public positions is to be narrowed down by elaborate technicalities and microscopic examination of every bit of the phraseology used in this article.
>
> Long ago, in the reign of George III, this question was fought out after a bitter controversy, with the fight for freedom in this country which was then fought between the people of this country and the judges of the country, and which led to the Act of Parliament which we lawyers know as Fox's Act. That Act establishes this one great prin-

ciple, the fundamental principle of justice in this country – that the question whether an article is a libel or not is not to be decided by the judge, however strong his views may be, but the question is to be decided by and left by him to the consideration and determination of the jury. That is the law of this free country.

For the defence, besides the defendant himself, Rufus Isaacs called as witnesses two of the six Liberal members of the Licensing Committee, the Bishop of Liverpool and Sir William Forwood, an ex-Lord Mayor and senior member of the City Council. Both of them testified as to Sir Edward's long and deep interest in temperance reform and the necessity for the reduction of licences in the city. Cross-examination of these witnesses was brief, and soon Rufus Isaacs was again on his feet making his closing speech to the jury.

The present criminal procedure, he urged, could only be justified by the imputation of dishonest motives in the discharge of public duty. But since there was no such imputation in this case, as Sir Charles Petrie, who was one of the prosecutors, had made clear in his evidence, an ordinary civil action for libel should have been brought. After analysing the article in detail, counsel went on: 'When you come to deal with it in the light of the facts which have been disclosed in this Court, don't you think, gentlemen, that the prosecutors are at the present moment feeling very considerable regret that they ever thought fit to bring these proceedings? Don't you think that in their heart of hearts and in their better moments, when political passions or partisanship are not in the ascendant, that they will themselves probably think at this moment – men of honour, all of them men of position – that they hope that your verdict will be one of acquittal of the defendant, so that they may not have upon their minds the burden of responsibility of thinking that they have brought down a high-minded and honourable man from the position which he has occupied to the credit and glory of the city to which he belongs.'

After Mr Justice Bray had paid a generous tribute to the leading defence counsel's oratory in his summing-up, the jury retired to consider their verdict. It only took them eighteen minutes to find Sir Edward Russell not guilty. The acquitted man was naturally delighted with what Rufus Isaacs had done for him. 'One of the many good results of my prosecution as a criminal,' he said afterwards, 'is that I have gained him as a friend.'

The final word was with the *Liverpool Post* which came out with a highly flattering editorial next morning, in which the editor's hand is perceptible. 'And perhaps the greatest result of all this episode in which we have been concerned will be that the magnificent championship of Mr Rufus Isaacs, worthy of Erskine and Lord Russell of Killowen, acknowledged by the very Bench to have conferred distinction on the Northern Circuit and on the whole Bar, will arouse the Press to a sense of its rights, the country to a recognition of the Press's service to right and reform, and juries to a feeling that they must imitate the wisdom, the courage, and the high morals of the jury which acquitted Sir Edward Russell.'

3

A few days before the Russell trial began, Mr A. J. Balfour resigned office as Prime Minister, and the King sent for Sir Henry Campbell-Bannerman, the Leader of the Liberal Opposition in the House of Commons, to form a Government. 'C.B.', as he was popularly known, was then in his seventieth year and in failing health, but he responded to the invitation with enthusiasm and quickly completed a new Administration. Two of Rufus Isaacs's colleagues at the Bar joined the Cabinet, Asquith becoming Chancellor of the Exchequer and R. B. Haldane War Minister, while his old master Lawson Walton became Attorney-General. Lloyd George obtained Cabinet rank as President of the Board of Trade, and two of the others who had spoken for the Liberal candidate at the Reading by-election were given junior ministerial office, Winston Churchill as Under-Secretary for the Colonies and Herbert Samuel in a similar post at the Home Office. The Prime Minister's next step was to ask the King to dissolve Parliament. The ensuing General Election was held in January, 1906, and was a landslide victory for the Liberals.

At Reading Rufus Isaacs had the advantage of being known in the constituency, whereas he had a new Conservative opponent, Mr G. H. Johnstone, who was a stranger to the electors. In the result Isaacs more than doubled his by-election majority, defeating Mr Johnstone by 697 votes. 'I do feel now that Reading has a second time chosen me as her representative,' he said after the declaration of the poll, 'that you intend me to remain.' It was a prophetic utterance since he was to be returned in three more successive elections, on one occasion being unopposed. He enjoyed the rough-and-tumble of electioneering, and he gave the inevitable heckler as good if not better than he got. For instance, while addressing a public meeting in the Town Hall during his first General Election campaign, a man in the body of the audience kept shouting 'Down with the Jews!' At first the candidate ignored these offensive interruptions, but as the monotonous refrain continued, Rufus Isaacs suddenly stopped speaking and faced the interrupter, at whom he pointed his finger in scorn. Then he declared with a note of fire in his voice, 'When I came to Reading, I said – as I say now – that I am a Jew and proud of it.' He then went on to speak of the sufferings of his race and of the English ideals of justice and fair play. By the time he had finished, even his political opponents were applauding him. No more was heard from the anti-Semitic heckler.

The new House of Commons was very differently constituted from that in which the Member for Reading had served for the previous two years. The Liberals won 377 seats, besides which they could count on the support of 83 Irish Nationalist and 53 Labour Members, while the Conservative and Unionist Opposition was reduced to 157. Not since the Election of 1832, after the first Reform Bill, were the Liberals in so strong a position. The Government thus felt it could safely introduce the mass of new legislative reforms foreshadowed in the Election campaign and in the King's Speech. This included a Trades Disputes Bill designed to reverse the judgment in the Taff Vale case which, it will be remembered, had held that trade unions could be sued for the acts of their agents and their funds made liable to meet the claims of successful plaintiffs in civil actions for damages brought against them.

In its original form the Trade Disputes Bill, which was introduced by Lawson Walton, the Attorney-General, and aimed at securing the unions against such damages, contained a clause excepting from immunity those tortious acts which could be proved to have been committed with the authority of responsible union officials. The bill also legalized 'peaceful picketing' and otherwise relaxed the law of conspiracy in relation to trade disputes.

This did not go far enough for the Labour Members, one of whom, Keir Hardie, now proceeded to bring in a Bill of his own based on the doctrine of complete immunity. Not wishing to alienate his Labour supporters, Campbell-Bannerman gave way to their pressure, and Lawson Walton was instructed to redraft the official measure in the sense of Keir Hardie's Private Member's Bill which it was to supersede. In the Second Reading Debate on the revised Government Bill

Rufus Isaacs was selected by the Government Whips to speak third, on account of his specialized knowledge of the subject, immediately following the Opposition Leader, Mr Balfour. It was an effective speech from an expert on trade-union law and practice. The decision of the House of Lords in the Taff Vale case had virtually amounted to a change in the law. Such a change must have the sanction of the people of the country, he pointed out, and the recent General Election had proved that there was no such sanction. Therefore, it was now for Parliament to legislate in accordance with the declared will of the people and to remove the unions from the unfair position to which the Taff Vale decision had relegated them.

In this first session of the new Parliament, the Commons sat well into August. Much of Isaacs's time was taken up with the committee stage of the Trade Disputes Bill, which dragged on throughout the summer. During the discussion on the crucial clause relieving unions from tortious liability Rufus Isaacs noticed one of the new Liberal Members rise from his place for the first time. He recognized the maiden speaker as a young barrister, who was already making a name for himself as a junior, named John Simon. Although his performance on this occasion contained none of the fireworks which had marked the Conservative F. E. Smith's maiden speech earlier in the session, Isaacs was greatly impressed by the quiet mastery of the subject which young Simon showed. They were soon to get to know each other very much better.

The four years that the 1906 Parliament lasted coincided with Rufus Isaacs's last years in private practice. They were also professionally his most lucrative, his annual earnings during this period averaging £30,000. The Middle Temple had recognized his leading position in 1905 when the Benchers of his Inn of Court elected him to their number. Now, with the disappearance of Sir Edward Clarke from the Temple through ill health and the departure of Asquith and Haldane to high political office, Rufus Isaacs became one of the two foremost practitioners at the Bar. The other was Sir Edward Carson, who had been Solicitor-General in the late Balfour Government and was now free to return to private practice. The friendliest of rivals, they were to be pitted almost daily against each other in the courts during the next four years. Their professional incomes during this period were phenomenal, their clerks usually refusing any brief marked below 500 guineas. It is unlikely that such large sums in the aggregate will ever again be earned at the English Bar.

One of the cases constituted a record in fees. It was an action entitled *Wyler and the Ibo & Nyasa Corporation Ltd.* v. *Lewis and Others,* in which damages for conspiracy were claimed in connection with the affairs of the corporation in Portuguese Nyasaland. Isaacs was for the plaintiffs and Carson for the defendants, and each leader had a fee of 1,000 guineas marked on his brief, together with a daily 'refresher' of 250 guineas. The trial, which came on in the spring of 1908 before Mr Justice Phillimore and a special jury in the King's Bench Division, lasted for thirty-three days, and another eighteen days in the Court of Appeal, so that the two leaders received over £12,000 each for that one case. The plaintiff Wyler occupied the witness-box for eleven days of the trial, yet it was a matter of little public interest. The dispute was purely a commercial one between two groups of financiers over certain concessions in Portuguese West Africa. Largely owing to Isaacs's superior financial knowledge the jury awarded the plaintiffs the enormous sum of £64,472. But Carson took the case to the Court of Appeal, where the findings of the lower Court were reversed, in spite of a speech by the respondent's leading counsel lasting nine days, probably the longest which has ever been delivered before that tribunal and certainly the longest ever made by Rufus Isaacs in the whole of his career.

Rufus Isaacs and Edward Carson were the two most outstanding leaders of their time; they had certain qualities of advocacy in common, but they differed greatly in method and technique, just as Norman Birkett and Patrick Hastings did in a later generation of barristers. Each was eloquent and each could be devastating in cross-examination, but while Carson was dominating and masterful, Isaacs was suave and coaxing. It was not a case of the bludgeon and the rapier, for Carson had a ready wit which Isaacs never attempted to rival. Isaacs, on the other hand, had a remarkable facility for mastering and memorizing intricate details, particularly financial figures, as well as a discretion and tact in handling judges and witnesses in which he could and did outshine the Irishman. There were also differences in physique and temperament. Isaacs was medium-sized and always appeared composed, his wig and gown in place. Carson was tall and lantern-jawed, and his manner frequently alternated between depression and excitement. He always wore his wig, which was an old one and looked too small for him, resolutely pushed to the back of his head. Isaacs was usually cheerful and physically fit; Carson was a prey to hypochondria and ill-health.

One of the most remarkable Court scenes between the two giant protagonists took place during the hearing of the so-called 'Soap Trust Case' at Liverpool Summer Assizes in 1907. The action was brought by Mr William Lever, M.P. (afterwards Lord Leverhulme), and the well-known firm of soap manufacturers of Port Sunlight against Lord Northcliffe, formerly Mr Alfred Harmsworth, and his Associated Newspapers group, particularly the *Daily Mail*, which had conducted a press campaign over a period accusing Mr Lever of forming a soap trust to exploit the consumer by cornering the raw materials market and raising the retail price of the finished article. As a result of this vindictive campaign, Lever Brothers Ltd. suffered trading losses to the amount of £40,000, while the value of their shares on the Stock Exchange fell by £200,000. F. E. Smith, who was asked for an opinion at very short notice, is said to have faced a stack of newspapers and other documents nearly four feet high, and after ordering two dozen oysters and a bottle of champagne sat up all night, eventually delivering the following terse opinion: 'There is no answer to this action for libel and the damages must be enormous.'

When the action came to trial Smith was led by Carson, while Rufus Isaacs was the leader for the defendant newspapers. The truth of Smith's opinion became abundantly clear at the end of the first day after Carson had opened the case for Lever Brothers Ltd., and Mr Lever had gone into the witness-box.

Next morning as Carson and his client motored to the Assize Court from Mr Lever's house, refreshed after an excellent dinner and a good night's rest, Carson expressed the view that Isaacs had probably spent a disturbed night, not knowing what to do. 'I'll wager he's been on the telephone to Harmsworth,' said Carson, 'and he'll be on the steps of the Court to make me an offer.'

There sure enough, when they drove up to St George's Hall, was 'poor Rufus', as Carson called him, looking tired and worried. His client was not with him. 'Well, Rufus,' said Carson, smiling broadly. 'Where's Harmsworth? Are you going to make us an offer?'

By this time Rufus Isaacs had realized that the prospect of gaining a verdict for the defence was hopeless. He felt, too, that if the case continued and went against him, as it inevitably must, not only would the damages be colossal, but the reputation of his client's newspapers would suffer considerably. There was nothing for it but surrender, and he had accordingly advised Northcliffe, who had agreed.

'We'll give you £10,000,' said Isaacs.

Carson and Lever treated this offer with contempt, and they all went into Court.

As the case was about to be resumed, Isaacs was seen whispering to Carson. 'You can't stop me withdrawing my defence and going to the jury on an assessment of damages alone.' Carson shook his head.

Isaacs then rose and with a marked display of magnanimity announced that in view of Mr Lever's evidence and the impression made by it upon himself and his friends in the case, it was impossible for his clients to continue their defence; he would therefore withdraw it without any reservations, leaving the jury only the question of the amount of the damages.

Carson now pretended to be surprised by this move, although, as we have seen, he had been in reality expecting it. 'The course adopted by my learned friend has taken me completely by surprise,' he declared, addressing the Bench. 'I ask for time to bring witnesses on the question of damages to the Court.'

To this proposal the judge agreed. Then, there followed an amazing scene, in which Isaacs in audible tones made repeated offers for a settlement, one after another being rejected.

'Look here, Ned, you can have £15,000.'

Carson communicated this offer to Lever. 'I won't have his £15,000,' said the plaintiff.

The offer was increased by instalments to £40,000 and eventually to £50,000. 'What do you say to that, Mr Lever?' asked Carson.

'That's a substantial offer,' said Lever. 'I'll take it.'

This was the largest sum hitherto awarded to a successful litigant in the English courts. Although Northcliffe had to find a great deal more by way of costs and further sums in settlement of similar claims against other newspapers in his group, he was grateful to Rufus Isaacs for settling as he did a series of claims in a matter in which the newspaper proprietor had undoubtedly overreached himself, since the campaign against Levers had been waged on his instructions.

As a result of this case he and his leading counsel became firm friends.

It is only fair to add, however, that Northcliffe, with his particular knowledge of American financial and business methods and also his friendship with the 'trust busting' President Theodore Roosevelt, was deeply suspicious of trusts. He took the view, quite legitimately, that such concentrations of economic and industrial power were not necessarily in the public interest and might well be against it, as he assumed to be the case of the Lever soap trust. 'We already have the tobacco trust operating here,' said Northcliffe at the time. 'Where is it going to end?' Reporting the verdict, the *Daily Mail* said that 'a somewhat embittered controversy' had been entered into in 'a no doubt mistaken sense of public duty'.

Rufus Isaacs could not help laughing when the outspoken weekly *Truth* parodied the well-known advertisement for Pears' Soap in a cartoon in which a tramp was seen writing a testimonial to the manufacturers: 'Six weeks ago I *abused* your soap, since when I have *abused* no other.'

In January, 1908, Sir John Lawson Walton, the Attorney-General and Rufus Isaacs's old master in the Temple, died after a short illness at the age of fifty-six. The Solicitor-General, Sir William Robson, was promoted to the Attorney's office. To fill the vacancy of Solicitor the Prime Minister appointed Samuel Evans, a Welsh M.P. most of whose practice was on the South Wales Circuit. Although he was a year older than Rufus Isaacs, Evans was junior to him both in point of call to the Bar and as a 'silk', and the appointment caused considerable surprise to the Temple. But Evans had been in Parliament for the previous eighteen years without a break, during which period he had rendered valuable political service to the Liberals; no doubt the Government Whips took the view that he should be rewarded and the Prime Minister agreed. Rufus Isaacs was naturally disappointed since he felt that he had a strong claim to the office. However, he was still on the near side of fifty and the fact that he had to bide his time for the next couple of years was no great hardship, particularly as his professional income was augmented by a further £60,000 or so in the interval.

One noteworthy case, in which Isaacs was opposed by Carson at this period, was in reality uncontested. It was an action brought by Mr Lloyd George, who by this time had become Chancellor of the Exchequer, against the owners of *The People* newspaper for the repetition of a gross libel on his private reputation.

In the summer of 1908, another weekly journal *The Bystander* had hinted that, in addition to his political difficulties over budgetary expenditure for the armed forces, the Chancellor was in trouble over a woman. After a writ for libel had been issued against *The Bystander*, the magazine had admitted that there was no foundation for this statement, which it unreservedly withdrew, at the same time making a public apology and paying 300 guineas at Mr Lloyd George's request to the Caernarvon Cottage Hospital.

But that was not the end of the matter. Some years previously, Lloyd George, who was notoriously fond of the ladies, had been mentioned in a divorce suit brought by a Welsh doctor against his wife, who had made a signed 'confession' that she had misconducted herself with Lloyd George in her husband's house in Montgomeryshire and that he was the father of her expected child. Fortunately Lloyd George was able to show from the division lists in the House of Commons that on the night he was supposed to have been in bed with the doctor's wife he was several hundred miles away voting in Westminster. Nevertheless the rumours about Lloyd George's private life persisted after *The Bystander*'s apology until they found permanent expression in several articles which appeared in *The People* early in 1909.

The articles did not mention Lloyd George by name, but they left no doubt in the reader's mind that the Chancellor was the person referred to. In short, the articles alleged that he was about to figure as co-respondent in another divorce suit, that it had been ascertained that there was no doubt as to his guilt, that he had committed adultery with a married woman, that the resultant Court proceedings must inevitably involve him in social and political ruin and degradation, that his friends were making extreme efforts to avert the catastrophe, but the injured husband insisted on going on. Later another article appeared headed 'The Price of Peace', which stated that Lloyd George's friends had succeeded in their efforts, that the suit would be conspicuous by its absence from the list of causes for trial in the Divorce Court, and that the price the Chancellor had to pay to secure this result was £20,000.

The matter came before Mr Justice Lawrence in the King's Bench Division on March 12, 1909. For the plaintiff Lloyd George, Rufus Isaacs led F. E. Smith, now K.C., and Raymond Asquith, whose father had become Prime Minister on Campbell-Bannerman's resignation in the previous year.

After Isaacs had set out the circumstances of the libel, he called the plaintiff, who was in Court with his wife. Two questions were put to Lloyd George in the witness-box. Had he read the allegations in *The People*? 'Yes.' Were they true in substance or in fact? 'The paragraphs are an absolute invention,' said the Chancellor of the

Exchequer in a loud, firm voice, his hands gripping the ledge of the witness-box. 'Every line of them.'

Carson then rose to offer no defence whatever. The articles had appeared without his clients' knowledge, he said. 'The defendants had no desire that their paper should be the means of circulating such a scandalous libel, and the more so having regard to the position of importance and dignity held by Mr Lloyd George.' Counsel added that, as soon as they had heard about it and as soon as he himself had been retained by them, they had done everything possible to mitigate the mischief caused by the articles. He consequently offered Mr Lloyd George a 'most sincere and frank apology, without reserve of any kind', and admitted that the statements in the articles were 'unfounded and absolutely without justification'. The proprietors of *The People* also paid Lloyd George £1,000 damages which he likewise handed over to charity. This time it was the Llanystumdwy Village Hall which benefited.

The plaintiff whose private reputation had been so strikingly vindicated by this action had every reason to be grateful to his friend Rufus Isaacs, particularly for having the hearing of the case expedited. In approving the settlement, in open Court, Mr Justice Lawrence explained why he had taken this 'unusual course', though the pleadings had only been completed the day before. 'The Chancellor of the Exchequer was actually framing his Budget, and he could not do his duty to his Office or his country with such a charge hanging over his head.'

4

The Budget, on which Lloyd George was working at the time of his action against *The People*, was to be the longest and most controversial in British political history. Deliberately designed to bring the issue of the constitutional powers of the House of Lords to a head, it contained far-reaching taxation proposals, including a novel tax on land values, heavy increases in liquor and other duties and the imposition for the first time of a 'super-tax' in addition to income tax on all incomes over £5,000. The Budget was duly embodied in a Finance Bill, and the fate of this measure in the Lords was to make constitutional history. 'Let us reject the Budget and damn the consequences,' said the Conservative Viscount Milner. And that is exactly what their Lordships did. On November 30, 1909, the Lords threw out the Finance Bill by an overwhelming majority – 350 to 75. The Prime Minister, Mr Asquith, thereupon advised the King to dissolve Parliament so that an appeal to the country could be made. The consequent General Election took place a few weeks later, in January, 1910.

At Reading, where he fought his third electoral contest, Rufus Isaacs put the constitutional issue very clearly in his election address.

> By the unconstitutional and revolutionary action of the House of Lords this Budget, passed by an overwhelming majority of the representatives of the people in the House of Commons, has been rejected by the Peers. Thus the House of Lords has, for the first time in the history of our constitution, which is based upon usage, practice and custom, asserted a right to force a dissolution of Parliament by refusing to assent to the necessary supplies, and has revived a claim to control the finances of the country which we all thought had been disposed of in favour of the House of Commons, once and for all, long ago. In my view, careful and deliberate provision should be made to prevent any possible recurrence by the House of Lords with the Budget or the finances of the country. Never again should the Budget be liable to rejection by the Peers.

> In my view, the taxation imposed on the people through their representatives in the House of Commons should be preserved to the people's protectors, their duly elected Members of Parliament.

> I would also suppose a definite limitation of the power of the Peers to mutilate and reject measures passed by the House of Commons and am in favour of steps being taken to ensure that the will of the people must and shall prevail.

The Conservative candidate, Major Leslie Renton, had formerly sat in the Commons as a Liberal and he had only recently been converted to Toryism. But in spite of this apparent handicap, he succeeded in reducing Isaacs's majority to 207, a narrow enough margin, in a total poll of 10,000. In the two previous elections Isaacs had got some support from disgruntled Conservative voters, but at the 1910 Election they seem to have reverted to their former party allegiance out of dislike for Lloyd George's radical Budget proposals. Incidentally, Lloyd George, who came down to speak for the Liberal candidate, was the target of a bizarre incident. At the mention of the word 'robber' in his speech, the Chancellor of the Exchequer was suddenly and unexpectedly interrupted by the apparition of two dishevelled suffragettes, who had hidden under the platform for seventeen hours and then emerged, shouting 'You are a robber because you take away the women's money and don't give them the vote!' They were then forcibly hustled out of the hall by the stewards, glowing with a sense of martyrdom.

At this Election Rufus Isaacs supplemented his original poster slogan 'Rufus for Reading' with another and more up-to-date version, 'What's the matter with Rufus? He's all right!' This aroused the admiration, among others, of the Conservative newspaper magnate Lord Northcliffe, who wrote the victor a note after the declaration of the poll, saying that he had waited by the telephone for the Reading result 'with more party disloyalty than I care to confess and I congratulate you heartily on a splendid win'. He added: 'Today I motored through the constituency and was immensely struck by the brilliance of your poster-artist. "He's all right." I never saw such a splendid show.'

The result of the General Election, although it left Mr Asquith still in occupation of 10 Downing Street, was a serious loss of strength to the Government. Its commanding majority over all parties in the House of Commons disappeared, the Liberals being now only 275 strong as against 273 Conservatives and Unionists, while Labour won forty seats and the Irish Nationalists eighty-two. Thus the Irish Nationalists held the balance of power at Westminster, and they were ready to trade their support for the Government in the division lobby in return for the Bill to give Ireland Home Rule which Mr Asquith was prepared to introduce.

Lloyd George had foretold during the Election that Rufus Isaacs would soon be sitting with him on the Government Front Bench in the House of Commons. The prophecy came true two months later when the Solicitor-General, Sir Samuel Evans, was made President of the Probate, Admiralty and Divorce Division of the High Court, and Rufus Isaacs was offered and accepted the vacant post of Law Officer. The appointment was generally well received in the profession. As the *Law Journal* put it, 'the great powers which this brilliant advocate and acute judge of men and affairs has implied to the vindication of private rights will now be employed in the service of the State; and there can be no doubt that his cool judgment and shrewd intelligence will be an advantage to the country in general, as well as to his party, at this period of serious constitutional crisis'.

Appointment to the office of Solicitor-General traditionally carried with it the honour of knighthood. In the case of the new Law Officer, there was a slight delay in the sovereign formally dubbing him 'Sir Rufus', owing to the sudden death of King Edward VII. In fact, Sir Rufus Isaacs was the first person to receive the accolade at the hands of the new monarch. As they shook hands after the ceremony, King George V said simply: 'How much pleasure it would have given my father to do this!'

In those days, under a statute dating from the time of Queen Anne, acceptance of a ministerial post in the Government obliged the recipient to offer himself for re-election in his constituency.[1] At first Isaacs thought that the Conservatives might try to recapture the seat in view of his slender majority; but as another General Election was felt not to be so very far away, the local Conservatives decided to save their fire and allow him to be returned unopposed.

The post to which Rufus Isaacs had been appointed on March 7, 1910, was an honour not only to him but also to his race, for he was only the second Jew to become a Law Officer of the Crown.[2] At the same time, it involved a substantial drop in his income, since, as has been seen, he had been averaging £30,000 for many years in private practice at the Bar. The Solicitor-General's salary was £6,000 a year, and he was also entitled to fees for Court work undertaken on behalf of the Crown. But these fees were modest by comparison with what Isaacs had previously been earning, and in the six months that he held the office they amounted to some £2,200.

The change in his financial circumstances was illustrated by a revealing incident which took place shortly after his appointment was announced. A messenger arrived from the Treasury at his Chambers with a bulky brief tied up in white tape and marked '10 and 2', that is ten guineas for the Solicitor-General and two for his clerk. 'Sir Rufus does not take ten-guinea briefs,' the clerk remarked airily. The messenger did not appear in the least put out. He quietly placed the Crown brief on the table in front of him. 'He'll take that one,' he said, 'and he'll take dozens more like it before he's finished!'

The most conspicuous case in which he had to appear for the Crown in the Courts as Solicitor-General was one he had inherited from his predecessor, and it caused him a great deal of trouble and anxiety, particularly since it was the only one in which his professional conduct was ever criticized.

[1] Since 1925 this requirement has been no longer necessary.

[2] The first was Sir George Jessel, who was appointed Solicitor-General by Gladstone in 1871.

The central figure in this remarkable case, which was subsequently to be made the subject of both a play and a film,[1] was a thirteen-year-old naval cadet named George Archer-Shee, who had been expelled from the Royal Naval College at Osborne, Isle of Wight, after being accused of stealing a five-shilling postal order from a fellow cadet whose signature he was alleged to have forged on the back of the order before cashing it at the local post office. The boy strenuously asserted his innocence. 'All I can say is I never did it,' he declared over and over again. His family believed him. However, his father was compelled to remove him from the college after the boy had been subjected to the test of writing the name of the other cadet, Terence Back, on a piece of paper and a handwriting expert had compared it with the signature on the postal order and pronounced the writing to be that of the same hand.

Young George had an elder half-brother, Major Martin Archer-Shee, M.P., who suggested that they should consult Edward Carson, whom he knew in the House of Commons. After he had questioned George in his chambers for three hours on every aspect of his story, the Irish advocate was completely satisfied as to his veracity. 'I saw nothing in his answers or demeanour when undergoing a very unpleasant ordeal,' said Carson afterwards, 'to lead me to the suspicion that he was otherwise than an honest and truthful boy.'

On Carson's advice, the family demanded a judicial inquiry from the Admiralty. As a result, Mr George Elliott, K.C., was sent down to Osborne and also Mr R. D. Acland, K.C., the Judge Advocate of the Fleet; but at neither of the investigations conducted by these gentlemen was the alleged culprit allowed to be legally represented, and there was consequently no opportunity for cross-examining any of the witnesses produced against him. In these circumstances it was scarcely surprising that the Admiralty should have refused to alter its decision and reinstate the boy.

Had George Archer-Shee been a fully fledged naval officer, he would have had the right, enjoyed by every member of the forces, of being tried by court-martial. Unfortunately this procedure could not be invoked in the case of a cadet. After careful consideration, Carson advised that the only course was for the boy to sue the Crown through his father for breach of contract, using the procedure known as a petition of right and claiming that the Crown had broken its agreement to furnish him with a complete course of naval training.

[1] *The Winslow Boy* by Terence Rattigan.

Thus the case came before Mr Justice Ridley in the King's Bench Division of the High Court on July 12, 1910, Sir Edward Carson leading for the plaintiff, and Sir Rufus Isaacs, who had by this time become Solicitor-General, for the Crown.

The objection had been taken in the written pleadings on behalf of the Crown by way of demurrer, no doubt on the advice of the previous Solicitor-General, that the action was not maintainable in law. Of course, it was open to Rufus Isaacs to waive this objection when the case came to trial. Indeed his personal inclination was to do so, but on reflection he came to the conclusion that it was his duty as a Law Officer of the Crown to persist in making it. Consequently at the out-set he argued that a petition of right would not lie, relying on the immunity of the Crown from legal proceedings and the absolute right which he claimed the Crown had to dismiss anyone who had entered its service. In reply Carson contended that this point should have been taken before the trial and decided in one way or the other. 'The plaintiff has gone to great expense in getting up the case on the facts,' he added, 'and I am surprised that the Crown should have taken this very unusual course.'

Mr Justice Ridley said that, though it might perhaps seem a hardship on the plaintiff, he felt that the Crown had to have the point of law decided first.

'The Crown is shirking the issue of fact,' Carson protested. 'It is a public scandal. The Crown can, I suppose, be high-handed out of Court, but in open Court it is not to be tolerated.'

The Solicitor-General thereupon submitted that he was entitled to judgment, and after some further argument the judge ruled in his favour.

Carson was furious at what he felt to be the most palpable injustice. 'This is a case of the grossest oppression without remedy that I have known since I have been at the Bar,' he said, looking disdainfully at the Solicitor-General and the other Crown counsel.

'All I can say is that there have been various inquiries,' said Rufus Isaacs.

'Only a hole-in-the-corner inquiry in which the boy was not represented,' answered Carson.

'That is not so.' This time it was the Solicitor-General's turn to protest. 'Mr George Elliott, K.C., went down.'

'Yes,' said Carson, bitterly. '*That* was our inquiry.'

'Assisted by the Admiralty,' observed Isaacs.

Carson turned towards his opponent. 'It's a gross outrage by the Admiralty, Mr Solicitor,' he exclaimed indignantly.

Here the judge intervened to reprove Carson. 'I do not think you should say that,' he said. 'I know nothing of the facts. I have merely decided the point of law.'

Carson's reply was to pick up his papers and stalk angrily out of Court.

Carson immediately lodged an appeal, which through his unrelaxing efforts came before the Court of Appeal in less than a week. This time the Court ruled against the Solicitor-General, and the Lord Justices unanimously sent the case back for rehearing, with directions that the facts should be tried by a judge and jury before the legal objections were argued at all. Carson appeared personally before the Lord Chief Justice to apply for a speedy trial, and as a result the case came on nine days later before Mr Justice Phillimore and a special jury.

In the event the jury were not asked to decide the issues of fact. On the fourth day of the trial, after young Archer-Shee had most convincingly withstood a long and gruelling cross-examination by the Solicitor-General, lasting for most of two days, Rufus Isaacs rose to announce that the Admiralty had given in. 'I say now, on behalf of the Admiralty,' he declared, 'as a result of the investigation which has taken place, that I accept the declaration of George Archer-Shee that he did not write the name on the postal order; that he did not take it, and that he did not cash it; and that consequently he was innocent of the charge which has been brought against him. I make that statement without any reservation of any description, intending it to be a complete acceptance of the boy's statements.' He added that, on the other hand, Sir Edward Carson accepted the statements of the Admiralty that all those responsible for what had happened had acted in good faith.

Although the boy's character was thus effectively cleared, there was no further reaction on the part of the Crown. No offer came from the Admiralty to reinstate young George Archer-Shee at Osborne, nor from the Treasury to compensate George's father for the expense he had been put to over the litigation. It was not until the matter had been raised in the House of Commons that the First Lord of the Admiralty, Mr Reginald McKenna, agreed to leave it to a tribunal composed of the Solicitor-General, Carson, and Lord Mersey, the leading Admiralty lawyer. This body eventually made an award of £7,120 by way of costs and compensation.

Rufus Isaacs was the target of considerable criticism in the Press and in Parliament for the line he had initially taken in this case. Looking at the Archer-Shee case now with the advantage of hindsight, it would no doubt have been better if the Solicitor-General had waived the Crown privilege, regardless of precedent, which in any event was of persuasive rather than binding authority. As a matter of policy too, it was hardly expedient in the circumstances for the Crown to put forward the argument of privilege. Unfortunately, at the stage at which he entered the proceedings, the Solicitor-General felt that he had to pay attention to precedent, and he was unable to find a single case in which there had been a waiver of the Crown Prerogative, allowing such a case to be brought. Rufus Isaacs admitted afterwards that he would have been only too glad to have said, as Law Officer, 'Try the case.'

'My difficulty was this,' he said. 'I stepped into the matter when the record was already completed, when the plea of the demurrer was already on the pleadings, and there was that plea on the very threshold of the case which had to be dealt with, and I should have been wanting in my duty if I had said, "This is an unpleasant matter for me to have to argue. I do not care to have to take this point in a case where a boy is trying to vindicate himself; therefore I will waive the right of the Crown, and will allow the case to be tried."'

It is worth noting that the demurrer was never overruled in the Court of Appeal; it was merely abandoned by the Solicitor-General at the express request of the judges, who were moved by Carson's argument that the facts should be tried first. Indeed the demurrer could not have been overruled, as it was undoubtedly sound in law. Today the Crown could adopt precisely the same tactics if a similar case arose and it so wished.[1]

[1] For further details of the Archer-Shee case with original documents, see the present writer's *Carson* (1953), pp. 263–76.

4

Attorney-General

1

For their annual summer holiday in 1910, Rufus and Alice Isaacs tried a new watering-place, which had become extremely fashionable through the visits of Edward VII in the last years of his reign. This was Marienbad, a picturesque spa in what was then the Austrian province of Bohemia. Besides the Solicitor-General, his wife and their son Gerald, the English society that summer included Lord Dunedin and Lord Justice Vaughan Williams from the Bench, Charles Gill from the Bar, Colonel Mark Lockwood and T. P. O'Connor from the House of Commons, and Squire Bancroft, Herbert Beerbohm Tree and Charles Hawtrey from the stage. It was a lively and an amusing gathering and Rufus and Alice Isaacs found it so congenial that they determined to go back the following year. Indeed they were to remain faithful to Marienbad until the First World War put an end to these curative jaunts in Central Europe.

On his return to chambers, Rufus Isaacs found the Temple buzzing with the usual rumours about legal changes and appointments. One of these which concerned him personally was a vacancy in the Court of Appeal, and he was not surprised when he heard that the Attorney-General, Sir William Robson, who had been overworking and badly needed a rest, had been selected to fill it. The consequential changes in the Law Officers' posts were announced shortly before the opening of the Michaelmas Term at the Law Courts. Rufus Isaacs became Attorney-General, while the brilliant and outstanding young 'silk' John Simon – he was only thirty-seven – was appointed Solicitor.[1] Thus, after only seven months as junior Law Officer and while still under fifty years of age, Rufus Isaacs became the head of the English Bar, a distinguished position which in those days carried with it a

[1] *The Times,* October 7, 1910. No one had become Solicitor-General at such an early age since the appointment of John Scott (later Lord Chancellor Eldon) in 1768. Scott was the same age as Simon at the time.

virtually prescriptive right to the reversion of any high judicial office, including the highest, which might fall vacant.

When he came to write his memoirs, Lord Simon (as he was then) recalled the duties of Attorney-General and Solicitor-General in the light of his own experience with Rufus Isaacs.

> To be one of the Law Officers of the Crown in England is to have a view of the working of almost every Cabinet office without full respon-sibility for Ministerial decisions. It is also to have an exceptional opportunity of estimating the equipment and character of your legal colleague, for you do your work in almost daily contact with him on terms of special intimacy. The innumerable opinions which have to be provided as advice to various Government Departments are almost always written and signed jointly, and the most important litigation in which the Crown is a party is conducted by one or other and often by both of them appearing together. Moreover, an English Law Officer is constantly wanted in the House of Commons to help in promoting a Government Bill or to explain a difficult clause, and this needs a fraternal sharing out of the work between the pair, and not infrequently the presence of both on the Front Bench. How much a Law Officer does in the wider field of general politics varies with the individual....[1]

Throughout the summer and autumn of 1910, there had been a lull in party political warfare due to the inter-party Constitutional Con-ference which met at Asquith's suggestion with a view to reaching an agreed compromise settlement of the Irish Home Rule issue. After twenty-one sittings the Conference eventually broke down on November 10, 1910, without reaching any agreement, and the Prime Minister immediately advised the King to dissolve Parliament so that another General Election could be held in the following month.

The final results which were declared a few days before Christmas left things very much as they were, the Liberals losing two seats and the Conservatives and Unionists one, while Labour had two gains and the Irish Nationalists three. With Liberals and Conservatives almost evenly matched, the balance of power in the House of Commons

[1] Viscount Simon. *Retrospect* (1952), pp. 85–86. Simon at first sought to decline the customary Law Officer's knighthood, 'as it seemed at that date to stamp the holder as a mere Government lawyer and nothing more'. But he had to agree to become Sir John, after Asquith told him of the precedent which had been established in Gladstone's time, when Henry James and William Harcourt similarly refused to be knighted in 1873, but were overruled. 'Mr Gladstone replied that the honour was compulsory: it was, he said, by such means as the knighting of High Court Judges and Law Officers that the dignity was main-tained at its proper level.' Simon, op. cit., p. 75.

lay as before with John Redmond and the 85 Irish Nationalists. At Reading, Rufus Isaacs succeeded in holding the seat for the Liberals, but with a considerably reduced majority. The fact that his majority fell from 207 to 99 was due, at least in part, to his energetic Conservative opponent, Captain Leslie Wilson, R.N., a future Conservative Chief Whip and Governor of Bombay. It cannot often fall to a Member of Parliament to be returned three times in one year, and also in the course of four contested elections never to fight the same candidate twice. But that was the lot of Rufus Isaacs. Following his third return as Member for Reading in December, 1910, he was reappointed Attorney-General.

During the election campaign Lloyd George had almost completely lost his voice, and in consequence he was ordered abroad for a holiday. As there was a period of several weeks before the meeting of the new Parliament, the Chancellor of the Exchequer invited Rufus Isaacs to join him, also Charles Masterman, then Under-Secretary at the Home Office, and Mrs Masterman, at Cap Martin in the south of France. The Chancellor particularly wanted their advice and help on the Insurance Bill, the first measure of its kind providing for health and unemployment insurance, which he was to introduce in the coming session, and it seemed that they might just as well talk over its provisions in the winter sunshine of the south of France as in the London fogs. The party was completed by two senior civil servants, John (later Lord) Bradbury, the principal Insurance Commissioner, and William Braithwaite, Secretary of the National Health Insurance Joint Committee.

On the subject of Lloyd George and Rufus Isaacs together and the way they behaved to her husband and herself, Mrs Masterman recorded in her diary:

We all had breakfast, and indeed every other meal together, and it must be said that George was setting the scale of expenditure very high. He was extraordinarily generous towards Charlie and me, on one pretext or another, and he did his best to pay for nearly every meal we had. When he was not trying to, Rufus was. When we moved to Nice and Charlie and I made efforts to get cheaper rooms, he engaged a suite and tried to insist on our paying only what we had paid at Cap Martin, where we had to put up practically in the servants' room. Of course we would not consent to it, and Rufus who has been a poor man himself was quick to notice, and very ready to help if we looked at all dubious at any of the expenditure. . . .

'RUFUS'
Cartoon by 'Spy' in *Vanity Fair,* February 14, 1904

IN THE COURT OF APPEAL

George used to listen interminably to Rufus Isaacs's description of his cases and appreciated them enormously. But the difference between the two men was extremely marked. Whenever George began to tell us of his experiences among his Welsh preachers, Rufus simply could not understand why he was so interested in them. To him these things seemed simply ridiculous. On the other hand, one could see that Isaacs had an extremely high standard in his profession, a high standard of honour and of permissible things to do. . . .

It was very curious to watch George and Isaacs discussing the Insurance Bill. George was inclined to judge everything by his own experiences in Wales. Rufus very naturally knew but little about the subject.

On a motoring visit to Avignon, a characteristic incident took place in the hotel. Some travelling musicians were playing, the leader of the orchestra being an old man who performed on the fiddle, accompanied on a harp. No one in the hotel was paying much attention, but Lloyd George, who like most Welsh people loved music, applauded loudly. The old man obviously pleased at this notice, groped among his music for a little, and then played, first, 'God Save the King', and afterwards a Scotch air and then, for Lloyd George's special benefit, 'The Ash Grove'. Lloyd George was delighted and when the old man had finished, he asked Rufus Isaacs to compliment him and ask him as a return civility to play the 'Marseillaise'. This the fiddler did with great verve. The proprietor of the hotel and the waiters came to the door, and even the chambermaids came out of the bedrooms and leaned over the gallery to hear the music. 'The finest tune in the world,' Lloyd George commented. At the next table there were two Englishmen, who amused the Lloyd George party. 'What is that?' one of them asked his companion, as the musicians began to play their country's national anthem. 'Oh, a French song, I think!' was the answer.

Mrs Masterman's summing up of the Attorney-General deserves quotation. 'It was during these drives, I think, that Rufus Isaacs gave his most amazing exhibitions of vitality. We usually started early in the morning. It was very cold at the time. Rufus was either talking or singing the whole time. Other people fell asleep in turn, but never he. Among other things he sang me the Hebrew version of the 'Song of Miriam', which he learned at school. George stared at him open mouthed. "You are an astonishing fellow. I never knew anybody like you," was his comment.'[1]

[1] Lucy Masterman: *C. F. G. Masterman* (1939), pp. 179–83.

D

A recent case, which no doubt formed a topic of conversation during this holiday, was the first of its kind and one of the first in which Rufus Isaacs appeared in Court as the senior Law Officer. It was concerned with 'official secrets' and in this particular instance had more than a hint of espionage about it. The Attorney-General's role was to lead the prosecution of a twenty-three-year-old lieutenant in the German army named Siegfried Helm on charges of unlawfully making sketches of the defences of Portsmouth Harbour. The trial took place before Mr Justice Eldon Banks at Winchester Assizes on November 14, 1910. On the advice of his defending counsel, Travers Humphreys and Percival Clarke, the accused pleaded guilty.

This was the first time that there had been a prosecution of an officer of any foreign state under the Official Secrets Act in England. Incidentally it demonstrated the inadequacy of the Act for dealing with spies in time of peace and was to lead directly to the passing of much more stringent legislation by Parliament. In order to convict anyone under the original Official Secrets Act of 1889, the prosecution had to establish proof of intent; in other words, if the prosecution wished to bring home a felonious act of espionage, it had to show that the accused intended to communicate to a foreign State information which had been wrongfully obtained. This was difficult to do, since the accused could always say that his presence in a prohibited place was purely accidental and his intentions were perfectly innocent. It was for this reason that the prosecution was obliged to drop the more serious charge against Lieutenant Helm of intending to pass on the sketches he had made to the German military intelligence service, and merely proceeded on the relatively minor charge of unlawfully making drawings of the fortifications in question.

The Attorney-General began by briefly informing the Court of the facts of the case. Lieutenant Helm, of the 21st Battalion of the Nassau Regiment of the German Army, came to England in August, 1910, to spend a few weeks' holiday. On September 3 he went to Portsmouth and stayed there. On September 5, he was seen by two officers of the British Army, who were riding on Portsdown Hills, to be taking measurements and making observations outside Widley Fort. At their request, Helm handed his sketch-book to the two English officers. On examination, it was found to contain nine drawings of fortifications, notes on the positions of guns and searchlights, details of distances, and diagrams showing the field of fire of defending artillery. The officers thereupon asked him to accompany them to Portsmouth, which he did, and he was handed over to the police. He was remanded in custody for four weeks and during this period he admitted that he had been unlawfully sketching and expressed 'unfeigned regret', adding that he was unaware he was doing anything wrong and promising not to offend again. On October 4 he was released on bail.

In these circumstances Rufus Isaacs asked the Court to deal leniently with the young German. The object of the prosecution had been attained, he said, 'inasmuch as it had now been shown quite clearly that the taking of the sketches in the way Lieutenant Helm took them and the acts that he committed were offences against the law of England and punishable by His Majesty's judges.'

The result was that Mr Justice Banks took the course expected of him and bound over the potential spy. Indeed he addressed him in almost sympathetic terms. 'I trust,' he said, 'that when you leave this country you will leave it with a feeling that, although we may be vigilant, and perhaps, from your point of view, too vigilant, in the detection of offenders against our laws, yet in the administration of those laws we are just and merciful, not only to those who are subjects of this realm, but also to those who like yourself seek the hospitality of our shores.'

The evidence was stronger against another German Army lieutenant, Max Schultz, whom it fell to the Attorney-General to prosecute at Exeter Assizes in the following year. Schultz, who held a commission in the 13th German Hussars and was a Doctor of Philosophy, was caught in Plymouth, where he had been living for several months on a houseboat and gathering information on naval matters for communication to his Government. During this period he struck up an acquaintance with a local solicitor named Samuel Hugh Duff. Schultz told Duff that he had a friend in the German News Agency, who had asked him to look out for foreign correspondents, and he offered the solicitor £1,000 a year if he would act as such a correspondent. When Duff heard the kind of news that he was expected to provide, he became suspicious and went to the police. Schultz told him that the Agency was only interested in naval news, and he asked him to find out the opinion of officers based on Plymouth on the possibility of war between Britain and Germany, what ships were going out of commission, how much coal and ammunition was available at the port, and similar questions.

The counter-espionage branch of the War Office (M.I.5) was called in, and while the case was being investigated the solicitor was instructed to feed the spy with false information, a course to which he consented somewhat reluctantly. When the security men eventually pounced on Schultz in his houseboat, they found the key to the code used in the telegrams he had been sending to Germany, as well as other incriminating documents.

At his trial, Schultz continued to protest that the information he had been collecting and transmitting was solely for the benefit of the German Press. But the jury disbelieved this unlikely story, and it took them only four minutes to convict him. In sentencing Schultz to twenty-one months' imprisonment in the second division, the Lord Chief Justice, Lord Alverstone, rather naïvely remarked that relations between Great Britain and Germany were most amicable. He was sure, he said, that 'no one would repudiate or condemn the practice of which the prisoner had been found guilty more strenuously than the leaders of Germany'. Yet the First World War was less than three years away.

The cases of Helm and Schultz showed very clearly the need for strengthening the existing law of official secrets. A new Official Secrets Act, which the Attorney-General helped to draft, was consequently introduced into Parliament and passed in 1911. It cast the onus of proof upon the accused to satisfy the jury that his purpose was a right one, if he was found in a place where his presence prima facie was 'prejudicial to the safety or interests of the State'. At the same time, the prosecution had to show that any information which he communicated or attempted to communicate to a third party 'might be directly or indirectly useful to an enemy'.

At the urgent request of the Government, who by this time had become thoroughly alarmed at the extent of German espionage in Britain, particularly as revealed by the Schultz case, the House of Commons passed the measure through all its stages in a single afternoon – it had previously passed the Lords without amendment – and it received the Royal Assent a few days later. There were some protests about 'upsetting Magna Carta', and the Attorney-General, admitted that the measure was 'a very startling innovation upon our ordinary legal precedents'. However, he promised the House that it would do nothing to disturb 'the ancient liberties of this country'.

It is under the Official Secrets Act, 1911, that espionage charges are now brought in time of peace. Whatever criticisms were levelled at it when it was rushed through Parliament, the Act has certainly proved a potent weapon against the 'foreign agent' and those whom he may employ.

2

Within a few weeks of his becoming Attorney-General, Rufus Isaacs was officially asked to advise on a remarkable and indeed unprecedented prosecution, which personally concerned the wearer of the Crown. The subject matter was a foul and malicious libel about King George V's private life. The libel, which had been going the rounds by word of mouth for many years, alleged that Queen Mary was not the King's lawful wife and that His Majesty was a bigamist. It appeared in the issue of a journal called *The Liberator* for November, 1910, in the form of an article entitled 'Sanctified Bigamy'. This journal, which was printed in Paris but circulated in England and overseas, was devoted to the dissemination of Republican propaganda under the direction of an American editor, Edward Holden James, assisted by an English agent, a young anti-monarchist agitator named Edward Mylius, who distributed *The Liberator* in England, and in the case of the libellous article had also supplied the information on which it was based.

The article began by stating that during the year 1890, in the island of Malta, the King had contracted a lawful marriage with the daughter of an English Admiral, Sir Michael Culme-Seymour, and that offspring had been born of this union. Having pointed out that at the time of this alleged marriage the Duke of Clarence, who subsequently died, was the heir to the throne, the article continued:

It is now that we are offered the spectacle of the immorality of the Monarchy in all its beastly monstrosity. In order to obtain the woman of Royal blood for his pretended wife, George Frederick foully abandoned his true wife, the daughter of Sir Michael Culme-Seymour, of the British Navy, and entered into a sham and shameful marriage with the daughter of the Duke of Teck in 1893. The said George Frederick, not having obtained any divorce from his first wife, who, by the common law of England and by the law of the Christian Church remained, and if she still lives remains, his true wife, committed the crime of bigamy, and he committed it with the aid and complicity of the prelates of the Anglican Church.

This is the sickening and disgusting crime which has been committed by the English Church which has married one man to two women. Our very Christian King has a plurality of wives, just like any Mohammedan Sultan, and they are sanctified by the English Church. The daughter of Sir Michael Culme-Seymour, if she still lives, is by the unchangeable law of the English Church, as well as by the common law of England, the rightful Queen of England, and her children are the only rightful heirs to the English throne.

In the following month, *The Liberator* returned to the charge with this crisp comment:

> The *Daily News* of London tells us that the King plans to visit India with his wife. Would the newspaper kindly tell us which wife?

Shortly before *The Liberator* article appeared, there had been a reference in an Australian newspaper, *The Brisbane Telegraph*, to the bigamy story, which the English Sunday *Reynolds' Newspaper* had cautiously repeated. This produced a letter from the King's Private Secretary Sir Arthur Bigge (later Lord Stamfordham), who wrote to that newspaper strongly denying on his authority the existence of any morganatic marriage. Mylius sent a cutting of this letter which *Reynolds' Newspaper* had published to the editor of *The Liberator* in Paris. 'I do not attach much credence to the statement made by Bigge and published in *Reynolds*',' the editor had replied. 'If there was no marriage, why do not these people explain why for years everyone has passed the word around that there was a marriage?' Later the editor wrote another letter, explaining his method of attaining this praiseworthy object: 'In writing the bigamy article, I decided to publish the facts at once without waiting for further verification. The best and quickest way to get at the truth is to begin to agitate the matter. If we have not stated the facts correctly, we will hear what the other side has to say.'

It would be difficult to imagine a more cruel and impudent libel upon the Sovereign. Apart from the fact that the seventy-four-year-old Admiral Culme-Seymour had a daughter – in fact he had two – there was no truth whatsoever in any of the allegations. What 'the other side' had to say was the direct result of a memorandum from the Law Officers, whose opinion the King asked should be taken as to the best method of demonstrating the falsity of the libel. The memorandum was duly laid before His Majesty and later deposited in the Royal Archives at Windsor Castle. This highly interesting document is published here, by permission, for the first time.

We have carefully read and considered *The Liberator* article of November 1910, and have come to the following conclusions:

1. The article is clearly a criminal libel upon the King, but it would not be advisable to institute a prosecution unless the accused can be shown to be in a more responsible position than that of a mere distributor. Even then, no prosecution should be commenced unless affirmative evidence is forthcoming at the trial to demonstrate exhaustively the falsity of the libel.

2. The evidence which the Director of Public Prosecutions informs us can be obtained will establish:

(*a*) that Sir Michael Culme-Seymour had two daughters only;

(*b*) that the King, then Prince George of Wales, was never at Malta when either daughter was there, inasmuch as he had left Malta in 1889 whereas the Admiral first arrived there in 1893, after which date his daughters first arrived there;

(*c*) that the elder daughter, now Mrs Napier, met the Prince on two occasions only – the first, in England when she was 8 years old, and the second, after her marriage, when the King (then Duke of York) with the present Queen (then Duchess of York) and the Prince of Wales (then Prince Edward) visited her father at Portsmouth;

(*d*) that the younger daughter died in 1895 and had never met the King.

The witnesses to the above facts would be Admiral Sir Michael Culme-Seymour, Mrs Napier, and if necessary Capt. Napier and Capt. Culme-Seymour, all of whom, we understand, are available witnesses, and are willing to give evidence if the King should so desire. Official witnesses could prove the movements of the King.

3. We have also carefully considered whether, as an alternative, a prosecution could successfully be instituted by the Director of Public Prosecutions on the complaint of members of the Culme-Seymour family for a libel upon that family. If this were a practicable course, it would afford the same opportunity for demonstrating the falsity of the story, but we have come to the conclusion that it is by no means certain that a conviction would follow, and obviously it would be very undesirable that the prosecution should fail for any reason however technical. It seems to us that it might, and probably would, be contended that the libel was upon the King, and not upon any member of the Culme-Seymour family, for in the libel the family is treated as the injured party. Moreover, the defence might be open to an accused person that the libel referred to the dead, and not to the living, daughter; in which case the further difficulty would arise that the prosecution would have to establish that the article was published with a malevolent purpose to vilify the memory of the deceased and with a

view to injure her family. For these reasons, a prosecution founded upon the complaint of any member of the Culme-Seymour family would, in our judgment, be highly undesirable.

4. This being our view, it follows that any prosecution, in whatever form, must be upon the ground that it is His Majesty who is attacked. A prosecution would lie for seditious libel: but inasmuch as in such a proceeding evidence of the falsity of the libel could not be given, a prosecution for seditious libel would, in our judgment, be most inadvisable.

The proper form of procedure, if a prosecution were resolved on, would be by criminal information for libel filed by the Attorney-General on behalf of His Majesty in the King's Bench Division of the High Court of Justice.

5. It is not necessary, in a prosecution for publishing a libel on the King, that His Majesty should give evidence. There is no precedent for the Sovereign appearing as a witness in his own Court, and, upon the authorities, there is some doubt whether he can do so. Apart altogether from this last consideration, we are distinctly of opinion that His Majesty should not take so novel a course.

6. We think it right to point out that a certain and immediate effect of any prosecution will be to give a world-wide publicity to the false and defamatory statements of an article which is contained in a very obscure leaflet of very limited circulation; and we think that it is a matter calling for the most serious consideration whether it is wise to institute proceedings which would evoke all the attention and comment attracted by a State trial.

Against this consideration must be set the fact that the evidence is now available of living witnesses conclusively to establish the falsehood of these statements, and that for the purposes of proof in a Court of Justice these conditions – inasmuch as one witness is 74 years of age – may not long continue.

Rufus D. Isaacs
John Simon

Nov 23, 1910

As the Law Officers pointed out, it was open to the Crown to charge Mylius with having published a seditious libel. In this event the prisoner would have been unable to plead, as he was to do at the outset of his trial, that the contents of the article were true in substance and in fact, since under British law an attack upon the Sovereign is a crime whether there is reason in the attack or not. This would have made it impossible to bring evidence in disproof of the libel. But apart altogether from this consideration, the King had no wish to take advantage of his privileged position, so that it was decided to proceed by way of criminal information, as indeed any of his subjects might do if they had been criminally libelled. This was an alternative procedure to the commoner form of proceeding by indictment; there were not the usual preliminaries before a magistrate and grand jury, and in this case it meant the accused would be tried in the Lord Chief Justice's Court at the Law Courts and not at the Old Bailey. As will be seen, it also gave him the opportunity of raising a point of law, which was his only defence.

There was one constitutional difficulty, as the Law Officers also pointed out. The King was willing and anxious to give evidence on oath refuting the allegations. He could, for instance, prove quite easily that he had never been in Malta in 1890 or indeed at any time when the Culme-Seymour family were there. But all the Law Officers' researches were unable to produce any occasion where the Sovereign had been allowed to go into the witness-box. Consequently, in order to establish his case, the King was obliged to rely on other evidence.

In case Sir Arthur Bigge should be called and asked by the defendant Mylius whether the King was not willing to come and give evidence, the Attorney-General drafted an answer for his use:

> If it were not constitutionally impossible, he would gladly come, but he is not willing to violate the Constitution. And he has been most definitely advised that it would be unconstitutional for him to tender himself as a witness.

The trial of Edward Frederick Mylius, accused of criminally libelling King George V, took place before the Lord Chief Justice, Lord Alverstone, and a special jury in the Royal Courts of Justice on February 1, 1911. The two Law Officers appeared with the Treasury junior counsel, Mr Richard Muir, and Mr Sidney Rowlatt, later Mr Justice Rowlatt, for the prosecution. The defendant Mylius was not professionally represented, although it was clear that his opening statement, with which he considerably startled the Court, had not been framed without legal assistance. At the solicitors' table, in front of the Crown counsel, sat the Home Secretary, then Mr Winston Churchill, who had an official interest in the trial. Mrs Churchill, also an interested spectator, was accommodated with a seat in the judge's private gallery.

Before the jury were sworn, the prisoner made a remarkable request. 'I wish to ask if the King is present,' he said. Asked by the judge to repeat what he had just said, the young man in the dock proceeded to elaborate it. 'I demand his presence,' he declared, 'on the grounds, first that every accused person has the right to be confronted with his accuser in Court; secondly, that no action for libel is usually taken without the prosecutor being in Court, where the jury can see him; and, thirdly, that there is no proof that the prosecutor is at present alive.'

This was the prisoner's second attempt to get the King into Court. He had already tried unsuccessfully to have a subpoena served on the King to attend the trial and give evidence. The Lord Chief Justice addressed Mylius sternly. 'You are perfectly well aware that the King cannot be summoned here. The King is not present.' The judge thereupon ruled that the trial should proceed.

There was a tense and strained atmosphere in the crowded courtroom, as the Attorney-General rose to open the case to the jury.

> Gentlemen [he began], I am very anxious that you should understand from the outset that in these proceedings in this prosecution no complaint has been lodged because of the Republican sentiments and views which this gentleman and those associated with him in this leaflet may choose to advocate. A man is free in this country to advocate political opinions, even to raise the question of the proper form of government for this country. He is probably freer in this country than in any country in the world to publish his views and to circulate them; and so long as he keeps within the law, which is framed on very broad and generous lines, no complaint is made against him, however much you and I may differ from every sentiment that is expressed in the paper. But I want you quite clearly to appreciate that this prosecution is not in respect of any observations of that character which may have been made in this leaflet.

The Attorney-General went on to examine the facts of the case. After he had been speaking for about ten minutes the atmosphere in Court became more relaxed when it was seen how baseless the defendant's charges were. Since Mylius had pleaded justification, the onus of proof was on him, as Rufus Isaacs pointed out; but the prosecution did not intend to wait for that but would immediately call witnesses of their own in refutation. The Attorney-General now asked the question, would the King be one of them? 'The Solicitor-General and I,' he continued, 'after careful consideration, have come to the conclusion that His Majesty has not the right to vindicate his character on oath – an advantage possessed by all his subjects. This is not a private privilege which the King can waive at pleasure, but it is an absolute incapacity attached to the Sovereign by the Constitution by reasons of public policy.' There was, in fact, no precedent for the reigning monarch giving evidence in the Courts, and the reason was obvious. It was not, of course, a personal liability, for King Edward VII, as Prince of Wales, had given evidence in the Mordaunt divorce and the Tranby Croft cases: it was due to the fact that the Courts are the King's Courts, and clearly a man cannot be subpoenaed to give evidence in his own Courts.

The case against Mylius was that he had circulated the libel with the full knowledge of its contents, that he had taken part in the writing of the article or in supplying the information on which it was based, and that he was aware that he and the editor had failed to get any information of the sort which would have been required to support the story. Also, he must have been aware, the Attorney-General went on, that the object of the libel was to destroy the respect felt for the Monarch by his subjects. And in order to do this, the rumour, which had been set at rest by Sir Arthur Bigge's statement, had been deliberately revived and circulated with an indifference to the facts clearly demonstrated by James's letters to Mylius.

Rufus Isaacs concluded his speech to the jury with these memorable words:

It is not for the Monarchy that the protection of this Court has been sought by means of this case. The Monarchy in this country rests upon foundations more secure than any that could be undermined by the attacks of James or the defendant Mylius. But the protection is sought for the King as a man, for the King as a husband, for the King as a father. Your protection is sought for the honour of the King.

In submitting this case to you, I do not ask you to deal with it in any other way than you would the most ordinary case as between one citizen and another. The same rules of evidence and the same considerations must apply. You have to determine this case, and you will determine it, upon the evidence that will be laid before you. You will judge it fairly and impartially. You will, I am sure, consider everything that can possibly be said or may be urged either as defence or in any other way by the defendant. But you will also, I know, bear in mind this: that the King is none the less entitled to the verdict of a jury and to the protection of an English Court of Justice in any attack made upon his honour because he happens to be the King of England.

The Crown witnesses were then called. The first was a detective who proved that he had seen Mylius post copies of *The Liberator* with the defamatory article from Notting Hill post office. He was followed into the witness-box by Admiral Sir Michael Culme-Seymour, who confirmed that he had two daughters. Elizabeth, the elder, was married and was now Mrs Napier; Laura, the younger, was dead. The first time they visited Malta was in 1893, when he was Commander-in-Chief of the Mediterranean Fleet. The Admiral swore the King was never in Malta at any time when he and his daughters were there. Indeed, Laura had never spoken to the King in her life and had only seen him once at a garden-party in London. The married daughter had only spoken to him once, and Mrs Napier herself confirmed this in her evidence.

The next witness was the Crown Advocate of Malta, who had charge of all the marriage registers in the island. He pointed out that under Maltese law registration of marriages was compulsory. He went on to say that he had personally searched the registers for the period between 1886 and 1893.

'Will you tell us,' Sir John Simon asked him, 'whether in all those registers, through that series of years, there is any entry of a lady bearing the name of Seymour, or Culme, or Culme-Seymour?'

'There is not,' answered the witness.

'Is there any entry in those registers which gives the slightest suspicion or support to what is here suggested?'

'Not the slightest.'

The other witnesses included Mrs Napier's husband and also her brother. But the prisoner declined to cross-examine any of the prosecution witnesses with the result that the case for the Crown was finished before the luncheon adjournment. When the Court reassembled, Mylius was asked whether he wished to call any evidence. He replied that he preferred to address the Court first on a point of law. But the point he now raised, on its face a procedural one, was merely a pretext for making another attempt to get the King into the witness-box.

There are two forms of criminal information. One is an information filed *ex officio* by the Attorney-General, the procedure followed in this instance. The other is an information filed by the Master of the Crown Office at the instance of a private individual. In the case of the latter, the individual instigating the prosecution must swear affidavits and personally appear in Court. Mylius now protested that the second procedure should have been followed in his case. However, the Lord Chief Justice overruled his contention, pointing out that there was no power to subpoena the King to appear as a witness, and in any event Mylius had adduced no facts in his plea of justification which the King alone could prove. The accused thereupon put up no further defence.

'You said you wished to call evidence,' Lord Alverstone reminded him.

'That is my evidence, my Lord.'

'Do you wish to say anything more, Mr Mylius?'

'No, my Lord,' replied the prisoner. 'I rest my case there, as I have been denied the constitutional right of a fair trial.'

In his summing up, the Lord Chief Justice referred to Mylius's contention. 'As a matter of fact,' he said, 'the evidence that could be obtained in such affidavits is before you today in the fullest measure. But that is not the ground on which I declined to accede to Mr Mylius's application. It is the right of the Attorney-General in any matter of libel or public wrong, which he thinks sufficient to justify a criminal information, it is his right – and in one sense his duty – to file a criminal information.'

The jury had no difficulty in arriving at their verdict. Without leaving the jury-box, they found Mylius guilty.

'Mr Mylius,' the judge turned to the prisoner, 'you have no right to say anything to me, but if you have anything to say before I pass sentence upon you, I will hear you. But you must direct it solely to that.'

'My Lord,' replied Mylius sullenly, 'I have made my protest, and I have nothing more to say.'

The Lord Chief Justice thereupon sentenced Mylius to twelve months' imprisonment, adding that he did not think it necessary in the circumstances to pass a heavier sentence.

There was the usual buzz of conversation and shuffling of feet which marks the end of any Court case. But it was not the end. The Attorney-General was seen to rise in his place, holding a sheet of black-edged writing-paper in his hand. Suddenly everyone was silent, as everyone in the court-room strained their ears to hear what Sir Rufus Isaacs had to say.

'Now that sentence has been passed in this case,' he began, 'there is a matter to which I should like to refer, and which I did not think your Lordship would have thought it right for me to mention until after the verdict and sentence had been passed. I hold in my hands at this moment a document, under the hand of His

Majesty the King, from which with your Lordship's permission I will read.'

The judge nodded approval from the Bench, as the Attorney-General raised the paper and continued slowly and deliberately.

I am authorized by His Majesty to state publicly that he was never married except to the Queen, and that he never went through any ceremony of marriage except with the Queen. And further that His Majesty would have attended to give evidence to this effect had he not received advice from the Law Officers of the Crown that it would be unconstitutional for him to do so.

'That statement, my Lord, is signed by the King himself.'

The Attorney-General's words were received with a prolonged murmur of approval by the spectators in Court, a demonstration which the Lord Chief Justice made no move to suppress. The result of the trial was immediately conveyed to Buckingham Palace, where the King and Queen Mary were anxiously waiting to hear it. Later that evening the King wrote in his diary: 'The whole story is a damnable lie and has been in existence now for over twenty years. I trust that this will settle it once and for all.'

Queen Alexandra was equally relieved by the news. 'Thank God that vile trial is over,' she wrote to her son from Sandringham, 'and those infamous lies and foul accusations at an end for ever and cleared up before the whole world. To *us* all it was a ridiculous story your having been married before. . . . Too silly for words – but as the public seems to have believed it, this trial was the only way to let them hear and know the truth, and so have your good name vindicated for ever. . . . It is hard on the best people like you, who really have steered so straight in your life, to be accused of such base things. . . . It only shows how unfair the world is and how the wicked love to slander the upright and good and try to drag them down to their own level.'[1]

To mark the King's appreciation of their services in vindicating his honour in the Mylius case, both Rufus Isaacs and John Simon were appointed Knights Commander of the Royal Victorian Order, an award in the personal gift of the Sovereign. A few weeks later, on July 5, 1912, the Attorney-General was sworn a member of His Majesty's Privy Council.

[1] Harold Nicolson: *King George the Fifth* (1952), pp. 143–44.

3

In his Presidential Address to the Medico-Legal Society in 1937, Sir Travers Humphreys, one of the greatest of modern English criminal lawyers said, discussing the trial of Frederick Seddon and his wife on a charge of murder by poison, 'I venture to recommend to any young barrister in search of a model cross-examination and to any medical man who aspires to become an expert witness the perusal of this interesting trial.'[1] The cross-examination in question was administered by Sir Rufus Isaacs when leading for the prosecution in one of the most interesting and celebrated of poison trials in England. It was the most deadly of an accused person which Travers Humphreys could recall – 'all the more deadly because it was perfectly fair'. Certain it is that it set the seal on the male prisoner's fate. Yet remarkably enough, the trial of the Seddons was the only murder trial in which Isaacs appeared in the whole of his career at the Bar. His presence in Court was due to the custom which required a Law Officer to lead for the Crown in all poison trials, and his experience in this one so unnerved him that he determined never to figure in any similar trial in future if he could possibly avoid it. In fact, he never did.

The trial was distinguished by several peculiar features, particularly the concluding scene between the judge and the prisoner in the dock, a scene unprecedented in the long history of English criminal trials. For one thing, the case against the Seddons depended entirely upon circumstantial evidence; there was nothing to show that either of the Seddons had administered poison to their alleged victim. What proved the husband's undoing was his insistence on going into the witness-box and testifying in his own defence. Had he refrained from doing so, the jury might well have acquitted him. But, as things were, if ever there was a case of a man convicting himself on a murder charge out of his own mouth, it was Frederick Henry Seddon. At the same time, while the evidence against him was also tendered against Mrs Seddon, the jury were to give her the benefit of the doubt and find her not guilty. Indeed there is no case of comparable gravity in which two people have been accused of the same offence on the same evidence, but in which the jury returned different verdicts. In many ways the trial was unique. Among other features, it is the only trial at which a photograph was successfully taken of the scene in the

---

[1] Travers Humphreys: *Criminal Days* (1946), p. 118.

court-room at the moment the judge assumed the black cap and proceeded to pass sentence of death.

Seddon, aged forty at the time of the trial, had been employed for the past ten years by the London and Manchester Industrial Assurance Company as an area superintendent of canvassers, whose duty it was to collect the weekly contributions due to the company. He lived with his wife and five children in a fourteen-room house, 63 Tollington Park, Finsbury, then a north London suburb of unimpeachable respectability. A mean and miserly man he had by the practice of extreme thrift saved a capital sum which brought him in a private income of about £400 a year. He was a lay preacher, also prominent in his local Masonic Lodge, and no doubt regarded in the neighbourhood as a thoroughly deserving citizen. He had originally bought the house in Tollington Park as an investment, but being unable to find a tenant for it, he had decided to live in it himself with his family and to let out part of it to lodgers, at the same time using the basement as an office. It was in reply to his advertisement for lodgers that a forty-eight-year-old maiden lady, Eliza Barrow, whom he was subsequently accused of poisoning, arrived in July, 1910, and took the top floor at a weekly rent of 12s. 6d., besides a further sum of 7s. for service, which was provided by Seddon's daughter Maggie.

Miss Barrow was an even more pronounced miser than her landlord. She was also a woman of slovenly and offensive personal habits. She brought with her a young boy named Ernest Grant, whom she had more or less adopted; also a married couple called Hook who were related to him. But shortly after her arrival she quarrelled with the Hooks and Seddon gave them notice on her behalf. Indeed she had a most quarrelsome nature; whilst previously staying with some cousins of hers named Vonderahe she had been known to spit in her hostess's face. She had about £3,000 of her own, which was mostly invested in India Stock, and the lease of a public house. She worried a lot about her money, and with some reason, since the India Stock had recently depreciated a good deal and the Liberal policy of licensing and taxation threatened the public house. It was not long before Seddon discovered that she had financial worries and took advantage of them. He persuaded her to hand over her entire fortune to him in return for an annuity of £155. For her part she thought she had got a good bargain, since her income was now about £30 more than she could have obtained from an insurance company or a savings bank. Seddon paid the annuity punctually each month in gold until her death fourteen months after her arrival. She hoarded as much of this gold as she could, augmenting her supply of coin by withdrawing £216 from her savings-bank account as a result of a scare about the solvency of these institutions. After her death, Seddon said that he had raised objections to her keeping so much gold in the house, and that she had replied, 'I know what to do with it.'

On September 1, 1911, Eliza Barrow became ill. The Seddons' family doctor was called in and diagnosed epidemic diarrhoea. She vomited and had pains in the stomach in addition to the diarrhoea. After about a week she showed signs of improvement. At the same time she made a will leaving her property to the boy Grant and appointing Seddon sole executor. But, while she began to get worse on September 13, the Seddons do not seem to have taken her illness very seriously, although Mrs Seddon prepared her meals at this time and sometimes poured out her medicine. On the same day, Seddon's sister and niece came to stay in the house and he himself went to the theatre, returning home with the characteristic story that the box-office clerk had cheated him of sixpence. At about 11.30 young Grant, who somewhat surprisingly had continued to sleep in the same bed as Miss Barrow during her illness, called down to the Seddons, 'Chickie' – that was what he habitually called her – 'Chickie is out of bed.' The unfortunate woman had in fact crawled out of bed and was sitting on the floor in agony and wailing, 'I am dying.' The Seddons sent the boy to another room, and while Mrs Seddon sat by the bedside, Seddon took up his vigil on the landing outside the room, reading a paper, smoking a pipe and occasionally going down-stairs to fetch himself a drink. After a while Miss Barrow fell into a deep sleep. Towards dawn her breathing became heavier, and at 6.30 a.m. she died.

Seddon immediately began to search for her money, but according to his own account he only succeeded in finding £4 10s. in the dead woman's cash box and £5 10s. hidden in a drawer. Later in the morning Seddon advised the doctor of her death, and the doctor, without visiting the house again, gave him a certificate that Miss Barrow had died of the complaint he had originally diagnosed. Seddon then went to see the undertaker to arrange for the funeral; and, although there was a document among Miss Barrow's papers entitling her to be buried in a family vault at Highgate, he told the undertaker that he only had £4 10s. to pay for the funeral and out of this sum the doctor's fees had also to be met. As a result the unfortunate woman was given the cheapest funeral possible and her remains were interred in a public grave. As a final example of his meanness, Seddon accepted a commission of 12s. 6d. from the undertaker for introducing the business. On the day Miss Barrow died, Seddon went about his business as usual. He was seen by two of his insurance canvassers counting out gold, and to one of them he made the only joke with which he has been credited. 'Smith,' he said, holding up a bag of gold, 'here's your week's wages.' 'I wish you meant it, sir,' the man replied, not realizing it was blood-money.

None of Miss Barrow's relatives was informed of her death, although the Vonderahes lived a short distance away. Seddon afterwards swore that he had sent Mr Vonderahe a letter with this news, also letting him know the date of the funeral, and he produced a copy of the letter which he allegedly wrote; but Mr Vonderahe said he had never received it, and in the circumstances it is unlikely that Seddon ever posted such a letter, which incidentally contained no mention of the fact that Miss Barrow was to be buried in a public grave. A request for an interview by Mr Vonderahe was evaded by Seddon, who put him off with the excuse that he had to go away and it was not until some weeks later that they met. Meanwhile the suspicion of the Vonderahes was aroused, particularly after they heard about Miss Barrow's will appointing Seddon sole executor. In the result they communicated with the police, further inquiries were instituted, and eventually an order was made to exhume the body. At the subsequent post-mortem examination, Dr William Willcox, the Home Office analyst, found that the corpse contained two and a half grains of arsenic. When he received a summons to attend the inquest and give evidence, Seddon consulted a local solicitor, Mr Walter Saint. The solicitor briefed a young counsel, Mr Gervais Rentoul, whose work had impressed him on another case, to represent Seddon at the inquest. It was all very awkward, Seddon explained; the 'old girl' had been his lodger and must have drunk some of the water in which arsenically treated fly-papers used in her room had been soaked, which accounted for the poison subsequently found in her body. When the solicitor expressed surprise that 'poisonous things like that' could be bought at an ordinary chemist's, Seddon sent his daughter Maggie to a near-by chemist's to prove it. But the chemist, when he heard her name, refused to supply her. At the same time, she was being watched by the police, who knew that another chemist in the neighbourhood called Walter Thorley had supplied a packet of these fly-papers to a fair-haired girl on August 26. Thorley went to the police station and identified Maggie Seddon as the girl who had made the purchase from him. Meanwhile, on December 4, before the inquest resumed, Seddon was arrested for the murder of Miss Barrow by administering arsenic. 'Absurd!' he exclaimed. 'What a terrible charge, wilful murder! It is the first of our family that have ever been accused of such a crime. Are you going to arrest my wife as well? If not, I would like you to give her a message for me. Have they found arsenic in the body? She has not done this herself. It was not carbolic acid, was it, as there was some in her room, and Sanitas is not poison, is it?' Six weeks later Mrs Seddon was also arrested, and in due course both were sent for trial.

The trial began before Mr Justice Bucknill at the Old Bailey on March 12, 1912, and owing to the large number of witnesses – forty-five for the prosecution and thirteen for the defence – it lasted for ten days. The Attorney-General, Sir Rufus Isaacs, led a most formidable prosecuting team, consisting besides himself of Mr Richard Muir, the Senior Treasury Counsel, and two future High Court judges, Mr Sidney Rowlatt and Mr Travers Humphreys. Marshall Hall appeared for the defence of Seddon and in fact led the defence of both the Seddons, although Mrs Seddon was nominally defended by Mr Gervais Rentoul, who had represented both accused at the inquest and the preliminary police court proceedings.

In opening the case for the prosecution, the Attorney-General employed phraseology which was to be followed in subsequent murder trials where the evidence against the accused was wholly circumstantial. He invited the jury to consider in the case of each prisoner their interest in causing Eliza Barrow's death, their opportunity for administering the fatal poison, and their conduct both before and after the alleged murder. He then proceeded to outline the facts in the case. It was a masterly as well as exhaustive opening and when he sat down after speaking for two hours, Marshall Hall leaned over and whispered to a colleague. 'They're all out for a conviction, aren't they?'

Nothing which could be called in any way spectacular occurred until the fourth day of the trial, when Dr Willcox, the last of the prosecution witnesses, went into the box. The prosecution's case was that Miss Barrow had died from acute arsenical poisoning, and that the fatal dose had been administered by the Seddons within twenty-four hours of her death. This was supported by the expert evidence of

Dr Willcox, who described how the amount of arsenic found (2·01 grains) had been arrived at. Point 63 of a grain had been found in the liver and intestines by weighing. It was not practicable to ascertain, by weighing, the rest which was widely distributed throughout the system. Recourse was consequently had to a chemical test known as Marsh's test, by which when a minute quantity of arsenic is extracted from a small part of, say, the stomach, the total amount of arsenic in the stomach is ascertained by multiplying the minute portion in proportion to the stomach's total weight. In cross-examination, Marshall Hall attacked this experiment, obliging the Home Office analyst to admit a possibility of error due to the fact that he had made no allowance for the loss of water due to evaporation. Having thus exposed the weakness of the experiment in an important particular, Marshall Hall went on to question the witness about the amount of arsenic found in the dead woman's hair, particularly at the distal end, i.e. the end away from the roots. On this point Dr Willcox admitted that the amount of arsenic found there might well mean that the arsenic had been taken more than a year ago, thus supporting Marshall Hall's line of defence that Miss Barrow had died from epidemic diarrhoea aggravated by chronic as distinct from acute arsenical poisoning.

If Marshall Hall had sat down at this stage and then prevailed upon his client not to go into the witness-box, it is more than likely that the man in the dock would have been acquitted, as well as his wife. As Dr Willcox subsequently told Marshall Hall's biographer, Edward Marjoribanks, 'He very nearly tied me up. I don't think I've ever been so nearly trapped as I was then – it was extraordinarily clever of him.' But it was as well for the ends of justice that Marshall Hall should have devoted some further questions to driving home his point about the hair. This gave Dr Willcox the opportunity to put his finger on the true explanation, which was that Miss Barrow's long hair had become contaminated by the blood-stained fluid in the coffin. Although Marshall Hall poured scorn on this explanation, it was to be substantiated when Dr Willcox was recalled to the witness-box before the end of the trial to describe how with the aid of another doctor he had conducted a further experiment by which a strand of hair taken from a living woman had been soaked in the fluid and was found to contain arsenic just as Miss Barrow's had done. Thus the effect of this crucial part of Marshall Hall's brilliant cross-examination was completely destroyed.

From the date of his first interview with Seddon, Marshall Hall had been strongly opposed to calling him as a witness. 'If the evidence does not convict this man,' he said at the time, 'his conceit will.' He told his instructing solicitor that, while he must not prevent Seddon from going into the witness-box, he must warn him clearly of the dangers. Just before the case for the prosecution concluded on the fifth day, Marshall Hall walked over to the dock and repeated this warning. But Seddon's mind was made up. Although he had heard the Attorney-General's masterly opening, he was convinced that he could get the better of him. Indeed he was longing for the fray. And so, after Marshall Hall had briefly examined two witnesses, who testified to Seddon's habit of keeping large sums of gold coin in the house, he called the male prisoner.

For the next two hours Seddon answered his counsel's questions clearly and well, thus bearing out the view subsequently expressed by Marshall Hall that he was the ablest man he had ever defended on a capital charge. There came the final question.

'Did you ever administer or cause to be administered to Miss Barrow any arsenic in any shape or form whatever?'

'I never purchased arsenic in my life in any shape or form. I never administered arsenic. I never advised or instructed the purchase of arsenic in any shape or form. I never advised, directed, or instructed the administration of arsenic. That I swear.'

4

The Attorney-General then rose to question the prisoner.

Throughout the long cross-examination, which lasted for most of two days, Rufus Isaacs never once raised his voice, putting his questions with studied courtesy and always addressing the witness as 'Mr Seddon'. The deadly tone was set by the first two questions, which were phrased with the utmost skill.

'Miss Barrow lived with you from 26th July, 1910, till the morning of 14th September, 1911?'

'Yes.'

'Did you like her?'

'Did I like her?' the prisoner repeated.

'Yes, that is the question.'

No wonder Seddon hesitated before replying, for the question placed him in a dilemma. If he said yes, then he would expose himself as a hypocrite in view of his arranging for the cheapest possible funeral. On the other hand, if he said no, he would immediately prejudice himself in the eyes of the jury. In the circumstances he gave the best answer he could.

'She was not a woman you could be in love with, but I deeply sympathized with her.'

Questioned about her personal effects at the time of her death, Seddon agreed that all they amounted to in value was £16 odd, including £10 in gold, although she had brought at least £165 in notes into the house, since £5 notes to that amount had been cashed by Mrs Seddon, who had incidentally given a false name and address at the shops at which she cashed them 'because she did not want everybody to know who she was'. Seddon also agreed that he had taken over all her property in exchange for an annuity of £2 to £3 a week.

'This has turned out a remarkably profitable investment from the monetary point of view?'

'Only from that point of view.'

'On your statement you had paid out altogether £91?'

'Yes.'

'And the whole of the property fell in to you?'

'I was already in possession of the whole of the property.'

Asked what security he had given Miss Barrow, the witness said it was his personal obligation to pay as evidenced by the annuity certificate he had drawn up, signed by himself and witnessed by his wife.

'Do you wish the jury to believe that you do not know the difference between making an obligation to pay the money and giving security for the payment of it?'

To this the witness replied by asking a question himself. 'But isn't a legally drawn up certificate security on my estate?'

'Do you not know that is only a personal obligation on you?' rejoined the Attorney-General.

'I understand it is recoverable by law.'

'Well, I have given you an opportunity of dealing with it.'

On the subject of Miss Barrow's will and the money she withdrew from her savings-bank account the witness's replies were equally unsatisfactory.

'Do you mean to tell my lord and the jury,' the Attorney-General asked him, 'that from the time you made that will until after the death, on 9th October, when you saw Mr Vonderahe, you never thought about that savings-bank money or what had become of it?'

'It had puzzled me what had become of it, certainly.'

'Why did you not tell the relatives?'

'Because I was puzzled to know what had become of it,' Seddon repeated stubbornly.

'Was not that a very good reason why you should tell the relatives?'

'At the time of the interview it never entered my head.'

'I do not think you are doing yourself justice by that answer,' the Attorney-General remarked dryly. 'Just let me recall to you what you have said. You make the will on 11th September; she dies on the morning of the 14th; you have inquiries made by the Vonderahes on 20th September and 21st September. You have an appointment with Mr Vonderahe, the male relative, the husband, to whom you are going to give an account, on 9th October. I have asked you whether it had occurred to you during the whole of this time as to what had become of this money which had been drawn on 19th June?'

'It had certainly occurred to me as to what had become of it, but I did not consider that the Vonderahes were entitled to the full details, without he showed that he was the legal next-of-kin.'

By this time the witness had lost much of his brash self-confidence, as the Attorney-General pounded away with his questions.

'You knew that in ordinary prudence you ought to take care – to have some relatives there before you got the keys and looked in her cash box?'

'I did not think so,' answered Seddon in a surly tone. 'She had already spoken about what she thought of her relatives. I do not see why I should if she did not want her relatives.'

'You are an experienced man of business. If you had nothing to conceal, what I suggest to you is that the first thing you would do would be to get some independent person into that house before you proceeded either to open her cash box and before you carried her out of the house to be buried?'

Seddon was now beginning to look distinctly uncomfortable. 'There was an independent person in the room,' he replied lamely.

'Who was that?'

'Mrs Rutt, the charwoman, who laid the body out.'

Time and again in this long cross-examination the Attorney-General returned to the question of the missing money, and each time Seddon's answers were less and less convincing.

'Did you think anybody had taken her money out of her cash box when you found only £4 10s. there?'

'I did not know. She had workmen coming into the room off and on. She had a window cleaner.'

'When was the last time she had workmen in the room before she was taken ill?'

'I could not say.'

'Did you ever think any of her money had been stolen?'

'I don't know what she had done with her money,' Seddon continued to answer stubbornly. 'She was a peculiar woman when you mentioned these matters to her that I did not go into details with her. She had a funny temper.'

'Her funny temper could not show itself after death?' Rufus Isaacs queried with a hint of sarcasm.

'No, but you are asking me what had become of her money during life.'

'No, I am not. I am asking you what had become of her money after death.'

To this sharp rejoinder all that Seddon could answer was, 'It was not there.'

The Attorney-General gave the witness no respite from this line of questioning.

'Did you think when you had made your very thorough search during the whole of that day that somebody had been stealing her money?'

'I didn't know what she had been doing with it.'

'Did it cross your mind that somebody may have stolen it?'

'No, I don't think evil of people like that. I am not so ready to think evil of people.'

'Not even of the workmen or the window cleaners who came into her room?'

'I have nothing to support the idea that they had.'

'Did you not think that it was a matter in respect of which some inquiry must be made?'

'No.'

'Do you realize how much money, according to your statement, there must have been in gold of hers during the eight months before her death?'

'Yes.'

'What do you make it?'

'£165, less anything she had spent.'

'According to your view,' the Attorney-General continued to press the witness, 'you had nothing whatever to conceal from her relatives?'

'I couldn't explain what had become of that money,' Seddon repeated.

'Why did you not tell the relatives that you could not explain it?'

'I told him he had not shown me that he was the next-of-kin.'

'Is that your reason?'

'Yes, I did not go into details beyond what I had already given him.'

'Now, Mr Seddon, just think a minute. If you have any other explanation to give, give it.'

'I told you that I did not give a thought to the matter.'

'And that is your only explanation to my lord and the jury of your not having said anything to the relatives about that money being missed?'

'Yes.'

'That the man who asked you was not the legal next-of-kin?'

'And that I could not say where it was.'

'Was not that the very reason why you should have told him you could not tell where it was?'

'It did not enter my head for to go into details.'

'Did you ever tell the police?'

'No.'

At last Seddon became rattled. It was when the Attorney-General questioned him about the bags of gold he had been seen counting out in the basement. The prisoner threw up his hands in indignation.

'The prosecution are suggesting that I am dealing with the deceased woman's gold; that I should bring it down from the top of the house to the bottom into the office in the presence of my assistants and count it up. Is it feasible?'

'I do not want to argue with you,' commented the Attorney-General, 'but you know that people sometimes do very foolish things?'

'Well, I am not a degenerate,' Seddon began to shout. 'That would make it out that I am a greedy, inhuman monster.'

'What?'

'That I am a greedy, inhuman monster,' the prisoner repeated his words, 'or something with a very degenerate mind, to commit a vile crime such as the prosecution suggest, and then bringing the dead woman's money down and counting it in the presence of my two assistants and flouting it like that. The suggestion is scandalous. I would have all day to count the money.'

Seddon was finally questioned about the arsenical fly-papers in the house. He did not know they were poisonous, he said, except to insects. He saw them only twice in Miss Barrow's room, the night she signed her will and the night she died. He added that he had only heard of poisoning by arsenic taken from fly-papers after he had been arrested.

'Can you account for the arsenic having got into her stomach and intestines?'

'It is all a Chinese puzzle to me.'

Even then, at the end of this six-hour cross-examination, Seddon did not realize how he had entrapped himself by his answers. It was not until the Attorney-General analysed them and summed up their cumulative effect in his closing speech to the jury that the terrible truth dawned upon him. Meanwhile his wife had followed him into the witness-box. But whereas Seddon had antagonized the jury, Mrs Seddon excited their compassion as a household drudge who meekly did her husband's bidding at all times. 'I never wish anybody dead,' she exclaimed on the verge of tears. 'I thought too much of Miss Barrow. I waited hand and foot on her. I did all I possibly could to get her better.' In a spontaneous outburst, she had even kissed the poor dead woman's face before the coffin lid was screwed down.

In his closing speech to the jury, one of his most eloquent, Marshall Hall suggested that after one of four saucers containing fly-papers in Miss Barrow's bedroom had been accidentally knocked off the mantelpiece and broken, Mrs Seddon had put the saucers on a soup plate because as she said she 'could not be bothered with having all these things about', and after pouring fresh water on to the plate with its contents had placed the plate on a table near Miss Barrow's bed. 'Here is arsenic in the house,' he said, 'there are those fly-papers in the house, containing, let us say, sixteen grains of arsenic, and the less water the more concentrated the solution. You have to remember that. I suggest to you in some way or other some portion of that, not sufficient to cause her death, but sufficient in the state in which she was to aggravate the symptoms from which she was suffering – some portion by some means or other got into this unfortunate woman's stomach, and so into her body. Gentlemen, that possibility has not been eliminated successfully. The prosecution have never called any sufficiently reliable evidence to prove that that opportunity was not taken advantage of, and that the arsenic was not, in fact, administered in that way.'

It was only at the end of his speech, which followed Marshall Hall's that the Attorney-General indicated the possibility that the jury might return different verdicts in respect of the two prisoners. 'It may be when you take the whole of this case into your consideration,' he said, 'you may think that the evidence shows beyond all reasonable doubt that one of these prisoners is guilty, but that you have some element of reasonable doubt with regard to the other. Supposing you come to the conclusion that you have no reasonable doubt with regard to the male prisoner, but that you have some doubt – you are not quite satisfied beyond all reasonable doubt – that the woman is guilty, then it would be your duty to acquit her.'

The Attorney-General's speech was criticized by some who heard it as 'a hanging speech'. It was, indeed, his first and only murder case, and he was not familiar with the atmosphere of murder trials. But both Marshall Hall and the judge subsequently paid tribute to its fairness, and cold and dispassionate as it appeared it can scarcely be said to have pressed unduly hard upon the prisoners, particularly Seddon who, as we have seen, was the main cause of his own undoing. Then, in his summing up, the judge was on the whole against Seddon but favourable to Margaret Seddon.

In this context, the subsequent comments of Travers Humphreys, who appeared with Rufus Isaacs, are apposite. 'The difficulty in the way of the Crown lay in the fact that the evidence pointed to Mrs Seddon as the actual administrator,' he afterwards wrote; 'no jury would convict her if they could find a way out, and our evidence left out, necessarily, the comparison of the two individuals which could only be made by a jury who had seen and heard them both. When that had taken place there was ample justification for the verdict of acquittal of the woman, a weak and probably ill-treated creature, on the ground that she may not have known that what she was giving to the sick woman contained arsenic.'

Rufus Isaacs's private opinion of the wife is also worth quoting. 'Her case was a terribly difficult one,' he told Marshall Hall afterwards. 'The chain was as complete as circumstantial evidence can make it, and you had a very hard task when it was so plain to all that the man had such a covetous nature, and was such a shrewd, cunning fellow.'

It took the jury precisely one hour in the afternoon of the tenth day of the trial to reach their verdicts – Seddon guilty and Mrs Seddon not guilty. At once Seddon turned to his wife in the dock and kissed her. 'Tell her she is discharged,' said the judge to the court usher, as she was led sobbing from the Court.

Asked whether he had anything to say for himself why the Court should not give him judgment of death according to law, Seddon pulled some notes out of his pocket and made a long speech, which the judge made no attempt to interrupt, even towards the end when the prisoner brazenly took advantage of the fact that they both belonged to the masonic brotherhood. 'The prosecution has not traced anything to me in the shape of money,' he concluded, 'which is the great motive suggested by the prosecution in this case for my committing the diabolical crime of which I declare before the Great Architect of the Universe I am not guilty, my lord.' He then made the secret sign which binds a mason to come to the aid of another in extremity.

This action completely unnerved the judge. But after a minute or two he pulled himself together and proceeded to pass sentence. His preliminary remarks were punctuated by a series of unprecedented interruptions on the part of the prisoner.

'This murder has been described by yourself in the box as one which, if made out, was a barbarous one,' the judge admonished him, '. . . a murder of design, a cruel murder. It is not for me to harrow your feelings.'

'It does not affect me,' said the prisoner. 'I have a clear conscience.'

'I, as minister of the law,' continued the judge, 'have now to pass upon you that sentence which the law demands has to be passed, which is that you have forfeited your life in consequence of your great crime. Try to make your peace with your Maker.'

'I am at peace.'

'From what you have said,' Mr Justice Bucknill proceeded, 'you and I know we both belong to one brotherhood, and it is all the more painful to me to have to say what I am saying. But our brotherhood does not encourage crime; on the contrary, it condemns it. I pray you again to make your peace with the Great Architect of the Universe. Mercy – pray for it, ask for it. It may be some consolation to you to know that I agree with the verdict that the jury has passed with regard to your wife. But that does not make it better for you. Whatever she has done that was blameworthy in this case, short of any criminal offence, if there was anything I feel she did to help you, not to murder, but, it may be at some time to deal improperly with these notes . . .'

'She has done nothing wrong, sir,' the prisoner broke in.

'I am satisfied the jury have done well and rightly in acquitting her,' the judge repeated. 'I am satisfied that they have done justice to you.

And now I have to pass sentence. . . . And may the Lord have mercy on your soul!'

Marshall Hall spent two more days in arguing Seddon's appeal against the verdict in the Court of Criminal Appeal; but the Court presided over by Mr Justice Darling dismissed the appeal without calling upon the Attorney-General in reply. The Home Secretary refused to recommend a reprieve, and Seddon was duly hanged, preoccupied with money matters and protesting his innocence to the last. 'I solemnly swear before my Creator, to whom all secrets are revealed that this is a true statement,' he wrote to his wife on the eve of his execution in Pentonville Prison, 'and the Law, in its seeming blindness and misguided justice, has condemned an Innocent Man.'

In spite of her acquittal people continued to regard Mrs Seddon as a murderess, and in an endeavour to silence these accusations she agreed to sign a 'confession', subsequently published in the *Weekly Despatch* to the effect that she had seen her husband give Miss Barrow arsenic, and that he had threatened to kill her with a revolver if she gave him away. When it was subsequently pointed out to her by another popular weekly, *John Bull*, that she had by her action exposed herself to the risk of being prosecuted for perjury, she retracted what she had written and said it was untrue. She was obviously a woman easily influenced. Meanwhile she had got married again, and with a new husband and a new name departed to begin a new life in the anonymity of Australia.

Whatever may be the merits of Mrs Seddon's 'confession', there is no doubt that Seddon did keep a revolver in the house. One of his legal advisers who went to the house before his arrest noticed a picture, not perhaps in the best of taste, hanging on the dining-room wall, which depicted a husband shooting his wife's lover. 'There,' said Seddon, pointing to the picture at the same time as he threw down the revolver on the table, 'that's the sort of man I am – only I would have shot them both!'

5

Shortly after the Seddons' trial, Rufus Isaacs encountered an acute professional disappointment which temporarily clouded his hitherto happy relations with the Prime Minister and which might have permanently embittered them but for the outcome in the shape of a consolation prize proposed by the Government Chief Whip and accepted by the Attorney-General. The matter arose out of the sudden and unexpected illness of Lord Loreburn, the Lord Chancellor.

Loreburn suffered a severe heart attack during the Whitsun recess and his doctors advised that he should resign immediately. It so happened that Asquith was out of the country at this time, cruising in the Admiralty yacht in the Mediterranean. The Lord Chancellor, who wrote to the Prime Minister's office, was informed that the matter must await Asquith's return in about a week's time. But next morning (June 4) he felt so ill that he sent in his resignation and summoned his friend and Cabinet colleague Lord Haldane, then Secretary of State for War, to his bedside, telling him what he had done and begging him to go at once and break the news to the King, as he was too unwell to go himself. Haldane hurried off to Buckingham Palace, where he was at once received in audience. To the King's question, 'Who is to succeed?', Haldane said he did not know as the Prime Minister was away. 'My choice, if the Prime Minister agrees,' the King remarked jocularly, looking at Haldane, 'would be a man who was quite capable of combining three offices – Ambassador in Berlin, Lord Chancellor and War Secretary. I know one who would do them all easily!' Haldane replied that no doubt the Prime Minister would make his recommendation when he returned.[1]

Meanwhile, the Government Chief Whip, the Master of Elibank, sent Asquith a wireless message informing him of Loreburn's resignation, which the Prime Minister answered simply: 'Consult Haldane as to who should succeed him at the War Office.'

Before leaving London on the same day for a convalescent visit to the seaside, Loreburn handed over the Great Seal of his office to Haldane, acting on the suggestion of the King's Private Secretary that it would be best to give the Seal into the temporary safe-keeping of a Cabinet minister. As Parliament was due to reassemble on the following Tuesday, June 11, and as it would consequently be necessary for the Lord Chancellor to take his place on the Woolsack in the House of Lords, a meeting of the Privy Council was arranged for the Monday afternoon at which the Great Seal could be formally transferred and Haldane could receive it at the King's hands, after he had surrendered his own seals of office as War Minister. It was also arranged that the new Lord Chancellor would be sworn in by the

[1] Haldane Papers. Cited by R. F. V. Heuston in his *Lives of the Lord Chancellors* 1885–1940 (1964), p. 166.

Master of the Rolls at the sitting of the Law Courts on the following morning.

Although the utmost secrecy was preserved before the official announcement was made, it was inevitable that Rufus Isaacs should get wind of these proceedings. He probably first heard what was afoot from the Chief Whip and he would naturally receive a summons to attend the extraordinary Privy Council meeting. The news certainly came to him as a great shock, his immediate reaction being that the Woolsack should have been offered to himself instead of to Haldane. On the face of it, he had a strong claim to fill the vacancy.

While the Attorney-General had indeed no prescriptive right to the office of Lord Chancellor when it fell vacant, nevertheless it had been the almost invariable practice for three centuries for the Attorney-General to be promoted in these circumstances; in fact, Sir Francis Bacon as Attorney-General had successfully insisted on the succession in the reign of James I. Rufus Isaacs considered that his being passed over might be regarded as a reflection on his Hebrew origin and the fact that he was at least nominally a practising Jew by religion. He even hinted privately to John Simon at resignation. Consequently Simon took it upon himself before the new nomination was made public to write a memorandum to the Prime Minister setting out the reasoning which seems to establish that a Jew can lawfully be appointed Lord Chancellor. 'As to this there can, I consider, be no doubt,' Simon remarked afterwards: 'what formerly excluded a member of that faith was the requirement of an oath taken "on the faith of a Christian". That requirement vanished in 1867.'[1]

As soon as Asquith returned to Downing Street on June 10, he sent for Simon whom he irreverently nicknamed 'the Impeccable' and told him 'with some vigour' that he agreed that the Attorney-General 'was qualified, but that he had long ago decided that if opportunity offered, he would appoint Haldane, who was an ideal choice'. The Attorney-General, who saw the Prime Minister on the same day, received a similar explanation, which did not particularly please him when he asked for the office.

According to the second Lord Reading, in his life of his father, Asquith told the Attorney-General that ever since the formation of the Government there had been 'an understanding' between him and Haldane that, if Haldane would agree to accept the War Office 'in the

[1] Simon, pp. 88–89.

first place' he should have the reversion of the Woolsack. 'Sir Rufus, who had never been aware of this private compact, was indignant, not only for personal reasons but on account of the break in the traditional rights of his own office, and did not hesitate to express to Mr Asquith his resentment at this disregard of his claims as Attorney-General to promotion.'[1]

It is only right to state that the researches of the present writer have failed to unearth any evidence of such a compact. It would appear that the second Lord Reading's statement is based on a misapprehension of what occurred at the time of the break up of the Balfour Government and the succession of Campbell-Bannerman as Prime Minister at the end of 1905.

There was indeed a private compact to which Asquith and Haldane were parties, but it was of a somewhat different character and it had long since been terminated, remarkably enough by Asquith himself. In September, 1905, the three Liberal Imperialists, Asquith, Haldane and Sir Edward Grey, met at Relugas, Grey's fishing lodge near Inverness. There they agreed together that none of them would take office in a Government formed by Campbell-Bannerman unless the leadership of the House of Commons was in other hands. The so-called Relugas Compact, the details of which were communicated to King Edward VII, envisaged Asquith as Chancellor of the Exchequer and Leader of the House of Commons, Grey as Foreign Secretary and Haldane as Lord Chancellor, all serving under Campbell-Bannerman, who would take a peerage and sit in the Lords. In due course 'C-B' had been sent for by the King and invited to form a Government. Asquith was the first to opt out of the compact, when he consented to become Chancellor of the Exchequer, giving as his reason that the General Election was 'before and not behind us' and that an independent Liberal majority in the new House of Commons was 'at most a probability'. Also, the new Prime Minister proved unexpectedly obdurate, refusing to go to the Lords, at any rate for the time being, and insisting on remaining in the Commons as Leader of the House. On the other hand, 'C-B' agreed to Grey becoming Foreign Secretary, but, in spite of the strongest urging by Asquith to give the Woolsack to Haldane, he insisted on appointing Sir Robert Reid, later Lord Loreburn, a former Liberal Attorney-General, to be the new Lord Chancellor. (There was a strong sentimental attachment between the two men, who unlike Asquith and Haldane had

[1] Reading, Vol. I, p. 224.

WITH LADY ISAACS
In 1912 *(Radio Times Hulton Picture Library)*

WITH SIR JOHN SIMON

Leading the procession of King's Counsel at the opening of the Law Term in 1913 *(Radio Times Hulton Picture Library)*

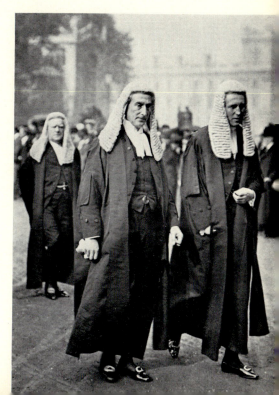

THE CENTRAL CRIMINAL COURT, MARCH 14, 1912

Frederick Henry Seddon being sentenced to death by Mr Justice Bucknill.
This is the only known photograph of the passing of a death sentence in the English courts.

both displayed pro-Boer sympathies during the South African War.) At the same time Haldane was offered the choice between becoming Attorney-General or else the political head of one of the great departments of state such as the Home Office. After some hesitation and consultation with Grey, who had already been offered and had refused the Foreign Office, Haldane who had likewise been offered and refused the Home Office, agreed to become War Minister if his friend would reconsider the Prime Minister's offer to him. In the result Grey did become Foreign Secretary, while Haldane went to the War Office, although they neither of them initially desired these offices.

There is no doubt that Haldane, who had set his heart on being Lord Chancellor, felt that he had been let down by Asquith, although he acknowledged at the time that 'Asquith had done his very best about the Chancellorship.'[1] For his part, Asquith who may have had some qualms of conscience, determined that he was under a strong moral obligation to offer Haldane the Woolsack if he should ever have the opportunity, but there was no compact in the sense of what had been agreed at Relugas. In the event, the way was made easier when Haldane at Asquith's request went to the Lords in 1911 in order to strengthen the Government representation in the Upper House, while retaining his War Office portfolio.

Haldane's appointment as Lord Chancellor was publicly announced on the evening of June 10, 1912, after the Privy Council had met and the Great Seal was handed over by the King. At the same time, so that the Attorney-General should not continue to feel slighted, what Sir John Simon described as 'a happy issue' was reached at the instance of the Government Chief Whip who suggested that Rufus Isaacs should be invited to join the Cabinet. The Prime Minister immediately agreed, and the announcement was made two days later. Thus Rufus Isaacs was enabled to join the inner circle of Government without changing his office and he took his place at the famous green baize-covered table at 10 Downing Street.[2]

No holder of the office of Attorney-General had ever previously been admitted to a seat in the Cabinet. Although he appreciated the honour at the time, he later came to the conclusion that the inclusion

[1] R. B. Haldane: *An Autobiography* (1929), p. 188.
[2] The second Lord Reading states in his biography of his father (Vol. I, p. 224) that the suggestion that he should join the Cabinet came from himself. But, according to Simon, the idea was put forward by the Master of Elibank, who told Simon that he had done so: see Simon, *Retrospect*, p. 89.

E

of the Attorney-General in the Cabinet was in principle a mistake. This view was shared by his Solicitor-General when Simon eventually succeeded to the senior post eighteen months later and was asked to continue the combination of duties. 'The Cabinet from time to time needs the legal advice of the Attorney-General on some aspect of an urgent and complicated political question, either international or domestic, and this advice often requires research and reflection. If the Attorney-General is a party to the earlier deliberations of the Cabinet out of which the need for technical guidance has arisen, it may be difficult for him to approach the problem ultimately presented to him as a lawyer with an entirely open mind.'[1]

Unknown to Rufus Isaacs at this time, a much more serious disturbance to his peace of mind than the loss of the Woolsack was in the offing and was to cause him many months of the most painful anxiety. It could be described in a single word which was to become a veritable nightmare in newspaper posters and headlines through the country – Marconi.

[1] Simon, pp. 89–90. The precedent was followed during the First World War in the case of Carson and F. E. Smith, when they held the office of Attorney-General: but it was subsequently dropped and has not been revived.

5

Lord Chief Justice

1

Commendatore Gugliemo Marconi, whose name was to become synonymous with 'wireless' and a household word, was the son of an Italian businessman in Bologna and an Irish mother. His earliest experiments in wireless and telegraphy were carried out in his home with the aid of peasants in the surrounding countryside. In 1896, at the age of twenty-two, he achieved a crude form of communication by wireless and he offered his invention to the Italian Government. When this was refused, he immediately went to England, where he made the acquaintance of the Chief Engineer at the Post Office and others interested in his novel invention. In the following year, he formed a company in London to exploit it, taking out the necessary patents and buying up others in the wireless field, including Edison's. In 1901 he made history by transmitting signals across the Atlantic for the first time. In the course of the next few years the Marconi apparatus was fitted to ships of the Royal Navy and also to some merchant vessels, which resulted in considerable saving of life at sea, notably when the liner *Titanic* struck an iceberg in the North Atlantic on her maiden voyage in April 1912.

Although technically Marconi's invention was a great success, the experimental research had been extremely costly, involving the expenditure of some £500,000 during the first ten years of the company's existence. No dividend had been paid, nor was there any immediate prospect of one. Meanwhile the £1 shares dropped to 6s. 3d. and Marconi's original backers were naturally disinclined to put up any more capital, while the chances of getting any return for their money seemed so remote. Hence the inventor looked round for an experienced businessman with knowledge of finance and the City, who could take over the work of managing director, while leaving Marconi free to concentrate on research and technical development.

In the autumn of 1909, his brother-in-law, the Hon. Donough O'Brien, introduced him to Rufus Isaacs's younger brother Godfrey, to whom the inventor took a strong fancy and who seemed to him with his City connections and acquaintance with finance houses in London and on the Continent to be just the man for the job.

Although Mr O'Brien had recently had some business dealings with Godfrey Isaacs and thought highly of his capacities, it must be admitted that Godfrey's various commercial enterprises, which ranged from gold mines in Wales to taxi-cabs in Australia, had not been notably successful and several of his companies had been either compulsorily wound up or had gone into voluntary liquidation. Nevertheless, according to his nephew, the second Lord Reading, Godfrey Isaacs was 'a man of shrewdness, enterprise and energy, even if he had not justified the implicit faith which his father had always preserved in his ultimate success.'[1]

For the first six months it was arranged that he should serve as joint managing director with Marconi, so as to familiarize himself with the operation of 'wireless', of which he knew nothing. After August, 1910, he had assumed sole management of the company's affairs.

Within a few weeks of joining the Company's board, the new managing director submitted an enterprising scheme to the Colonial Office, which provided for the erection of eighteen wireless stations at key points throughout the Empire, the stations to be erected, operated and maintained at the Company's expense, for which the Company asked for twenty-year licences. The Colonial Office did not reply. Some months later, Godfrey Isaacs wrote again, and on this occasion he was informed that the matter would be considered at the Imperial Conference which was due to meet in the following year. Not satisfied with this answer, he wrote once more, in January 1911, pressing for an earlier and speedy decision, since the rival German Telefunken Company was known to be planning a similar chain of wireless stations covering the globe but not of course to be erected in British territory. As a result of his persistence, the matter was referred to an inter-departmental Standing Committee known as the Cables (Landing Rights) Committee, which in due course reported against the suggestion that the Marconi Company should own and operate the proposed stations. Instead the Committee recommended that the stations should be State-owned and that the Marconi Company

[1] Reading, Vol. I, p. 227.

should be asked by the Post Office to erect them, since it was desirable that the firm concerned in the construction work of such a confidential and important character should be British, besides which Marconi's were first in the field with such technical devices as tuning and wavelengths. 'I think it very undesirable to give Government patronage to foreigners,' wrote Mr Winston Churchill, then Home Secretary, to Herbert Samuel at the Post Office. 'At any rate, no Department for which I am responsible shall, with my knowledge, put any contracts abroad except in circumstances of a very special character, or to break, or to prevent the formation of, a ring among the home producers.'[1]

The Cables Committee's recommendation was duly endorsed by a sub-committee of the Committee of Imperial Defence in June, 1911, adding recommendations of its own to the effect that action should be taken by the end of the year and that the work should be carried out by Marconi's on a 'cost plus' basis, that is at cost plus a percentage to be agreed between the parties as a reasonable profit. There was a further delay when the matter was referred by the Postmaster-General to a third committee, the Imperial Wireless Committee, which in turn approved the project and instructed the Post Office to prepare terms for submission to the Company. When this had been done and the terms approved by the Cables Committee, negotiations were opened between the Company and the Post Office. In these, as Samuel later remarked, Godfrey Isaacs proved 'certainly a very tenacious negotiator'. Eventually, on March 7, 1912, just two years after Godfrey Isaacs had originally broached the subject with the Colonial Office, the Marconi Company's tender for the initial erection of six stations was accepted by the Postmaster-General, subject to ratification by the House of Commons.

Two days later Commendatore Marconi and Godfrey Isaacs sailed for New York. Subsidiary Marconi companies had been formed in a number of countries, including the United States, to exploit the Marconi invention. So far the American company had not been a success and at this time its shares were at a discount. Furthermore, it was having trouble with another company, the United Wireless Company of America, which had infringed its patents and against which it had brought suit. The trial of this action had been fixed to begin later that same month, and it was ostensibly for the purpose of attending the hearing that Marconi and the managing director made

[1] Samuel Papers, cited by John Bowle in his *Viscount Samuel* (1957), p. 88.

the Atlantic crossing. However, information had reached Godfrey Isaacs that the United Wireless Company was in such low water that the Company might be forced to settle the case out of court and that the American Marconi Company might consequently be able to acquire its assets. Marconi and Godfrey Isaacs were accompanied on the voyage by Mr Percy Heybourn, a partner in the Stock Exchange firm of Heybourn & Croft, who were the largest jobbers in the Marconi market.

While the party were on the high seas, the *New York Times* planned a surprise banquet in honour of the great inventor to take place on the night of his arrival. The newspaper asked a number of distinguished people for appropriate messages which would be read out at the banquet. Among those whom the newspaper approached, through its London correspondent, was the Attorney-General. Rufus Isaacs happened to be at Fox Hill when the telephone rang and was answered by his son Gerald. At that precise moment Rufus Isaacs was pre-occupied with legal difficulties arising out of the current coal strike in England, and according to his son he was none too pleased at being bothered. However, on learning that the Hon. Harry Lawson, M.P. (later Lord Burnham) and several other well-known people had already agreed to send messages, he asked the Press representative to hold on while he and Gerald hastily concocted a message which they considered adequate to the occasion.

> Please congratulate Marconi and my brother on the successful development of a marvellous enterprise. I wish them all success in New York, and hope by the time they come back the coal strike will be finished.

The message was duly sent off and read out with the others at the banquet, where it was received by means of Marconi's apparatus in the banqueting hall. Innocuous and trivial as it appeared at the time, the message was to assume a wholly unexpected and exaggerated importance in the light of subsequent events.

As soon as they landed in New York, Marconi and his managing director learned that the United Wireless Company was in liquidation and two of its directors had been arrested on a charge of fraud and were in jail. This gave Godfrey Isaacs the opportunity to acquire the tangible assets of the United Wireless Company that he had hoped for, since they included virtually the whole of the wireless business of America. Godfrey Isaacs therefore proposed that the authorized share capital of the American Marconi Company should be increased from the existing amount of 1,600,000 dollars to 10,000,000 dollars, of which 1,400,000 dollars should be used to buy up the assets of the American Wireless Company, while the balance of the new issue (7,000,000 dollars) would be earmarked for expansion of the Marconi operations in America.

Since the American Marconi Company had never paid any dividend and its shares were standing at a heavy discount, it was conceivable that the new issue would not be taken up even to the extent of the immediately necessary 1,400,000 dollars by the American public who had already lost money in wireless enterprises. Consequently the directors of the American Marconi Company not unnaturally refused to agree to the English managing director's scheme unless the English company was prepared to guarantee the whole amount of the 1,400,000 dollars required for the American Wireless Company purchase. Godfrey Isaacs was agreeable, since the English Marconi Company held the majority of the American Company's share capital already issued; but Commendatore Marconi was unwilling to saddle the English Company with such a heavy responsibility and he insisted that the managing director should be personally responsible for 500,000 of the initial new issue of 1,400,000 shares, leaving the balance of 900,000 to be guaranteed by the English Company.

Godfrey Isaacs immediately undertook to underwrite the amount and thereupon called in Mr Heybourn. He arranged with Mr Heybourn on the spot to place with him 250,000 shares at a par value of $5 (£1 1s. 3d.) on condition that Mr Heybourn would introduce them into the London and New York markets and supply the principal dealers in London at a price not exceeding 25s. Before leaving America Godfrey Isaacs was able to place a further 150,000 shares himself mainly with American banking institutions, leaving the remaining 100,000 for disposal when he got back to England. As Mrs Donaldson remarks in her excellent account of the Marconi affair, 'in view of the situation in America, it is impossible to believe he could readily have placed so many shares but for the great prestige the English Company had recently acquired through the agreement with the British Government'.[1]

Before leaving America, Godfrey Isaacs brought off another brilliant stroke of business, when he negotiated an agreement with the Western Union Telegraph and Cable Company for the reception and

[1] Frances Donaldson: *The Marconi Scandal* (1962), p. 51.

distribution of wireless messages in America, thus eliminating the necessity of competing with the principal cable company by setting up a separate system.

Well pleased with the success of his American mission, Godfrey Isaacs returned to London on April 8. On the following day, he invited his brother Rufus and his other brother Harry, who worked in the family fruit business, to a luncheon at the Savoy Hotel. After describing the course of events in America, he proceeded to offer them some of his own shares in the American Marconi Company at 21s. 3d., the price he had paid for them. According to his own account, the Attorney-General, who had been ignorant of even the existence of the American Company, asked a number of questions about its relations with the parent company in England. Godfrey hastened to reassure him, pointing out that, although the English Company was a large shareholder in the American Company, the American Company held no shares in the English Company and was in no way concerned with its profits or undertakings. It made no difference to the financial position of the American Company whose operations were confined to the United States, he went on, whether the acceptance of the English Company's tender to the Post Office ever matured into a formal contract or whether the proposed imperial wireless chain was ever established.

At this meeting Rufus Isaacs decided not to buy any of his brother's shares on the grounds, according to his subsequent explanation, that he thought the proposed issue of capital very high, and that, although he saw no objection to his buying the shares, he thought it better that he should have no dealings with his brother Godfrey in view of the latter's position in the English company and that company's relations with the British Government.

After Rufus had left the luncheon table, the two other brothers sat on for some time and continued the discussion. Eventually Harry agreed to take 50,000 shares at 21s. 3d. When he got home that night, his wife asked him whether he could get some shares for members of her family. Harry thereupon telephoned Godfrey and secured a further 6,000. Meanwhile Godfrey had no difficulty in disposing of the remaining 44,000 shares, of which he retained 2,500 for himself.

During the week following the meeting of the three brothers, there was an unofficial boom in American Marconis, although the shares were not yet officially quoted on the London market (owing to the excessive number of applications for the new issue), the shares reaching £2. At the same time, the shares in the parent company had rocketed within a few weeks from 15s. to over £9, a contributory factor undoubtedly being the terrible news of the sinking of the *Titanic* on the night of April 14, which impressed upon the public mind the advantages of the use of wireless communication at sea.

On April 17, Harry again met his brother Rufus and told him that in his view American Marconis, which then stood at around £2, were certain to rise higher, and that they were an excellent investment. At this interview Rufus let himself be persuaded to buy 10,000 of the shares which Harry had bought from Godfrey. Rufus insisted on paying the current unofficial market price of £2, although Harry offered to let him have them at the original price of 21s. 3d. which he had paid for them. To his mind, as the Attorney-General afterwards put it, there was a very real difference in buying in these circumstances from Harry rather than from his other brother.

That night Rufus Isaacs called on his friend Lloyd George, the Chancellor of the Exchequer, and the Master of Elibank, the Government Chief Whip, who was staying with the Chancellor at 11 Downing Street. There he told them of the transaction and offered them 1,000 shares each at the price he had paid for them, remarking that they need not bother to pay at the moment since the shares were not yet in existence, and that he would give them plenty of notice when he required the money. The two Ministers, thinking they were on to a good thing, gratefully accepted the offer.

Next day the American shareholders met and approved the proposed increase in capital, and on the same day the English Marconi Company issued a circular in London setting out the arrangements Godfrey Isaacs had made in America. Meanwhile, in unofficial dealings on the London market the price of American Marconis rose to £3, and next day, when dealings became official the price opened at 65s. and closed at £4. On that day Rufus Isaacs telephoned his brokers, and they advised him to sell, as in their view the shares were far too high. As a result, Rufus gave instructions to sell 5,000, at the same time telephoning his brokers' advice to Harry. Harry thereupon agreed to sell a portion of his shares, and in fact Rufus was able to sell 7,000 for the two of them at an average of 70s. On May 5 he sold a further 1,000 at 53s. 9d. At the same time Lloyd George and the Master of Elibank sold half their holdings. Later, however, they reinvested, buying together a further 3,000 shares.

Unfortunately these transactions, which there had been no attempt to conceal, contributed to some ugly rumours. These rumours spread about the City and were further stimulated by the news that the contract for the erection of the imperial wireless chain had been signed between the Post Office and the English Marconi Company. Briefly, the rumours crystallized into two allegations. The first was that the Attorney-General had used his influence at his brother Godfrey's instigation to persuade the Postmaster-General to accept the Marconi Company's tender, so giving that company a monopoly to the exclusion of all other rival wireless undertakings. The second allegation was that certain Ministers, notably Lloyd George, Rufus Isaacs and Herbert Samuel, had made immense fortunes by using their confidential and official information to buy Marconi shares, presumably those of the English company, at a low price and to sell them again at the height of the boom.

In due course these rumours reached the ears of the Prime Minister; but the matter did not strike him as anything more than gossip. However, in July, he asked the Master of Elibank, who was about to resign his office of Chief Whip on deciding to accept a peerage and embark on a commercial career, whether any members of the Government had been doing anything in the way of speculation. The Chief Whip replied: 'Rufus Isaacs, Lloyd George and myself have bought a few shares in an American company.' As Mr Asquith later reported to the King, he did not think that the word 'Marconi' was mentioned on this occasion. Nor, oddly enough, did he seem to remember afterwards a visit he received from the Postmaster-General about the same time, at which Herbert Samuel informed him of the transactions of the three Ministers in American Marconis, which he had in turn learned from the Attorney-General.[1]

'I went at once to inform the Prime Minister of what I had been

---

[1] Cf. statement of Sir Rufus Isaacs to the Select Committee (March 27, 1913): '... at the end of July the Master of Elibank had told the Prime Minister. I had myself told Mr Herbert Samuel. I do not mean by that that he knew all the details. What I told him was that I had bought American shares and that the Master of Elibank and Mr Lloyd George had an interest with me, and I told him that they had nothing to do with the contract; that the shares were bought some time before the contract had been announced and they had nothing to do with the English Company in this sense certainly – that they had no interest in the profits of the English Company or in the contract. That is about the substance of what I told him. We were discussing together the rumours, and he told me he had had nothing whatever to do with the shares of the Company or with any of the shares – discussing it generally – and then I told him what my position was.' *Evidence from the Select Committee on Marconi's Wireless Telegraph Company, Limited, Agreement* (1913), Vol. I, p. 53.

told,' the Postmaster-General later recalled. 'He felt more concern than I did, and said that he thought "our colleagues could not have done a more foolish thing".'[1]

2

The rumours about Ministers and the Marconi Company came to a head with the publication of an article strongly attacking Rufus Isaacs and Herbert Samuel in a journal called *The Eye-Witness*, which appeared early in August. The editorship of this journal, which had been founded and previously edited by Hilaire Belloc, had recently been taken over by Cecil Chesterton, a younger brother of Belloc's friend, G. K. Chesterton. It may be observed that *The Eye-Witness* was markedly anti-Semitic in content, and in an earlier issue it had charged the Attorney-General with paying himself exaggerated professional fees at the public expense and also with deliberately dragging out the proceedings of the *Titanic* Inquiry in order to earn the consequent 'refreshers'.

The offending article, under the heading 'The Marconi Scandal', contained the following remarks:

> What progress is the Marconi Scandal making? We ask the question merely from curiosity and under no illusion as to the inevitable end of the affair. Everybody knows the record of Isaacs and his father, and his uncle, and in general of the whole family. Isaacs' brother is Chairman of the Marconi Company, it has therefore been secretly arranged between Isaacs and Samuel that the British people shall give the Marconi Company a very large sum of money through the agency of the said Samuel, and for the benefit of the said Isaacs. Incidentally the monopoly that is to be granted to Isaacs No. 2, through the ardent charity of Isaacs No. 1 and his colleague the Postmaster-General, is a monopoly involving antiquated methods, the refusal of competing tenders far cheaper and far more efficient, and the saddling of the country with corruptly purchased goods . . .

[1] Viscount Samuel: *Memoirs* (1945), p. 75. In the account of the affair given by Asquith in his *Memories and Reflections* (1928), Vol. I., p. 209 *et seq.*, and supported by his official biographers, he implies that he had no knowledge of the dealings in the American Marconis until over six months later when the facts were first disclosed to the public as a result of the libel action brought by Rufus Isaacs and Herbert Samuel against the French newspaper *Le Matin*. However, it is quite clear from an entry in Lord Stamfordham's unpublished diary in the Royal Archives (April 4, 1913) that the Prime Minister informed the King of the details, while staying at Balmoral in August, 1912.

Another reason why the swindle, or rather theft, impudent and barefaced as it is, will go through is that we have in this country no method of punishing men who are guilty of this kind of thing. . . .

. . . Between January and March 1912, they [the shares] rose to just under 100s., which would be about their natural price, supposing the abominable scandal of the contract to be allowed to stand. After this price had been reached the news was deliberately allowed to leak out and the stock was thus forced up to a fictitious value. At the end of April they stood at £9. Then, of course, they sagged just as was intended.

Parliament had risen for the summer recess by the time this article appeared, and Rufus Isaacs, who had left with Lloyd George for his annual holiday at Marienbad, did not immediately see the issue which carried it. However, Herbert Samuel bought a copy at the railway station when he was about to catch the train for his home in Yorkshire. He wrote off at once to his colleague:

> The Gables,
> Saltburn.
> August 8, 1912

My dear Rufus,

As I was leaving King's Cross this morning, I saw on the bookstall a copy of today's number of Belloc's paper *The Eye-Witness* with an article headed 'The Marconi Scandal'. I found it to be a gross and unrestrained libel on you and myself. I had just time before the train started to address an envelope to you at the House of Commons and to put the article into it with a scribbled note. I have since obtained your address by telegraph, and this letter, enclosing another copy of the paper, will probably reach you before the first.

One's natural inclination is, of course, at once to have application made for a writ, and I am not at all sure that that is not the right course. There can be no possible doubt as to the result of the action. It is hardly necessary for me to say that during the long negotiations that preceded the conclusion of the contract there was no action of mine that I would wish withdrawn from any measure of publicity in the courts or in Parliament.

The circumstances that deter me from at once coming to the conclusion that proceedings ought to be taken are obvious ones: first, that this contemptible rag has a very small circulation, its pages are always full of personal abuse, its articles cannot influence any opinion which is worth having, and an action would give an immense publicity to the libel; secondly, *it would not be a good thing for the Jewish community for the first two Jews who have ever entered a British Cabinet to be enmeshed in an affair of this kind*; and thirdly, one does not wish to soil one's hands with the thing.

As there will in all probability be a Select Committee of the House of Commons in the autumn to inquire into the wisdom of the contract, the Report of that Committee will supply a sufficient answer.

On the other hand, it is a grave thing when Ministers are directly accused of corrupt action by a newspaper, no matter how obscure and scurrilous, for them to do nothing.

With your unrivalled experience of the law you are better able than I to judge what is best to do, and I will very gladly join you in proceedings if you think it advisable, or do nothing if you consider that the best course.

If you are of opinion that a writ should be issued and will wire to me to that effect, I will go to town and see a solicitor and start the proceedings on behalf of both of us if you wish. But in that event I should be glad if you would nominate the solicitor, as my own solicitor is my brother, and I think in a case like this it would be better to have someone else.

If you are in doubt as to the proper course, you might think it well to consult the Prime Minister, and in that case I should be glad if you would send on this letter to him.[1]

Four days later, Samuel received the following telegram from Rufus Isaacs in Marienbad: 'Agree with you but have sent your letter and have written to the chief.' At the same time, Rufus Isaacs wrote to the Postmaster-General:

I need not tell you, I am sure, that there is not one word of truth in the statements about myself. I never held a share or an interest direct or indirect in any Marconi Company until after the contract with the Government was announced. I then bought some American Marconis and hold some now – and except for that Company, which is entirely independent of this country and is a separate Company, I have not and never have had any financial interest of any kind in Marconi's.

Although you had never mentioned any question to me of the Government contract, I did hear that it would probably be signed in a day or so before the execution took place, and of course I knew the effect the announcement was bound to have on the market, just as I

---

[1] Samuel Papers. When he subsequently read this letter aloud to the Select Committee, Samuel omitted the words which I have italicized. 'There is one sentence in it which is not strictly relevant and which I would rather not read,' he told the Committee, 'but I will hand it to the Committee and I will mark it for them to see, and I think they will understand the reason why I do not wish to read it. It does not cast any reflection on anybody in any way.' *Evidence* (1913), Vol. I, p. 133.

knew from the first when my brother became Managing Director that the commercial development of the Company would be great and rapid, but I thought (as you would have thought in similar circumstances) that I would not touch the shares, and glad I am I took that view consistently from the first. I am not sure whether I ever told you this – that is why I write fully to you about it.

The text of Rufus Isaacs's letter to the Prime Minister has not survived. According to his evidence to the Select Committee, it was mislaid or destroyed. But he did give the Select Committee an interesting summary of it. 'What I did think was that my chief was entitled to know of the article, and was entitled to know also what my views were,' he said on this occasion, 'and I wrote to him and I told him exactly then my views about it, and I told him about the American shares – I do not mean that I went into figures, but I certainly told him that I had bought, as I knew that he already knew, American Marconi shares, of which Mr Lloyd George and the Master of Elibank had part, that I had sold some of them at a profit, that I held the greater part of the shares at that time that I wrote to him, and that they held their interests with me still, and were interested to the same extent – that is to say, they were holding shares at that time, and I got a letter from him in reply.'

Asquith's reply, returning the copy of *The Eye-Witness* and Samuel's letter, expressed agreement with his two Cabinet colleagues, but it made no mention of the share purchase transaction. It was written from Scotland where the Prime Minister had gone to stay as the guest of the King and Queen at Balmoral Castle.

August 15, 1912

My dear Rufus,

I return the enclosed. I have read carefully this scurrilous rubbish, and I am clearly of opinion that you should take no notice of it. Samuel gives some excellent reasons in his letter. I suspect that *The Eye-Witness* has a very meagre circulation. I notice only one page of advertisements, and that occupied entirely by Belloc's publishers. A prosecution would secure notoriety and might bring in subscribers.

We have broken weather here and but for Winston there would be nothing in the newspapers.

Yours always,
H. H. Asquith

At this time Winston Churchill, who had become First Lord of the Admiralty, was carrying on a violent controversy in the Press with the Conservative Party Leader, Bonar Law, on the subject of Ulster's position under the Irish Home Rule Bill. The reference was to provide one of the few instances of light relief in the course of the Attorney-General's evidence before the Select Committee, when Rufus Isaacs read it out.

Besides the two Cabinet Ministers, Godfrey Isaacs had also been libelled by *The Eye-Witness*, and at first he was keen to issue a writ. Before leaving Marienbad, Rufus Isaacs again wired Samuel, saying he was meeting his brother in Paris and that he 'discountenanced' any proceedings by him. A third wire reached Samuel from his colleague on August 31, confirming that the meeting between the two brothers had taken place, that they had 'definitely decided take no step' and that Godfrey Isaacs 'agrees our views'.

It is remarkable that the Prime Minister and his two Cabinet colleagues should have brushed aside *The Eye-Witness* as being of such little consequence. It is true that its circulation was small, but it was widely read by those whose opinions mattered. Indeed it was a journal of high literary quality, as one might expect from the fact that it owed its origin to Hilaire Belloc, and its contributors included the leading literary intellectuals of the day, such as G. K. Chesterton, H. G. Wells, Maurice Baring, Wilfrid Blunt, Arthur Quiller-Couch, A. C. Benson, Desmond MacCarthy, Arthur Ransome and J. C. Squire. Of course, it is always easy to speak or write with the advantage of hindsight, but looking back now there can be little doubt that those attacked would have done better to take immediate action in the Courts and thus silence their accusers. The result of the decision to ignore the offending article merely encouraged the editor to continue his attacks in subsequent issues. 'If Samuel and Isaacs force their deal through (as is exceedingly likely),' he wrote on August 29, 'it will be in the teeth of a public opinion that regards them simply as criminals.' The attacks continued throughout the recess and were taken up by other journals, notably *The National Review*, which was then edited and owned by the colourful L. J. Maxse, who detested Liberals and Jews with equal vehemence.

The Government motion, in the name of the Postmaster-General, to appoint a Select Committee of the House of Commons to investigate the circumstances of the Marconi contract and to report, was debated shortly after Parliament reassembled, on October 11. Although it was primarily an occasion for discussing the criticisms which had been levelled at the contract, it was generally expected that

Ministers would answer the accusations of corruption and gambling in the stock market. 'The reason why the Government wanted a frank discussion,' said Lloyd George, who intervened early in the debate, 'was because we wanted to bring here these rumours, these sinister rumours, that have been passed from one foul lip to another behind the backs of the House.'

When it came to his turn to speak, Rufus Isaacs seized the opportunity to deal at some length with the charges that had been brought. First of all, he disposed of the charge that he had used his influence to obtain a contract for the Marconi Company with the Government. 'I want to say in reference to myself,' he said emphatically, 'that I have never from beginning to end, in any shape or form, either by deed, act, word, or anything else, taken part in the negotiations in reference to this contract with my Right Honourable friend, the Postmaster-General, and I never knew there was such a contract in contemplation until a few days before, when I was told at a private social function by the managing director, who is my brother, that he did hope to get a contract with the Government and was in negotiation with them for it. That was a few days before I saw the announcement in the papers that there had in fact been a contract accepted.'

Next he passed to what he called 'a worse charge', namely that some member or members of the Cabinet, 'not named but hinted at', knowing that the shares would go up when the announcement of the contract was made, the shares being then around 14s. and subsequently rising to £9 after the announcement, bought shares of 'this company' at a low price in order to sell them at the higher price when the contract was announced. 'I desire to say frankly on behalf of myself that this is absolutely untrue,' the Attorney-General went on. '*Never from the beginning, when the shares were fourteen shillings or nine pounds, have I had one single transaction with the shares of that company.* I am not only speaking for myself, but I am also speaking on behalf, I know of my Right Honourable friend, the Postmaster-General, and the Chancellor of the Exchequer, who in some way or other in some of the articles have been brought into this matter.'

He then dealt with a charge which had been made in *The National Review* that he had misused his position as Attorney-General, in the interests of the Marconi Company, by opposing the application for an extension of patents by a rival concern, the Lodge-Muirhead syndicate. He pointed out that the application was one which was automatically submitted to him, and he decided that the Solicitor-General should appear; but, he added, Sir John Simon, in doing so, had made it clear that he did not appear to oppose but to put the relevant facts before the Court. Finally, he answered the Conservative back-bencher, Major Martin Archer-Shee, M.P., who had censured him for sending the telegram to the *New York Times* to be read at 'a dinner for the purpose of booming the Marconi Company', which he described as 'a great mistake and a most injudicious proceeding'.

'What happened was this,' Rufus Isaacs explained. 'They had made arrangements to have a Marconi apparatus fitted up on the table where the banquet was to take place, and as a matter of interest to the guests they wanted to see how long it would take to get the messages through to the dinner table. I confess I demurred at first, because I did not quite understand the object, but it was explained that it was nothing else than a congratulation. Mr Marconi and my brother, the managing director, were at the banquet, and so I sent a congratulatory telegram on the success of the Marconi enterprise in which apparently I was joined by Earl Grey and Lord Avebury. . . .

'They are not in the Cabinet,' interjected another Opposition back-bencher, Lord Winterton.

'And there was also the Honourable Member for Mile End (the Hon. Harry Lawson), who sent a congratulatory telegram of the same kind,' the Attorney-General continued, ignoring the interruption. 'It was a congratulatory telegram upon the Marconi enterprise and for the discovery of wireless telegraphy, which was going ahead by leaps and bounds, and I ended by saying that I hoped by the time they came back the coal strike would be finished. . . . I am reminded the telegram to which reference has been made was sent after March 7. The announcement had been made already in the public Press and the shares had already been going up, so that it had nothing to do with that.'

In his speech which followed, Herbert Samuel rallied strongly to his friend's support.

Neither I myself nor any of my colleagues have at any time held one shilling's worth of shares in this company, directly or indirectly, or have derived one penny profit from the fluctuation in their prices. It seems shameful that political feeling can carry men so far, that lying tongues can be found to speak and willing ears to listen to wicked and utterly baseless slanders such as these. The Committee which will be appointed will, I hope, inquire into every aspect of this question, and

Members of the Government will be most ready to appear before it. Every Member of the House may have full confidence that, whatever part of this transaction may come under the searchlight of examination, it will be shown that there is no uncleanliness in any corner.

It will have been seen that both Rufus Isaacs and Lloyd George had decided to keep quiet about their share purchases in the American Company, and the matter was not mentioned by either of them in the debate. But immediately afterwards Rufus Isaacs told the Solicitor-General in confidence. Simon was surprised, as he put it, 'that one who was so wise an adviser of others should not have seen that when wrongly accused of an investment which would have been quite improper, the correct course was to explain to the Commons at once what the different investment was that he had made and how the confusion might have arisen'. Accordingly he begged him to make a supplementary statement in the House next day. But Rufus Isaacs swept this plea aside. The actual transaction was 'irrelevant', he said, since the American Company was 'entirely independent financially'. Also, he added, 'there are others in this besides myself'.

The Prime Minister was absent from the debate, owing to indisposition. Discussing the subject some months later with his Prime Minister, the King said he 'regretted the Ministers did not make a clean breast of it in October'.

'It is easy to be wise after the event,' replied Asquith, defending the two Ministers. He added that in his opinion it was better to say or do nothing then, since 'the purchase of the shares was made after the contract had been signed'. Lloyd George later explained his own reticence by saying that it appeared to him at the time that 'the Committee afforded the better opportunity for presenting the whole of the facts.'

The matter was put in its right perspective by Lloyd George's friend Thomas Jones, later Deputy Secretary of the Cabinet. 'The legal training of the men involved probably served them ill at this juncture,' remarked Jones afterwards. 'The bare accusation alone was refuted. But it was not legal guilt which needed to be disproved; it was the confidence of the House in their integrity which had to be maintained or restored. To the plain man 'Marconis' were 'Marconis', whether British or American, and a complete statement on October 11, 1912, on the occasion of the debate in the House would have prevented much grief. The buying of the shares was an error of judgment, the failure to acknowledge publicly at the time of the inquiry the purchase of the American shares savoured of disingenuousness. . . .'[1]

3

When the Prime Minister was first pressed to appoint a Select Committee to investigate the circumstances of the Marconi contract, so he subsequently told the King, he resisted the proposal 'which he thought a mistake but eventually agreed to it'. An independent judicial inquiry, presided over by an eminent High Court judge, would have been more satisfactory in every way; for one thing, the proceedings would have been much shorter and they would almost certainly have resulted in the delivery of a unanimous report. On the other hand, a Select Committee of the House of Commons is constituted on strict party lines in proportion to the respective numerical party strengths in the House. Consequently in this instance some at least of the Liberal Members were inclined to whitewash the Ministers, while two or three of the Conservatives tended to disregard the judicial approach and treat the occasion as an excuse for making party political capital of the affair. This made any general unanimity of findings impossible.

The Committee which met for the first time on October 23, 1912, consisted of fifteen members in all. Of these six were Liberals, including the Chairman, six were Conservatives, two were Irish Nationalists and one was Labour. This gave the Government party members and their Irish and Labour supporters a majority of three over the Tories. The Chairman, Sir Albert Spicer, was a director of a firm of paper-makers and a respected back-bencher, and though he had considerable previous experience of committee work he was an amiable but weak personality, who soon proved himself quite incapable of controlling the proceedings of the Select Committee, particularly in the face of the onslaughts from Lord Robert Cecil and Mr Leopold Amery on the Conservative side. The activities of the two latter were offset by two of the Liberals, Mr James Falconer and Mr Handel Booth who were avowedly determined to prevent any disclosures damaging to the Ministers. To a great extent they succeeded.

The Committee's proceedings spread over seven months and occupied sixty-two days. They were just about the longest on record. In all

[1] Thomas Jones: *Lloyd George* (1951), p. 44.

sixty-six witnesses were examined; including Ministers, back-bench M.P.s, journalists, bankers, stockbrokers, and the great Commendatore Marconi himself. They answered 29,276 questions, of which many were tediously repetitive.

It had been generally expected that the Committee would immediately summon the Ministers before it, but a different procedure was followed, which may have been logical, but resulted in a long delay and incidentally much personal worry and anxiety particularly for Rufus Isaacs and Lloyd George before they eventually made their appearance in the Committee chamber. It was decided first to consider the contract itself and hear its critics, next to examine the journalists and others who had made charges of corruption and gambling, so that the case might be clearly established for the Ministers to answer, and finally to call the Ministers themselves.

The Committee was occupied with the question of the contract itself until the middle of January, 1913, when Lord Robert Cecil issued an interim Report, which recommended the establishment of a chain of imperial wireless stations as a matter of urgency and that a highly qualified technical committee should be set up to examine the merits of the rival systems, including Marconi's. As a result such a committee of experts was immediately set up under the chairmanship of Lord Parker of Waddington, and the Select Committee now passed to the task of examining the journalists.

It was at this stage that Rufus Isaacs informed the two Liberal members, Falconer and Booth, in confidence, of his transactions in the American shares so that they might be able to head off any awkward questions on this score, or, as Isaacs's son was to express it more euphemistically, 'in order that they might be forearmed when the journalists came to give evidence'. The Chairman, Sir Albert Spicer, was not told, and in consequence was extremely annoyed when he found out. In fact he was said to have written Asquith a letter resigning his position but to have later been persuaded by the Prime Minister to withdraw it. However, one of the Conservative members, Mr Harold Smith, brother of F. E. Smith, did resign in protest.

The first of the journalist witnesses was Mr W. R. Lawson, whose articles in *The Outlook* appearing just before Mr Cecil Chesterton's attacks in *The Eye-Witness* had been the first to draw attention to the rumours about corruption and gambling on the part of the Ministers.

'Do you think it is in the public interest to charge Ministers of the Crown with something like corruption?' Mr Lawson was asked.

'If Ministers of the Crown will allow lying rumours to go about for months at a time, how can they expect other people to take more care of their characters than they do themselves?' the witness answered. 'They did not choose to deny them. I have gone further and I admit I have incurred legal liability in putting them in that way, but I am quite prepared to take the risk of it. We expected when these articles were published that they would do what they immediately threatened to do, but never did. They should have taken these articles into Court at once.'

It was about this date, that is some time in January, 1913, that Rufus Isaacs and Lloyd George went to see the Prime Minister in his room in the House of Commons. What happened at this interview was later passed on by Asquith to the King. The two Ministers said they wished to speak to him on a very serious and disagreeable business. 'We told you we had bought the shares,' they said. 'Now we find ourselves in a terribly awkward position.' They went on to express their deep regret, admitted they were 'guilty of an error of judgment', and placed their resignations in his hands.

The Prime Minister was much taken aback, but absolutely refused to accept the proffered resignations, as 'they had done nothing affecting their honour as Cabinet Ministers or gentlemen'. But he did point out how very seriously he regarded their conduct – 'a gross error of judgment', 'lamentable', and 'so difficult to defend' were some of the phrases which he used in describing it to the King. His colleagues were also 'much upset', as well they might be.

Indeed the strain was becoming almost intolerable, while it now looked that with the other journalist witnesses waiting to give evidence the Ministers were unlikely to have an opportunity of facing the Committee and disclosing the details of their dealings in the American Company's shares until well after Easter. The opportunity was unexpectedly provided by the testimony of Mr L. J. Maxse, the editor of *The National Review*, who had his own suspicions about the American dealings. He said:

> I confess to sharing the general uneasiness as matters stand at present. Over four months have elapsed since the discussion in the House of Commons, but Ministers have done nothing whatever to dispel the mist of suspicion overhanging the affair. Mr Samuel stated that Ministers 'will be most ready to appear before the Committee'.

One might have conceived that they would have appeared at its first sitting clamouring to state in the most categorical and emphatic manner that neither directly nor indirectly, in their own names or in other people's names, have they had any transactions whatsoever, either in London, Dublin, New York, Brussels, Amsterdam, Paris or any other financial centre in any shares in *any* Marconi Company throughout the negotiations with the Government.

Although the implication behind the word 'any' which Maxse deliberately emphasized was not immediately seized upon by the Press, it was Maxse's statement which touched off an explosive chain of events. On February 14, Rufus Isaacs, who was about to leave for a short holiday in Paris, read a garbled account of Maxse's evidence before the Committee which appeared in the newspaper *Le Matin* in the form of a report from its London correspondent. Under the heading '*Scandale Financier En Angleterre*', it was alleged that Herbert Samuel and Rufus and Godfrey Isaacs had together entered into a corrupt arrangement, buying shares in the English Marconi Company at an average price of 50 francs before the opening of negotiations for the contract with the Government and selling them at a profit of as much as 200 francs a share when it was clear that the contract would be concluded.

Rufus Isaacs immediately wrote to the editor and demanded an apology. Four days later the paper printed an apology from its London correspondent, expressing regret that he should, in perfect good faith, by communicating current rumours to his editor, have 'possibly done an injury to three men of quite unimpeachable honour'. However, Rufus Isaacs did not consider the apology adequate and, on February 19, after consulting Samuel, he instructed his solicitor, Sir George Lewis of Lewis & Lewis, to issue a writ against the newspaper, asking that his old professional antagonist in the Courts, Sir Edward Carson, M.P., should be retained to lead for the plaintiffs. Meanwhile, the Postmaster-General thought it advisable to inform the Prime Minister of what had happened and to send him a copy of the relevant issues of *Le Matin*. Asquith agreed with what had been proposed but without any marked enthusiasm. 'The statements are so specific and personal that you were probably bound to take proceedings,' he wrote by return, 'though it is a little unfortunate that the peccant journal should be a French and not an English newspaper.'

On February 25, Samuel wrote to Sir George Lewis:

I heard last night from the Prime Minister, and whatever steps are necessary against *Le Matin* can now be taken to initiate proceedings. Perhaps, when you are writing to Sir Rufus Isaacs, you would be good enough to mention that I thought I had better acquaint the P.M. with what was in contemplation.

With reference to counsel, it is possible that Lady Carson's illness may prevent Carson from practising at present. For my part I should much prefer non-political counsel, but the decision must of course rest with Sir Rufus and yourself.

I am disposed to think that the sooner the case be brought on the better.

Although Carson as an ex-Law Officer sat on the Opposition Front Bench in the House of Commons, he had taken no part in the attacks on the Marconi contract which had been made by some of the Conservative Members. Nor for that matter had F. E. Smith, who was briefed as second leader, so that he could take over the conduct of the case at short notice in the event of Carson being called away to his dying wife's bedside.

At the preliminary consultation with counsel, it was decided that the Attorney-General must take the opportunity afforded by the case of disclosing the part played by himself and Lloyd George in their dealings in the American Marconis. 'The fact has to be stated,' wrote Samuel on the eve of the trial, 'and, although there was nothing dishonourable in what they did, it was certainly unwise, and the statement which Rufus Isaacs will make in the witness-box on Wednesday will undoubtedly give rise to a great deal of hostile comment. However, it can't be helped, and the Government must stand as best they can.'

The most powerful newspaper proprietor at this time was Lord Northcliffe, who in addition to the popular *Daily Mail* and *Evening News* also controlled *The Times*. It was obviously desirable to secure his goodwill, and to this end, Mr Winston Churchill, who had been let into the secret, agreed to act as an intermediary on behalf of his two ministerial colleagues. He immediately telephoned Northcliffe and asked to see him. Shortly afterwards he arrived in Northcliffe's bedroom, where he told him the whole story, explained that the revelation would be made and captured the Press Lord's sympathy. The result was that Northcliffe gave instructions that the matter should be handled in a friendly way by his newspapers. Indeed, when the proof of the leading article which George Freeman, acting editor of *The Times* in the absence of Geoffrey Dawson on holiday, had written immediately after the trial for publication next morning, was read over to him on the telephone, Northcliffe scrapped the leader and rewrote it himself in terms which although still critical were much more favourable to the Ministers.

The case of *Isaacs and Samuel* v. *Le Matin* came before Mr Justice Darling in the Law Courts on March 19, 1912. The Prime Minister's son Raymond Asquith, soon to be killed fighting in France, appeared as a junior Counsel with Carson and Smith for the plaintiffs. The defendant newspaper was represented by another Irish Unionist M.P., Mr J. H. Campbell, K.C., although no defence was offered.

In opening the case, Carson said that, had the charges been made in an English newspaper, the plaintiffs would have pressed for damages, but as it was a French newspaper circulating in France with only a relatively small English circulation and the allegations were printed merely as gossip and were not prompted by political or personal malice they were not doing so. After outlining the course of the negotiations between the English Marconi Company and the Government, Carson proceeded to deny that either Rufus Isaacs or Herbert Samuel had ever bought a share in this company, either in their own names or in any other names, nor had they had any other transactions whatever with regard to shares in this company. 'But there were other Marconi companies,' Carson continued in his most persuasive manner, 'and, although what I have said on this point entirely completes the matter as regards the truth or falsity of the libel, I must in regard to one transaction in one of the companies by the Attorney-General, which it is necessary to explain, ask your indulgence although it is a little outside the scope of the libel.'

There being no objection from the Bench, Carson went on to detail the whole transaction of the American shares. 'With regard to the purchase of 10,000 shares, in reality it turned out to be a loss,' he explained. 'He sold some of the shares, and amongst others 1,000 to Mr Lloyd George and another 1,000 to the Master of Elibank, who is now Lord Murray. They were intimate friends of his. Though at the time neither of them knew of the shares and probably never would have heard of them, it is right to say that he offered them the shares believing them to be a good investment, having nothing whatever to do with the shares in the English Company. They were offered and bought 1,000 each of these shares, and I am afraid it also turned out to be a loss for them. At all events, as regards the Attorney-General, the net result is that, having sold these and some other shares, some of them at a profit, he still has 6,400 of the shares, and, taking the whole is a loser of £1,000 to £1,500 at present prices.[1] Nor had there been any secrecy in the share dealings, Carson added. 'I only go into it all . . . on account of the position of the Attorney-General and because he wishes to . . . state everything and keep nothing back. That is the whole matter.'

The two plaintiffs then went into the witness-box and denied the allegations on oath, and Rufus Isaacs further supported his counsel's opening statement about the American shares. After Mr Campbell for *Le Matin* had conveyed the unqualified apologies of the newspaper 'for having made charges and insinuations which were absolutely devoid of foundation', it only remained for Mr Justice Darling to enter judgment for the plaintiffs with costs. 'I express no opinion and make no comment,' said the judge, 'not because I do not hold any opinion on the matter, but because I do not for one moment wish to interfere with the investigation that is going on.'

In this way the general public learned for the first time of the dealings by Rufus Isaacs and his two ministerial friends in American Marconis.

On the night of the trial, Herbert Samuel wrote:

> The case went very well in all respects, as we anticipated, and the newspaper apology could not have been more ample. The Court was crowded to overflowing, largely with reporters, of whom there must have been forty or fifty; and inside there were fully ten newspaper photographers standing in a row, so that one could appreciate the feelings of a man stood up against a wall to face a platoon of soldiers at a military execution.
>
> The statement about Rufus's and Lloyd George's American shares was received with equanimity, and although most of the posters of the evening papers are devoted to the case, only one, *The Star*, refers to that aspect of it, with a placard 'MARCONI LLOYD GEORGE SENSATION'. They will have to pass through a somewhat unpleasant time for a few days, and it will then be forgotten.
>
> If that Company, instead of being called the American Marconi Company had been named the American Wireless Telegraphy Company, no one would have troubled about it. However, as things are, Rufus Isaacs and Lloyd George's indiscretions will of course be the

[1] In fact, he lost over £1,700, while Lloyd George and the Master of Elibank each lost over £200. See letter from Rufus Isaacs to Lloyd George, December 27, 1913, cited from the Lloyd George Papers by Frank Owen in *Tempestuous Journey* (1954), p. 239.

basis of every possible misrepresentation, and knowing that, it has caused us all much anxiety since we knew of it. My own position remains, of course, quite unaffected.

In its second leader on the morning after the trial, as rewritten by the proprietor, *The Times* in accepting Rufus Isaacs's explanation commented that it might have saved a lot of trouble if he had made in the previous October in the House of Commons the statement he volunteered in court about his purchases in the American company. The article concluded with these words:

> We are of opinion that more delicacy might have been shown by Ministers involved in the selection of investments. But mere lack of judgment is a very different thing from the monstrous offences that have been imputed to them.

The Tory Press generally was not so lenient, regarding the transaction in the American shares as sufficient explanation of all the rumours and demanding that the Ministers should be called upon at the earliest moment to give a detailed account of their actions before the Select Committee. Meanwhile, the statement that the investment had resulted in a loss inspired the cartoonist Max Beerbohm to one of his most amusing efforts, in which the Attorney-General was shown surrounded by members of the Government in various supplicatory attitudes, underneath the following legend: 'Some Ministers of the Crown, who (monstrous though it seem) have severally some spare pounds to invest, implore Sir Rufus Isaacs to tell them if he knows of any stocks which they could buy without fear of ultimate profit.'

Both Rufus Isaacs and Lloyd George wrote to Northcliffe thanking him for his 'generous' and 'chivalrous' treatment of them in his newspapers. 'I know how such a matter might be used if there was a desire and intention to injure me,' wrote Isaacs, 'and, although the transaction is as innocent as any that has ever been effected, it might be twisted into an appearance to those who had not mastered the facts of something very unpleasant.'

'Letters of thanks to newspapers are very rare,' Northcliffe replied, 'and it was very pleasant to get yours. No one who knows your record in the City or at the Bar and your care of your innumerable kinsmen could feel that you had shown anything more than a lack of foresight in this business.'

However, opinion in Printing House Square was divided on the Marconi issue. When Geoffrey Dawson, the *Times* editor, returned from his holiday, he tried to persuade 'the Chief' that the action against *Le Matin* was really 'a put up job' between the Ministers and that newspaper. But Northcliffe would rightly have none of it. His admonitory letter to the editor, before summoning him to his presence to receive a further personal rebuke, is worth quoting:

I have no intention of being part of an attack upon a man because of his brother's faults. I have been so attacked myself. Nor have I any intention of being associated with an ascription of grave imprudence as roguery. . . .

Even if public opinion were as you say, which I entirely doubt, I am not in the least afraid of public opinion. I stood up against it in the Dreyfus case. I took my life in my hands prior to the Boer War, and in connexion with Mr Rhodes, when a pamphlet was placed in every seat in the House of Commons accusing me of being paid by Mr Rhodes. History has justified me in both cases. Rhodes was grievously indiscreet, but he was not corrupt. I am not comparing a Welsh solicitor and Jew barrister to C.J.R., but I see around me exactly the same malevolence from exactly the same kinds of minds as that with which I was faced before. . . .

May I say I was really surprised to hear you suggest that Cabinet Ministers connived at a put-up action between themselves and an obviously hostile newspaper. If you have watched the matter, you will see that *Le Matin* has reported this thing most malevolently, with many scraps and insinuations and attacks which have not been used here.[1]

4

In view of the disclosures by Rufus Isaacs and his leading counsel in the libel action against *Le Matin*, the Select Committee could no longer delay the calling of the ministers to testify before it. Accordingly the Attorney-General took his place in the witnesses' chair in Committee Room 12 of the House of Commons on the morning of March 25, 1912. During the next two-and-a-half days, when he was subjected to the most detailed and repetitive examination and cross-examination by various members of the Committee, he told his story and answered all their questions with exemplary patience, never once referring to a note and willingly producing his bank pass-books and other account books for inspection. His evidence revealed little that was not already known by this date, and as many of the facts which

[1] *History of The Times* (1952), Vol. IV, p. 1007.

he related have already been set out in the preceding pages it is unnecessary to repeat them. However a few passages deserve quotation.

Answering the Chairman, Sir Albert Spicer, at the outset, he emphasized that from the moment the Committee was constituted he was most anxious to appear before it, 'because I smarted very much under the suggestions that still went about', and from that time he had been waiting until the Committee thought right to summon him. Since it was for the Committee to determine its own procedure and say when it desired his evidence, he had not thought it right to ask the Committee to take his evidence out of the ordinary turn by reason of his position as a minister. 'For that reason,' he added, 'although I did once write a letter, on consideration I did not send it.'

'When you were making your speech on October 11th,' the Chairman asked him, 'did the thought occur to you that you might get rid of some of those rumours if you mentioned your investment in the American Marconis, because both being Marconis you could easily understand how one might get confused with the other?'

'It did not occur to me, and it does not occur to me now,' the witness answered firmly. 'I am obliged to you for putting the question. I find it very difficult, and always have found it very difficult, to understand how any person who had information – I will assume he had information, I do not know whether he had or not, but there were books and entries in books with my name, and contract notes and accounts – could with that information write the lies which were apparently built upon such foundation. That is what I want to know, and what I am entitled to know.'

'But,' the Chairman persisted, 'you felt that your investment in the American Marconis did not form a proper topic for remark in your speech?'

'Not in the speech,' the witness replied. 'Certainly I thought it proper to state it before the Committee. What I felt in regard to the speech was that I wanted to deal with the specific charges. I confined my speech entirely to dealing with the four specific charges made. . . . My view then was – and I have stated it quite plainly and clearly – that there was no truth in the rumours; but may I add, and it is very important, that at that time no one had ever suggested that any transaction in any other Marconi Company, either Spanish, Canadian or American, would in any way savour of corruption or be improper, or was in any way the subject matter of criticism of Ministers. That did not occur. *The whole of the suggestion from beginning to end was limited to speculation before the acceptance of the tender on the 7th March was announced in the public press on the 8th March.* That was the statement to which I directed myself, and which I wanted to contradict.'

In the Attorney-General's view, this was the gravamen of the main charge he had to meet. He had rebutted it during the debate, and he was to rebut it again and again in the course of his evidence before the Select Committee.

Asked by Mr MacMaster, one of the Conservative members, whether he had felt no obligation to disclose his purchase of American shares, the Attorney-General replied: 'It was not a question of making a disclosure, I had no objection to anybody knowing about the American shares.' In answer to a further question whether he had mentioned to any member of the Committee his transaction in American Marconis, he said: 'Certainly.'

Mr Falconer immediately jumped up and objected to this question, making a long rambling speech which was difficult to follow but from which nevertheless it was not difficult to infer that he was one of the members in question.

The Chairman thereupon ruled that the discussion should be continued in private. Next day, when Rufus Isaacs resumed his evidence, Mr MacMaster informed him that he was not bound to answer the question in any further detail, since the majority of the Committee had ruled that he was not to.

'Of course, all I have to do is to bow to your ruling,' replied the Attorney-General turning to the Chairman. 'But for myself I may say that I raise no objection to this or any other question that has been put to me.'

On the whole, apart from this incident, things went smoothly until near the end of the second day, when Rufus Isaacs was provoked into a passage of arms with one of the Conservative Members, Mr Leopold Amery. It was the only occasion throughout the proceedings that his customary calm deserted him and Rufus Isaacs became at all heated.

MR AMERY: Is it not conceivable that the mention by somebody of a dealing in your name in American Marconis could have passed from mouth to mouth till a number of people repeated it?

WITNESS: I do not dispute this. I should agree that if somebody sets a distorted version of a story about, the next person distorts it more, and then it is distorted more in a drawing-room or perhaps over the dinner table, and the people there go and tell it in confidence in what is called 'the best authority' to a number of other people at other dinner tables, and so it gets repeated. In the same kind of way we have heard a lot of other lies suggested with regard to myself lately of the worst possible description.

MR AMERY: That is a very probable account of how it happened?

WITNESS: That may have accounted for the kind of rumours and the gossip, but it does not account and it cannot account, and so far as I am concerned will never be able to account, for the lies which were told in the journals and magazines.

MR AMERY: Those things that appeared in certain magazines were definite, and as regards certain other papers you have just told us a little while ago the statements were not definite; they were suggestions of the kind that if there are rumours, Ministers . . .

WITNESS: What did you think when you read them?

MR AMERY: Those articles?

WITNESS: Yes. I will take Lord Robert Cecil's view. I will take yours as fair-minded men: what did you think when you read those articles? Did you not think they contained definite insinuations and suggestions of corruption on the part of myself, Mr Herbert Samuel and the Chancellor of the Exchequer?

MR AMERY: Well, I don't know that I ought to be answering questions from a witness?

WITNESS: Quite right. I only put it in that form to bring home to your mind what I have said. Take the *National Review*; take the *Outlook*.

MR AMERY: Those are the only ones I read till after this Inquiry.

WITNESS: I leave out *The Eye-Witness*. I do not consider that. It is not worth discussion. I am only taking those which are responsible papers. Take those and read those articles. Is there any man who reads those articles today who would not think that what was meant was that we had all been guilty of corruption – the basest charge which could be made?

MR MACMASTER: Or impropriety?

WITNESS: No, do not let us get off to that.

LORD ROBERT CECIL: I do not wish to intervene . . .

WITNESS: Let me finish what I was going to say. I will not be stopped. I am being charged with something; and all I am saying with regard to it is this – and if I appear heated I am sorry, but it is not very easy – all I mean to say is we cannot have – at least I ask you, Sir, and I ask the Committee, to say that we cannot have a confusion between a charge of corruption and a charge of impropriety. One concerns the honour, and the other the judgment of a man.

LORD ROBERT CECIL: Everybody admits that. That is quite plain and there is no dispute about it.

WITNESS: That is all I meant.

LORD ROBERT CECIL: We are not trying the journalists.

WITNESS: But you are trying me.

LORD ROBERT CECIL: We are not trying anybody. We are inquiring into the facts.

The Attorney-General was followed into the witness-chair by Lloyd George. The Chancellor of the Exchequer began with a long statement about the Treasury's connection with the Marconi contract. He then proceeded to lay down the rules which, in his view, should guide a Minister in the choice of his investments, and to declare that he had in no way infringed any one of these rules. He then dealt with the accusations that he had made a large fortune and was a very wealthy man. In fact, he said, his total investments brought him in £400 a year. ('That is my great fortune.') He added that the only other property he had was a small house in Wales that cost £2,000, and which he had paid for out of his salary as Chancellor of the Exchequer. The house at Walton Heath where he lived, and which the Press photographers had made look like a palace, belonged to somebody else.[1]

Towards the end of the day, Lord Robert Cecil began to question the Chancellor about his share purchases for which he had not paid, and Lloyd George gave the impression that he did not understand the full significance of the transaction.

'You bought these shares on the 17th April? You bought with the Master of Elibank, as the Attorney-General has explained to us, shares between you two, as I understand?'

'Yes.'

'And you sold also between you two, let us take it, the 2,000, and – do not bother about the two for the moment – you sold 1,000 on the 20th?'

---

[1] The house was rented by Lloyd George from his friend Sir George Riddell, chairman of the *News of the World*, later Lord Riddell.

'Yes.'

'You bought or made yourself liable for £4,000 for the purchase, 2,000 shares at £2?'

'Well,' replied Lloyd George, by this time somewhat confused by the questions, 'I was liable for £2,000.'

'I am taking the whole transaction together,' Lord Robert Cecil went on, 'because the Attorney-General explained to us . . .'

'Well, I wish you would take it the other way, because it looks such a huge transaction to make me liable for £4,000. It really frightens me, a liability for £4,000.'

'The only reason I did so,' Lord Robert Cecil explained, 'was because the Attorney-General would not allow me to take them separately.'

'I know,' replied Lloyd George with a flash of native wit which drew a laugh from the Committee. 'He is more accustomed to big figures than I am!'

'I will do my best to get it separately.'

'I am a solicitor, and he is a barrister, Lord Robert.'

'I am afraid that is not conclusive,' observed Lord Robert blandly. 'You bought, or rather you made yourself liable because you did not pay, for £2,000?'

'Yes.'

'You sold 500, and that, of course, gives you for the 500 . . . ?'

'I can tell you exactly what I got. The total is £1,565.'

'Then the Attorney-General, as he has explained to us, sold for you later on . . . ?'

'No, not later on.'

'5,000 were sold on the 19th April?'

At this point Rufus Isaacs who had been listening to the proceedings intervened to make a correction, '7,000 on the 19th and 1,000 on May 3rd at $2\frac{11}{16}$ths.'

'So that in the first transaction you gained a certain number of hundreds of pounds?'

'Oh, yes,' Lloyd George answered in a rueful tone. 'I wish I had left it there.'

'That transaction you have referred to as an investment?'

'Yes.'

'Not exactly an investment,' Lord Robert went on. 'You would not call it that?'

'It does not cease to be an investment because you sell it at a profit,'

SIR JOHN SIMON
From a photograph taken when he was Solicitor-General

GODFREY ISAACS

said the Chancellor. 'I meant it to be an investment, and for a whole day I refused to sell, against the advice of my broker, because I wanted to stick to it. He pressed me again on the 20th and then I sold. It was an investment which it is true I got rid of very quickly at a profit.'

'At a profit and without in fact any money passing. That is generally the distinction drawn, is it not?'

'No money could pass because I had not the shares at that time. I had only the call for the shares.'

'I quite understand,' said Lord Robert. 'No money could have passed because the shares had not been delivered?'

'No.'

'But as a matter of fact no money did pass. You resold before the shares were delivered and before you had taken them up?'

'That is so,' Lloyd George agreed.

At this point the Committee adjourned for the week-end before the Chancellor's evidence had been completed. By this date his friend Charles Masterman had become Financial Secretary to the Treasury and was naturally in close consultation with both Lloyd George and Rufus Isaacs at every stage of the Committee proceedings. They met during the week-end, as Mrs Lucy Masterman recorded in her diary[1].

> There was a really very comic, though somewhat alarming, scene between Rufus and George on the following Sunday. George had to give evidence on the Monday – the following day – and Rufus discovered that George was still in a perfect fog as to what his transaction really had been, and began to talk about 'buying a bear'. I have never seen Rufus so nearly lose his temper, and George got extremely sulky, while Rufus patiently reminded him what he had paid, what he still owed, when he had paid it, who to, and what for. It was on that occasion also that Charlie and Rufus tried to impress upon him with all the force in their power to avoid technical terms and stick as closely as possible to the plainest and most ordinary language. As is well known, George made a great success of his evidence.

Much of the remainder of Lloyd George's evidence turned on the question, to a large extent a theoretical one, whether his dealings on the Stock Exchange were speculations or investments. The Chancellor was anxious to rebut the charge of 'gambling', which would naturally shock the Nonconformist elements in the Liberal Party. He had never

[1] Masterman, p. 255.

F

speculated, he said in answer to Lord Robert Cecil's further queries, because he had never had much cash and he had a family.

'You said just now that you had never speculated. I wish to be quite clear that you and I understand the word in the same way.'

'I know it is a word which is capable of all sorts of interpretations,' Lloyd George explained. 'I meant gambled.'

'Tell me if we are agreed about this,' continued Lord Robert. 'I understand an investment to be buying either shares or any other security for the purpose of receiving the dividends?'

'Yes.'

'A permanent investment?'

'Yes, that was my view of this transaction, certainly.'

'I understand a speculation to be buying in order to sell again?'

'I have never done that,' Lloyd George replied with marked emphasis. 'Never in my life!'

The Chancellor of the Exchequer went on to explain that, 'if you put money into a concern intending it to be an investment and something happens which you never expected and your broker advises you to sell, that does not mean that you did not originally buy them for an investment'.

A less favourable impression was caused by Lloyd George's admission that he had subsequently bought 3,000 shares in the American Marconi Company on behalf of himself and the Master of Elibank, without immediately informing Rufus Isaacs, at which date the market value of the shares had dropped considerably. In so far as he still held some of the shares in the original dealing with the Attorney-General which he had not taken delivery of and which he had not paid for, Lloyd George had, however unintentionally, come very near to 'bearing the market' in American Marconis.

Rufus Isaacs made a dramatic intervention in the course of his colleague's evidence. Although Lloyd George had not been libelled by *Le Matin*, his name had been mentioned in the subsequent Court proceedings. This appeared to Lord Robert Cecil sufficient justification for putting to the witness the story which had recently been repeated in the *Daily Herald* that the action against *Le Matin* was 'a put-up job' and 'was not a real proceeding at all'. The Attorney-General immediately asked whether the question should not be addressed to himself and he was accordingly allowed to answer it. 'It is absolutely untrue,' he declared. 'I never knew of it until the day I was going away. . . . I did not know a word about it until it was brought to me. I certainly could not think anybody would invent such a suggestion – that anybody should suggest that I had put forward a specific lie like this to be circulated all over the country where I have many friends and relatives, and that I should have done it for some purpose which I do not appreciate.'

'I think it really the limit to quote the *Daily Herald*,' Lloyd George remarked.

'I only do it to call attention to any rumours which had been published,' Lord Robert Cecil somewhat lamely explained.

'Yes, you know the *Daily Herald* and its position.'

'I do not,' said Lord Robert.

'A paper with absolutely no position at all,' retorted Lloyd George.

Mr Herbert Samuel, who followed Lloyd George into the witness-chair, commented at this time:

> The Marconi business is more than ever the cause of interest. I have listened to almost all the evidence given by Rufus Isaacs and Lloyd George.... The position is, of course, a very uncomfortable one, but not more than uncomfortable. For my part I feel very great regret that members of our Cabinet should be in the position of having to appear before a Parliamentary Committee to discuss their private affairs in the presence of all the world. But facts being as they are, the case could not have been better handled than it was by these two.

5

The Committee continued its sittings for over two months more, and whenever public interest in the proceedings showed signs of flagging, it was revived by some fresh incident or development.

First, there was the resignation of Mr Harold Smith from the Committee, as already mentioned. After another of the Conservative members, Major Archer-Shee, had revealed in the House of Commons that Mr Falconer and Mr Booth had been told of the American share purchases, Mr Smith wrote an indignant letter to Sir Albert Spicer, which was later published in *The Times*:

> Two members have been publicly charged with having received and withheld from the Committee most vital information, which, had it been communicated to their colleagues, must have very much short-ened, and, I submit, materially altered our proceedings. These two members have not denied the charge, and one of them has publicly objected to a question which was put to a witness with the object of

testing its accuracy. This objection was withheld by a majority of the Committee, which is thereby precluded from obtaining information to which, in my judgment it is entitled.

I desire for the present to refrain from all comment. I can only draw my own conclusion with the result that I cannot see my way to attend further meetings of the Committee.

Next there was the case of Cecil Chesterton, who had started a new journal, *The New Witness*, following the bankruptcy of the financial backer of *The Eye-Witness*. In a series of articles entitled 'Ghastly Record', he branded Godfrey Isaacs as a vile conspirator, a corrupt man, a thief and a knave, who had attempted to enrich himself by public plunder with the help of his brother, the Attorney-General. To advertise the series Chesterton employed a squad of sandwichmen to parade up and down outside the House of Commons while the Select Committee was sitting, their posters carrying the legend 'Godfrey Isaacs: Ghastly Record'. This led the outraged managing director of the Marconi Company to prosecute Chesterton for criminal libel. Rufus Isaacs and Herbert Samuel again went into the witness-box, as well as the prosecutor, and repeated what they had said in the case of *Le Matin*. In the result Chesterton was convicted and sentenced to a fine of £100 as well as having to pay the heavy costs of the prosecution, in which Carson and F. E. Smith appeared for Godfrey Isaacs, the judge making it clear that he would have sent the defendant to prison had he not sworn that he honestly believed in the truth of the libels he had published.

After the verdict, Rufus Isaacs wrote to F. E. Smith: 'I am more deeply grateful to you for all you have done in my brother's case, and for the triumphant result. I thank you very, very warmly and not least for your courage and loyalty. The Bar will ever remember the part Carson and you played in the matter. You have both behaved so generously and indeed magnificently.'

Incidentally, Carson and Smith were both attacked by their fellow Conservatives for being 'trapped' into accepting briefs in the *Matin* and Chesterton cases, Sir John Stirling-Maxwell accusing the Ulster leader in particular of carrying chivalry too far when he lent his assistance to 'those Marconi knaves or fools or both – I do not know which they are'. Both counsel defended themselves in the pages of *The Times*, which had likewise questioned their conduct. 'We are given a monopoly of advocacy not for this person or that person, or this side or that side,' Carson rejoined, while Smith declared that although he had spent twenty years of his life 'in strenuous contention on behalf of the Conservative Party', he had not surrendered to that or any other party 'and I never will, my independence of judgment in matters of professional propriety'.

Then there was Mr Ellis Powell, the editor of the *Financial News*, who admitted before the Select Committee that a third minister had been rumoured as having dealt in Marconi shares and that this was Mr Winston Churchill, although the witness was careful to add that he believed this particular rumour to be absolutely false. This statement resulted in Mr Churchill hurrying to Committee Room 12 and stoutly denying the charge. 'I have never at any time, in any circumstances,' he declared, 'had any investment or any interest of any kind, however vaguely it may be described, in Marconi telegraphic shares or any other shares of the description in this or any other country of the inhabited globe – never! And if anybody at any time has said so, that person is a liar and a slanderer; and if anybody has repeated this statement and said he had no evidence and believed it to be false, but there it was, the only difference between that person and a liar and a slanderer is that he is a coward in addition.'

Finally, the breach of confidence on the part of a clerk employed by Lord Murray's stockbroker who had absconded revealed the fact that Murray (the former Master of Elibank) had bought 3,000 shares on a 'trust account', which turned out to be Liberal Party funds. 'No one in the Cabinet knew of these dealings, which have caused dire dismay in the Liberal Party,' Lord Riddell noted in his diary at the time. 'L.G. and Rufus were astounded.' Lloyd George, who was 'evidently very depressed' by the news, told the newspaper proprietor: 'I knew nothing of this. Murray never said a word. He believed in the American Marconis as an investment. No doubt he thought he was doing well to invest the Party funds in that way, if he did so.' In fact, Murray had invested £9,000 of the Party funds in American Marconis, in addition to which the absconding broker failed to account for £30,000 entrusted to him by Murray as Government Chief Whip. Unfortunately Murray had removed himself on business to Bogota, of all remote places, which L. J. Maxse sarcastically described as 'fourteen days hard mule-riding from the nearest wireless office', and had declined to return so as to be examined by the Committee, and his evidence was never taken. But henceforth hecklers at Rufus Isaacs's and other Liberal meetings now bawled 'Bo-go-ta!' in addition to 'Marconi!'

Meanwhile it became known that Percy Illingworth, Murray's successor as Chief Whip, had been aware of the share transaction for some time, since his name appeared in the stockbroker's ledger as co-trustee of the account. Consequently there was an embarrassing moment for the Chief Whip the day this piece of news became known through his evidence before the Select Committee. When he entered the House of Commons and walked up the floor to take his place on the Government Front Bench, an unidentified member of the Opposition shouted at him, 'Where's your co-trustee?' According to the *Illustrated London News* (June 14, 1913), 'Mr Illingworth, who had then reached a point opposite the Mace, pulled up suddenly, and turning to face the Unionist benches as though he would read by the face who it was had called out, remained stock still for a full minute, Ministerialists raised the cry "withdraw"; but the Chief Whip ended the demonstration with a gesture and the affair closed.'

When the Select Committee set about its Report, the procedure followed was as inept and prolix as all its previous proceedings. In fact, there were three separate Reports, although only one was official, this being the Majority Report which was produced on strictly party lines. Originally the Chairman drafted a report on behalf of the Liberal Members, while Lord Robert Cecil and Mr Amery collaborated on an alternative draft as an amendment subsequently published under Cecil's name. There was much common ground between the two draft Reports, the differences being to a considerable extent differences of emphasis. Both documents unequivocally repudiated the charges that Ministers had been influenced in their public duties by private or personal considerations, and that they had used privileged knowledge to gamble in Marconi shares. Both recorded the opinion that the purchase of shares in the American company had been indiscreet, and both regretted the lack of frankness with the House of Commons in the debate of October 11, 1912. Both censured the Ministers for their conduct, but the Cecil-Amery Report did so in much more severe language than that employed by Sir Albert Spicer. The harshest censure was reserved for Godfrey Isaacs, although it appeared incidentally in the body of the Report.

We feel compelled to state that Mr Isaacs's account both of his own position with regard to these share dealings and with regard to the whole of the transactions connected with the introduction of these American shares upon the London market was not satisfactory. Owing to a decision of the majority of the Committee we were precluded from recalling Mr Isaacs in order to explain the discrepancy between his statements and the records produced.

The conclusions of the Cecil-Amery Report contained the following paragraphs:

We are of opinion that the Attorney-General acted with grave impropriety in making an advantageous purchase of shares in the Marconi Company of America upon advice and information not then fully available to the public given to him by the managing director of the English Marconi Company, which was in course of obtaining a contract of very great importance – a contract which even when concluded with the Government had to be ratified by the House of Commons. By doing so, he placed himself, however unwittingly, in a position in which his private interest, or sense of obligation, might easily have been in conflict with his public duty.

We think that the Chancellor and the then Chief Ministerial Whip, in taking over a portion of the Attorney-General's shares on the same advice and information, are open to the same censure; and we hold this to be also true of the purchase of shares for the Liberal Party funds by the Chief Whip, so far as such purchase was due to the same advice and information.

The Cecil-Amery draft Report was duly voted on and rejected by the Committee. Thereupon Mr Falconer, who was along with Mr Handel Booth the principal 'whitewasher' on the Committee, while nominally accepting the Chairman's draft, proposed and succeeded in getting carried so many amendments to it that it became completely unrecognizable. Seven-and-a-half out of nine pages of Sir Albert Spicer's findings were struck out, while in place of his comparatively mild strictures on the Ministers was substituted a virtually complete exoneration. Mr Falconer's report then became, by a majority of eight votes to six, the official Report of the Select Committee of Inquiry. The main conclusion was that '*all the Ministers concerned have acted throughout in the sincere belief that there was nothing in their action which would in any way conflict with their duty as Ministers of the Crown*'.

Such a blatantly whitewashing document could not be expected to satisfy the Conservative Opposition in the House of Commons. The Report was published on June 13, and a motion of censure was immediately put down on the Order Paper by Mr George Cave, K.C., a leading back-bench lawyer, later Lord Chancellor, in the following terms:

That this House regrets the transactions of certain of His Majesty's Ministers in the shares of the Marconi Company of America, and the want of frankness displayed by Ministers in their communications on the subject to the House.

It was arranged that, after the motion had been moved and seconded, Rufus Isaacs and Lloyd George should immediately follow with their speeches and then withdraw from the chamber. The Prime Minister also let it be known that he would intervene during the debate in defence of his colleagues. 'If Lloyd George and Rufus Isaacs play their cards well, show the proper spirit, I will let the Opposition have it,' Asquith told his wife. 'They shall sweat under what I've got to say!' The two Ministers did play their cards well, and the Prime Minister stood loyally by them.

The Attorney-General spoke first. Although he found speaking in these circumstances 'a great strain', as he subsequently told Lord Riddell – after all if Mr Cave's motion by some quirk of fate should be carried it would mean the end of his public career – his admission that he had acted mistakenly made a good impression on the House. 'I say now that if I had all the facts present to my mind at the time I entered into the transaction,' he declared, 'if I had known then all I know now, if all had been disclosed to me which subsequent events have revealed, if I had realized that men could be so suspicious of any action of mine, if I had thought that such misrepresentation could possibly exist, I state quite plainly that I would not have entered into the transaction. . . . I say solemnly and sincerely that it was a mistake to purchase those shares. The mistake arose from the fact, as I say, that it never occurred to me that I should be suspected, and I did not know all that I have subsequently learned.'

After the two Ministers had withdrawn, the debate continued for the greater part of two days and exhibited a large measure of party rancour. The Prime Minister was as good as his word, asserting that he did not think he had ever heard, or that anybody had ever heard, 'a franker or more manly explanation' than that put forward by his two ministerial colleagues. 'Their honour, both their private and their public honour, is at this moment absolutely unstained,' he said. 'They have, as this Committee has shown by its unanimous verdict, abused no public trust. They retain – I can say this with full assurance – the complete confidence of their colleagues and of their political associates. We ask the House . . . to say . . . that, having heard their statements with regard to this particular transaction in which their honour is not involved, though their judgment may be impeached, the House accepts those statements and desires to put that acceptance on its records.'

By arrangement with the Government Whips, Sir Ryland Adkins, a Liberal back-bench lawyer, moved an amendment to leave out the substantive words of Cave's motion and to substitute the following:

> That this House, after hearing the statements of the Attorney-General and the Chancellor of the Exchequer in reference to their purchase of shares in the Marconi Company of America, accepts their expression of regret that such purchases were made and that they were not mentioned in the debate of the 11th October last, acquits them of acting otherwise than in good faith and reprobates the charges of corruption brought against Ministers which have been proved to be wholly false.

In the ensuing division, at which the party Whips were on, Cave's motion was defeated by 346 votes to 268, a Government majority of 78. Sir Ryland Adkins's amendment was then agreed to without another division. In the vote on the substantive motion, Carson and F. E. Smith on the Government side abstained on account of their professional appearance in the two law cases arising out of the Marconi affair. Eight members of the Irish Nationalist Party likewise abstained, as also did five Labour Members. At the same time three Liberals voted with the Opposition.

What *The Times* said in a leading article next morning probably reflected all but the most bitter and partisan opinion in the country.

> We should be sorry if, as a result of this wretched business, either Sir Rufus Isaacs or Mr Lloyd George were driven from public life. And after the present severe lesson there is reason to hope that they will be far more useful public servants than before.

Speaking of the two Ministers, Northcliffe remarked to Riddell at this time: 'I hope our friends appreciate the action of my papers.'

'Yes,' replied Riddell. 'They say you acted like a gentleman.'

Such to all intents and purposes was the end of the Marconi affair, although both Rufus Isaacs and Lloyd George were to feel the effects of its backwash for some considerable time to come. Other newspapers were not so friendly as *The Times* and the *Daily Mail*, and the campaign against the Attorney-General in particular was continued by various organs of the Press. The possibility of Rufus Isaacs being appointed to succeed the ailing Lord Alverstone as Lord Chief

Justice was roundly condemned, particularly by the ultra-Conservative *Morning Post*. Furthermore, certain newspapers chose to rake up the old and long-forgotten incident of the Attorney-General having stated in his application for membership of the Stock Exchange that he was over twenty-one, when in fact he was under age. He immediately went to see the Prime Minister and told him the facts, which he followed up with a letter in which he offered his resignation, 'if you think my position as a member of the Government has been or may be weakened or the value of my services impaired.'

To this Asquith replied as follows:

> 12, Downing Street,
> Whitehall, S.W.
> 2 August, 1913

My dear Attorney-General,

After a public career of 25 years you have earned and enjoy the respect and admiration of a great profession and the complete confidence of your political colleagues and friends.

The attempt to which you refer in your letter to impair the reputation which you have so honourably acquired by raking up an incident of 34 years ago when you were a boy will do harm only to those who have made it. I am glad but not surprised to find that it has received no countenance in any quarter of the Opposition which commands or deserves respect.

I need not assure you I count on your continued and much valued co-operation in the service of the State.

> Yours always sincerely,
> H. H. Asquith[1]

One outcome of the Marconi affair was that it gave the Prime Minister the opportunity to formulate a set of rules to govern ministerial conduct in future. He divided them into rules of obligation and rules of prudence. One of the former was that 'Ministers should scrupulously avoid speculative investments in securities as to which, from their position and their special means of early or confidential information, they have or may have an advantage over other people in anticipating market changes.' The most pertinent rule of prudence was that 'in these matters such persons should carefully avoid all transactions which can give colour or countenance to the belief that they are doing anything which the rules of obligation forbid'. It was this rule of prudence, said Asquith, which 'in my opinion and in the opinion of my right honourable friends and colleagues was not fully

[1] Asquith Papers.

observed, though with complete innocence of intention, in this case'.

The long months of anxious waiting, while their political careers hung in the balance, left their mark on both Ministers. Lloyd George lost weight, his face grew lined and he took to wearing spectacles in public. Rufus Isaacs, according to Lord Riddell, 'looked tired' and 'his hair, which was raven black, is showing tinges of white'. To his intimates and family he was sadly changed. His son has recorded that one day at the height of the controversy he happened to come into his chambers in Garden Court and found him sitting at his desk, his head resting on his hands, gazing silently before him. Then, looking up at his only son and heir, he said: 'I had hoped to hand on so much to you, and now it looks as if I shall have nothing to hand on to you that you will want.' After it was all over he was never heard to refer to the matter again. 'It was as if he had determined to blot out of his memory so harrowing and embittering an ordeal.'[1]

The last word on the affair may be left with Winston Churchill, who like Asquith had stood most loyally by the two Ministers. At a dinner-party which he gave at Admiralty House in the following year, when the matter was still fresh in people's minds, young Mr Duff Cooper, who was among the guests, was delighted when Winston Churchill solemnly assured his ministerial colleagues present that 'if that affair had been properly handled by the Opposition it might have brought down the Government'.

At this Percy Illingworth, the Government Chief Whip, remarked that 'the Tories had been too stupid to handle it properly'.

'Some of them were too stupid,' Winston Churchill agreed. But, he was careful to add, 'frankly, some of them were too nice.'[2]

6

Just before the House of Commons rose for the summer recess in 1913, Bonar Law asked the Prime Minister whether the Lord Chief

[1] Reading, Vol. I, p. 273.

[2] Duff Cooper: *Old Men Forget* (1953), p. 35. Thirty years later Churchill would still talk about the affair. During his convalescence at Marrakesh in 1943, his doctor records in his diary that 'after luncheon, Winston wearing an immense sombrero, slumps in a deck-chair and decides with Max [Lord Beaverbrook] that the Marconi case was a squalid business. They go over again how F.E. and Carson rescued Lloyd George. . . .' Lord Moran. *Winston Churchill: The Struggle for Survival* (1966), p. 156.

Justice had resigned and whether Asquith had advised the appointment of any successor. The Prime Minister replied that Lord Alverstone had not resigned and that the last communication he had
received from him had led him 'to entertain the hope that he would in
course of time be able to resume his active duties.' In fact, this was a
vain hope. By the time Rufus Isaacs had returned from his annual
holiday in Marienbad, Alverstone had written his letter of resignation.

To the Attorney-General's suspense of mind was added a sharp
attack of gout which kept him indoors for some days. Early in
October he went down to Walton to help Lloyd George with a speech
with which he was to launch his campaign for the taxation of land
values. Riddell, who was there with the Mastermans, remarked
sympathetically *à propos* of Rufus Isaacs's indisposition that gout
'often attacks great lawyers'. The Attorney-General replied: 'That
does not make it less painful!' None of them apparently had any
news of the vacant Lord Chief Justiceship, although the new Law
term was to open very shortly.

A few days later, Rufus Isaacs received a summons to Downing
Street. Exactly what passed between the Prime Minister and the
Attorney-General on this occasion is not known, apart from the
fact that Asquith confirmed his decision to offer Rufus Isaacs
the vacant place on the Bench. No doubt the pros and cons of the
appointment were carefully considered, as they had been a little time
before when Asquith raised the matter with the King, who had found
it 'most embarrassing'. As the King's Private Secretary expressed it,
'if the P.M. does not recommend him, it will be tantamount to
condemning his action', and 'if Mr Asquith *does* recommend him,
he will be equally condemned by the other side'. At the same time
the King and his Prime Minister agreed that if Rufus Isaacs was not
appointed Lord Chief Justice, he could not remain in the Cabinet.

The matter was settled by the middle of October, when the King's
approval was obtained and the appointment formally accepted.

His next act was to motor over from Fox Hill to Lord Alverstone's
house in Surrey. He found the retiring Lord Chief Justice 'very ill,
very thin and very worn-looking', but his mind was quite clear. They
had a short talk together, and then, as he was leaving, Alverstone
shook his successor warmly by the hand, and holding it in his for a
few moments said: 'I feel I ought to tell you that if there was an error
of judgment in connection with the Marconi affair – which I do not

say there was – I was disgusted at the disgraceful manner in which the incident was used for party purposes, and that all along you had my deepest sympathy.'

During this interview, Gerald Isaacs, who had accompanied his father in the car, remained in it outside the house. When his father reappeared, the son noticed that he was overcome with emotion, being 'for some moments quite unable to speak'.

Two days later, on October 22, the new Lord Chief Justice of England was sworn in to his office in the Law Courts in the presence of the Lord Chancellor and most of the other judges as well as many members of the Bar. Unfortunately the ceremony did not go off quite perfectly.

After the swearing in was completed, the Lord Chancellor made a short speech introducing the new Lord Chief Justice and bidding farewell to his predecessor. Having welcomed Sir Rufus Isaacs with some decidedly complimentary expressions, ('He is a man of the highest honour'), the Lord Chancellor then passed on to pay tribute to the departing Lord Alverstone. Suddenly a barrister, who had come into Court intending to protest at the new appointment, shouted out, 'Speak for yourself, Lord Haldane!', evidently under the impression that the Lord Chancellor was still eulogizing Rufus Isaacs. The interrupter then hurriedly left the Court, his departure being somewhat roughly accelerated, so we are told, by some of his fellow barristers close to him.

On the whole the appointment was well received in the Temple. Among the letters of congratulation delivered to the new Lord Chief was one from his old friend and opponent in the Courts, Sir Edward Carson, who had recently befriended him in the Marconi cases. 'My dear Ned,' the new judge wrote in acknowledgement, recalling Carson's action, 'you behaved to me with all that nobility which is characteristic of you. There I must leave it – it almost overwhelms me.'

The majority of public opinion was fairly summarized by *The Times* in a leading article at the time of his appointment:

> For our part, we trust and believe that his career on the Bench, when it comes to be reckoned up, will be no less distinguished than his astonishing career at the Bar. Meanwhile it can only be regarded as a great misfortune that an absorbing controversy should have brought hesitation and discord into what would otherwise have been a unanimous chorus of approval.

While the appointment was naturally criticized by some of the Conservative Press, particularly the *Morning Post*, nothing exceeded in ferocity the attack by a popular and highly regarded literary figure, Mr Rudyard Kipling, who was moved to write what must surely be one of the most vitriolic poems in the English language, in which he likened the new judge to another Jew, one Gehazi, the servant of Elisha in the Old Testament story. Although the poem did not appear in print until some years later, its text was freely passed round London society at the time.[1] Only the first two stanzas and the last four lines need be given here.

> 'Whence comest thou, Gehazi
>   So reverend to behold,
> In scarlet and in ermines
>   And chain of England's gold?'
> 'From following after Naaman
>   To tell him all is well,
> Whereby my zeal hath made me
>   A Judge in Israel.'
>
> Well done, well done, Gehazi,
>   Stretch forth thy ready hand,
> Thou barely 'scaped from judgment,
>   Take oath to judge the land,
> Unswayed by gift of money
>   Or privy bribe more base,
> Of knowledge which is profit
>   In any market-place.
>
> Stand up, stand up, Gehazi,
>   Draw close thy robe and go,
> Gehazi, Judge in Israel,
>   A leper white as snow!

On the other hand, the new Lord Chief Justice was comforted and reassured to receive 'a very kind and charming message' from Buckingham Palace. 'Please tell the King,' he wrote to Lord Stamfordham, 'that he has given me the loftiest encouragement to serve him and the State and that I shall ever treasure and remember his words.'[2]

The first time he met Lord Riddell after he had taken his place on the Bench, Riddell found him 'delighted by his promotion'. Rufus

---

[1] 'Gehazi' was first published in *The Years Between* (1919) when its subject was still Lord Chief Justice. Although plainly libellous, he chose to ignore it.
[2] November 17, 1913: Royal Archives.

Isaacs said to him, 'It is difficult to realize at once what a great honour has been conferred upon me.' Since the post traditionally carried with it a barony, this led to a discussion of his title. Near to Fox Hill was a little village called Earley, sometimes spelled Erleigh, where Rufus Isaacs had bought some land. The choice of title lay between Lord Erleigh of Reading or Lord Reading of Erleigh. He told Riddell that he would probably take the latter, as a compliment to his constituency, to which he now had to bid farewell. In fact this was what he eventually did. The announcement of his peerage was included in the following New Year's Honours List, and he was duly created Baron Reading of Erleigh in the County of Berkshire.

He also told Lord Riddell when they met that he had been looking through Campbell's *Lives of the Chief Justices* and that he was 'much impressed by the succession of brilliant men who have occupied the position'.

'I hope you are going to have your portrait painted by a good man so as to go down to posterity in proper form,' said Riddell. 'A great artist can make his sitters look almost immortal.'

'I want to be painted in my robes,' replied the new Lord Chief, 'so that the picture may make a good engraving.'[1]

'Has it occurred to you,' Riddell went on, 'that you are very like Lord Mansfield in appearance? You have the same high cheekbones, and, if I may say so, a nose that looks as if it had had a knock.'

'Well, mine did have one,' Rufus Isaacs laughingly replied, thinking back to his early days in the boxing ring. 'I am glad you think I resemble Mansfield.'

The new Lord Chief Justice was able to put off his first circuit until there was an opportunity of doing the Midland, which did not occur until the following Summer Assizes. His choice was dictated by the fact that the first assize town he would visit as a judge would be Reading and that he could consequently sleep for the first few nights of the circuit at Fox Hill.

On returning from his first circuit, Reading spent a day with Riddell and Lloyd George and told them something of his experience on the Bench. Riddell made the following entry in his diary afterwards:

[1] It had long been the custom for Lord Chancellors and Lord Chief Justices to be painted in their robes with a view to the issue of engravings, for which, as Riddell noted, 'the legal profession have a special fancy'. By this time, however, photography had rendered the publication of engraved portraits superfluous. A portrait of Lord Reading in his robes as Lord Chief Justice was painted by Oswald Birley and is reproduced as the frontispiece to this book.

The L.C.J. repeated that trying criminal cases was hateful although necessary work, particularly sexual cases. He gave a graphic description of the trial of a girl charged with concealment of birth. She was a respectable girl, a mechanic's daughter. She had been deceived by a promise of marriage. The man had disappeared. In the dock she was broken with grief and shame. The Chief said, 'Having read the depositions, I endeavoured to catch her eye as she sat there sobbing her heart out, but could not attract her attention. I wanted to convey to her that she had at least one friend in Court.' Ultimately, owing to the evidence, he was able to tell the jury that the prisoner must be acquitted.

The Chief told the story well and was visibly affected. When he had finished, I said, 'You earned a lot of good marks in the Recording Angel's diary this week, Chief.' He had made my eyes glisten, and as I looked at him I saw his were glistening too. He is very kind-hearted.

'I like the work,' he told Lloyd George at this time, 'but feel the loss of the old constant companionship and never-ceasing turmoil on which all are involved who work intimately with you. Only those who have lived in it can appreciate the loss of it.'

At this date Lord Reading was looking forward to the ordinary judicial routine of London and circuit work, pleasant long week-ends and the vacations at Fox Hill, with his annual cure in the summer at Marienbad. But as events turned out, his judicial routine was to be considerably disturbed, and he was suddenly to undertake a variety of very different public duties normally quite unexpected of a Lord Chief Justice.

The courts rose at the end of July and Reading went off to Fox Hill. The possibility of war breaking out in Europe between Austria and Russia following the murder of the Austrian Archduke Franz Ferdinand determined him to cancel his usual visit to Marienbad, but he still hoped for a pleasant vacation at Fox Hill with plenty of golf. Then on the morning of the August Bank Holiday Monday, his telephone rang from London. It was Lord Riddell, who told him that things were serious and that Germany and France might be at war at any moment. Britain might well be involved, although at the moment the Cabinet was divided on whether or not to intervene. Riddell added that his friend should return to London as soon as possible, as Lloyd George, who was wrestling with problems of currency and a proposed moratorium, would like to have his financial advice.

By the time Reading had arrived at Riddell's house for dinner, the other guests being Lloyd George and Masterman, Germany had invaded Belgium and it was a foregone conclusion that Britain would be dragged into the conflict.

'When I came here today I did not appreciate the position,' Reading remarked gloomily to his host, when he heard the latest news. 'I seem to have come into another world.'

7

Lord Reading's special war-time duties, which he was called upon to perform in varying capacities, will be described in the next chapter. For the present, his work as Lord Chief Justice may be conveniently considered here, particularly a number of important trials and appeals where he was the presiding judge. Two of these trials became leading cases in the law of treason and one of the appeals the leading case on the legislation of enemy aliens.

The accused in the first treason trial was a naturalized British subject of German birth named Ahlers, who at the time of the outbreak of the War on August 4, 1914, was German consul in Sunderland. On August 5, when a state of war officially existed between Britain and Germany, Ahlers assisted two German subjects of military age with money and information in order to enable them to return from England to Germany. As a result he was arrested and tried before Mr Justice Shearman at Durham Assizes on the charge that he 'with force of arms, unlawfully, maliciously and traitorously, was adhering to, aiding and comforting the German Emperor against our Lord the King'. While pleading not guilty, Ahlers argued that he acted without any evil intention and in the belief that it was his duty as their consul to assist German subjects to return to Germany. But, in his summing up, the judge directed the jury that, if they found on the evidence that he had thus assisted the King's enemies at a time when he knew that war had been declared, then it was their duty to find him guilty and that it was no defence in law for him to say that he believed that he was lawfully entitled to act as he did. In consequence the jury convicted Ahlers and he was sentenced to death.

Ahlers appealed, and in December, 1914, the matter came before a full bench of the Court of Criminal Appeal, consisting of the Lord Chief Justice and Justices Darling, Banks, Lush, and Atkin.[1] Lord Reading, who delivered the judgment of the Court, took the view,

[1] *Rex* v. *Ahlers* [1915], 1 K.B. 616.

unanimously supported by his judicial brethren, that the trial judge's direction to the jury was insufficient and unduly prejudicial to the prisoner and that the jury should have been told to consider whether the prisoner's acts were done with the deliberate intention of assisting the King's enemies or whether he was merely doing his duty as consul, as he had pleaded in his defence, in which latter event he would not be guilty of treason. Furthermore, proper consideration had not been given to the modern practice of nations by which enemy subjects should be allowed a reasonable time for departure, a principle to which effect had actually been given by an Order of the Home Secretary made under the Aliens Restriction Act and published on August 6 whereby alien enemies were allowed until August 11 to embark at certain ports without the necessity of a permit, although for some reason Sunderland had not been included in the list of ports. 'We cannot say that it follows from the evidence that the actions of the appellant were necessarily hostile to this country in intention and purpose,' said Lord Reading, 'although there was undoubtedly evidence upon which the jury might have so found.' In these circumstances the Court held that the conviction must be quashed, and so Consul Ahlers was set free instead of going to the gallows.

The other treason trial concerned a knight of the realm and a former member of the British Consular Service, who was likewise found guilty and sentenced to death. But in this instance the sentence was carried out, although not before it had created a storm of public controversy. This was the case of the fifty-two-year-old Irish patriot Sir Roger Casement, who after resigning from the consular service had gone to America and thence to Germany where he had endeavoured, with relatively little success, to recruit British prisoners of war in German camps to form an Irish Brigade to fight against England ostensibly for the liberation of Ireland from British rule. Casement's activities in the prison-camps constituted the overt acts of treason with which he was charged. His landing on the west coast of Ireland from a German submarine on the eve of the Easter Rebellion in April, 1916, and his capture and incarceration in the Tower of London caused a tremendous sensation as did his subsequent 'trial at bar' which opened on June 26 before the Lord Chief Justice and Justices Avory and Horridge and a jury in the Lord Chief Justice's Court in the Law Courts.

Since the trial has been described in detail elsewhere, notably by the present writer, it is unnecessary to do more than indicate briefly its salient features here.[1] The facts of Casement's alleged treasonable acts were not in dispute and the prisoner did not go into the witness-box and give sworn evidence in his defence. He was allowed to make an unsworn statement from the dock, but in this he made no attempt to controvert the facts proved by the prosecution. His defence, put forward with great vigour by his leading counsel, Serjeant A. M. Sullivan, who incidentally collapsed in the middle of his closing speech as the result of his exertions, was purely one of law on the construction of the medieval Statute of Treason under which he was charged, namely that he had been 'adherent to the King's enemies in his realm giving them aid or comfort in the realm or elsewhere'. Sullivan argued that to be guilty of high treason the accused must be shown to have adhered to the King's enemies inside his realm, whereas at all material times Casement had been outside the realm, to wit in Germany. In his summing up to the jury, the Lord Chief Justice was scrupulously fair to the prisoner, but, since he rejected Sullivan's construction of the statute, his direction to the jury really left them with no alternative but to convict.

> You have to determine whether the prisoner was contriving and intending to assist the enemy. If what he did was calculated to aid and assist the enemy, and he knew it was so calculated, then, although he had another or ulterior purpose in view, he was contriving and intending to assist the enemy. It is necessary that you should pay particular attention to this direction, which is a direction of law to you. The questions of fact upon it, of course, you will determine for yourselves, but it is necessary that you should understand that . . . if he knew or believed that the Irish Brigade was to be sent to Ireland during the War with a view to securing the national freedom of Ireland, that is, to engage in a civil war which would necessarily weaken and embarrass this country, then he was contriving to assist the enemy.

Casement was found guilty and sentenced to death. In due course, his appeal was dismissed by the Court of Criminal Appeal (Justices Darling, Bray, A. T. Lawrence, Scrutton and Atkin) which upheld Lord Reading's interpretation of the Statute of Treason. The Home Secretary refused to recommend a reprieve, after the Cabinet had three times considered the case, and Casement was duly hanged in Pentonville Prison. As Mr Justice Darling said in delivering the judgment of the Court of Criminal Appeal, 'The subjects of the King

---

[1] See *Trial of Sir Roger Casement* (1960) edited by H. Montgomery Hyde; also Penguin edition (1964).

owe him allegiance and the allegiance follows the person of the subject. He is the King's liege wherever he may be, and he may violate his allegiance in a foreign country just as well as he may violate it in this country.'

It fell to Lord Reading to hear a number of civil actions arising out of the rights and liabilities of alien enemies in time of war. The most important of these, which is still the leading case on the subject, was that of *Porter* v. *Freudenberg*, which was considered by the entire Court of Appeal, over which the Lord Chief Justice presided, together with the Master of the Rolls, Lord Cozens-Hardy, and five Lords Justice, in January, 1915. The appeal was the result of an action by Porter to recover from Freudenberg, a German national, the rent due under a lease for the premises in London in which Freudenberg had carried on business as a mantle manufacturer before the outbreak of the War, which had made Freudenberg an alien enemy. At the time of the trial Freudenberg was resident in Berlin. The principal question which the Court had to decide was whether Freudenberg could be sued, and if so whether he had the right to enter an appearance and defend the action and also to appeal against any decision given against him. The Court unanimously decided that he had. 'To deny him that right would be to deny him justice,' said Lord Reading delivering the judgment of the Court, 'and would be quite contrary to the basic principles guiding the King's Courts in the administration of justice.' On the other hand, an alien enemy cannot himself sue, his right being suspended during the progress of hostilities, and until after peace is declared. 'The rule of law suspending the alien enemy's right of action is based on public policy, but no considerations of public policy would justify preventing the enforcement by a British or neutral subject of a right against the enemy.'[1]

The ruling that an alien enemy has the right to defend himself when sued in time of war was denounced in certain sections of the Press at the time as being unduly favourable to enemy aliens, as also was another decision shortly afterwards to the effect that the payment of a debt to a company registered in England, whose shareholders were with a single exception German nationals resident in Germany, was not a payment to the enemy alien shareholders for their benefit. The Company was a subsidiary formed by a German company to promote the sale in the United Kingdom of motor tyres made in Germany by the German company. All its directors were German subjects resident

[1] [1915], 1 K.B. 875, pp. 880, 883.

in Germany, and the whole of its shares (except one) were held by German subjects residing in Germany. As the Lord Chief Justice pointed out, once a corporation has been created in accordance with the requirements of English law it is an English company, notwithstanding that all its shareholders may be aliens. 'It is undoubtedly the policy of the law as administered in our Courts of Justice to regard substance and to disregard form,' he said. 'Justice should not be hindered by a mere technicality but substance must not be treated as form or swept aside as technicality because that course might appear convenient in a particular case.'[1]

Another significant war-time case which it fell to the Lord Chief Justice to try concerned two naturalized British subjects. Both were German Jews by birth and both had attained to considerable eminence in the business and social worlds of their adopted country. The elder, Sir Ernest Cassel, who was naturalized in 1878, had been an intimate friend of King Edward VII and moved in court circles; his granddaughter was to become Lady Mountbatten. Sir Edgar Speyer, who was ten years younger than Cassel and was naturalized in 1892, was not a courtier, but he shared the other's interests in banking, commerce and the arts. Both were instrumental in financing London's underground railway system, both entertained on a lavish scale, and both gave most generously to charitable and educational causes. Cassel was sworn a Privy Councillor at the time of King Edward's accession, while Speyer, who was a Liberal in politics and a friend of Asquith, had his name added to the Privy Council Roll five years later. On the outbreak of the War both men were attacked on account of their origins in the current wave of anti-German feeling. So far as the elder man was concerned, his loyalty to Britain was beyond question, and he had virtually no interests in Germany. Speyer did have strong German business connections, while his brother James in New York was notoriously sympathetic towards the German cause. Consequently of the two, Speyer suffered the more, his critics even going so far as to suggest that he used his house on the Norfolk coast in order to signal messages to German submarines. Lady Speyer was especially indignant at being ostracized by her former friends and she urged her husband to take some counteraction. The result was that in May, 1915, Sir Edgar Speyer wrote to Asquith, saying that he considered it 'due to his honour as a loyal

---

[1] *Continental Tyre and Rubber Co. (Great Britain) Ltd.* v. *Daimler Co. Ltd.* [1915], 1 K.B. 893, p. 903.

British subject' and to his 'personal dignity as a man' to retire from all his public positions. He accordingly asked the Prime Minister to accept his resignation as a Privy Councillor and to revoke his baronetcy. Speyer does not seem to have been aware that Privy Councillorships and baronetcies, being honours conferred by the Sovereign, cannot be relinquished in the manner he suggested. Anyhow Asquith wrote to him in reply: 'I have known you long and well enough to estimate at their true value these baseless and malignant imputations upon your loyalty to the British Crown. The King is not prepared to take any step such as you suggest in regard to the marks of distinction which you have received in recognition of public services and philanthropic munificence.'

The matter might have rested there, had it not been for the action of an obscure Scottish baronet, Sir George Makgill, who had come to the conclusion as the result of his constitutional researches that neither Cassel nor Speyer was by reason of his foreign origins entitled to continue a member of the Privy Council. In November, 1915, Makgill obtained a rule nisi in the King's Bench Division, calling upon the two men to justify their membership of the Council. In December a divisional Court presided over by the Lord Chief Justice discharged the rule, and the decision was affirmed on appeal in July, 1916. There were long, technical arguments on whether the proviso in the Act of Settlement of 1700, expressly disqualifying alien-born persons from membership, was still law. Briefly, what was finally decided in the matter was that the proviso which had been abolished by the Naturalization Act of 1870, had not been revived, contrary to the argument of Makgill's counsel, by the British Nationality and Status of Aliens Act of 1914. As far as the law was concerned, therefore, Cassel and Speyer were entitled to remain Privy Councillors.[1]

Unlike Cassel, who was satisfied with the decision of the Court and settled down to a dignified retirement in Bournemouth, Speyer still felt aggrieved. He resigned all his offices and went to join his brother in New York. Here he identified himself with strongly pro-German and anti-British elements, and furthermore was held to have indulged through his business connections in trading with the enemy. His presence was later to prove an embarrassment to Lord Reading when he became British Ambassador in Washington. Consequently, Speyer's certificate of naturalization was revoked in 1921, following the report of a statutory commission set up in London to consider his

[1] [1916], 1 K.B. 595.

case, and his name was struck off the roll of Privy Councillors. He died in Berlin, eleven years afterwards, a sad and embittered man.

After his return from the Washington Embassy in 1919, after an absence of two years from the Law Courts, Reading resumed his judicial duties for a brief period. Although they are out of strict chronological order, it may be convenient to mention two of the cases in which he gave judgment at this time.

The first case involved a claim by a married woman named Elizabeth Scott for maternity benefit under the original National Health Insurance Act of 1911. Mrs Scott was properly insured through her husband having paid the necessary contributions to an approved society, but the child was born while the husband was on active military service in France and she admitted that he was not the father. The society thereupon refused to pay the benefit on the ground that the child was illegitimate. However, the Court held, by a majority of two to one (Mr Justice Darling dissenting) that the benefit was payable irrespective of the paternity of the child. 'It is well known that there are cases in which the husband takes the wife back notwithstanding that she has committed this serious fault,' said Reading in his judgment. 'Why should she in such a case be deprived of the maternity benefit? What is there in the statute which says that she should be deprived of the maternity benefit in such a case?'[1]

The other case was to become a leading one in the law of murder. A man named Beard suffocated and killed a girl while raping her. He was drunk at the time; and, although drunkenness is ordinarily no defence to the commission of a criminal act, it can be in certain special circumstances where a particular intent is necessary. Since murder falls within this category, the question for the Court to determine was, had Beard committed murder? Or did the state of intoxication preclude his forming the intent or 'malice aforethought'? In fact, Beard was convicted and appealed. In the Court of Criminal Appeal, the Lord Chief Justice followed a recent case (*Rex* v. *Meade*) which had decided that, where the evidence shows that the killer is too drunk to form the intention, the killing is not murder but manslaughter, and the Court accordingly reduced the verdict to one of manslaughter. However, the Crown in turn appealed to the House of Lords, which restored the original verdict. In a notable judgment, reversing Lord Reading's decision, the Lord Chancellor, Lord

[1] *Scott* v. *The Northumberland and Durham Miners Permanent Relief Fund Friendly and Approved Society* [1920], K.B. 174, p. 191.

Birkenhead, held that although Beard was too drunk to form the intent to kill, he had not been too drunk to form the intent to commit rape; and since rape is a felony, and since by the doctrine of constructive malice killing in the course of committing a felony is legally murder, Beard was guilty of murder.

A curious feature of the case was that Lord Reading sat both in the Court of Criminal Appeal and in the House of Lords. It might have been expected that in the circumstances he would have delivered a dissenting judgment defending the decision he had given in the lower court. But, on the conclusion of the Lord Chancellor's judgment, he contented himself with saying: 'My Lords, I agree with my noble and learned friend on the Woolsack and have nothing to add.' Reading had therefore the unusual, possibly unique experience of publicly acquiescing in the reversal of his own judgment.[1]

No Lord Chief Justice of England has probably spent less time in his Court than Reading. But this was not his fault. It was the result of the First World War. Nevertheless his dual role did create an anomalous position, and there were some who said that he should have resigned his high judicial office on becoming an Ambassador.

Perhaps the best as essment of his work as Lord Chief Justice came from the pen of his friend and colleague 'F.E.' (Lord Birkenhead):

> In that high office he displayed many admirable qualities. He was always courteous, patient, assiduous, and industrious. But he did not, perhaps, realize upon the Bench the high expectation of his judicial qualities which his skill in arguing legal points had seemed to justify. Indeed, to argue points of law with high distinction does not always make it certain that he who so argues will deliver judgments with equal distinction. It may be that, if events had allowed him to end his career in the placid atmosphere of the Law Courts, he would have become a great Lord Chief Justice. But the constant interruptions and preoccupations of his judicial career, produced partly by the war, but partly, I think, by his own impatience of a sedentary judicial career, denied the opportunity of creating a lasting judicial reputation.[2]

There is one quality which Lord Birkenhead might have added to the list which he enumerated. It is not one which judges always

---

[1] *Director of Public Prosecutions* v. *Beard* [1920], A.C. 479. Since the doctrine of constructive malice was abolished by the Homicide Act, 1957, Reading's decision, were it given in similar circumstances today, would probably stand.

[2] Birkenhead: *Contemporary Personalities* (1924), pp. 108–10.

possess in the abundant measure shown by Lord Reading in his judgments, undistinguished though they may be in pronouncements of law when compared, for example, with Lord Birkenhead's. That quality is humanity. Or, as Lord Reading himself expressed it, 'I would always prefer to be known as a just man rather than a great lawyer.'

High Commissioner

1

When he came to compose his *War Memoirs*, Lloyd George wrote in the warmest terms of the 'invaluable aid' he had received at the Treasury from Lord Reading in the many conferences and meetings which took place during the first critical weeks and months of the Great War. 'His knowledge of finance, his mastery of figures, his dexterity and calm and sure judgment helped at many turns.' The Chancellor's lack of technical knowledge of the City at this time made this help abundantly necessary. Lloyd George's peculiar position was well summarized by his friend and fellow countryman Tom Jones:

> With the advent of war the Treasury immediately became the centre for the determination of urgent questions of monetary policy, of which neither the Chancellor nor his able staff, with Sir John Bradbury at its head, had any previous experience. The Chancellor had to learn in the midst of a raging world financial crisis. It was the London money market which moved commodities round the world through the medium of bills of exchange. The Chancellor had never seen a bill of exchange and knew little or nothing of the delicate and complicated mechanism by which international trade is regulated. Lloyd George sought guidance from the Governor of the Bank of England and other financial experts to help him through the maze.[1]

The resulting emergency measures were the most novel and far reaching which had ever been taken in the field of public finance. Towards the end of November, 1914, when the crisis had subsided, Lloyd George told Reading that he thought the Government's financial arrangements the most remarkable of all its operations and suggested that the Lord Chief Justice should write a book recording and describing them. 'Reading has made notes which he says may be

[1] Lloyd George, Vol. I, p. 69; Jones, p. 50.

useful hereafter,' Riddell noted in his diary at the time. 'Finance is the only direction in which novel expedients have been tried.'[1]

The news of general military mobilization on the Continent at the end of July, 1914, caused alarm and near panic in the City of London, which was then the financial centre of the world. In particular, the Banks and bill brokers who held bills to the nominal value of several hundred millions of pounds on behalf of foreign traders were threatened with financial disaster as well as the accepting houses. One of the first emergency measures was to declare a general moratorium. Bank Rate rose for a short time to 10 per cent. The Stock Exchange was closed and the Bank Charter Act suspended so as to enable the issue of bank notes without regard to the fixed ratio of fiduciary notes to gold prescribed by the Act. The Chancellor appealed to the public not to hoard gold coins, then the general currency, and to forestall a possible run on gold the Treasury was empowered to issue notes in denominations of £1 and 10s. These came to be popularly known as 'Bradburys' from the signature of the permanent head of the Treasury which they bore on their face. So as to enable the necessary notes to be printed, the Bank Holiday which fell on August 3, was extended for three more days. Fortunately no abnormal demands were made upon the banks when they reopened their doors, and with the reduction of the Bank Rate to 5 per cent there was, so far as the general public were concerned, a return to 'business as usual'.

The special Treasury Committee, under the Chancellor's chairmanship, which sat in almost continuous session throughout the unprecedented series of Bank Holidays and for many days thereafter included Lord Cunliffe, the Governor of the Bank of England; Sir Edward Holden and Lord Revelstoke, Chairmen respectively of the London City and Midland Bank and Baring's; besides Sir John Bradbury, Lord Reading, Sir George Paish, a leading economist, and Mr Austen Chamberlain, the Opposition 'Shadow' Chancellor, who took the chair when Lloyd George was absent at Cabinet meetings. To facilitate his work, much of which consisted in helping, along with

[1] Riddell, Vol. II, p. 42. Reading's notes do not appear to have survived. The second Lord Reading, who had access to his father's private papers in preparing his biography of his father, shows no evidence of having seen them. Some years later Reading told Lloyd George: 'Such records as I kept, apart from the formal documents that were issued by the Treasury . . . would be useless without my own interpretation. I was so impressed at the time with the danger of notes possibly falling into wrong hands through some mischance that I wrote little that could be understood by any but myself.' Reading to Lloyd George, July 26, 1923 (Lloyd George Papers).

Sir John Simon, the Attorney-General, to draft the necessary emergency legislation for presentation to Parliament, Reading was given a room at the Treasury. One of the most important items of legislation thus drafted, which was later to form a precedent for similar legislation in the Second World War, was the Courts (Emergency Powers) Act designed to relieve the hardships of debtors who could not meet their obligations owing to war conditions.

In particular, Reading was employed by the Chancellor to bring the banks into line with Government policy. For instance, during the first weeks of the War news reached Lloyd George that there was an agreement pending between the banks to restrict further advances and not to accept any new customers who wished to transfer their accounts from other banking institutions. In those days there were many more banks than today when the majority of business is concentrated in the hands of the 'Big Five' joint stock banks. Reading let the Chancellor's reaction become known through Sir Felix Schuster, Governor of the Union Bank (later amalgamated with the National Provincial) and an expert on the technical side of banking and bill-broking.

In order to effect a speedy rehabilitation of the discount market, which had virtually collapsed, and so get foreign trade moving again, the Government with the advice of Reading and the other experts introduced two remedial measures. Under the first, the Government undertook to guarantee the Bank of England against any loss which it might incur by discounting any approved bills which had been accepted before the proclamation of the moratorium, thus relieving the bill brokers and discount houses from all liability in respect of them. The result was that during the next few weeks bills were discounted to the value of over £100 millions. Of course, the acceptors still remained liable for the bills at maturity, and it was to help them that the second measure was devised, by which the Bank of England was authorized to advance funds to meet the bills when they matured; at the same time all claims against the acceptors for repayment were postponed for one year after the end of the War. By this means the accepting houses were given sufficient time to recover the sums due from their clients and they were enabled to carry on their business free from immediate financial embarrassment. Finally, there was the plight of the provincial traders who were in the habit of supplying goods to their Continental customers on credit and without receiving bills of exchange in return. Here the Government agreed to put up 50 per cent of the sums involved provided that the traders' local banks, who were best fitted to judge their customers' commercial standing, were willing to advance a further 25 per cent.

Reading devoted the whole of the Long Vacation to this work, and after the opening of the Michaelmas Law Sittings he would go down to his room in the Treasury after the Courts rose for the day and continue his work there. He would also coach Lloyd George on the speeches and statements he had to make to the House of Commons, cautioning him not to involve himself in technical details. On the technicalities of the discount market, for instance, he warned the Chancellor to be very wary 'because several men in the House know this part of the subject and might correct you'. ('You will probably find the House wants to hear very little of the details – it wants a broad statement. As it cannot criticize effectively, it will be bored by detail, and you are not enamoured of it!!') He also warned Lloyd George of the dangers of referring to the possibility of some banks being ruined; it was enough to mention the bankruptcy of some traders with consequent loss to the banks. ('There is nothing so sensitive as the public with money in the banks at these times. Perhaps I exaggerate the importance of the reference but I do not think so and you may be criticized as Chancellor for the suggestion. . . .')

Some recent historians, notably A. J. P. Taylor, take the view that the alarm was overdone and that all the emergency measures were not justified by subsequent events, particularly in respect of the moratorium, since far from defaulting, many foreigners as things turned out were only too anxious to meet their obligations under the bills of exchange drawn upon them by English traders.[1] Certainly as regards the £500 millions' worth of bills guaranteed, the Government's eventual loss was relatively small, but this could not be foreseen at the time the guarantees were given any more than that the withdrawal of golden sovereigns from the banks would be much less than was anticipated. Reading was strongly opposed to the continuance of the moratorium once the other emergency measures were seen to be operating effectively. It was largely as the result of his urging that the moratorium was brought to an end on November 4, exactly three

[1] A. J. P. Taylor: *English History 1914–1945* (1965), pp. 4–5. Cp. Lord Keynes: 'Foreign balances in London were insignificant and were greatly outweighed by what foreigners owed us on acceptance credits. The financial crisis of 1914 was due, not to our being unable to pay what we owed abroad, but to foreigners being unable to pay us. It was not sterling that crashed in that month, but the dollar (which went temporarily over 6 to the £).' Cited by Sir Roy Harrod in *The Life of John Maynard Keynes* (1951), p. 205.

months after the War began, and trade with neutral countries was restored to its normal channels.

As Chancellor of the Exchequer Lloyd George was given the credit by the public for having 'saved the City'. In this he realized how much he owed to Reading's constant advice and he acknowledged it when the crisis was over with the gift of a cigarette holder. Reading replied in characteristic language:

I am unfeignedly glad you think my assistance has been of value to you. Whatever its quality it was and always will be most willingly given whenever it is required. I have always felt proud that I was able to help at such a critical period. Then the work fascinated me, and added to it all the close companionship of former days delighted me.

Shall I tell you my innermost thoughts? It was joy that I who so unintentionally had caused you trouble should be able to help in however small a capacity to put you on your highest pinnacle where you now are and must remain till a taller one is made for you.[1]

Their companionship was further expressed in a journey which Reading and Lloyd George made to France at this period in company with Sir John Simon to see what was being done in the way of increasing the production of munitions, a subject in which the Chancellor had begun to take a vigorous interest. It was their first experience of the physical proximity of war. Winston Churchill, who by this date had moved from the Home Office to the Admiralty, promised that if they would go over by submarine he would supply one of the latest craft; but when they arrived at Newhaven where they were to embark at midnight – the whole town in darkness and their way lighted by a guard with a small oil lamp, as Reading was later to recall – they found an old and small destroyer called the *Flirt* of some 300 tons, in which they eventually made the crossing in extremely rough weather, pursuing a zigzag course to avoid a U-boat reported off Cherbourg.

At Dieppe they found a convoy of motor-cars waiting to transport them to Paris. Near Beauvais they saw the first British troops in charge of a subaltern wheeling a bicycle. On their way they encountered many signs of German artillery bombardment, notably at Senlis much of which was in ruins. Elsewhere, such as Creil, the French had blown the bridges so as to cover their retreat, and the visitors had to cross the river by pontoon. Paris, which they reached in the evening, looked a deserted city. The Government was still at Bordeaux, whither

[1] Reading to Lloyd George, January 2, 1915; Lloyd George Papers.

it had fled during the panic in August, and all the Ministers and Deputies, with the notable exceptions of Briand and Clemenceau had likewise quitted the capital for the comparative safety of the south. In Paris, where the Hotel Mirabeau was specially opened for their accommodation, they discussed the production of arms and munitions with General St Clair Deville, the inventor of the famous 75-millimetre gun, who told them that the Renault car factory and other factories and workshops had been turned over to their production. Unfortunately, as in England, there was a great shortage of skilled workers owing to the call-up of military personnel and indiscriminate recruiting, and in France it was extremely difficult to get back men who were scattered over a wide front in different units. The possibility of purchases from American sources was discussed, and later Reading undertook to go into this question with the Ordnance Department in London, where the munition requirements to meet the expected duration of the War put by Lord Kitchener, the War Minister, at three years, were seriously underestimated. They also met General Joseph Gallieni, the Military Governor of Paris, whose unexpected attack with the Paris Defence Force on Von Kluck's right flank at the first Battle of the Marne was largely responsible for saving the capital; he was able to give them an accurate picture of the military situation which had originally been envisaged as a series of great pitched battles with periods of rest and preparation in between but was now developing into continuous fighting on a more or less fixed front, or, as Lloyd George described it, 'a siege operation on a colossal scale'.

From Paris they motored to Amiens, the General Headquarters of the Northern Army of France under the command of General Castelnau, who took them on a tour of the front and introduced them to his various divisional commanders, also bringing them to within about twelve hundred yards of the German front line of trenches. It was the first time that the three Englishmen had heard the screech and burst of shells overhead, 'fired with murderous intent against human beings', as Lloyd George put it, and the sound made them shudder. At St Pol they lunched with General Foch, the victor of the Marne, whom they met for the first time and liked. Asked by Lloyd George if he had any message for the British Cabinet, the General replied, 'Tell them there will be no more retreats.' Further asked if there would be any more advances, Foch answered after a pause for thought, 'That depends on the men and material you will be able to throw into the battle line!' He then repeated the advice he had given to the Belgians, 'If you want to keep your country, dig yourselves into it, and hang on to it!'

At General Balfourier's Divisional Headquarters, a captured Prussian guardsman happened to be brought in while they were there. He was wounded in the arm and evidently in pain. Reading addressed him in German and ascertained that he came from Berlin and was a well-educated man.

'Well, you need not worry,' General Balfourier broke in. 'You will be taken to hospital and looked after just as well as our own men.'

'Your men are well treated by us, too,' replied the German.

'At any rate,' the General went on, shrugging his shoulders, 'for you it is now only a question of time. When the War is over, you will be free to return to your home.'

'Ah!' said the prisoner with weary longing. 'Home is the only thing that matters in life!'

While they were being shown round the front Lloyd George asked a young French officer who was their guide whether the stories of German cruelty to women were true. 'No,' he answered. 'They leave them alone as a rule.' He added with a cynical shrug, 'They do not appreciate women!'

Before returning to England, the party paid an unexpected call at the headquarters of the British Expeditionary Force at St Omer. They found that General Sir John French had gone on a tour to the north where 'some fighting' was reported. Lloyd George sent the British commander a message that on no account was he to return to headquarters since they had given him no advance notice of their visit. The General's A.D.C. read them a message which had just been received from the General and which indicated that the fighting looked as if it might develop into a great battle. In fact, it was the beginning of the terrible first Battle of Ypres.

In the following King's Birthday Honours, Reading was created a Knight Grand Commander of the Bath (G.C.B.) 'for special services during the Great War'. In conveying his thanks to His Majesty through the King's Private Secretary, he wrote: 'I shall always esteem it an acknowledgment of such war services as I have been able to perform, and am proud to think that they were deemed worthy of such recognition. All are, I am sure, willing to help, but it is given to few to have the opportunity.'[1]

[1] Reading to Stamfordham, June 6, 1915: Royal Archives.

CARTOON BY MAX BEERBOHM ON THE MARCONI AFFAIR

'Some Ministers of the Crown, who (monstrous though it seem) have severally some spare pounds to invest, implore Sir Rufus Isaacs to tell them if he knows of any stocks which they could buy without fear of ultimate profit.'

From left to right: Winston Churchill, Colonel Seely, Asquith, Sir Edward Grey, Sir Rufus Isaacs, Reginald McKenna, Augustine Birrell, John Burns, Lewis Harcourt. *(From* Fifty Caricatures *by Max Beerbohm, published by William Heineman Ltd)*

'MR LLOYD GEORGE AND HIS GUARDIANS'
C. F. G. Masterman and Sir Rufus Isaacs.
(*From* Fifty Caricatures *by Max Beerbohm, published by William Heinemann Ltd*)

2

In May, 1915, Asquith's Liberal Government became a coalition, the transformation being brought about by the immediate failure of the Dardanelles Expedition to knock Germany's ally Turkey out of the War by capturing Constantinople, and also by the increasingly heavy British casualties on the western front, particularly at the battle of Festubert, where Sir John French excused his failure to penetrate the fortified German line by reason of a shortage of shells. In the Cabinet reshuffle, Lloyd George became Minister of Munitions, while his place at the Exchequer was taken by Reginald McKenna, supposedly a sound Free Trader, who was obliged in two successive war-time budgets to swallow his Cobdenite principles and introduce duties on a wide range of imports in order to conserve shipping space, the so-called 'McKenna duties', which were to be retained long after he had left the Treasury. Although the various portfolios were fairly evenly distributed between the parties, the Liberals retained most of the key posts. Sir Edward Grey, for example, stayed at the Foreign Office. Bonar Law, the Conservative leader, might have become Chancellor had he pressed his claim, but he was content to be Colonial Secretary. At the new Chancellor's request, Reading kept on his room in White-hall where he continued to advise on the various problems of war finance, such as the purchase of arms, food and raw materials abroad.

By the beginning of 1915 the War was costing the country £3,500,000 a day and Great Britain's credit balance of some £90 million in the United States had been practically wiped out, while both the pound sterling and the French franc were falling on the New York exchange. The acquisition of dollars for the continued financing of the War was now only possible through dipping into the Bank of England's gold supply, selling British-owned American securities or raising a loan in the United States. As soon as he became Chancellor, McKenna several times urged upon Lord Cunliffe, the Governor of the Bank of England, the need for providing more cash in hand for immediate payments; but the dictatorial Cunliffe told him in effect not to meddle. 'Mr Chancellor,' he used to say, 'this is a matter of exchange and the responsibility here lies with me.' Then, suddenly one hot summer afternoon, the roles were reversed.

The Governor sought out McKenna in his room in the House of

G

Commons and showed him two telegrams from J. P. Morgan & Co., the well-known New York bankers who acted as the Government's financial agents in America. The substance of the telegrams, which were addressed to Morgan's London house, Morgan, Grenfell & Co., was that orders for £52 million of war material had been placed by the British armed services with contractors in the United States, that the contracts were waiting to be signed, and that before signature $65,000,000 (£13 million) must be paid down. Any delay in payment, the cables added, would seriously damage British credit in America. The truth of the matter was that Britain's till at Morgan's was empty.

When he heard this sorrowful tale, the Chancellor is alleged to have remarked, 'But Mr Governor, this is what you call a matter of exchange. Is it not for you?'

According to Lord Beaverbrook, who is the authority for this story, the worried Governor replied, 'Oh, don't talk like that! What is to be done?'

'Leave it to me!' said Mr McKenna. And in that sentence, commented Lord Beaverbrook in his *Politicians and the War*, was contained the nullification of Lord Cunliffe's claim to supreme control over national finance.[1]

The Chancellor acted promptly and courageously. The same evening he invited the heads of the Prudential Assurance Company to come and see him urgently. When they arrived, McKenna asked them how much the Prudential had got in American securities. The answer was 40,000,000 dollars. 'Will you give them and let me settle later?' said the Chancellor. The Prudential directors said they would. 'Then let the Bank of England have them by ten o'clock tomorrow morning.' This was accordingly done, the Bank of England supplied another £5 million in gold, and the whole 65,000,000 dollars handed over to Morgan's. Thus the situation was saved, and the contracts were enabled to be signed with the required down payment.

The Governor reported to the Prime Minister what had happened. Asquith then saw Reading and also Edwin Montagu, the brilliant young Financial Secretary of the Treasury, who had previously been the Prime Minister's Parliamentary Private Secretary and with whom he was considerably more intimate than he was with Montagu's immediate chief. Next day he wrote to the latter.

[1] Beaverbrook, Vol. I, p. 154.

10, Downing Street,
London, S.W.
July 25, 1915.

The Governor of the Bank came to see me again yesterday morning, and I have had the opportunity of talking over the situation with the Chief Justice and Montagu.

The result is that I feel a good deal of disquietude.

Without going into details there are two or three points which seem to me to be clear: (1) that it is of primary importance to our credit that none of the American contracts should be dropped through inability to provide exchange for the moment. I understand that provision has now been made for the immediate case; (2) that the process of acquiring and collecting American securities here for export should be conducted as quietly and unostentatiously as possible; (3) that every possible effort should be made to withdraw gold from circulation and accumulate it, so that a substantial reserve will always be available for export; (4) that both Russia and France should have it made clear to them that they must be ready to part with substantial contributions of gold, if they expect us to continue to render them effective financial help.

All these are matters which cannot be put through without delicate handling, and the closest and most cordial co-operation between ourselves and the Bank of England. The Governor has rendered us invaluable service during the past year. He has (like most people) limitations of outlook and faults of temper. But I am satisfied that, though not nimbler either in thought or expression, his deliberate judgment is always well worth taking into account, and that he is perfectly straight.

In regard to Morgan's, while I do not doubt that they have made and will continue to make all that they can out of us, I see no reason to think that they have been acting unfairly, still less treacherously. The original contract with them may or may not have been wise, but it would be bad policy to swop horses now, or to make them suspect that we distrust them.

I have spoken with the frankness which I always use to you, and which you never resent.

On the face of it, this was an extraordinary letter for a Prime Minister to write, and no wonder it upset McKenna. The use of the word 'disquietude', and the implication that Reading and Montagu, who occupied near-by rooms in the Treasury – Montagu was in effect the Chancellor's Under-Secretary and might have been expected to sustain his chief – both sided with the Prime Minister, seemed to convey a reprimand. McKenna replied on the following day:

> Your letter has caused me not less surprise than pain. I am at a loss to understand what can have been said to you by the Governor of the Bank, the Chief Justice and Montagu to lead you to write it. Nothing that I am conscious of having said or done could make you think it necessary to recommend the course of action suggested in the four propositions in your letter, in the correctness of which I concur so fully as to think that the neglect of them would be most culpable.
>
> I should be glad of an opportunity of meeting the Governor, the Chief Justice and Montagu in your presence in order that I may know the precise terms of their complaints.

Asquith realized the unfortunate impression which his letter had caused, and he immediately sought to mollify his offended colleague with an assurance that he knew the Chancellor attached as much importance to the four 'points' as he did, but he thought it 'not amiss to put them down on paper' in the order of what seemed to him for the moment their relative importance. 'Nor is there (so far as I am concerned) any question of charges or complaints,' he added. 'All the three persons I named were loud in their praise of the efficiency and rare knowledge which you have brought to the discharge of your new office.' What had 'principally disturbed' him, the Prime Minister concluded was 'the evidently quite genuine feeling of the Governor (who wished to resign, or at any rate go into temporary retirement, ideas which I promptly knocked on the head) that you had lost confidence in him and in his judgment, and found co-operation with him difficult'.[1]

'Your second letter has taken a load off my mind,' McKenna replied. 'I don't mind what others may say or think, but I do mind very much if you are dissatisfied with me and I read your first letter as meaning that you thought the Governor's grumblings were justified.' Indeed the grumblings were mutual, and co-operation between the Chancellor and the Governor practically ceased in consequence. Meanwhile Lord Cunliffe recovered the measure of power which he had seemingly lost over the sale of the Prudential securities by promoting an Exchange Committee with himself as chairman and full control over all Government financial assets and securities. The Committee was also empowered to look into the question of raising a dollar loan, and Morgan's were asked to advise on the amount

[1] Stephen McKenna: *Reginald McKenna* (1948), pp. 237–38.

likely to be obtainable on the security of notes of the British and French Governments.

To the intense disappointment and indeed consternation of both the British and French Governments, a reply was received from Morgan's on August 18, 1915, that the maximum amount of help likely to be forthcoming in the shape of a loan was £20 million, although the joint needs of the two countries for their immediate requirements was ten times that figure. Even so, Morgan's had been warned by the State Department with the assent of President Wilson shortly after the outbreak of the War that 'in the judgment of this Government loans by American bankers to any foreign nation which is at war are inconsistent with the true spirit of neutrality', and this remained the accepted policy a year later. The only course left was to try the effect of a personal approach. It was hurriedly agreed between the Quai D'Orsay and Downing Street to dispatch an official Anglo-French Financial Mission to New York and that the mission should be led by one of the British members. When the matter came before the Cabinet, Lloyd George proposed with the assent of McKenna that the Lord Chief Justice should head the mission, and so it was generally agreed. After consulting his judicial brethren, Reading decided to accept the assignment and arranged that Mr Justice Darling as the senior puisne King's Bench judge should act as Lord Chief Justice during his absence.

As colleagues on the British side, Reading chose Sir Edward Holden, Chairman of the London City and Midland Bank and a former Liberal M.P., Sir Henry Babington Smith, an experienced ex-Treasury official and President of the National Bank of Turkey, who had also been Secretary of the Post Office, and Mr (later Sir) Basil Blackett of the Treasury, a currency expert, who acted as secretary to the mission. The French representatives were M. Octave Hombert of the Quai D'Orsay and M. Ernest Mallet, a well-known private banker and a regent of the Bank of France.

3

The Anglo-French Financial Mission embarked on board the s.s. *Lapland* on September 1, 1915, and reached New York Harbour nine days later. The crossing was not without anxiety, since Reading was conscious of the risk of the ship being stopped by a German vessel and the surrender of the mission demanded. However, all went well and the mission was met on arrival by the redoubtable J. P. Morgan in person and his partner Henry P. Davison, who welcomed them ashore with an invitation to meet some fifty prominent American bankers in Morgan's library the same afternoon.

Although it was his first visit to the United States, Reading had already met J. P. Morgan in the houses of Morgan's American cousins in England, Mrs Lewis ('Lulu') Harcourt and Mrs Walter Burns, so that he was already quite well acquainted with the famous banker. But while he was on easy social terms with Morgan, he had never met him officially and he soon realized the difficulty of his task in the prevailing economic climate of America, as shown by his first cable home.[1]

To Reginald McKenna

New York. September 12, 1915. Great activity since arrival. We have met most leading bankers. Situation is very difficult and will require much time and effort.

Press have talked of big loan in collateral of American securities. Have emphatically informed Morgan that suggestion impossible. We want £200 million sterling.

Later the same day he sent the Chancellor a further cable:

Have told Morgan we want £200 million sterling. We meet tomorrow to begin business. Will inform you of progress which must be slow and laborious. American public unaccustomed to such loans even for small accounts. Negotiation very delicate.

The Biltmore Hotel, where the Mission made their headquarters, became the centre of much hard bargaining and long drawn-out argument during the next two weeks. The first public reactions to the idea of the loan were distinctly unfavourable, especially as no tangible collateral security was offered such as British- and French-owned American stocks; indeed the only security suggested was the mere word of the two countries to honour their obligations and there was a good deal of anti-loan propaganda fostered by German and Irish-American elements in the country.

To Reginald McKenna

New York. September 17, 1915. German opposition developing by threatening withdrawal of deposits and resignation of directors to

[1] Foreign Office Papers. America (War) F.O. 371/2589–90: Public Record Office.

prevent bankers subscribing to loan. These figures make situation difficult and progress slow. We are pursuing our way very cautiously but too early to express opinion as to result. We are working in complete accord with Morgan's.

Serious difficulty is that investor is not tempted by 5 per cent to which he is unaccustomed, as he can readily get more on sound American securities. We may be able at utmost to raise £100,000,000 sterling by loan if we can come to terms which may involve cost to Exchequer equivalent to 5½ per cent. . . . Please remember difficulties here.

The difficulties were indeed formidable, since no internal loan of any considerable size had been launched in America since the time of the Civil War half a century previously. Fortunately for the Financial Mission the atmosphere began to change when it came to be realized that without such a loan as was now being sought the farmers of the Middle West and the South would have no market for their meat, cereals and cotton, and many of them would be bound to suffer severely if they were left with a large glut of produce on their hands, which they could not dispose of to their habitual British and French customers. When this view was conveyed to President Wilson by Mr William G. McAdoo, the Secretary of the U.S. Treasury, and also by Mr Robert Lansing, who had succeeded the isolationist William Jennings Bryan as Secretary of State, the Government changed its attitude from opposition to benevolent neutrality. The only American politicians who came out publicly against the loan were Bryan and Senator Lewis of Illinois. The latter whose knowledge of economics was somewhat hazy, appeared to be obsessed with the idea that it was proposed to pack up gold to the value of a billion dollars for transportation to England and France. This operation, he explained, would 'take one half of all the available cash in the country from the people' to be lent to nations which were spending fifteen million dollars a day. As Sir Cecil Spring Rice, the British Ambassador in Washington, noted at the time, the Senator's '*naïveté*' in financial matters is good humouredly commented on in the Press and endeavours are made to explain to him the difference between a war loan in gold and a credit arrangement for the benefit of American commerce.'

At the end of a week's arduous discussion, Morgan's proposed the issue of five-year 5 per cent bonds convertible at the holder's option, to be declared at the end of four years, into 4½ per cent bonds

redeemable between 1930 and 1940. On these terms Morgan's felt
they could form a syndicate to underwrite a loan of £100 million.
'We are insisting on £150 million sterling but meet with great
difficulty,' Reading cabled McKenna. This proposal was approved
by the Chancellor on behalf of the Cabinet. 'Liability to repay whole
in five years need not in all the circumstances disturb us,' McKenna
cabled back on September 22. 'We are in full agreement with you in
desiring larger amount but will not risk failure of negotiations on that
account.' Reading accordingly gave way on the amount, and Morgan's stated they were ready to form a syndicate to underwrite a loan
of 500,000,000 dollars at a price of 96 to the syndicate and 98 to the
public provided the mission gave their immediate agreement. The
authority to close the deal was forthcoming from London on
September 24, although McKenna warned that '£100 million will not
be enough to see us right through'. It was also agreed that the pro-
ceeds of the loan should be spent in the United States. Accordingly
Morgan's went ahead with the issue which was moderately over-
subscribed. In the event the whole of the $500,000,000 was repaid in
full at the end of the five-year period.

Between the announcement of the terms on September 28 and
the formal signing of the loan agreement on October 14, Reading
busied himself with meeting as many influential Americans as he
could either at small private luncheons or at larger dinners such as
were given for him by representative leaders of banking and commerce in Chicago and the Pilgrim Society in New York. As Spring
Rice wrote to Sir Edward Grey at the Foreign Office, 'it is fortunate
you have Lord Reading to consult about the United States. He "got
on" to everything and everybody here first class. I think he will be a
most useful adviser.' Meanwhile McKenna cabled enthusiastically
from London: 'Reports received here indicate that the loan is a
brilliant success. I congratulate you and your colleagues most warmly
and wish to express the very sincere thanks of the Treasury for the
present relief to our American liabilities.'

Undoubtedly the most important private individual whom Reading
met during this time was Colonel Edward M. House, then the
President's closest confidant. House, a fifty-seven-year-old Texan of
independent means with a whiff of the frontiersman about him, had
given the controversial ex-college professor invaluable help in his
journey first to the Governor's executive mansion in New Jersey and
then to the White House; and Wilson, who was elected the first

Democratic President for twenty years, thereafter consulted him at every turn, particularly in the matter of foreign relations. They were both men of sincere liberal views and hated war, House's detestation of armed conflict dating from his boyhood days during the Civil War in his native Houston, where he remembered his father standing guard over the family storehouse with a shot-gun while returning Confederate soldiers looted the surrounding buildings. Unlike his gregarious and sociable Republican predecessor William Howard Taft, Wilson led a comparatively withdrawn life and received few visitors outside Government and official circles, and even these were restricted. But it was known that anything said to House reached the President's ears soon afterwards, and the Colonel was much courted in consequence. His meeting with Reading took place at his own suggestion over lunch in a Wall Street banker's mansion. After lunch their host left them together and they had a long conversation, ranging from the arming of merchantmen on the high seas to criticism of America and particularly of the President in the English Press.

Diary of Colonel House[1]

Reading asked me when he could see me again and whether I thought it would be all right for him to call upon the President before leaving the country. I replied that the President had made it a rule to see no one who came from the belligerent countries upon matters relating to the war, but that his official position as Lord Chief Justice of England might make it possible. I promised to develop this and, if agreeable to the President, he could make a formal request through the British Ambassador.

I gave him my telephone number and told him it would be perfectly all right to come to my apartment whenever he pleased. I explained that I could not call upon him, but it would cause no comment if he came to me. He understood and promised to avail himself of the opportunity.

Next day Reading reported to the Prime Minister by telegram.

New York. October 3, 1915. Have had important conversation with influential person, which strongly confirms opinion I had formed and expressed for myself and all the Mission in telegrams of yesterday.

The attitude of at least four-fifths of the American people is most friendly, but they are very sensitive especially to criticism from England as to American greed and mercenary motives. I am convinced that there is genuine desire to help the Allies and that many welcome loan as an opportunity of helping.

[1] House Papers: Diary, October 3, 1915.

It was necessary to fix a low price in order to be assured of success of loan of hitherto unprecedented magnitude. Americans do not understand foreign investment. They are unaccustomed to lend except upon collateral security. They can get a yield of $5\frac{1}{2}$ to 6 per cent on unimpeachable stock, and their transactions as compared with international transactions in England are very small. There is no cohesion or organization among the many thousands of banks throughout the country, and again there has been violent and organized German opposition and also the opposition of pacifists. . . .

I am most anxious to prevent as far as possible harsh criticism of Americans with regard to this loan. It would not only be unjust but could do a great harm. There are possibilities of future assistance of a similar kind to be borne in mind. This is the first step and a big one and I do not want the Opposition papers to taint the American with British criticisms.[1]

At the Pilgrims' Dinner given to the Mission in New York, the chair was taken by Mr Joseph H. Choate, a distinguished lawyer and former American Ambassador in London. 'Lord Reading is going home with $500,000,000 in his pocket,' he said in toasting the principal guest. 'He has dealt splendidly with the American people.' To this Reading replied in appropriate terms. 'We feel tonight we are at home,' he told the American Pilgrims. 'We came as strangers and you have received us as relatives. You have clasped us to your hearts and made us realize more than ever what the great bond of humanity is.'

Reading also paid a short visit to Washington, where he called at the White House and was reported to have been received 'very graciously' by President Wilson. (This was the result of Colonel House's friendly intervention.) Spring Rice, the British Ambassador, thought it best not to accompany him, 'as the President is anxious to avoid unnecessary conversations with diplomatists which lead to misunderstandings in the Press'. Afterwards Reading went to the Supreme Court where he was welcomed by Chief Justice Oliver Wendell Holmes and invited to take a seat on the Bench which he did for a short time. In the evening the Ambassador gave a dinner for him

[1] The account of the meeting in Colonel House's diary contains the following: 'I called Reading's attention to the growing discontent and criticism of the President's policy in the English Press. I cited several cartoons and much written matter. He was exceedingly sorry, but thought it was almost impossible to control the Press in such matters. The Government knew and appreciated the President's position, but the lay public did not; consequently the criticism. He spoke as if he would take the matter up with his Government and find whether something could not be done to right it.' *The Intimate Papers of Colonel House*, Vol. II, p. 73.

at the Embassy to which his famous American opposite number and the other Justices of the Supreme Court were also bidden.

Next day Reading returned to New York for the signing of the loan agreement, which took place in the presence of a great company of bankers in the Morgan Library, Reading and M. Hombert for France affixing their signatures to sixty-one copies, one for each member of the underwriting syndicate. Twenty-four hours later the Mission was on the high seas bound for home.

On the day he sailed Reading accepted an invitation to have breakfast with Colonel House. The latter noted in his diary the same day (October 16):

> Reading and I agreed to keep in touch with one another and he is to write in an unofficial way as often as necessary to have me fully informed. . . .
> Reading was somewhat fearful that the Germans might stop the *St Louis* and take him off as a prisoner of war. He told me in confidence that he had cabled Balfour to have the *St Louis* met so that he might be transferred to a British ship.

After Reading and the others had departed, the British Ambassador paid a final tribute to the Mission's leader. 'It was to a very large extent due to the personal qualities of Lord Reading that the operation of floating the loan was brought to a successful conclusion. Spring Rice cabled to Grey at the Foreign Office. 'He made an impression on all who met him such as is rare in the case of visiting Englishmen.'

4

On the same day as Reading and the rest of the Financial Mission sailed for England, Colonel House addressed a letter to Sir Edward Grey, with whom he had begun a confidential correspondence, on the subject of a negotiated peace. 'In my opinion,' he wrote, 'it would be a world-wide calamity if the War should continue to a point where the Allies could not, with the aid of the United States, bring about a peace along the lines you and I have so often discussed. What I want to know is that, whenever you consider the time is propitious for this intervention, I will propose it to the President. He may then desire me to go to Europe in order that a more intimate understanding as to procedure may be had.' House went on to state that after conferring

with the British Government he would 'proceed to Berlin and tell them
that it was the President's purpose to intervene and stop this destructive war, provided the weight of the United States thrown on the
side that accepted our proposal could do it'. He added that 'if the
Central Powers were still obdurate, it would *probably* be necessary for
us to join the Allies and force the issue'.[1]

When Grey learned that this proposal was to be taken in conjunc-
tion with his own proposal for a League of Nations after the War to
preserve international peace, and that President Wilson had approved
of the whole idea, he was enthusiastic. The upshot was that Colonel
House arrived in England early in the following January and spent the
next fortnight in a round of talks with Asquith and various of his
Cabinet colleagues including Grey, Balfour, Chamberlain, McKenna
and Lloyd George. He began with the Foreign Secretary, with whom
he raised the question of Spring Rice's position in Washington. ('I
touched lightly upon the British Ambassador and his temperamental
unfitness for the position he occupies. I did not push this further but
will perhaps take it up later.')[2]

The meeting with the Munitions Minister was arranged by Reading. ('He said he knew that neither George nor I would be willing to
open our minds fully to one another unless we were alone.') The
following entry in House's diary throws a revealing light upon it.

January 14, 1916. I dined at the Savoy Hotel with Lord Reading and
Mr Lloyd George. They had a private dining-room, 'Princess Ida'.[3]

Lloyd George had been to see 'The Birth of a Nation' and was much
interested in my account of the reconstruction period in the South.
During dinner, while the waiters were present, we discussed matters in
general, such as the American political situation and the coming
[Presidential election] campaign. I found George as ignorant as ever
of our public men and affairs. When the waiters withdrew, he began to
state the purpose of our meeting.

George believes the War could go on indefinitely, and will do so
unless the President intervenes; but he does not think intervention, to
be effective, should be offered until around September first. . . .

He was insistent that the Turkish Empire must go, and that Poland

[1] House, Vol. II, p. 90. According to House, President Wilson, who was
shown the letter for his approval, inserted the word 'probably'.

[2] House Papers: Diary, January 6, 1916.

[3] The private dining-rooms in the Savoy Hotel are named after the titles
of the Gilbert and Sullivan comic operas, originally performed at the adjacent
Savoy Theatre.

should again become a nation. We discussed all these matters at considerable length. His mind acts quickly, largely upon impulse, and he lacks the slow reasoning of the ordinary British statesman. He was interested in my forecast concerning Asia, and in my conviction that Great Britain should make her plans some day to leave that continent. I thought that China in the future might play the same role Turkey has in the past, and be the cause of innumerable bloody conflicts.

The Lord Chief Justice sat by and said nothing, leaving George and me to thresh it out alone. What I was most interested in was George's insistence that the War could only be brought to an end by the President, and that terms could be dictated by him which the belligerents would never agree upon if left to themselves. Fantastic as this may seem, there is some truth in it; and if the President had taken my advice and increased the army of the United States in the early months of the War, as I strongly urged him to do, he would be in a position today to do what George wishes him to do this coming autumn.[1]

In spite of his ignorance of American affairs – he had never visited the United States – Lloyd George greatly impressed Colonel House with his enthusiasm and energy. A few days later House noted: 'I wish Lloyd George was Prime Minister, with Sir Edward Grey as Foreign Minister, for I believe we could then do something. The Cabinet are all too conservative, and boldness is needed at this time. George has this quality, I believe. . . .' Twelve months later House's wish was to be realized as regards Lloyd George, but in the new Coalition Government Grey was to be dropped from the Foreign Office.

On his return to London from Berlin, where he found the German leaders convinced that they could win the War in the military sense and consequently unwilling to agree to any peace terms which would satisfy the Allies, Colonel House resumed his meetings with his English friends. On the morning after his arrival, Reading called at his hotel and told him that Lloyd George wished to see him again and continue the conversation they had during House's earlier visit. House asked him to arrange it, and they agreed that Reading would try to arrange a dinner for a few nights later to which, in addition to Lloyd George, he would invite the Prime Minister, Grey and Balfour. 'I urged him to be expeditious,' House noted later the same day, 'and to tell those mentioned that, if the work we had in mind was to be accomplished, there must not be the usual British delay.'

As a preliminary to the dinner-party, Reading invited Lloyd George

[1] House Papers. Partly quoted in House, Vol. II, pp. 125–26, 128–29.

to meet House at a small dinner he gave for them at home. House recorded his impressions as follows:

> It is evident that Lloyd George is somewhat distrustful of the Prime Minister, Grey and Balfour, and they are equally so of him. Neither group wants the other to have the advantage, and both are afraid to go as far in the direction as I am pushing as their inclination would lead them for fear capital might be made of it by the others.
>
> Both Reading and George assured me that a peace proposal would be the most unpopular move that could be thought of in England. George said England was aroused for the first time. John Bull was grown fat and lazy, and he was working off his flesh and getting as lean and fit as an athlete, and had no fear of the result. George believes the War has done the nation good – greater good than harm; that it had aroused the best in the people and that they will come out of it rejuvenated, with better impulses and purposes.[1]

The larger dinner took place as planned at Reading's house in Curzon Street, and the details were subsequently recorded by the American guest in his diary.

February 14, 1916. The dinner at the home of the Lord Chief Justice was for 8.30 o'clock. I arrived first, then Lloyd George, Grey, Balfour, and Asquith in order. Reading had the Prime Minister to his right, me to his left, Sir Edward next to me, and Balfour next to the Prime Minister, and Lloyd George at the other end of the table.

The conversation was general while dinner was being served, and was largely about English domestic affairs. When the butler withdrew, there was general discussion of the War, the mistakes that had been made and possible remedies. They talked quite freely before me, discussing the questions of ammunition on hand, the wasteful way in which the Russians were expending what Great Britain was sending them, the general morale of the troops, etc., etc.

I gave it as my theory that the Germans would probably attack the Allies on the west and perhaps at Verdun, and would attack quickly, not waiting for the spring weather to open. My reasons for believing this were that they could not get into the Russian field until the end of April, and the fact that they were not pushing matters in the Balkans convinced me that they would almost immediately open a violent offensive on the western front. My theory is that the Germans are still at their highest point of efficiency, and if they could strike a decisive blow, break through and capture either Paris or Calais, it might conceivably end the War.

[1] House Papers: Diary, February 11, 1916.

It was 10.30 before they got down to the real purpose of the meeting. 'Let us get the setting just as we all now think it might be,' said House, interrupting Lloyd George who had begun to talk on much the same lines as he had done at the Savoy. 'Sir Edward and I in our conference this morning thought it would be impossible to have a peace conference at Washington, and I have promised that the President will come to The Hague, if invited, and remain as long as necessary. Then let us assume that the conference is at The Hague and that the President is presiding over it. With that setting, please proceed with what you think would happen.'

The next hour was spent in discussing the hypothetical peace conference and the territorial changes to the map of Europe which should be made, the restoration of Belgium, Serbia and Poland, the surrender of Alsace and Lorraine to France with territorial compensation to Germany outside Europe, the acquisition by Russia of an outlet to the sea, the partition of Turkey, and the liberation of the remaining Italian communities from the Austrian yoke.

It was growing late, and I drew them back to the point of our meeting; that is, when should the United States demand that the War should cease and a conference be held? I drew George out upon this subject and thoroughly committed him to the idea that the President should act in this capacity. But he was rather chary of naming a definite time. Grey was evidently leaning towards an immediate venture in this direction. The discussion then ran as to how the Allies could best be approached and what had best be done about them.

Asquith asked my opinion as to the proper time. I thought if the Allies could make an impression on the German lines of sufficient importance to discourage Germany, that would be the psychological moment. Asquith agreed with me heartily, and it seemed to be tentatively agreed by all that this course should be followed. I asked them, however, to consider this feature: if the Allies made a deep dent in the German lines, the opinion in Allied countries would be enheartened and they would feel they must go further. Therefore there would be considerable public feeling against peace proposals. Asquith thought this would not be true unless the success of the Allies was greater than he now considered possible.

Lloyd George and Balfour were inclined to take the risk which I held before them, and postpone action until some time later.

It was now twelve o'clock and the Prime Minister made a move to go. While the conference was not conclusive, there was at least a common agreement reached in regard to the essential feature; that is, the President should at some time, to be later agreed upon, call a halt and demand a conference. I did not expect to go beyond that, and I was quite content.

At their meeting again next day in the Foreign Office, Grey congratulated House upon committing Lloyd George 'so thoroughly' to the proposition of intervention by the President. 'He said he did not wish to do this himself, and he was wondering how it was possible to bring it about.' The Foreign Secretary added that he knew the idea would be unpopular in the country, so unpopular that he expected to have the windows of his house broken by angry mobs; nevertheless he was ready to face it because he felt it was right.

Diary of Colonel House

February 17, 1917. The Lord Chief Justice called this morning.

He came to say that in his opinion the conference at his home the other evening was a great success. Like Sir Edward Grey, he thought it remarkable that Lloyd George, Balfour and Asquith should talk so freely before one another. He considered a great work had been accomplished by getting them all committed to the general proposition in the presence of each other. There was no way now by which one could attack the other to his disadvantage. This is because Reading knows, as I know and they know, that peace discussion at this time would be about as popular in England as the coronation of the Kaiser in Westminster Abbey.

I told Reading that both Grey and Balfour had complimented Lloyd George upon the breadth of vision and courage displayed. They both said they had not believed it was in him. This, however, I did not add. Reading thought the Prime Minister had committed himself much more strongly than he thought he would. He thought Asquith had in the back of his mind the feeling that the President was being represented by proxy, while whatever he, Asquith, said was at first hand. He could not repudiate, while the President might conceivably do so.

Reading considered it inadvisable to tell the other members of the Cabinet at present. In this I agree with him. He said it would leak, and would probably lead to a certain cabal getting together to defeat the object we had in mind. I was going directly to see Grey and told Reading I would call this to his attention.

A few days later, Reading called once more on House and told him that he had seen Asquith alone and that the Prime Minister had spoken to him much more strongly in favour of the peace-conference proposal than he had done at the dinner-party. He had also learned from Asquith that it was the intention to make a push on the western front 'at the earliest possible date' so that President Wilson's proposal might come as soon as possible. 'I feel the responsibility I have taken in this matter,' House noted the same day in his diary, 'for it is upon my assurance that the agreement will be carried out that they are preparing for this quick and powerful offensive.'

On the same day Grey initialled the memorandum of the agreement he had drawn up with House. The first paragraph read as follows:

> Colonel House told me that President Wilson was ready, on hearing from France and England that the moment was opportune, to propose that a Conference should be summoned to put an end to the war. Should the Allies accept this proposal, and should Germany refuse it, the United States would probably enter the war against Germany.

In handing House a copy of the memorandum, the Foreign Secretary told the President's representative that he intended giving one to each member of the Cabinet but at House's 'strong protest' presumably in the interests of security he agreed to read it to them instead. House also asked Grey to send Reading to the United States on receiving a cable from House to this effect, in order that Reading might go with House to the President and take back direct word of any modification or amplification of the agreement. House made this request as a precautionary measure for his own protection. 'The President might agree, and I would cable as much to Grey; then something might arise to cause the President to change his mind and I would be censured here in unmeasured terms. Meanwhile the Allied Governments might have gone ahead with this understanding in mind, and followed a course which they would not have done had they not had the agreement with us.'

Two days later, on February 25, Colonel House sailed back to America. In his luggage were two photographs, one of Grey and the other of Reading, both presented by their subjects. Reading's, in his robes as Lord Chief Justice, was conveyed 'with all good wishes to Mrs House and you from Lady Reading and myself for a safe and speedy voyage and arrival home'. The gift marked the beginning of a close personal and political friendship which was to last until Reading's death and which incidentally was to be largely responsible for his eventual appointment as British Ambassador to the United States.

Unfortunately the promising peace plan, which was immediately approved by President Wilson on House's arrival in Washington, came to nothing. In his *War Memoirs*, Lloyd George has attributed its failure to a combination of the President's fear of public opinion in the United States and Grey's fear of the Allies in Europe. The real reason, however, was the rapidity with which the Germans forestalled the projected Allied military offensive on the western front by launching an attack on Verdun, just as House had prophesied they would. By the time the inconclusive fighting had eventually abated on the bloodstained banks of the Somme the House-Grey Memorandum was out of date; the Germans, who still hoped for victory, would never have accepted the peace terms envisaged, while the President was preparing to fight an election on the policy of keeping America out of the War and for the time being he could not risk an intervention which might well bring in the United States on the side of the Allies. Conditions were to change after he had been sent back to the White House for a second term and Germany renewed its policy of unrestricted submarine warfare with an increased fleet of U-boats early in 1917, thus eventually bringing America into the war.

5

A significant change in the composition of the Asquith Cabinet and consequently in the conduct of the War was suddenly precipitated by the tragic loss of Lord Kitchener, when the cruiser in which he was travelling on a mission to Russia struck a mine off the Orkneys and the War Minister and all his staff accompanying him were drowned. As a result of securing the Conservative leader Bonar Law's support for the vacant portfolio, Lloyd George withdrew his threatened resignation, and Asquith was reluctantly obliged to appoint his brilliant colleague to this key post. In doing so, the Prime Minister must have been aware that he was signing his own political death-warrant. 'We are out,' noted Mrs Asquith on the day on which Lloyd George was gazetted Kitchener's successor at the War Office. 'It is only a question of time when we shall have to leave Downing Street.'

The mission on which Kitchener lost his life was of crucial importance to the Allied war effort, since it was essential to reach an understanding with Russia on such questions as strategy, finance and supply, if that country was to be saved from collapse. It was obviously necessary to find a successor to undertake this mission, as well as at the War Office. Lloyd George suggested Sir William

Robertson, Chief of the Imperial General Staff. But Robertson made difficulties, pleading that the Somme offensive was in full blast and that he was very busy with the arrangements involved. Time slipped by, and Lloyd George made a determined effort to settle the matter before Archangel became ice-bound for the winter. He begged Asquith to send Robertson and to let Reading go with him to deal with the financial questions. 'As to Sir William Robertson,' he told the Prime Minister, 'his standing here is well known to the military authorities in Russia, and for the moment they are the only people who count in Russia. . . . As for Lord Reading, he has the high standing and necessary diplomatic gifts and knowledge of finance which would enable him successfully to achieve an understanding with Russia.' However, Robertson persisted with his refusal, having by now become suspicious that Lloyd George was trying to get rid of him. Indeed this accusation was actually made by one of Lloyd George's ministerial colleagues to his face at a meeting of the War Council. 'The P.M. took no action,' Lloyd George told his friend Lord Riddell. 'That hardened me. I felt I could not go on with benefit to the nation under such circumstances.' Thus the projected Robertson-Reading mission to Petrograd did not materialize.

In September, 1915, Lloyd George spent a fortnight in France and Reading accompanied him as his interpreter. 'I think it is delightful of you to have thought of me when you were about to visit the front,' Reading told the War Minister at the end of the trip. 'As always I enjoyed being with you apart from everything else.'[1] They dined with the French General staff in an underground cavern below the citadel at Verdun. Afterwards Lloyd George told his friend Lord Riddell it was one of the most impressive things he had witnessed.

> L.G. says that when the toast was drunk he could see tears trickling down the faces of many of the men. He is enthusiastic about our guns, and expressed his satisfaction that Joffre had come to him to ask him for the loan of some of them. L.G. had a conference with Joffre, Haig and Cavan[2] in a small hut which Cavan used for his conferences. The noise of the guns was deafening. . . . L.G. thinks we are doing well, but that the War may last for a considerable time. The public know only half the story. They read of the victories; the cost is concealed.[3]

There was another side of the picture less flattering to the British

---

[1] Lloyd George Papers.
[2] The Earl of Cavan, who commanded the Guards Division.
[3] Riddell, Vol. II, p. 210.

War Minister. Sir William Robertson told Sir Maurice Hankey, the Secretary of the War Cabinet, that Lloyd George made the worst possible impression on his recent visit to France. He spent most of his time with the French. He asked Foch's opinion of the English generals, whom he himself criticized severely. Foch promptly telephoned the whole thing to Haig and Joffre. Consequently when he went to see Joffre, the latter refused to see him without Haig.[1]

This story leaked out to the Press and Lloyd George was bitterly attacked in the *Morning Post*. However, he insisted that it was not true, and his Parliamentary Under-Secretary Lord Derby loyally backed him up with the King. 'Lloyd George absolutely denies (and Reading who was his interpreter confirms this) that he ever asked any French general what he thought of our generals, or that he in any way compared our forces with those of the French to the disadvantage of the former.'[2] Nevertheless the story was widely believed at the time and has received some confirmation from Haig.

Mrs Asquith's prophecy was fulfilled just six months after it was uttered. This is not the place to detail the course of events which led to the end of the First Coalition Government and the replacement of Asquith by Lloyd George in the Premiership, except in so far as Reading was concerned in the story; this has been told elsewhere, notably by Lord Beaverbrook, a spectator at close quarters, in his *Politicians and the War*. The prime mover in the political campaign and backer of Lloyd George was Reading's old friend and adversary in the Courts, Sir Edward Carson, who had previously resigned his office of Attorney-General and his seat in the Cabinet as a protest against what he considered to be the inefficient conduct of the War. He was supported outside the House of Commons by Northcliffe who loathed Asquith; the Prime Minister in turn disliked the popular Press as epitomized in the *Daily Mail* and had always refused to meet Northcliffe and even to speak to him. On the other hand, Reginald McKenna, the Chancellor of the Exchequer, had come equally to detest Lloyd George, and he did his best to foment the differences between the opposing leaders. In the final struggle Reading and Edwin Montagu, who had succeeded to Lloyd George's job as Minister of Munitions with a seat in the Cabinet at the unusually early age of thirty-six, were the only prominent individuals in public affairs to keep on friendly terms with the two rivals for supreme power.

[1] Lord Hankey: *The Supreme Command* (1961), Vol. II, p. 555.

[2] Randolph Churchill: *Lord Derby* (1959), p. 223.

Briefly, the crisis began on December 1, 1916, with a proposal from Lloyd George to Asquith for a reconstructed War Committee of three or four, including himself as Chairman but excluding Asquith, for the day-to-day conduct of war policy, although Lloyd George was willing that Asquith should continue to be Premier with nominal responsibility for the new War Committee's activities. The same afternoon Asquith turned down Lloyd George's proposal, insisting that the Prime Minister must be the Chairman of the War Committee whatever changes might be made in its composition or functions. ('He cannot be relegated to the position of an arbiter in the background or a referee to the Cabinet.') The next development occurred that evening when Lloyd George was dining by invitation of Lord Cunliffe, the Governor of the Bank of England, in the public restaurant of the Berkeley Hotel. The other guests were Edwin Montagu and his wife, and they were joined after dinner by Reading. Suddenly Sir Max Aitken (Lord Beaverbrook) appeared and carried off Lloyd George to a secret meeting with Bonar Law. This encounter determined Bonar Law to call a Conservative Party meeting and demand Asquith's supersession.

Next morning, Montagu breakfasted with Reading, and in the afternoon the two men went to see Lloyd George in his room at the War Office. However, they were unable to move him in the matter of insisting on the Chairmanship of the War Committee besides the removal of Balfour from the Admiralty upon which he had also insisted. Failing this, Lloyd George had made up his mind to resign. Immediately afterwards Montagu wrote to the Prime Minister:

> The situation is probably irretrievably serious. I have just come from L.G., with whom I have spent an hour of hard fighting, but it seems to be of no avail and I fear he has committed himself. I have done everything in my power and you know that Rufus has also done his best. Rufus has been with him throughout and I left him there. He [Lloyd George] says that he submitted proposals to you which are not acceptable to you, and that you have submitted proposals to him which are not acceptable to him. We then tried to arrange a compromise, but so far none is possible.[1]

Having persuaded Lloyd George to postpone taking action for at least twenty-four hours, Reading walked across Whitehall to Downing Street where he saw Eric Drummond, one of Asquith's private secretaries. With some help from Montagu, they worked out a

[1] S. D. Waley: *Edwin Montagu* (1964), p. 104.

compromise designed to leave Asquith as Prime Minister and President of the War Committee but at the same time let Lloyd George run it, which was in effect tantamount to running the War, subject to no more than Asquith's nominal control. Meanwhile Asquith had gone off to Walmer Castle in Kent for the week-end, and it was arranged that the compromise in the form of a memorandum was brought down to him there by Maurice Bonham-Carter, another of his private secretaries and also his son-in-law.

Sir Maurice Hankey, the Secretary of the War Cabinet, was also consulted, and he recorded in his diary that night how he had walked home with Reading and discussed the situation.

> We both agreed that the whole crisis is intolerable. There is really very little between them [Lloyd George and Asquith]. Everyone agrees that the methods of the War Committee call for reform. Everyone agrees that the Prime Minister possesses the best judgment. The only thing is that Lloyd George and Bonar Law insist that the former and not the Prime Minister must be the man to run the War. . . . The obvious compromise is for the Prime Minister to retain the Presidency of the War Committee with Lloyd George as Chairman, and to **give** Lloyd George a fairly free run for his money.

His private secretary's unexpected appearance at Walmer brought the Prime Minister hurrying back to London on the Sunday morning. Later that day he wrote: 'I was forced back by Bongie [Bonham-Carter] and Montagu and Rufus to grapple with a "Crisis" – this time with a very big C. The result is that I have spent much of the afternoon colloguing with Messrs Lloyd George and Bonar Law, and one or two minor worthies. The "Crisis" shows every sign of following its many predecessors to an early and unhonoured grave. But there were many wigs very nearly on the green.' The meeting with Lloyd George and Bonar Law seems to have resulted in a satisfactory understanding on the basis of the 'compromise'. The same evening Asquith dined with Montagu who persuaded him that in order to make matters clear to the public he should announce that the Government would be reconstructed. The announcement was in fact given to the Press from Montagu's house, and it appeared in the newspapers on Monday morning.

Unfortunately *The Times*, which carried the announcement in common with the other morning newspapers also contained a markedly hostile first 'leader'. Asquith erroneously attributed this to

Northcliffe on the basis of information supplied by Lloyd George, since it stressed the fact that the Prime Minister was not to be a working member of the new War Committee. (Actually the leading article had been written by the editor, Geoffrey Dawson, after consulting Carson, without any help from Northcliffe.) It caused Asquith to have second thoughts about the previous day's 'arrangement' with Lloyd George and Bonar Law and to doubt its feasibility. As he now told Lloyd George, 'unless the impression is at once corrected that I am being relegated to the position of an irresponsible spectator of the War, I cannot go on'.

After Lloyd George had made it clear that he could no longer serve under Asquith, even in a reconstructed Government, and that it was his duty 'to leave the Government in order to inform the people of the real condition of affairs, and to give him an opportunity, before it is too late, to save their native land from a disaster if the present methods are longer persisted in', Asquith immediately submitted his own resignation to the King, who thereupon sent for Bonar Law as the leader of the Conservatives. After Bonar Law had failed to form an all-party administration, in which Asquith refused to join, he advised the King to send for Lloyd George as 'the man whose leadership was most likely to win the War'. Lloyd George duly became Prime Minister on December 7, 1916. Asquith, who might have become Lord Chancellor had he wished, declined to serve under his former colleague. He moved across the floor of the House of Commons to the Opposition Front Bench, where he became the leader of the Liberals who did not join the new Coalition, such as McKenna and Walter Runciman, to be known as the Asquithian Liberals.

According to the second Lord Reading, his father's part in the negotiations during the political crisis which led to Lloyd George's becoming Prime Minister caused a temporary estrangement between himself and Asquith, who seems to have misunderstood Reading's role of honest broker. Immediately after the crisis was over, Edwin Montagu, Asquith's intimate friend and former Parliamentary Private Secretary, wrote: 'Northcliffe and McKenna worked hard against Asquith's and George's desire [to co-operate], and against men like Reading and myself, who throughout the time have tried to bring them closer together. They have won: we have failed: and the country in its direst hour has to avail itself of Lloyd George's capacity in the position where I do not think he is best used, and loses the unimpaired judgment, the firm courage, the unruffled, imperturbable steadiness of Asquith.'[1]

Some months later, by which time the United States had entered the War and Lloyd George was contemplating a further reconstruction of his Government, soundings were made to Asquith to come in. On this occasion Reading acted as the intermediary, having contrived to get himself invited to the country-house party which the Asquiths had at Whitsun. After Reading had departed, Asquith set down a memorandum of their conversations, which was preserved amongst his private papers. An interesting human document, hitherto unpublished, it records in forthright language what the ex-Premier really thought of his successor and why he could never serve under him, in spite of the temptations of the Lord Chancellor's official salary – £10,000 a year and a pension of £5,000 – to a man who though not indigent was far from being well off judged by the standards of the times.

Secret[2]

The Wharf,
[Sutton Courtney]
Whit Monday,
May 28, 1917

We came down here for Whitsuntide on Friday, and among our guests was the Lord Chief Justice, who arrived that evening and left this afternoon. I soon found out that he had come on a political mission – whether self-imposed, or inspired by others, or (as is more probable) a little of both, I cannot say. He twice sought me out for private confabulation on the subject.

The first time (on Saturday morning) he began by referring to McKenna's acceptance of a Bank Directorship from which he inferred that Holden the Chairman had marked McKenna out, with his own assent, as his successor. He (the Lord Chief Justice) and others had drawn the conclusion that this meant McKenna's abandonment, for the time being at any rate, of politics for business: and 'this' he remarked 'would remove a great obstacle in the way of possible reconstruction of the Government'.

I replied that he and his friends were living in a fool's paradise: that I was sure from what McKenna had said to me that he had no such intention: that he had accepted the directorship, partly for pecuniary reasons, partly to fill his time, and partly to familiarise himself with the routine of City business. I added that in my opinion McKenna

[1] Waley, p. 103.
[2] Asquith Papers (*Author's italics*).

(and also Runciman), whom I know to be almost equally obnoxious in some quarters, was an indispensable member of any really capable Administration.[1]

My friend was a little discouraged by this unpromising opening, but proceeded to throw out other feelers. Bonar Law, e.g., was anxious to get away from the Exchequer, Balfour would soon find the Foreign Office too much for him; the War Cabinet could well drop one or two of its present members, &c. &c. I said that if he wanted my opinion, without going into individual cases, I regarded the whole thing as a hopeless and unworkable experiment. A ridiculous and insupportable weight was cast upon two or three not over-competent men, while the administrators of most of the great departments were deprived of all responsibility, and even of any real knowledge of what was going on. Self-respecting statesmen could not be expected to take part in such a crazy adventure.

This (Monday) morning the Lord Chief Justice returned to the charge, with something more like a frontal attack. He said that he, and many others, regarded my active participation in the Government as essential, and he hinted that this was the view of the Prime Minister. I gathered that I could have almost any post I chose except that of the head of the Government.

I answered that I must use preferably plain language, since he had raised the subject. I was quite ready to go on giving the Government full support so long as they carried on the War in the proper spirit, and use my influence within my party, and in the country, in the same sense. *But he and others had better understand clearly, and at once, that under no conditions would I serve in a Government of which Lloyd George was the head. I had learned by long and close association to mistrust him profoundly. I knew him to be incapable of loyalty and lasting gratitude. I had always acknowledged, and did still, to the full his many brilliant and useful faculties, but he needed to have someone over him. In my judgment he had incurable defects, both of intellect and character, which totally unfitted him to be at the head.*

The Lord Chief Justice with rather a wry face acquiesced. To some further vaguely tentative overtures, I replied that I could not associate myself with what he called 'the counsel' of any Government unless I had supreme and ultimate authority.

It is hardly surprising that in the circumstances no further attempt should have been made to bring Asquith into the Government. Apart from his personal attitude towards Lloyd George, he could hardly

[1] McKenna had joined the board of the Midland Bank. Two years later he succeeded Sir Edward Holden as Chairman. He lost his seat in the House of Commons at the General Election in 1918 and never returned to politics.

have joined an administration from which such close political friends as McKenna and Runciman were excluded, although two of his former lieutenants did bring themselves to accept Lloyd George's invitation; these were Winston Churchill, who went to the Ministry of Munitions and Edwin Montagu who became Secretary of State for India.[1] As between Asquith and Lloyd George, Reading had always been on more intimate terms with the latter, although he did his best to maintain friendly relations with the ex-Prime Minister to whom after all he owed both his appointments as Law Officer and his appointment as Lord Chief Justice. However, as to Lloyd George's fitness to run the War in preference to Asquith, there was never any doubt in his mind. For the continuance of his extra-judicial contribution to the war effort, it was inevitable that Reading should now look to Lloyd George.

The confidential information on political subjects with which Reading supplied the new Prime Minister extended to the international field. On June 21, 1917, for example, he wrote to Lloyd George about King Alfonso XIII of Spain.

It has been brought to my notice from a very reliable source that the King of Spain's mental attitude to the Allies' cause is affected by the fear that success of this cause would add to the perils that beset monarchical institutions in his own country. This view is based in the main upon the idea that you desire to substitute Republican for Monarchical forms of Government and apparently irrespective of the freedom that exists under a limited monarchy.

I am assured that this plea is tending to affect his policy and that if it could be removed from his mind it would assist the cause in Spain.

Knowing your views it occurs to me that a few words from you may help to reassure him. I have the opportunity of passing this on so that they could be rapidly but *confidentially* transmitted to him. Do you see your way to sending them to me for this purpose?

What answer, if any, the Prime Minister returned to this letter, is not known. One would like to think that some appropriate message was sent to Madrid, if only on account of the work which the Spanish

[1] Lloyd George did not inform the Conservative members of the Coalition of these appointments in advance, an omission which annoyed Bonar Law. Lord Beaverbrook, in his *Men and Power* (pp. 136–37) reproduces a letter from Reading to Lloyd George dated July 22, 1917, confirming Bonar Law's reaction to the Churchill appointment in particular – 'his point being that he wasn't told it was to be made before it was actually given to the Press. He is not complaining of it but nevertheless is aggrieved. I thought it right to let you know.' The incident illustrates Lloyd George's autocratic methods as Prime Minister.

King had accomplished in negotiating the repatriation of Allied prisoners of war, including 8,000 British combatants from German and Austrian camps.

On August 18, 1917, the Lord Chief Justice wrote again, a little plaintively, to Lloyd George from the hotel in Harrogate where he had gone to take the waters:

> This is the first Long Vacation in which I have had no war work to do. I should be very glad to do anything that would be of service and would have liked to have been a member of the Committee to deal with the constitution of the House of Lords. Whilst I was Attorney-General, I had much to do with this matter and collected some information about Second Chambers. Can it be managed?

Unknown to Reading, strenuous efforts were being made by his friends on the other side of the Atlantic at that very moment to secure his services in a much more immediately important task than that which he had sought for himself in the field of parliamentary law reform. These efforts which had been exerted for more than a month were about to bear fruit. Within a week of writing to Lloyd George, he had received an invitation from the Prime Minister and the War Cabinet to go out to the United States as High Commissioner primarily to take charge of the delicate and complex Anglo-American financial relations which had recently developed and which were beyond the capacity of either the British Embassy or the special War Mission headed by Lord Northcliffe. He was also asked to survey the whole field of British representation in the United States in the light of the changed conditions occasioned by the War, and to report back to the Cabinet. In promptly accepting this assignment and agreeing to embark with his wife for the United States at a few days' notice, Reading was unaware of the prolonged endeavours which had been made to persuade the Government in London to consent to his appointment.

6

Northcliffe had arrived in New York early in June, 1917, with instructions from the War Cabinet to co-ordinate all British war activities in such matters as shipping, food supply, munitions and War Office and Admiralty business in the United States in order that 'all possible measures are taken to render America's resources available in the most effective manner and with the least possible delay'. The impact of Northcliffe's dynamic personality upon the American scene soon made itself felt, particularly by the use of propaganda designed to bring home to the American people the enormous expenditure in personnel, material and money by the Allies in Europe. 'I am glad that I came because I believe I am doing some good,' he wrote home after he had been in the country for several weeks. 'The work, however, exceeds anything I have ever done in my life. It requires labour, tact, versatility and the digestion of an ostrich. Business is conducted here entirely at golf clubs, restaurants and houses. Everything here is personal. Everything depends on personal relations with those you meet.' When he told people that the War was costing fifty million dollars a day, they were aghast. At the same time Northcliffe reported to Lloyd George that 'members of the Cabinet should understand that our attitude towards the United States Government is that of beggars. The majority of people with whom one comes in contact (though not the President or Colonel House) have no notion of the immense sacrifices we have made or are making. I do not know who was responsible for the concealment of this information in the early days of the War, but whoever it was he has rendered our position here, as beggars on behalf of the British nation, most difficult.'[1]

In addition to Great Britain's share of the American loan negotiated by Reading in 1915, which amounted to £50 millions, Britain owed America through Morgan's about £140 millions secured by collateral, which was liable to be sold wholly or in part in the event of the British Government's failure to repay the loan after due demand had been made. This so-called 'Demand Loan' was a constant source of worry both to the Government at home and Northcliffe on the spot, who feared that liquidation with the accompanying difficulty of selling large amounts of American securities would be disastrous to exchange and the credit of the British Government. 'If loan stops, war stops' was the constant theme of Northcliffe's cables home. Since the United States entered the War, Great Britain had advanced nearly £194 millions to her European Allies which included the financing of Russian purchases in the United States. 'This is a staggering amount and indicates the load Great Britain has been carrying for her Allies,' Colonel House had written to President

[1] Reginald Pound and Geoffrey Harmsworth: *Northcliffe* (1959), pp. 562, 565.

Wilson at the end of June. 'It seems to me that we should have some definite understanding with England as to what money she will need in the future and how far she can count on us. It seems absurd to be giving her comparatively small amounts, the frequent publication of which make a bad impression on our people. Would they not stand one large amount better than these lesser amounts constantly brought to their attention?'

A misunderstanding over the financing of the Russian purchases, which Britain mistakenly thought was to be taken over by the United States, produced an acute financial crisis threatening the liquidation of the 'Demand Loan' with disastrous consequences. This was averted at the last moment by House's intervention with William McAdoo, the Secretary of the U.S. Treasury, who agreed to accept the issue of short-term British Treasury bills with the sale of some collateral to meet the loan payments due on July 1. 'We seem on the verge of a financial disaster which would be worse than defeat in the field,' Balfour had cabled House on June 29 in alarm. 'If we cannot keep up exchange neither we nor our Allies can pay our dollar debts. We should be written off the gold basis, and purchases from the U.S.A. would immediately cease and the Allies' credit would be shattered.'

House noted in his diary on July 12:

Wiseman telephoned for nearly an hour explaining his conversation with McAdoo, and telling of the financial crisis which, for the time, has been averted. He thought McAdoo spoke too slightingly of the Allies, which was one cause of the friction existing between his Department and the Allies' representatives in this country. Wiseman said if McAdoo spoke to the others as he did to him, he did not wonder at their irritation. Asked for a specific example, he said that McAdoo complained that Great Britain, France, Russia and Italy were constantly coming to him for funds. He spoke as if they were a lot of beggars with their hats in their hands. . . .

Great Britain is sensitive because, for a century or more, she has held the first financial place in the world. Balfour's cable to me is a most extraordinary document and, when the history of these times is written, will be looked upon with amazement.

McAdoo now insisted that if the loans were to continue, the Allies must correlate their demands preferably through an English financial expert of high political standing. House was in complete agreement with this request. 'In my opinion,' he said, 'the best temporary solution would be to send Lord Reading or someone like him, who has both a financial and political outlook, and give him entire authority over financial questions, Northcliffe to retain charge of all commercial affairs. . . . What is really needed is someone who can dominate and compose the situation and who would have the entire confidence of the President.'

Before obtaining the approval of President Wilson's Secretary of the Treasury, House broached the subject with Northcliffe, who jumped at the idea.

> He [Northcliffe] spoke of Lloyd George's intimacy with the Lord Chief Justice, saying that Reading was 'the Colonel House of their Government'. We decided that the Lord Chief Justice would be a good man to come over and negotiate with McAdoo upon financial questions. We discussed many other names but finally rested on Lord Reading who was suggested by me. Before finally asking for Reading, it was agreed that I should see McAdoo and discuss it with him.[1]

Northcliffe immediately cabled London warmly endorsing the suggestion, repeating the request several times during the next few weeks. But his cables went unanswered. Afterwards Northcliffe noted: 'I cabled on July 13 and repeatedly at the expressed wish of the U.S. Government, who knew that he [Reading] had worked at the Treasury with George and McKenna, but he was not informed of my cables till August 23. The delay has cost us many millions of pounds.' Irked by the delay, House suggested to Colonel Sir William Wiseman, the brilliant young chief of British Intelligence in the United States, with whom he had recently established intimate relations, that he should go to London and carry the matter through. At first Wiseman demurred to the suggestion, since he knew no one in the Cabinet with the exception of Balfour. Nor had he ever met the Lord Chief Justice. However, he accepted an invitation to talk the matter over with Northcliffe at dinner in the country house Northcliffe had taken outside New York. There Northcliffe told Wiseman to sail by the next boat and calling for a secretary dictated a sheaf of letters of introduction to various Ministers and others. Sir Arthur Willert, *The Times* correspondent, who was present at the dinner also provided Wiseman with a letter to Geoffrey Dawson, asking him to lend all possible help. As they got into their motor-car to return to New York, Northcliffe shouted to Wiseman, 'Don't fail to bring Reading back

[1] House Papers; Diary, July 16, 1917.

with you!' Six weeks later Reading and Wiseman landed together in New York.

At this time Sir William Wiseman, tenth baronet, who derived his title from a creation of King James I, was only thirty-two. Since his arrival in the United States eighteen months previously, after being gassed in Flanders and invalided out of the Army, he had carved out a unique position for himself, not only as head of all British secret intelligence, security and counter-espionage operations, but also as the intimate friend of Colonel House, whose private secretary he virtually became, as well as the trusted confidant of the President who gave him free entry to the White House and opened his mind to him as he did with no other foreigner. Wiseman had his own codes and ciphers for communicating with his intelligence headquarters in London, and both House and Wilson had already begun to use him as a confidential channel of communication with the British political high-ups in preference to the stuffy and neurotic Spring Rice in the Washington Embassy. Wiseman was gifted with a remarkable political sagacity, and it was this characteristic, as House was quick to grasp, which particularly appealed to the President, besides a common liberal viewpoint. The gift equally impressed Northcliffe when he met Wiseman for the first time and, after Wiseman had gone, made the obvious remark that he was 'well named'. ('He is young, alert and knows these people well.')

While Wiseman was still on the high seas on his way to London with the object of bringing Reading back with him, Northcliffe cabled to Winston Churchill:

> I have long believed war can only be won from here. The position is most difficult and delicate. Sir William Wiseman, Chief of our Military Intelligence here, should reach England in a few days. He is the only person, English or American, who has access to Wilson and House at all times. He had an hour and a half with Wilson last week and a day with House. The Administration is entirely run by these two men. Wilson's power is absolute and House is a wise assistant. Both are pro-English.

In the course of a visit he paid to London later in the same year, House told the Foreign Secretary how highly he thought of Wiseman. 'I told Mr Balfour of the help Sir William was to all of us, and to what degree he had my confidence,' House noted at the time. 'I had no secrets from him, and he has access to all my papers with about as much freedom as any of my secretaries.' A little later, House wrote in his diary:

> I have given Wiseman immense leverage by putting him in touch with the President and with the leaders of his own country. They do not quite understand why I have done this, but it is because of his ability, loyalty and trustworthiness. He has qualities which are rarely met with in one man.

During his month's stay in England Wiseman was sustained by a steady stream of telegrams from Northcliffe to the Prime Minister and members of the War Cabinet. Nevertheless he encountered the greatest difficulty in convincing the Cabinet and the other interested authorities of the delicacy of Anglo-American relations and also in persuading them of the importance of sending a man of Reading's calibre to Washington. On August 9, Northcliffe's brother Harold (Lord Rothermere), whom Northcliffe had asked to make independent soundings about Reading, reported that the Prime Minister was 'quite afraid to utilize his services' and that Lloyd George 'fears a revival of the Marconi allegations'. ('I shall be surprised if you see Reading in America.') Three days later, Wiseman cabled an interim progress report to Northcliffe:

> I have now discussed the American situation with the King, Prime Minister, Bonar Law, Balfour, Milner, Carson, constantly keeping in touch with Geoffrey Dawson whose advice has been invaluable.
> My conclusions are as follows: The Government realizes every day more clearly the importance of the United States and are coming to the view that she must be treated as our most important ally. There is, however, need for this to be kept constantly before the Cabinet owing to the great distance of America and to the fact that members of the Government have little personal knowledge of Washington affairs.

That the approval of Reading's appointment continued to hang fire appears to have been partly due to Lloyd George's hesitation for the reason mentioned and perhaps still more to the opposition of Bonar Law, the Conservative Chancellor of the Exchequer, whose permanent officials at the Treasury wanted someone from their own ranks rather than an 'outsider', and who himself felt that, if a politician should be sent, then it should be a Conservative in preference to a Liberal. Meanwhile Northcliffe kept up the pressure. ('I am semiofficially informed that delay about Reading is causing irritation.') Sir Arthur Willert, *The Times* Washington correspondent, happened to be with Northcliffe when a message came through from Wiseman in London reiterating the fact that 'the Treasury does not understand the American situation'. Willert later recalled Northcliffe's comment at the time: 'They don't want to understand it because to understand it would be to admit that London is now second fiddle to Washington.'[1] With his usual acumen Northcliffe had got to the real heart of the matter in a single sentence.

Finally, on August 24, in response to a message from London relayed through Northcliffe asking House whether it was essential that Reading should come, House answered categorically: 'Yes, I think it is essential to have Reading or someone like him.' On the same day Bonar Law told Wiseman that the matter had at last been agreed and that he would ask Reading to undertake the mission. 'I do not know Reading personally,' Wiseman cabled Northcliffe with this welcome news, 'but dare say his sound impartial judgment will help on general questions besides finance, and on his return he will be able to give sound advice to the Cabinet.' Wiseman went on to suggest that Northcliffe should cable Reading urging him to accept and to discuss the matter with Wiseman. 'I believe his appointment will be another step to better co-operation and making Washington real war headquarters,' he added. '*Cabinet actually thought Wilson might be persuaded to come here!*'[2]

Rothermere to Northcliffe

London, August 27, 1917. I hear now that it is most likely Reading will go to America. I happened to meet Bonar Law at Margate last week-end, and he told me that the American Government as well as yourself were urging that he should be sent. Although Bonar Law did not say so, I conclude that there is going to be a change in the Embassy at Washington. Why do you not suggest Reading for the job? He is dying to get away from the Bench.[3]

Before he sailed, Reading spent a couple of days with Lloyd George at Great Walstead, a house near the pretty Sussex village of Lindfield, which Lord Riddell had taken at the Prime Minister's suggestion, 'so that he may get some short holidays and at the same time keep in touch with his work'. Also staying in the house besides Riddell were Sir Maurice Hankey, the Secretary of the War Cabinet, and Philip Kerr (later Marquess of Lothian), Lloyd George's Private Secretary.

[1] Sir Arthur Willert: *The Road to Safety* (1952), p. 119.
[2] House, Vol. III, p. 123, author's italics.
[3] Pound and Harmsworth, p. 576.

H

Reading asked that 'some knowledgeable official' who was *au fait* with the problems of the War Cabinet should go with him to America. At first the Prime Minister suggested that Hankey should go, but eventually decided that he could not spare him and left it to Hankey to nominate someone. Hankey thereupon selected Lt.-Colonel (later Sir) Ernest Swinton, D.S.O., the Assistant Secretary of the War Cabinet and Committee of Imperial Defence, who was the inventor of the tank, besides being the author of *The Green Curve* and other lively war stories under the pseudonym of 'Ole-Luk-Oie'.

According to Hankey, the Prime Minister was 'in a peevish, changeable mood, worried by the shocking weather and afflicted with neuralgia. . . . To add to our troubles the wind broke the telephone lines, and I had to walk with Riddell two or three times to the telegraph office at Lindfield. . . . All day long Lloyd George was in a most capricious mood and Kerr and I drafted about ten letters from Ll.G. for Reading to take to President Wilson, but before we had finished one draft he would invariably get a "brainwave" and want a new one.' The letter further redrafted by Kerr was considerably toned down by Hankey, since 'Lloyd George had insisted on his [Kerr's] putting in all his complaints against the military management of the War; his protests against Western Front policy; his desire to knock out Austria and Turkey; and a new, and not very well thought-out scheme for an Allied Council and General Staff in Paris to direct the War.'[1]

Reading and his staff were due to embark on the morning of September 4. Consequently a special meeting of the War Cabinet was held after dinner on the previous evening, for which Haig was specially brought over from France, to approve the much redrafted letter for the American President, which had now become, in Hankey's words, 'in the main . . . a carefully worded plea to President Wilson to take part in the Allied Councils'. The important communication was then entrusted to Reading's safe hand for delivery at the White House.

Acting on Wiseman's suggestion, Northcliffe cabled Reading at some length, again emphasizing (1) 'that the Americans have no conception of our sacrifices, in men, ships, and money'; (2) 'that they are as yet unaccustomed to the huge figures of war finance', and expressing his anxiety that 'we should get a firm contract with the United States Government for the regular allocation, for the duration

[1] Hankey, Vol. II, pp. 694–96.

of the War, of the monies we require.' He added the following sentences:

It is obvious that our Cabinet has no conception of the situation here, especially of the American attitude towards us, which is now that of the rich relation towards the poor. The situation during the rest of the war will require the most delicate handling. Whenever we raise any objections, which we do with the utmost tact, we are told that unless we comply with the suggestions made loans will not be forthcoming. The financial supplies are doled out in driblets. Each driblet is advertised in 2,000 newspapers.

Reading replied that he was 'much impressed' with Northcliffe's telegram and that he was preparing to leave within the next week. He added that he had seen Wiseman who would be accompanying him on the voyage. He himself would hold the rank of High Commissioner.

Meanwhile Colonel House expressed keen delight when he heard the news of the Reading mission. 'There is no one so well equipped for the work in hand,' he wrote of the approaching visitor. 'A great jurist, he possesses a knowledge of finance which is at the moment essential if order is to be brought out of the present chaos. He has a fine diplomatic touch which will ensure against unnecessary friction. The jangled nerves of many high-strung individuals will be soothed by this imperturbable negotiator. He has also the confidence of the British Prime Minister as perhaps no other man has, and that in itself is a compelling reason for his appointment to such a mission.'

7

Reading and his wife and the rest of the party arrived safely in New York during the second week of September, 1917. Besides Swinton and Wiseman he was accompanied by the brilliant young economist John Maynard Keynes, then working in the British Treasury, where he had become head of the department dealing with external finance at the age of thirty-three. On reaching Washington, the Readings established themselves in a small house in Sixteenth Street, which the Embassy had found for them and provided with an adequate staff for the purpose of entertaining. Later they moved to a larger place in Massachusetts Avenue. Keynes wrote as soon as they were settled in: 'I live in a small but comfortable private house with Lord and Lady Reading, both of whom I like immensely.'

Sir Arthur Willert dined there with his wife a few days after the Readings' arrival in Washington. He afterwards recalled the picture of their host 'with his dark aquiline face, which would have made up well as that of an elderly Hamlet, graceful body, strong shoulders, delicate sensitive hands toying with a chicken wing, sipping gingerly from a glass of good claret, gently drawing them out, elegant in evening dress – a tail-coat, though the dinner was small and the evening warm.' Lady Willert's comment when they left was 'A lovely antique, a piece of ivory, the conventional host of another century.'

Yet, if there was an old-world courtesy about his manners, there was nothing antiquated about his methods as a negotiator and advocate, in which he outshone Northcliffe. Several American bankers described him to Spring Rice, the British Ambassador, as 'exceedingly adroit'. Indeed his reputation for cleverness was so high that a good deal of anxiety was expressed, according to Spring Rice, lest 'he should put one over on Mr McAdoo', the U.S. Secretary of the Treasury.[1] But he did not employ such tactics in his negotiations; his methods were always candid and straightforward, as Mr McAdoo himself acknowledged. However, Reading took great pains in preparing a 'case' to argue, just as he had done in his days at the Bar. In his excellent account of Anglo-American relations at this period, *The Road to Safety*, Sir Arthur Willert has compared and contrasted the High Commissioner's methods in negotiation with those of Northcliffe:[2]

> Advanced middle age had left his energy unimpaired. As a nego-
> tiator and advocate he was Northcliffe's superior. Northcliffe's methods
> were pyrotechnical, and the fuses did not always go off; he relied upon
> the inspiration of the moment and his own forcefulness, rather than
> upon preparation. Reading was always perfectly prepared. He had the
> great lawyer's power of mastering a case quickly, unravelling its
> complications and marshalling in the right order the arguments most
> likely to impress the other side. Sometimes I was called in to assist in
> this preparation where politics were concerned, and in my mind's eye
> there is still the picture of Reading pacing softly about the room or
> standing in front of the mantelpiece, deciding how to start some con-

[1] Sir Cecil Spring Rice: *Letters and Friendships*, ed. Stephen Gwynn (1929), Vol. II, p. 410.

[2] op cit., p. 123.

versation, how his interlocutor would be likely to meet his presentation of the case, what his own answer would be, and so on.

I used also to think that the fact that he was a Jew and Chief Justice of England helped considerably. It 'spotlighted' his ability, and British open-mindedness. It impressed Americans that a Jew should plead the British cause with such sincerity and feeling.

His first official call was upon McAdoo, who was to place it on record that Reading 'saw the problem in the large' and that 'it was a great relief to me to have a man of his fine ability, common sense and good judgment with whom to discuss the complicated questions that were constantly arising. . . . Our relations were soon established on a plane of complete candour and confidence.' Besides the reduction of the Demand Loan, an immediate problem was posed by the imminent breakdown of British purchases in Canada. Hitherto the United States had insisted that the American loans must be applied exclusively to the purchase of goods inside the United States. Reading now asked McAdoo to make an exception in the case of essential purchases such as wheat, meat and munitions. By the time Reading had his first interview with President Wilson in the White House, on September 20, after a somewhat irritating delay, the proposed arrangement had been agreed in principle.

Diary of Colonel House

September 20, 1917. There has been a great to-do in Washington over the failure of the British Embassy and the State Department to make an early engagement for Lord Reading to call on the President. The fault lies partly with the State Department and partly with Spring Rice. Reading is furious and got Wiseman, who was in Washington yesterday, to ask my good offices. I telephoned Frank Polk [Assistant Secretary of State] and the matter was straightened out in good order; in fact, it was in process before I telephoned.

Lord Reading to Sir William Wiseman[1]

1008 16th Street,
Washington, D.C.
September 21, 1917

Please thank Colonel House for having arranged the interview with the President. I was with him for half-an-hour – he received me cordially and we had a satisfactory conversation getting at once to essentials. I was struck by the promptness with which he discarded [the] fringe and at once went to the kernel of things. . . .

[1] Wiseman Papers.

The President received the suggestion in general terms that we were anxious that there should be a more thorough co-operation of America with us in a more sympathetic manner than I had expected, doubtless as a result of his interviews with our friend [House]. . . .

I was very pleased with the interview.

Diary of Colonel House

September 22. Wiseman brought a letter from Lord Reading telling him of his interview with the President and expressing satisfaction with what the President had said. Reading gave me the credit of arranging the interview so promptly, which I did not deserve, and also for the cordial manner in which he was received, which, perhaps I did deserve. He wishes to see me at once, and Sir William telephoned him if he would take the 12.30 today I would see him upon the arrival of his train. . . .[1]

Strangely enough the larger part of his time was taken up by a discussion of his troubles with Sir Cecil Spring Rice and proposed remedies. . . . Reading feels he is in a precarious position with Spring Rice working against him at every turn, and in a perfectly unbalanced way. We agreed it was best for him to ask his Government to recall Spring Rice, giving the reason Lord Reading's presence here and the consequent possibility of a vacation for the Ambassador, and also the desire of the Government to confer upon him certain honours because of the United States' entrance into the War on the side of the Allies.

I spoke to Reading of the narrow escape the Allies had in keeping back their true condition from us. We went in barely in time to save them. This, I thought, was because they had not trusted us. I recalled to him that I urged them a year and a half ago to let us know when their condition became serious. He also recalled that I had tried to get them to allow us to intervene for peace, promising to side with the Allies in the event Germany would not consent to reasonable terms. Reading condoned their action, or lack of action, by saying that they had been totally misinformed as to conditions here; that while I had told them the truth, everyone else was giving a distorted view, particularly as to the President's mind, and they feared to act. This comes again to Spring Rice's door, for he has been the backbone of misinformation. Page has been an able second. Both of them took their views from enemies of the President and I think became unconscious enemies of their two countries.

Reading is to write a despatch to his Government on the question of

[1] Northcliffe asked Reading to stay with him in his house outside New York, but Reading politely declined. 'I thought it would be better not,' he told Wiseman, 'as House and I would want to meet and talk alone.' He therefore asked Wiseman to engage rooms for him in the Plaza Hotel.

recalling Spring Rice, and is to submit it to me for approval. We agreed that he, Reading, is to remain here as long as it was possible for him to do so consistent with his position as Lord Chief Justice, and that they would send Grey, Cecil or Asquith, preferably in the order named. Asquith, he thought, would be an admirable selection were it not for Mrs Asquith, good woman as she is. There was danger that her caustic tongue would set Washington by the ears before she had been there a month.[1] Cecil he considered the best of the Tories, even though he was a narrow churchman.

A few days later, House wrote to Lloyd George:

The coming of the Lord Chief Justice has already resulted in good. Lord Northcliffe is helping to make his visit a success, and I am sure your sending him will be justified.

About the same time Wiseman gave his opinion to Sir Eric Drummond, who had become Balfour's Principal Private Secretary at the Foreign Office:

There are serious financial problems unsolved, but Reading is approaching them in the right spirit and is a very acceptable person to all the Administration. House as usual is very helpful, and I believe we are now tackling the situation properly. While I cannot say that there is any popular enthusiasm for the War, there is a very solid determination to carry on with all the resources of the country until the German military power is crushed. The position of the President remains very strong. Feeling towards the British is improving. . . .

A week or so later Wiseman reported that Reading had made:

. . . the very best impression on McAdoo and all others concerned. It is now admitted that the British Treasury is properly represented for the first time, and our other Allies have had to recognize that he has immediately become the dominant figure in finance.

This opinion was enthusiastically endorsed by Northcliffe who cabled the Prime Minister from New York on September 30:

Reading is working indefatigably, amidst great difficulties. He was able to obtain fifty million dollars for Canadian wheat, which really was an inroad on the basic principle that every cent of money advanced to the Allies should be spent in the United States.

[1] House also described the ex-Prime Minister's wife at this time as having 'perhaps the most irritating personality in all the world'. House Papers (Diary, November 13, 1917).

This achievement of Reading is in my opinion one that could not be brought about by anyone not possessed of Reading's ability, charm and tact in handling these difficult people. Reading, by his frankness in concealing nothing from them and by his sympathetic understanding that they are harassed day by day by the Allies for money and also by politicians and Press, will, I am convinced, be able to achieve all that is humanly possible.

Reading dined with House in New York the same evening. 'I have confidence in Reading, as he seems to have in me,' House noted in his diary, 'and it is not difficult to open our minds to one another.' House added that Reading was sending a message to the Prime Minister and Balfour 'practically demanding that they bring Spring Rice home, or relieve him, Reading, of further duty'. House used to take Reading driving in Central Park, which they found a convenient and unobtrusive way of continuing their conversations. 'I find Reading a calm, clear-minded statesman with more of the political than the judicial mind,' House noted after one of these motor drives. 'These talks with him have been of much value to me, because I have become saturated with the British official point of view.' And again: 'Reading has rather a quaint vocabulary and phraseology which I find attractive. He remarked that it was a curious situation here with Wiseman and myself really directing British policy in the United States. He said the British Government was accepting Wiseman's advice, knowing that I was advising him.'[1]

While Reading was able to tide over a critical situation and secure the necessary credits for Britain, he was conscious of the increasing difficulty in obtaining supplies for the Allies as the demands of the American service departments became greater for their own requirements. As he expressed it in a memorandum on the whole supply question which he wrote for the War Cabinet in London, 'the growing lack of co-ordination between the programme of the Administration here and the programme of the Allies is probably, on every ground, the biggest question in front of us. But I have some reason to believe that the matter is engaging the attention of the Administration and I shall take any further opportunity of emphasizing to the President the risks, lest hastily considered orders by United States War Departments spoil our efficiency before they themselves are ready.'

[1] House Papers: Diary, October 2, 3, 1917.

Lord Reading to Prime Minister

1008 16th Street,
Washington, D.C.
September 27, 1917

I am satisfied that the Administration is absolutely sound for the war, in spite of suggestions to the contrary which have reached me from some quarters. I am also satisfied that their power and authority is very considerable. During the past three weeks they have been getting their measures through Congress with really remarkable success and political opposition has been very quiet. There is plenty of latent opposition which a mistake would bring to the surface. The labour situation has threatening elements in it.

In many respects the Administration is much ahead of the country. It is not right to assume therefore that they have quite a free hand or, when they act in a manner which from our point of view is ill advised, that this is not the result of their hands being forced by influences of opinion the importance of which has escaped our attention. It is my strong feeling that we ought to trust the Administration, and support them, and to avoid any act which would give a handle to their detractors.[1]

At his first meeting with the President, Reading had presented Lloyd George's personal letter to Wilson. The letter contained the British Prime Minister's views, expressed in the cautious language of the Cabinet Secretary, as to the comparative failure of the Allies during the past year; this was attributed mainly to the military collapse of Russia and also to the fact that the direction of Allied military operations lacked what Lloyd George called 'real unity'. He advocated the concentration of attacks upon the front of Germany's allies, since that was the weakest part of the enemy line. ('They are weak not only militarily but politically. They are also very anxious for peace, so that a comparatively small success might produce far-reaching results.') He went on to state that in his opinion 'it will be necessary to establish some kind of Allied Joint Council, with permanent military and probably naval and economic staffs attached to work out the plans for the Allies, for submission to the several Governments concerned.'

Consequently he urged that the United States should be represented at the conferences of the Allies, not merely because the decisions made there would vitally affect the American Army in Europe, but because 'the presence at the deliberations of the Allies of independent

[1] Wiseman Papers.

minds, bringing fresh views, unbiased by previous views, might be of immense value in helping us to free ourselves from the ruts of the past.' The appearance of the vanguard of the American Army had produced a tremendous effect, especially in France. 'I would ask you to consider, therefore, whether it is not of the utmost importance that the purpose and ideals as well as the wisdom of America should be manifested in the Council Chamber as well as the battlefield if we are to preserve unshaken through this difficult winter season the resolution of the Allies to go on with the War until Prussian military despotism over Germany is broken, by revolution from within or defeat from without.'

At the same time, Lloyd George had sent a letter to Colonel House by the hand of Wiseman. 'I think it is essential to the cause of the Allies that a representative of the United States of the first rank should come over here officially as soon as possible to take part in the deliberations of their future plans of campaign,' wrote the Prime Minister. 'Needless to say it would be a source of the utmost satisfaction to us if you were to come yourself.'

The President's initial reaction was against sending American representatives to sit in the councils of the Allies because he felt, as Wiseman put it, that 'the United States had not enough experience in the war'. However as a result of the information given to him by House through Wiseman and Reading, Wilson changed his mind and decided that the United States should be represented. At first he thought of sending House as special representative to stay in Europe until the end of the War. However, on further reflection, the President decided that there should be no permanent American Commission in Europe, but that House should go over for a short visit, taking with him representatives of the different supply boards and of the Army and Navy, who would be able to discuss with their 'opposite numbers' in England and France the technique of co-ordination.

Thus the matter was settled in principle by the time Reading had his next interview with the President, on October 12. House was present, and noted in his diary how the meeting went off:

October 13, 1917. Reading came at noon and remained for an hour. . . . Reading knew what the President intended to propose, and the President knew what Reading expected. He seemed pleased with the President's reception. I walked to the door with him and he asked me to meet him at five o'clock at the British Embassy for a further conference.

At this conference, I definitely decided that I would attend the Allied War Council. Reading was pleased and offered me his house in London. He also offered to cable his Government asking them to send the *Mauretania* or *Olympic* to Halifax to take me over.

I have made it clear to both the British and French Governments that we wish to go in the simplest way possible. There must be no banquets, no receptions, but merely conferences to transact business as speedily as possible.

October 18. Reading is restless at being left here while I am in Europe. I think he believes there will be no way for him to get decisions, should an impasse occur. When I am here he feels that a way out is always at hand, and I think he is nervous over the thought of my leaving. He does not wish his mission to be a failure. The truth is, in getting the President to send me to the Allied War Council, he has accomplished the main purpose of his visit. He desires to return to England with me.

Strangely enough, after Reading left, Northcliffe came in. He spoke of 'what a charming and capable man Reading is'. I wondered whether he felt this or whether he did it for a purpose. He knows the people I like, and he has never yet failed to say a word in their praise.

As soon as he had received confirmation from the Foreign Office, and seen Robert Lansing, the American Secretary of State, Reading wrote formally to the President.

> 2315 Massachusetts Avenue,
> Washington, D.C.
> 15th October, 1917

Dear Mr President,

I communicated the substance of our recent conversation to my Government and have today received a reply which I thought right to bring immediately to your notice.

I am now authorized by the French and British Governments to express their earnest hope that it will prove possible for your Government to send a representative to Europe to discuss important military and other questions of vital interest to cobelligerents. My Government has learnt with the utmost gratification that the invitation is likely to receive your favourable consideration.

The British Ambassador and I waited upon the Secretary of State this morning and conveyed this message to him. I understand that the French Ambassador, as the doyen of the Diplomatic Corps, will without delay, present the formal invitation to the Secretary of State.

My Government is also extremely pleased to learn that it may hope for the invaluable presence of Colonel House as the representative of the United States.

> I am, Dear Mr President,
>
> Yours sincerely,
>
> Reading.

About the same date Wiseman sent Drummond an interesting assessment of Reading's position as High Commissioner:

> Reading has made an excellent impression here, but there are one or two difficulties in the situation. In order to avoid hurting the feelings of Spring Rice the full importance of Reading's mission and credentials were not made public. I now think that this was a mistake. The impression got about in Washington (whether by accident or design I do not know) that he was nothing more than a Treasury representative; indeed that he only came out to settle the question of the Morgan overdraft. He has found it rather difficult to rectify this. . . .

It was, indeed, rather difficult. Reading's mission had shown the need for the several branches of British representation in the United States to work under one supreme head to avoid petty jealousies and overlapping or duplication of functions. Now there were three representatives, all outstanding in their different spheres, and none altogether happy at the presence of the others. Spring Rice, the Ambassador, disliked Northcliffe and his propaganda activities; as a professional diplomatist, he also resented Reading as another 'outsider'. At the same time Northcliffe was never at ease with the Ambassador and made no secret of his intention to get him shifted. Reading also found Spring Rice unhelpful, and while his relations with Northcliffe were outwardly friendly he never trusted him as much as appeared on the surface. On the other hand, it is true that Northcliffe acknowledged Reading's negotiations in Washington as 'a victory of a magnitude financial and political that will one day be realized – I cannot yet reveal it.' Nevertheless the Press magnate saw to it that his newspapers gave himself the lion's share of publicity. This is confirmed by the confidential reports from Colonel Arthur Murray, M.P., Assistant Military Attaché in the Washington Embassy, to the Foreign Office. Murray, who was a brother of the Master of Elibank, maintained friendly relations with both Reading and Northcliffe as well as with Wiseman.

Lt.-Colonel Arthur Murray, M.P. to Sir Eric Drummond

British Embassy,
Washington, D.C.
October 23, 1917

Northcliffe, whilst in conversation and so on, giving Rufus every credit for what the latter is doing appears determined that he (Rufus) shall not be allowed to eclipse Northcliffe in the eyes of the public. Northcliffe, in other words is quite willing and anxious that Rufus should continue his good work, but in the eyes of the public Rufus's work must be in a sense subsidiary to the work of Northcliffe and Rufus must not be allowed to come out too much into the limelight.

Two things have happened which have brought this to my notice, and Rufus is conscious of it, and has talked to me about it. *You* of course will understand that he talks freely to me as an old friend, and has not and would not speak to anyone else here about it. Nor, I think, would he like it 'passed around', and I pass it on to you only in order that you may be fully seized of the *personal* situation.

As to the actual methods: Rufus's recent visit to Canada where as you know he was the 'guest of honour', and pulled off a 'big thing', was announced in *The Times* (London) and the Press over here in which Northcliffe has a 'pull' as 'a visit to Canada of Lord Northcliffe accompanied by Treasury Officials *and* Lord Reading!' Secondly: Rufus addressed a most successful meeting in New York last week for the Liberty Loan. There was no report of it in the *New York Times*. In nosing about quietly to discover the reason for this I found that Northcliffe had kept out (by the means at his hand) any report of the meeting, because, as he said to my informant, he thought that too much publicity would harm the work that Rufus is doing!

It is difficult to convey by letter a personal situation such as this without perhaps creating the impression that there is at the same time a sense of antagonism between the two. This is not so, though *privately* Rufus is a bit sore. I feel sure you will understand the situation – and you ought to know it. I have said nothing of this to anyone – *not even to Wiseman.* . . .

In my humble opinion, Rufus in pulling off the 'War Council' has achieved one of the biggest things of the War. The vital importance of the immediate allocation of shipping to various urgent needs over a long period ahead impresses itself upon one more and more every day. A section of public opinion here is out to send as large a number of American troops across as quickly as possible without regard to other (and Allied particularly) demands for shipping. If there is sent across a larger number of troops than ought, having regard to other urgent requirements, to be sent across, the demands for shipping to keep and maintain them there will grow, and the situation *vis-à-vis* Allied necessities would become acute.

November 1. I had a long talk with Rufus yesterday, and saw Northcliffe immediately afterwards. It will be quite clear to *your* mind that there can be no free, frank and open discussion between the two as to any possible new arrangements, and Rufus has *not* divulged to Northcliffe what is in his mind. I cannot of course say what may happen on the voyage across! Perhaps the rolling waves of the Atlantic may induce confidences, but I doubt it!

. . . You will doubtless hear from Northcliffe himself what place he would like in any rearrangement! So far as I can gather, he would like to be the supreme British head of the new organization whatever be its form.

Looking ahead it seems to me that the successful issue of the War will in a large measure depend on the proper control, management and handling of the situation out here. For the supreme control you may have a better man than Rufus – if so I hope you will send him. But I much wonder whether you can find a man more suited in every way for the job.[1]

8

Reading, Northcliffe and Wiseman arranged to travel to England on the same ship at the beginning of November, 1917, so as to be in London with the House mission which sailed a few days previously. Before they left, Reading cabled to the Prime Minister on the impossibility of providing sufficient shipping to carry the intended number of United States troops and maintain them in the field at the same time as furnishing the supply requirements of the Allies.

General view is that Allies must determine which is the more urgent need, soldiers or supplies, and Ministers say that the matter must be discussed at conference in Europe. . . . For your consideration I suggest that great importance should be attached to political value throughout different States of soldiers fighting in Europe and that every effort should be made to maintain United States programme even if it be at the expense of some supplies.[2]

At Northcliffe's urgent request, a melodramatic exit was arranged for him by Wiseman which his two travelling companions did not

[1] Lloyd George Papers. A. C. Murray: *At Close Quarters* (1946) pp. 5–6.
[2] Lloyd George Papers.

share. He had his luggage labelled for Canada, went to the station pretending to catch the train for Ottawa, then was smuggled in a police car on board the *St Paul* in New York Harbour. 'The secret service people think that if the Germans knew that Reading and I are on the *St Paul*,' he remarked at the time, 'efforts will be made to catch us by submarine, or put infernal machines in the coal!' However, all went well and the *St Paul* safely made the crossing in nine days. Also, contrary to Colonel Murray's expectation, the Atlantic rollers did inspire confidences between the two men. According to Northcliffe's official biographers, Northcliffe talked more than once with Reading on the homeward voyage about the enhanced importance of the Washington embassy as a result of America's entry into world politics. 'There was need to bring all the British activities in the United States, political, diplomatic, financial, under one directing head. Reading knew that he was likely to be asked to take over the supreme responsibility. He was hesitant about accepting it. Northcliffe strongly urged him to do so. Reading's success at Washington could not be questioned; but he was undoubtedly aware of strong prejudice against him, and also against his German-Jewish wife, which did not exist in England, and he may have discovered that while McAdoo had welcomed his coming, the President had not shown the same interest.'[1]

Chesterfield House, with its art treasures and fine library, a few doors from Reading's home in Curzon Street, was placed at the service of Colonel House, and Wiseman saw to it that the central heating, telephones and other facilities were up to American standards. Both Northcliffe and Reading called on House the day after their arrival. They were somewhat depressed by the War news as well they might be, since Italy had been virtually eliminated by the defeat at Caporetto by the Austrians, while in Petrograd Lenin and the Bolsheviks had taken over the Government from Kerensky and were about to sue for peace. House noted in his diary, (November 13):

> Strangely enough Reading, just as he did the last time I saw them in New York, followed Northcliffe. I saw him only for a moment, but suggested that he help in every way possible to bring about a better coordination. Reading's influence with Lloyd George is greater perhaps than any other man's in England, and it is on this I am playing. Both Reading and Northcliffe are to scout round for a day or two and gather what news of importance seems worth bringing to me.

[1] Pound and Harmsworth, p. 590.

Two days later House recorded with pleasure that Lloyd George was going to preside at a meeting of British and American service and technical experts at No. 10 Downing Street.

It is to take place in the same room in which the British Cabinet declared war against the United States under the administration of Lord North.

'It is planned to urge Lloyd George to help bring about co-ordination in our working forces,' House noted the same day, 'and we have picked Lord Reading to see that it is properly done.' He went on to describe how this arrangement was implemented when Reading visited him at Chesterfield House.

I called Reading's attention to the importance of Lloyd George working cordially with me. If he did, I thought his Government could not be overthrown. In saying this I intended a covert threat which I think Reading caught.

At this stage the Prime Minister and Wiseman came in. George greeted Reading with enthusiasm, saying how delighted he was that he should have happened to be here at this time. He was just the man he wished to be present, for he had something very disagreeable to ask me. I marvelled that a man of George's ability should undertake so patent a farce.

He made a long speech urging me to consent to a postponement of the Inter-Allied Conference. I listened quietly, for Reading had told me in advance of his coming what he would say, and I had told Reading that I would consent to postpone the conference for a week but not longer. Reading and I had talked it out, so all the arguments George gave were repetitions. Because of the Italian situation, because of the lack of a French Ministry, it would be futile to have a conference before the two situations composed themselves.

George wished to postpone it until a more distant date but I insisted upon naming the 29th of November and this was finally agreed upon. . . .

I now have both Reading and Northcliffe, Lloyd George's closest friends, working to force the Prime Minister to coordinate the work we have in hand. Northcliffe delights in this. He is as eager as a hound on a trail. Today he refused another offer from George to become a member of the Cabinet.

On November 16, House reported to the President:

Northcliffe has been splendid. . . . With this combination of Wiseman, Reading and Northcliffe, things are now being accomplished with more rapidity than I ever experienced here. . . . I cannot tell you how splendidly and cordially the Commission are working together, and what a fine impression they have made here.

The same evening Lady Reading gave a dinner-party for Colonel and Mrs House in Curzon Street, the other guests being the Prime Minister and his wife and Sir William and Lady Wiseman. After the ladies had left the table and the port was passed round, House endeavoured with little success to pin down Lloyd George on the subject of Britain's war aims. A few days later, when the same company dined at Chesterfield House, he had better results.

George and I did practically all the talking, Reading as usual being the listener. . . . What Great Britain desires are the African colonies, both East and West; an independent Arabia, under the suzerainty of Great Britain; Palestine to be given to the Zionists under British or, if desired by us, under American control; an independent Armenia and the internationalization of the Straits. . . .

Reading had been prepared to return to his duties on the Bench, but it was now announced that he would continue to assist the British War Cabinet on financial matters and in that capacity would attend the Conference of the newly created Supreme War Council, which had been convened in Paris at the end of November. Before leaving for Paris, he was summoned to Buckingham Palace, a pleasant surprise arranged by Lloyd George, who had asked the King to advance him a step in the peerage in recognition of his services in America. The King was quite agreeable, but it was with some reluctance that he made Northcliffe a Viscount at the same time.[1] The successful High Commissioner was thereupon created Earl of Reading, also becoming Viscount Erleigh, so that his son could have a courtesy title, as is customarily borne by an earl's eldest son and heir.

Immediately afterwards Reading attended the two plenary sessions of the new Supreme War Council at Versailles and he also participated in various informal talks with Lloyd George, House, and the French and Italian Ministers, meeting for the first time the Allied war leaders, Clemenceau, Pétain, Orlando and Sonnino. It emerged that Austria had been putting out peace feelers, and with House's

[1] Colonel House noted in his diary (November 27, 1917): 'Wiseman tells me that the King talked to him of Northcliffe in a most denunciatory way. However, he was compelled to make Northcliffe a Viscount the next day. He must have done it with a wry face.' (House Papers.)

support Lloyd George got the others to agree that these should be investigated. The British Prime Minister suggested that Reading should go to Geneva and meet the representative of the Austrian Government there. 'Lloyd George and I walked together from the Foreign Office to the Hotel de Crillon,' House noted in his diary on December 1. 'He was full of the proposed peace with Austria. One would think that it was as good as done. His imagination runs away with his judgment.'

House's diary for December 1 continued:

Lloyd George and Reading dined alone with me. We had a pleasant evening together. They were both in good form and George was happy over the conclusion of the Conference. Just why he was happy, excepting that the Conference had adjourned and he was returning to England, is more than I can fathom for, certainly, we have not done half of what we should have done. The Supreme War Council has taken up but few of the matters which properly should have come before it and instead of sitting for one morning it should have sat for a week. . . .

After dinner we took up the question of Reading going to Switzerland to meet a representative of the Austrian Government to discuss the making of a peace with Austria. George asked Reading to go. Reading thought it would not do for him to go because everyone would wonder what the Lord Chief Justice of England was doing in Switzerland. George declared he could go under an assumed name, such as Brown, and no one would know who he was. Reading thought it was beneath the dignity of the Lord Chief Justice to go under an assumed name. He also thought that questions would be asked which he could not answer. George, in reply, cheerfully recommended that he lie about them. Reading again did not object so much to the lying as he did to the Lord Chief Justice telling a lie. I was greatly amused with the entire procedure. . . .

In trying to persuade Reading, George declared there were only three men he knew in the world who could successfully undertake such a delicate mission, and those three, if he would pardon the inclusion of himself, were sitting around the table. This pleased Reading, but it did not convince him that the Lord Chief Justice of England should lie and masquerade under the name of Brown. . . .

George is constantly ridiculing Northcliffe. He again asked if I would not agree to take Northcliffe back if he would agree to let Roosevelt [the Republican ex-President] come to England. I replied that I had learned to like Northcliffe and that he could send him to America and we would welcome him.

The Prime Minister goes home in the morning, leaving Balfour in charge. I am glad, for while he lacks the force and energy of George he has what is needed at this Conference, and that is, character and a commanding historic background.[1]

The members of the American War Mission were back in the United States by the middle of the month. Very shortly afterwards House received a cable from Wiseman forecasting that Northcliffe would not return to Washington and that Reading would replace him as head of the British War Mission, and that he would also replace Spring Rice as Ambassador. The forecast turned out to be correct.

On January 7, 1918, it was officially announced in London that the Earl of Reading had been appointed Ambassador Extraordinary and High Commissioner on Special Mission to the United States and that Sir Cecil Spring Rice had been recalled 'for consultation'.

[1] House Papers; partly quoted in House, Vol. III, pp. 279, 283.

7
Ambassador

1

The news of the change of Ambassador in Washington was conveyed by Balfour to Spring Rice in a Foreign Office telegram which, though courteously worded, was nevertheless blunt and impersonal. Nor was it accompanied by any announcement of other employment or recognition of his past diplomatic services. Although Balfour apologized for its necessary 'telegraphic bluntness', the message came as a painful shock to Spring Rice, since he was given to understand that the Government expected Lord Reading to stay at Washington for as long as his other duties permitted. It is unusual to recall an Ambassador by telegram and to announce his successor in the same message. Spring Rice, who was a person of highly sensitive temperament as well as being a sick man, took the news badly, while his friends felt, in the words of one of them (Senator Lodge), that 'he was hurried away from Washington in a manner which seemed harsh, and certainly proved to be needless, since Lord Reading did not come for some weeks'. A recall in such circumstances inevitably looked like a censure, and that was how Spring Rice regarded it.

'Poor "Springy" felt his dismissal very keenly,' Wiseman wrote at the time. 'He chose to put the worst interpretation on the cables from the F.O. and thinks he was discharged at a moment's notice. The truth is that he is in a very bad state of health, and sees everything through jaundiced eyes. He always distrusted the President and the Administration, and was not able to disguise it.' Unfortunately there were considerable grounds for this criticism. Cecil Spring Rice was a diplomatist of the old school, wedded to the traditional methods of diplomatic intercourse, and quite out of tune with the demands of war-time Washington. True, he had many political friends, but his friendships had been formed in the days of Roosevelt and Taft and were all among the Republicans. It was uncongenial enough for him to have to deal with a Democratic

Administration, and worse to be obliged to cope with an inaccessible President and an unorthodox chief lieutenant in the person of Colonel House to whom on one occasion he was obliged to apologize for losing his temper with him. Nor was he any more enamoured of the President and his Cabinet. He was given to remarks of caustic wit, and one of them, which went the rounds of the capital and reached the White House, did him no good. 'If the President is the shepherd of his people, then McAdoo is his crook!' On the other hand he was a cultivated man of pronounced literary gifts and it is only fair to add that before his health began to deteriorate, Spring Rice carried out his instructions with considerable tact, whatever his private views may have been about the new régime in the White House, and all the important issues in dispute between Great Britain and America were decided as Great Britain wished. In this respect Reading frankly acknowledged his predecessor's achievement. 'I believe it to be the case that the Allied Governments were never forced to recede from their position in any important question owing to American opposition,' Reading wrote after Spring Rice's death, 'and the result is in itself sufficient proof of the sagacity with which the negotiations were conducted during the period of American neutrality.'

Immediately after receiving Balfour's telegram, Spring Rice sought an interview with the President, with whom he put as good a face as he could upon the news of his replacement. On January 4, 1918 he reported back to Balfour:

The President gave me an audience yesterday. I communicated to him your telegram announcing Lord Reading's appointment here. He read it and said he fully understood the circumstances. I pointed out to him how necessary it was to have some one who had been in close touch with the British Government to be present here and that he must have full control....

I said that as soon as Lord Reading arrived he would have the advantage of speaking freely with one who could interpret the policy of the British Government. Speaking only for myself, I said that I knew quite well what your personal wishes were and what was your personal conviction. I knew that you believed the hope and salvation of the world lay in a close and cordial understanding between those who were of the household of our language. I said that we could almost endure with equanimity all the horrors of this terrible struggle if they led in the end to a close, sure and permanent understanding between the English speaking peoples. If we stood together we were safe. If we did not stand together nothing was safe.

He then prepared to leave Washington for the homeward journey, a journey which he was fated not to complete alive. On January 12, the day before his departure, he wrote a farewell letter to the former Secretary of State, William Jennings Bryan, enclosing a poem which he had composed in the form of a sonnet, 'I Vow To Thee, My Country,' words destined to be spoken and sung and broadcast on many occasions on which England has remembered her dead who have made 'the final sacrifice' in the Great War. His send-off at the Union railway station was a painful affair. 'Springy was utterly weary and broken,' noted his friend Shane Leslie who was present. 'Owing to intense cold the train delayed and delayed. Every quarter of an hour his haggard face appeared at the window beckoning his staff to retire and be done with him. Sad and unhappy scene but we all stuck to it in spite of freezing tears. It appears that he had no letter of gratitude from Balfour or the Foreign Office, nor any Order of Distinction or the least reward.'

In fact such a letter was written in the leisurely manner of the Foreign Office, but the ex-Ambassador did not live to receive it. He and his wife broke their homeward journey at Ottawa to spend a week or two with the Governor-General, the Duke of Devonshire. While he was there he suffered a sudden heart attack in the night and died in a few minutes. 'My own belief,' said his close friend Senator Lodge when he heard the news, 'is that the sudden cessation of his work and responsibilities, in which his heart was bound up, caused a reaction and a loss of will to live, as they term it now, which in the old days used to be termed a broken heart.'

Reading's appointment was generally well received on both sides of the Atlantic.[1] A few days after the official announcement had been made, Mr Walter Hines Page, the United States Ambassador in London, wrote to President Wilson (January 16, 1918):

You know Lord Reading and have taken the measure of him, but the following facts and gossip may interest you.

He is one of the ablest Englishmen living – everybody concedes that. But, with that, agreement about him here ends. The very general Conservative view of him is that he cannot be trusted. See and compare the view taken of Disraeli, the other Hebrew Earl, by his political enemies. He is not so spectacular as old Dizzy was, but he is far sounder. I doubt if Dizzy was honest and I think that Reading is.

[1] Reading did not receive any salary as Ambassador, but he drew expenses from the Foreign Office.

After describing Reading's career first on the Stock Exchange, then at the Bar, and in politics and finally as a judge and a peer of the realm, Page continued:

> He is the son of a London merchant and he married a daughter of a merchant named Cohen. The Isaacs and the Cohen are now swallowed up in the Earl and Countess, and 'Reading' gives no hint of Jewry.
>
> Lord Reading does not give up the Lord Chief Justiceship. He remarked to me the other day that his Ambassadorship would be temporary. Lady Reading told Mrs Page that they expected to be gone only three months. But I take it that he will not return till the end of the War. . . .
>
> I think there is no doubt that to do a concrete job Lord Reading will succeed, during war time, better than any man who was considered for the post. . . .
>
> Of course the immediate problems to be met in the relations of the two Governments will continue to be financial – till we have to slacken our pace. The British, God knows, need money, but God knows also that they are not slow in making their wants known. I doubt if anybody, but the Germans, will ever wage war on less than twice what it ought to cost. But, if it could be more extravantly conducted than they (the British) conduct it, I can't imagine how it could be done.[1]

Wiseman returned to New York towards the end of January, 1918, preceding Reading by several weeks. On reaching his office he received what he called an 'S.O.S. from the Embassy who all expect to follow their Ambassador into exile'. Wiseman hastened to Washington to reassure the staff that they had nothing to worry about. ('As a matter of fact they will find that Reading is a most delightful chief to work for and very appreciative and considerate of his staff.') At the same time he took the opportunity provided by his visit to call at the White House for a talk with the President. In reporting this meeting to the Foreign Office, Wiseman remarked:

> I told him the purpose of Reading's coming was to tell him on behalf of His Majesty's Government what we thought ought to be done in the common cause and place at his disposal – in so far as one man was able – our experience in deciding these matters. He remarked that this arrangement ought to be very useful to him. He repeated the difficulty was to decide on the question of essentials and non-essentials and to determine the best priority. . . .
>
> From what he said I gather the President wishes to make a practice of sending for me for similar conversations. I propose with your

[1] Walter Hines Page Papers.

consent to inform him that this will be undesirable so long as Lord
Reading is in the country.

The last paragraph raised an important matter of procedure. On
thinking it over, Balfour authorized the following answer to Wiseman's suggestion:

> The suggestion you make is certainly correct, but had you not better
> discuss the matter with Reading before replying? The latter may find
> difficulty, owing to publicity and jealousy of Allied representatives, in
> seeing the President as often as desirable. Might it not be very useful
> for you to be available as an extra channel of communication?

In the event, Reading was to agree to the continuance of the
arrangement. Indeed he cheerfully accepted it in the circumstances,
and although he sometimes seemed to those who worked with him
like Arthur Willert to be irked by this extra and anomalous wheel to
his ambassadorial coach, he realized its value. Anyhow he personally
liked Wiseman and the combination worked well. 'Wiseman is
really an invaluable person to us and I am most sorry to lose him
even temporarily,' Reading was to write to Lloyd George when
Wiseman made a short visit to London in the following spring at the
instance of both the President and Colonel House. 'He supplies the
rarely satisfied need of one with whom you can talk and be sure you
will get some suggestion at least well worthy of consideration. Get
him to tell you about everything here – it will be worth your while.'

On his return to New York, Wiseman cabled the Foreign Office
(January 25, 1918) on the 'important changes' which he detected had
taken place since he and Reading had left nearly three months
previously.

> America's contribution to the War during the months has un-
> doubtedly fallen short of this country's expectation and is a shock to
> America's self-satisfaction. Administration appreciate valuable time
> has been lost on shipbuilding programme. This is partly due to muddle,
> but also largely due to difficulties with labour which are serious. Rail-
> ways are not capable of handling the full output of the country's
> industries which during the War have increased much more rapidly
> than railway development. Administration appears to be making real
> efforts to find more tonnage for War purpose by reducing non-
> essentials and trying to secure further neutral and interned ships.
> I believe Reading's firm insistence on our essential needs and helpful
> suggestions and sympathy for their difficulties will achieve far more

than the hostile criticisms of the Administration's methods which are too noticeable among certain British officials here.

President Wilson may be led but certainly not driven.[1]

On the same day Wiseman wrote privately to Sir Eric Drummond:

It is easy to be wise after the event – but one cannot help reflecting what might have been accomplished by a really big Ambassador in Washington who could have kept the realities of the situation before the Administration.

I am hoping a lot from Reading. He has a wonderful chance. If he is well backed up with a constant stream of information, and his recommendations are promptly acted upon, he can assume a great position in Washington and do very much to guide the Administration. I find them all willing enough to listen to suggestions if given in the right spirit, but they are very quick to resent criticism, and I think many of our people here have not had enough patience with them.

House's position has been considerably strengthened by his trip to Europe. . . . It seems to me that the American people quite generally accept the fact that he is the Government's adviser on foreign affairs. In the meantime he is quietly working away to try and break down the President's prejudices. . . .

We are all getting ready to make Reading a big success over here.[2]

Meanwhile Reading's preparations for leaving England were being constantly interrupted by conferences and meetings of the War Cabinet on the delicate question of American military assistance in the field. The question had been raised with House in Paris, when Robertson had proposed that either American troops should be incorporated by companies with British battalions or else American infantry battalions should be brigaded with the British forces to as great an extent as possible. House and the technical members of his mission were convinced that this was the best short-term solution to the Allied shortage of manpower. On the other hand, General Pershing, the Commander-in-Chief of the American Expeditionary Force in France, was anxious to preserve a separate and independent American force and he had the backing of American public opinion. The question was complicated by the amount of British shipping available for American troop transports. According to the official minutes of a meeting of the War Cabinet at 10 Downing Street, on January 14, 1918, to which Reading was summoned, the Ambassador

[1] Reading Papers (F.O. 800/222/U.S./1).
[2] Balfour Papers.

designate to Washington gave a gloomy picture of American ship-building. 'The difficulty appears to be that there is no system of delegating authority at Washington, and everything has to be referred to the White House for decision. Ex-President Roosevelt is daily attacking the Government for their delays in settling vital matters.' Reading added that 'sooner or later he thought that President Wilson must be guided by the British view. The difficulty was that every American mission sent to this country became very strongly anglicized. Admiral Sims was an instance in point. The President still hesitated to submit their advice to the American public, as American sentiment was so strongly in favour of separate national organizations.'[1]

A few days afterwards, General Tasker H. Bliss, Chief of Staff of the U.S. Army, arrived in London and saw Reading, who immediately reported to the Prime Minister that 'in the main he is ready to fall in with your and General Robertson's views as to assistance to be given by American troops in France'.[2] Reading went on to state:

> General Bliss said that he understood that General Robertson required 150,000 men; they could be brought here from America and landed in France by 1st March and he thought 30 days training would suffice so they would be in line on April 1st – always provided tonnage supplied to carry from here to France. He suggested that not too much should be said about requiring American soldiers to be placed in companies or battalions with British troops. He thinks it would be unwise to attack the national sentiment point unless absolutely necessary, and it would be better to get the troops over here quickly and then they could be used as required in an emergency. This notion is based on need for prompt action, and decisive move of the troops. He evidently wants to avoid a fuss there and thinks that if he can get the troops here as suggested by us, he will have no difficulty in disposing of them as they may be best required for use.
>
> He is *very anxious* that not a moment should be lost. I am anxious that you should strike at once. . . .

Eventually a compromise was reached at a meeting in the offices of the Supreme War Council at Versailles on January 29, 1918, between Pershing and Bliss on the one side and Lloyd George, Robertson and Haig on the other. It was agreed, in deference to Pershing's wishes, that British sea transport should be used to bring over the personnel of entire American divisions as Pershing wanted,

[1] Cited by Thomas Clement Lonergan in *It Might Have Been Lost!* (1929), pp. 66–67.
[2] Lloyd George Papers.

and not merely infantry battalions as proposed by Robertson. Furthermore, the infantry and auxiliary troops of these divisions should be trained with British divisions by battalions, 'or under such plan as may be agreed on'. The higher commanders and staff officers were to be assigned for training and experience with corresponding units of the British Army. This decision, which was communicated to Reading as he was on the point of leaving England, went some way towards improving matters, since in the event of a grave emergency it insured the presence on French soil of a considerable number of American troops who had received some training by officers with war experience.

Meanwhile Reading's appointment to Washington had been generally welcomed in the English Press and also in the ranks of his profession. 'It recalls a proud period when English judges were, as he is, versed in statecraft,' *The Times* observed in an editorial doubtless written by Geoffrey Dawson, 'and it gives evidence of a desire on the part of the Government to make use of indisputable financial and diplomatic ability.' The Bench and Bar of England likewise gave his mission their blessing in a brief but dignified ceremony in the Lord Chief Justice's Court. 'May success attend and crown your labours,' said the Solicitor-General (Sir Gordon Hewart) on behalf of the Bar, 'and may the unity of effort achieved by these labours bear before long as its fruit the peace which is victory and the victory which is lasting peace.' At the same time the new Ambassador was concerned lest he should be absent over long from his work in the English courts. Accordingly he addressed letters both to the Prime Minister and the Foreign Secretary on the question of his need to return to the Bench within six months at the most.

At six o'clock on the morning of February 1, as he was about to embark on board the White Star liner *Olympic* for New York, Reading was at his desk attending to some last-minute correspondence. He was conscious that the American Generals, particularly Pershing, were far from satisfied with their military contribution so far, barely one division of 25,000 men. 'I must put all my powers into my present task and indeed we must do our best to speed them up over there,' Reading wrote to Lloyd George. 'At the moment I think from all I hear they are suffering from shock of disappointment at their own delay in producing the goods. This may not be a bad moment to get them to make greater efforts.'[1]

[1] Lloyd George Papers.

2

Apart from the hazards of enemy submarines – five were known to be operating in the Western Approaches – the crossing was an exceedingly rough one. By the time the rolling and pitching *Olympic* had zigzagged her way out of the danger zone in safety, most of the passengers were lying prostrate in their bunks suffering from seasickness. Reading, whose thoughts were carried back to his days before the mast forty years earlier, seems to have quite enjoyed this voyage. He took the opportunity of a collection being made for the merchant seamen's charities to pay a tribute to their navy's courage and endurance in the dangers of war time, recalling with pride that he had once been for a short time 'an inconspicuous member of that noble fraternity'.

The staff who travelled with the Ambassador were the Private Secretary from the Foreign Office, Hubert Montgomery (afterwards Sir Hubert), Minister at The Hague; Colonel Swinton, who had been with Reading on his previous visit as High Commissioner, and Grimwood Mears, an old friend at the English Bar, later Chief Justice of the High Court of Allahabad – they were to act as assistants in military and civil matters respectively; and Lt.-Colonel C. K. Craufurd-Stuart, D.S.O. of the Indian Army, whose duties were to be those of Comptroller of the Household and social secretary.

It was a relief to all when the *Olympic* berthed safely in New York on February 10. Before disembarking, the Ambassador was handed a letter of friendly greeting from Colonel House, who had been summoned to Washington by the President. 'You cannot know how glad I am that you are back,' it read, 'and how warmly the American people welcome you. There is great work to do and I feel no one can do it better than you.'

The gaps in the Ambassador's political knowledge of events which had occurred during his ten days at sea were filled in by Wiseman. In response to a telegram from Balfour asking him to see the President and put to him the case for the brigading of American troops with British and French units, Wiseman had gone to Washington, called up the White House on the telephone and been invited to lunch. Besides the President, Mrs Wilson and her secretary, the only other person present was Newton Baker, the Secretary for War in Wilson's Cabinet. After the lunch, at which only generalities were discussed, the President invited Wiseman and Baker upstairs to his study. There Wiseman was asked to state his case which he did as best he could. Baker was sympathetic but non-committal, and Wiseman guessed that he did not wish to say anything definite until he had heard more of General Pershing's side of the matter. Then, to Wiseman's surprise, the President politely dismissed his War Secretary and sat down for a further talk with the young English Intelligence Chief. His words stuck in Wiseman's memory for long afterwards. 'It is a very serious thing for a President to override his Commander-in-Chief in the field, but if Pershing is standing in the way, he must be ordered to stand out of the way.'[1]

Wiseman made it clear that the President did not indicate that he was prepared to give Pershing such orders right away, but 'he was fully aware of the urgency of the matter and would do whatever he thought right'. Then the President remarked that the matter was to be brought up again at a meeting of the Supreme War Council which was to take place at Abbeville, and such was his disregard for military protocol that he actually suggested that Wiseman should go to Abbeville and explain his views to Pershing. 'Naturally I was taken aback,' Wiseman later recalled, 'and tried to explain that it would be very difficult for a British officer to take a message of that importance from the President to Pershing.' The President immediately agreed and asked Wiseman if he knew Mr A. H. Frazier, the President's political observer in France. 'I said I knew him well,' Wiseman's account continued. 'He then said that he would see that Frazier was instructed, but that he would like me to go to Abbeville and explain verbally to Frazier his, the President's, attitude in the matter. In fact, his attitude was that while, of course, he was as anxious as anyone for the prompt creation of an American Army in the field, under its own Commander, this must not be allowed to endanger the military situation; that he had no means of judging for himself the urgency of the problem, but that if the problem was as urgent as stated by Mr Balfour, there would seem to be grave risk if Pershing opposed the Allied request.' In the meantime, as Wiseman told Balfour in a telegram which he sent off the same night to the Foreign Office and which he showed Reading, 'the President repeats most earnestly that he will risk any adverse public criticism in order to win the War and he has told Pershing that he may put American troops by battalions in the British line or use them in any way which in his,

[1] Murray, p. 21.

Pershing's, judgment may be dictated by the necessities of the military situation'.[1]

The British Foreign Secretary's thanks and appreciation of the President's attitude were conveyed in a telegram to House, of which Wiseman received a copy for his and Reading's information.

A. J. Balfour to Colonel E. M. House

London. February 7, 1918. American soldiers must feel that they belong to an American army fighting under the American flag. It is only on these terms that the best can be got out of them or that they can count on the enthusiastic support of the American people. I know that these views were strongly pressed by General Pershing at Versailles, but I understand that proposals were made there which in his view would enable small American units to train, and, if need was considerable to fight in the immediate future in companies with French and British troops without interfering with or delaying the creation of a great American army. If so, early and much needed assistance would be given us on the Western Front without hindering the realization of legitimate American aims.

The other piece of news which Wiseman had to impart was that he had learned from House that the President intended to make an important speech to Congress on the following day, with the result that Reading determined not to linger in New York but to proceed to Washington with Wiseman immediately so that they could both go to the Capitol and hear what President Wilson had to say. The pretext for the President's speech was the declaration of war aims recently made by the German Chancellor and the Austro-Hungarian Foreign Minister, Count Hertling and Count Czernin, which had in turn been occasioned by Wilson's famous 'Fourteen Points' programme, including the public announcement for the first time of his plan for a League of Nations, and the principles of open diplomacy, freedom of the seas, removal of economic barriers, and reduction of armaments. But, whereas Czernin desired a general peace since Austria had little to gain and everything to lose by the prolongation of the War, Hertling was really only interested in concluding peace with the Russian Bolsheviks so as to free the German divisions from the Eastern front to reinforce their forces in the West, where he hoped that peace terms could be dictated by Germany within sight and sound of the battle in the context of the existing balance of power.

[1] House, Vol III, p. 444.

This idea President Wilson rejected utterly. 'The method the German Chancellor proposed is the method of the Congress of Vienna,' Wilson told Congress. 'We cannot and will not return to that. What is at stake now is the peace of the world. What we are striving for is a new international order based upon broad and universal principles of right and justice – no mere peace of shreds and patches.' He then went on to enunciate the four basic principles, in his view, for any lasting peace. Briefly, these were, first, the essential justice of each part of the settlement; secondly, no bartering of peoples and provinces; thirdly, every territorial settlement to be for the benefit of the populations concerned; and fourthly, national aspirations should be accorded the utmost satisfaction 'without introducing new or perpetuating old elements of discord and antagonism that would be likely in time to break the peace of Europe and consequently the world'.

After delivery of the speech, House who had accompanied the President to the Capitol drove back with him to the White House. Later the same day he made the following entry in his diary:

> After lunch I drove to Lord Reading's. He has retaken his old quarters at No. 2315 Massachusetts Avenue. I was delighted to hear him say, 'I would have given a year of my life to have made the last half of the President's speech.' I said he would surely want to know why the last half. The reply was that the first half was merely a reiteration of Czernin's and Hertling's positions, but the last half was a noble utterance, both from an oratorical viewpoint and from that of a statesman.
>
> Sir William Wiseman who was with Lord Reading and Gordon[1] announced it the best address the President has yet delivered.
>
> I returned to the White House, where the President was waiting to hear if I had any news from Reading. He was delighted when I told him what Reading, Wiseman and Gordon had to say. . . .[2]

On February 13, 1918, Reading called at the White House and presented his credentials. According to the President's daily diary kept by his secretary, the new British Ambassador was accompanied by a staff of nine and 'the usual formal compliments were exchanged'. To mark the occasion the Ambassador and his staff were photographed in a group outside the entrance to the Embassy.

'I am rather staggered by the amount of work to be tackled,' he

---

[1] Gordon Auchincloss, House's son-in-law, then working in the State Department.
[2] House Papers.

told Wiseman, 'but it will get easier when I have got the personnel properly to work.' An incident, trifling in itself, which occurred at this time as the result of a mistake on the part of one of the Embassy personnel, might have assumed more serious proportions but for the fortuitous presence of Colonel House. Lady Reading had written to Mrs Wilson, at the same time as her husband presented his credentials, asking when she might pay a formal call on the 'First Lady'. By some inadvertence the letter was put in the diplomatic bag for London, whence it was sent back to be received by Mrs Wilson some six weeks later. 'If I had not happened to be in Washington at the time and upon intimate terms with both parties,' House later recalled, 'it would have resulted in strained relations.'[1]

Two days later Reading was back at the White House to announce the news of his predecessor's sudden death which had just been received from Ottawa, and to inform the President that a memorial service was to be held in the afternoon of the following day. The President said that he and his wife would attend, which they did with members of the Government and diplomatic corps. The dead Ambassador's friend, Shane Leslie, who was also among the congregation described the scene at the time as follows:

> I wanted Wilson to do something public in Spring Rice's memory. The President could say nothing, but he specially attended the memorial service in St Alban's Cathedral, Washington. The new Ambassador Lord Reading and Secretary Lansing were also present. It was a lugubrious affair. The President sang the hymn open-mouthed but Reading refrained from vernacular relations with the Deity. . . . I think the scene in Washington Cathedral would have filled Springy with irony.

Reading now plunged into the seemingly endless round of meetings, conferences, negotiations, arguments, speeches, dinners and other functions, which is the common lot of an Ambassador abroad, the more difficult and onerous in Reading's case by reason of the unprecedented war-time conditions. As he told Lloyd George, 'I hardly ever go out in the day except to see Ministers and thank Heaven am kept very hard at work. I do not care to let the important things get out of my hands.' At the end of his first month at the Embassy, an interesting confidential progress report was placed on Balfour's desk in the Foreign Office by his Private Secretary.

[1] House Papers: Diary, June 21, 1918.

Sir William Wiseman to Sir Eric Drummond[1]

New York. March 14, 1918. Reading has done splendid work here. He found a good deal of confusion when he arrived owing to the North-cliffe régime at the War Mission and the entire lack of cooperation between the Embassy and the Mission. It is important you should remember that Reading, on his arrival, was faced with a number of awkward and unpleasant personal questions which you heard nothing about, but which had to be settled before he could get the machine to run smoothly. I do not suppose they are by any means settled yet, but the organization has certainly improved.

I think the only mistake he made was to bring out Swinton and Craufurd-Stuart. Both of them are exceedingly nice fellows, and every-body likes them, but it is a mistake for an Ambassador to have a military suite, which savours too much of the Viceroy or Governor-General. Moreover there is no real place for them in his organization, as the heads of the departments naturally decline to work through a military Secretary. On general principles, too, we ought not to have more soldiers out here than are necessary, and you know militarism, even in the mildest form, is not popular in America.

Immediately he arrived Reading was faced with the urgent problem of Food. The Americans, as you know, had fallen far short of their promised deliveries for January and February. This time it was not a question of ships, as there was enough tonnage available. The difficulty was that the Administration could not transport the food to the sea-ports. This was partly due to a general breakdown of the railroad organization, and partly due to the exceptionally bad weather which tied up a lot of the railroads for days at a time. The Government in control of the railroads took various measures to remedy this, and have succeeded to a large extent; but the truth is that the railways running from the Middle West farming districts and the great indus-trial centres to the eastern seaboard are not capable of handling the produce of the country. . . .

Reading is excellent in dealing with the Food Controller, Railways, Treasury and shipping people. He masters each complicated subject himself, and is very patient and tactful in dealing with the Ministers at Washington. He has established also a dominant position among the Allied Ambassadors, who seem willing to let him take the lead in joint negotiations. This, of course, is all very excellent. It is not easy work for a British Ambassador, as you can well imagine. At every turn he is met by the obvious but unpleasant truth that we are very largely in the hands of the American Administration – that they are in a position almost to dictate the war policy of the Allies. This would make any

[1] Balfour Papers.

lesser man irritable and disheartened, but Reading knows them well enough to realize that the President at any rate is in no mind to misuse his great power, or take advantage of difficulties in which the Allies may find themselves. But, of course, it does make negotiations very hard.

Politically they are so unfamiliar with European, in fact with international, affairs that the Foreign Ambassador must be very patient indeed. The Administration also seem inclined to be slow to face unpleasant truths; particularly they still cling to the hope that they may still 'talk' the Germans into a just peace. But this attitude must not be mistaken for any weakening in their determination to win. After they have done their talking, you will find they will go on fighting whatever the sacrifices may be. . . .

Wiseman's report reached London just about the time the Germans launched their great offensive on the Western Front. It began on March 21 with the object of splitting the British and French Armies and forcing France out of the war before the anticipated American reinforcements could arrive. On March 23, so-called 'Black Saturday', the British Fifth Army under General Gough, whose lines had been penetrated to a depth of thirty-five miles, was in full retreat to the Somme, and the Germans were moving on Amiens. The War Cabinet met the same afternoon and decided to dispatch the eighteen and nineteen-year-old men to France. But these were not enough to stem the German onslaught. More reinforcements were vitally necessary if the British lines were to be restored and Gough's forces not completely cut off from their French Allies.

Reading was now faced with the need for putting across a sense of urgency about the latest turn of the War to the American people. In this he was helped by the sudden swing in popular sentiment. A few days after the German breakthrough, he cabled the following appreciation to the Foreign Office:

Effect of the great battle on American public opinion is wholly advantageous to the Allied cause. Nothing has occurred since America entered the War which has stirred more fully the national feeling or united the people so thoroughly against Germany. Display of German military power is a shock to America and the people at large realize for the first time that the Allies in general and England in particular have been standing between her and German militarism. It has produced feeling of admiration and sympathy for the British, quite contrary to the usual attitude. People of America are for the War and anxious to know how they can most effectively help. They have realized as it were in a flash their own military shortcomings and time they have lost since they entered the War. This has already produced outburst in the Press and Congress which naturally enough takes form of attack on the Administration. . . .

To the Administration the battle has been no less of a shock. They had hoped and believed that the effect of the President's speeches had been to strengthen Liberal party in Germany and sap morale of the Army and influence of the military party. Today they are very conscious of their delusion and realize that there is no hope that speeches and propaganda will turn the German people against their military party or detach Austria from Germany. At last they face the fact that, if Germany is to be beaten, she must be beaten by force.

It so happened that the Ambassador had a long standing engagement to address the Lotus Club at a dinner in New York on March 27. The idea now occurred to him that if he could persuade the Prime Minister to send a suitable message of encouragement for him to read out to the Club, where the Press would be present, it would create an excellent impression.

As usual, the Prime Minister rose to the occasion. He immediately cabled the following to Wiseman's office in New York for Reading:

We are at the crisis of the War. Attacked by an immense superiority of German troops our Army has been forced to retire. The retirement has been carried out methodically before the pressure of a steady succession of fresh German reserves which are suffering enormous losses. The situation is being faced with splendid courage and resolution. The dogged pluck of our troops has for the moment checked the ceaseless onrush of the enemy and the French have now joined in the struggle.

But this battle, the greatest and most momentous in the history of the world, is only just beginning. Throughout it French and British are buoyed up with the knowledge that the great Republic of the West will neglect no effort which can hasten its troops and its ships to Europe. In war, time is vital. It is impossible to exaggerate the importance of getting American reinforcements across the Atlantic in the shortest possible space of time.

Lloyd George followed up this message in another cable in which he instructed Reading to urge upon the President the vital importance of pouring American troops into France as rapidly as possible. General Pershing had already consented to put his four divisions into the line so as to relieve the more experienced French troops for service on the front of attack. Reading was further to inquire whether

the President 'would agree to the brigading during the crisis, of all
other units that may become available with French or British
divisions'. The Prime Minister continued:

> You should explain to the President that we are engaged in what
> may well prove to be the decisive battle of the War. The Germans are
> concentrating the greater part of their available forces against the
> British front and are pushing their attacks with the greatest determina-
> tion. We have every hope of checking them, but our losses have been
> very heavy and will be heavier. . . .
>
> You should appeal to the President to drop all questions of inter-
> pretation of past agreements and send over infantry as fast as possible
> without transport and other encumbrances. The situation is un-
> doubtedly critical and if America delays now she may be too late.

The telegram reached the Embassy during the afternoon of March
28. As soon as it had been deciphered, Reading called for his car
and drove straight to the White House with a paraphrase of the
telegram in his hand. Meanwhile the President had been alerted and
instantly agreed to receive the British Ambassador.

Again luck favoured Reading. He was totally unaware at the time
that, but for the fact that House happened to be staying with the
President, his reception might have been considerably less cordial
than the event it turned out to be. House explains the reason in his
diary:

The White House, Washington. March 28, 1918. As I anticipated he
[the President] was much annoyed at Lloyd George's [first] cable to
Reading and at Reading's lack of judgment in reading it. I told him the
circumstances and tried to smooth the matter over, both as to Lloyd
George and the Ambassador. I told him George had been requested
to send the cable because of Reading's proposed speech, but that
Reading did not give him any intimation as to what to say.[1]

The President's point was that it was most discourteous and unusual,
as well as an undiplomatic thing, for an ambassador to give out
publicly a message from his Government directly to the people of
another country without addressing it to the head of that Government.
He said it was sufficient cause to send an ambassador home. . . .

Strangely enough Reading had an appointment with the President
within the hour, and he expressed his intention of telling Reading how
he felt. I dissuaded him from this, saying it was all meant in good part,

---

[1] As will have been seen, this was not so. On the other hand Reading had
apparently informed House of the text of the first telegram which he proposed
to read at the Lotus Club Dinner and House 'did not object'.

and that Reading himself had no diplomatic experience. I thought we ought not to be too critical since he was our sincere friend and doing the best he knew.

Eventually Reading and Wilson faced each other in the President's study.[1] The interview was brief. After he had read Lloyd George's second telegram, President Wilson said he would do anything he was asked. There was a short silence. Then the President explained quietly that under the Constitution he had the power to do this without consulting any members of his Cabinet and that he would give the necessary direction.

Reading thanked the President warmly and rose to take his leave. The President accompanied him to the door. Only as they said good-bye did Wilson's habitual reserve drop for a few moments. 'Mr Ambassador,' he said, putting his hand on Reading's shoulder in a gesture of unexpected warmth, 'you need say no more. I'll do my damnedest!'[2]

3

Next day, House called at the British Embassy and saw Reading. 'I told him of the President's feeling regarding the Lloyd George message and his speech,' House noted in his diary. 'I thought it advisable to do this in order to make him more careful in the future. He expressed his regret and hoped I had smoothed the matter over.'

The question now was how to get as many American reinforcements as possible across the Atlantic as quickly as possible. On March 29, the Prime Minister sent a further telegram to Reading asking him to see the President again and request the embarkation of 120,000 infantry a month for the next four months. He proposed that the battalions of these American regiments should be brigaded with British or French divisions for training and when trained should be reformed into regiments and sent to Pershing for use as he might require.

[1] Baker, Vol. VIII, p. 59. The second Lord Reading in his life of his father (Vol. II, p. 92) gives the date of this meeting as March 23. But this is not borne out by the President's list of engagements for that day. There is no doubt that the meeting took place on March 28, shortly after Lloyd George's second telegram had reached the Embassy.

[2] The authority for this story is Reading himself, who related it to Lord Birkenhead: see 'The Real President Wilson' in the London *Evening News*, November 2, 1928.

Please see the President about this at once. In no other way can the hundreds of thousands of trained and half-trained men now in America be made available in this struggle; for they cannot be organized into separate units in time. Should it go against us in their absence, the War might be over and the cause for which the President has so eloquently pleaded might be lost without America being given an opportunity to put in more than an insignificant fraction of her Army. I believe that the whole future of the War will depend on whether the Allies or the Germans are first in making good the losses of this great battle. . . . Unless we can refit as fast as they can, we shall simply give Germany the chance to deliver that knock-out blow with which its leaders hope to win the War.

'I hope your Generals are not as rattled as your politicians,' the President remarked to Reading when they met again, on March 30. On this occasion the President agreed substantially to Lloyd George's detailed proposals, telling the Ambassador that he would give directions for the transportation of the numbers of men requested, provided the shipping and equipment were available. He also approved in principle the method of employment of the troops suggested by the British Prime Minister, but left the details of their disposal and use to General Pershing. 'In principle he approves of employment of troops in manner desired, but leaves details to military chiefs,' Reading cabled back. This reply was to assume considerable importance owing to Pershing's refusal to accept the President's commitment in the sense of the British War Cabinet's understanding of how the promised American troop reinforcements should be used in France.

The same day, House again saw Reading. 'He is very nervous and anxious,' House noted afterwards, 'and Wiseman and I have to be constantly around to cheer him up. All through this terrible offensive Sir William has never lost his self-possession.' Indeed, according to House, everyone was 'rattled', with the exception of Wiseman, the President and himself.

A day or so later, the President received a visit from Wiseman, in the course of which he elaborated upon the meetings with the British Ambassador. Wiseman made a note afterwards of what the President had to say on the subject.

Remarking that he was glad the news from France was better, the President said he hoped Lord Reading had not misunderstood his remark the other day when he said that he hoped that our Generals were not as rattled as our politicians. He had detected, he thought a note of alarm which was almost panic in the telegram which he was shown, and all he meant to say was that such alarm was very contagious, and it would be a very serious thing if the people generally, and the troops in particular, were to catch any spirit of panic. It was, he thought, a good time to keep very calm.

His answer to Lord Reading, he observed, had been, of course, a foregone conclusion. He was prepared to do anything he possibly could to help. The number of American troops sent to France had, he said, been limited by the port facilities in France and the railroad facilities from the ports to the front. There had been, he said, enough men ready and enough ships to send over a considerably larger number. He hoped by sending them through England he could be able to get over at least 100,000 a month, and he hoped considerably more. . . .[1]

Lord Reading to Prime Minister

British Embassy,
Washington, D.C.
March 31, 1918

I need not tell you that the news of the retreat and the German success came upon the President as a great shock. He had come to the conclusion that the advance would not take place and consequently was startled when the huge attack developed. He is genuinely anxious to do all that is possible now – pray Heaven it may not be too late! He has always been most ready to help, but there have been deficiencies of administration which have most unfortunately retarded aeroplane programmes and the earlier months of shipping – the sending of troops across the water has been rendered difficult and indeed impossible by the want of proper accommodation at the French ports – as you know.

One of the consequences of recent military events has been that criticism of the Administration, which had already broken out in the Senate before the advance, has redoubled in intensity and indeed there is some danger of its clogging the machine. There is always the election of Congress in November and eyes are directed to that. There has been a little tendency, as I wired you, to use your cablegram to me for Lotus Club as enforcing this criticism and I have already told you my views upon it. I want, however, to make quite clear to you that it did a power of good. It stirred the country and did just what was wanted. Before I read it to the Club I showed it to House and told him that I had cabled asking for it – this is of course *quite confidential* and must not be told – and he did not object. . . .

It is essential we should have a President strong in authority and

[1] Wiseman to Foreign Office, April 1, 1918: Balfour Papers.

influence. The criticism of Opposition which began last winter and has developed strongly with regard to aeroplanes is useful so long as it is directed to greater effort but becomes harmful if directed to weaken the President and Administration. It has at present the evil effect that much war legislation is held up in Congress which ought to be passed so as to allow the Administration to get on with the War.

The effect of recent events is undoubtedly to strengthen the war spirit of the country – there is not the smallest sign of weakening. The indications are all the other way. The reports to me from the West are good. Swinton is out there speaking for the Liberty Loan. I lent him to the Administration for this purpose and he is doing good work.

Generally I think the next few weeks will show a distinct speeding up and closer knitting of the machine of government. You will probably say it is very late – alas! it is late, but provided the enemy be held in France we shall depend upon this country, and its work now becomes of even more supreme importance. . . .[1]

Meanwhile Lloyd George was worried about possible gaps between promises and performance in the dispatch of American troops judged by past experience. 'We have been let down badly once or twice before,' he cabled Reading on April 1; 'in fact, we are largely suffering because the Americans have fallen grievously short of their programme. They promised to have 17 divisions in France by March, they have actually only four, and these have only just gone into the line. . . .'

Next day he sent Reading a longer cable in which he reinforced his plea that the Ambassador should make every effort to see that the President's undertaking was implemented.

Prime Minister to Lord Reading

Urgent. Secret.

London. April 2, 1918. It is very difficult for you at this distance, without being in close touch with the realities of the position, to realize how success or disaster in this battle will be decided by the exertions which America puts forth in the next few weeks or even days. I believe that the German chances now depend mainly upon whether or not America can get her troops effectively into the line in time. The difference of even a week in the date of arrival may be absolutely vital. In this contest an advance of a week in the arrival of troops may win a battle, and the delay of a week may lose it. And remember that no troops can be put into the battle line for at least a month after they land. They must be put through the final training by men acquainted

[1] Lloyd George Papers; Lonergan, pp. 99–102.

with the conditions at first hand and this, I understand, is alone possible in France.

We have so often had large promises in the past, which have invariably been falsified in the result that I am sincerely apprehensive that this last undertaking may not be carried out in practice. In these circumstances everything depends upon your going beyond the ordinary province of an ambassador, and exercising personal supervision over the carrying out of the pledge. The War Mission of which you are the head will enable you to find out where delays are occurring. Immediately a hitch does occur we rely upon you to bring pressure to bear in the right quarter to secure its immediate removal. In particular I think that you ought to get Colonel House to give his whole time to this question, as if it were an election campaign, until it is certain that 120,000 American infantry are going, in fact and not merely on paper, to arrive in Europe in April and in each succeeding month afterwards. If you can get more so much the better. We can do with all you can send. I am told that there are barely 400,000 infantry in all in the whole of the United States with which to enable President Wilson to redeem his pledge of sending 480,000 men. If so, it is essential that there should be an immediate fresh draft on a large scale. . . .

Actually Lloyd George had been misinformed on the numbers and it was intended to call up fresh drafts at the rate of 150,000 a month; the first call was to be made in three weeks' time. 'We need have no fear that 480,000 will not be sent according to programme,' Reading assured the Prime Minister by cable on April 7. He went on to say that he had learned that U.S. War Secretary Baker, who was in Europe, had cabled asking the President whether he had ever agreed to the brigading of 480,000 American infantry with French and British.

President has replied that he agreed in principle that there should be brigading but did not commit himself to total and reserved details for Generals Bliss and Pershing.
I do not find any substantial difference between this and my report. . . . Only difference, if any, may be that President had in mind that Generals might not wish to brigade 480,000 although nothing was said about it in terms. Nevertheless I quite understood that any such question was left open if his military chiefs wished it as President was careful to leave all military details to them.

By this time Pershing was acutely suspicious that the French and British meant to rob him of his army and that once the American infantry got brigaded with European formations he would be unable to recover them. At all events he now flatly refused to accept the 120,000 a month transport programme, saying he could agree to no more than 60,000 infantry for which arrangements had already been made to be given priority in British shipping. This precipitated a first-class crisis, which called forth agonized cables from both the Prime Minister and the Foreign Secretary imploring Reading to seek a further interview with President Wilson. 'I am very unwilling to embarrass the President who has shown such a firm grasp of the situation with criticisms of his officers,' Balfour telegraphed on April 8. 'But it is evident that the difference of opinion between General Pershing on the one side and what we conceive to be the President's policy on the other is so fundamental and touches so nearly the issues of the whole War that we are bound to have the matter cleared up.' To this Lloyd George added next day:

> There is another great battle impending, and to make good the gaps it will make in the ranks of the Allies we are relying on American reinforcements. Our plans are dependent on 120,000 American troops for brigading with the Allied Forces being available each month. We cannot answer for consequences should Americans not arrive, or should difficulties over brigading be caused by hesitation or misunderstanding. The business of transporting and brigading 480,000 American troops with allied units is an imperative necessity, to which all questions of building up an independent American Army in Europe should come second while this crisis lasts.

From his side Reading handled the President with consummate tact and ability. First of all, he sought the advice of Colonel House and showed him the Foreign Secretary's telegram. When he had read it, House told him not to ask for an appointment at the White House until the following day and not to see the President until he (House) had written to him. This House immediately did, beginning with a summary of the cable which he had been shown. He made it clear that he sympathized both with the Allied leaders and with Pershing. 'Pershing's feeling that an American army under his command should be established and made as formidable as possible is understandable,' he told the President. 'Nevertheless, the thing to be done now is to stop the Germans and to stop them it is evident that we must put in every man that is available.'

Reading saw the President again in the afternoon of April 10 and immediately afterwards cabled the outcome of his interview to the Foreign Office:

I found President Wilson rather disinclined to answer specific points, although he was emphatic in his assurance to me that whatever it was possible for him to do to help the Allies in present situation would assuredly be done, but that he had to consult his military advisers and be guided by them as to details.

House made the following entry in his diary the same day:

> They had what Reading considered only a fairly satisfactory conference. He [Reading] sent for Gordon [Auchincloss] immediately and with his help framed a cable to his Government explaining the President's attitude. He is to give Gordon a paraphrase of this cable to send me.
>
> Reading is using Gordon as liaison officer between himself and me in exactly the way he used Wiseman. This indeed was our understanding when I insisted that Wiseman should go to England, to which Reading strongly objected until I proposed the idea of using Gordon in his stead.

At their interview, the President told Reading that he could take no further step until he had seen his Secretary of War who was on his way back from Europe. The Ambassador's cable continued with a sagacious piece of advice:

> Misunderstanding should be cleared up by President Wilson direct with General Pershing, doubtless with the assistance of Secretary Baker, and, it may be, with General Bliss. Forgive this warning. I give it for reason that otherwise President's task would be rendered more difficult if he wished to act after concluding, if he did conclude, that there had been some misapprehension in General Pershing's mind. But I need not dilate upon importance of this aspect to you.

On April 19, after Baker had returned, a memorandum was drawn up in the War Department reiterating the promise to transport 120,000 troops a month consisting of infantry and machine-gunners. Instead of assigning these troops to General Foch, who had been designated Supreme Commander or Generalissimo of the Allied Forces in the West, the memorandum stated that 'these troops will, under the direction and at the discretion of General Pershing, be assigned for training and use with British, French or American divisions, as the exigencies of the situation from time to time require'.

House was not very favourably impressed by the memorandum. He noted in his diary at the time:

It is a poorly worded and muddled sort of document, but I advised Reading to accept it cordially and to send a telegram to his Government commending it. I thought, if he did not, his Government would send cables to him which he would have to take to the President, and they might upset good relations now existing between himself, the President and Secretary Baker. The President and Baker are cordially endorsing the view which the British and French desire as against the view of Pershing and the Army, and I called Reading's attention to the importance of doing nothing to antagonize the President or Baker and throw them over on the other side.

Since Reading advised that these were the best terms that could be obtained, the War Cabinet accepted them, although they would have preferred it to have been left to Marshal Foch or the Supreme War Council to decide when the emergency was past. 'I think that the President means to hold to his original undertaking,' cabled Reading to Lloyd George on April 21, 'whilst giving effect to some objections raised by Pershing so as to make it more easily acceptable to the latter.' Unfortunately the arrangement failed to satisfy the intransigent American Commander. He immediately concluded a further agreement, this time with Lord Milner, who had succeeded Derby as British War Minister, to the effect that, after the six divisions had been shipped in May, artillery and other divisional units should be transported so that American divisions and corps when trained and organized should be utilized under an American Commander-in-Chief in an American army group.

The other Allied military leaders at the next meeting of the Supreme War Council, which took place early in May in Abbeville, failed to move Pershing. Indeed the American Commander would only consent to leave the six divisions with Haig 'as long as the emergency lasted' and insisted on the right to recall them at his discretion.

'I need not tell you how disappointed I am that the agreement with Secretary Baker has now been modified so materially by the new agreement between Lord Milner and General Pershing,' Reading cabled Lloyd George when he heard of this fresh development. 'Negotiations have proceeded on your side and an agreement has been made which does not make it easier for me in the future to make arrangements affecting the military assistance to be given. Of course the new agreement must be worked here to the best advantage, and if any change be desired it must, it seems to me come from your side. The authorities here did what we asked of them.'

On May 4, Lloyd George replied, giving Reading an account of
what had happened at the Supreme War Council meeting at Abbeville:

> I am just as disappointed at the Pershing agreement as you are. The
> whole difficulty arises from the fact that the American Government has
> issued no definite instructions to General Pershing. It has agreed to
> certain general principles, but has left the settlement of all the practical
> questions on which the value of the agreement [with us] really depends
> to Pershing. . . .
>
> Despite all our efforts and the strong appeal by General Foch, we
> could not move Pershing beyond the point of six divisions in May and
> June. I may add that Foch, who is much the greatest Allied General,
> was intensely depressed and disgusted. Wiseman who will report to
> you independently was very much upset, and Bliss, who was present
> throughout the discussions, sat absolutely silent and gave no support to
> Pershing. I hear privately that he has expressed to his colleagues com-
> plete disagreement with Pershing's attitude. . . .
>
> It is maddening to think that, though the men are there, the issue of
> the War may be endangered because of the shortsightedness of one
> General and the failure of his Government to order him to carry out
> their undertakings.

On the other hand, Lloyd George did not think that Pershing
would allow the War to be lost by refusing to let American combat
troops, once they were in Europe, be used where reinforcements were
vitally needed. Hence he urged Reading 'to make it his business,
whatever the agreement, to see that as many men as possible were
shipped across the Atlantic without delay, and as many as possible
called up in the States in readiness for the autumn battles'.[1]

Lord Reading to Prime Minister[2]

British Embassy,
Washington,
May 5, 1918

I appreciate the difficulties confronting you after the Milner-
Pershing agreement was made, but I cannot understand why the Baker
memorandum was discarded without reference to this side. It represented what the authorities here were prepared to insist upon. However,
it is of no use saying more about it; the subject must be irritating to

[1] Reading Papers, F.O. 800/224/Wg8; Lloyd George *War Memoirs*, Vol. II,
pp. 1825–26.
[2] Lloyd George Papers.

you, to use a mild phrase. Apart from the value of the agreement made here, the serious aspect is that it represented the President's views which have now been set aside in the main and I doubt whether we shall get such a stand made again. However, now I shall devote myself to trying to get the War Department to continue to send infantrymen, etc., as you ask me in your today's cable. . . .

There has been a tremendous awakening here. Your observations of the reports that you thought were being sent to the United States Government that we were exaggerating our necessities and the serious-ness of the situation explains to me the persistent optimism which prevailed here before the great drive began. Your telegrams to me and the Haig order to stand fast and all the later developments have made the U.S. realize better the gravity of the position and now throughout the country there is a war spirit which is increasing and will increase as their own troops get over and take their part. . . .

I shall be glad indeed to see Wiseman back and hear all from him. Unfortunately House has not been here for some time. I have seen him in New York but it is impossible for me to get there much. My place is here. . . .

May all good fortune accompany you and may you bring our country safely through these awful times.

Secretary Baker to General Bliss[1]

War Department,
Washington.
May 7, 1918

There is just a little disposition on the part of both British and French to feel that they are in a position to demand, or at least to insist, upon the fulfillment of expectations on their part as against a right on the part of the United States to pursue its own policy. For this reason I am very glad that we have from the first insisted upon leaving these ques-tions to the discretion of General Pershing, and in all my conferences with Lord Reading I have insisted that as General Pershing is the American Commander-in-Chief we must continue to be guided by his judgment of the military exigencies in France in the matter of the transportation of the troops there.

At the meeting of the Supreme War Council early in May, Foch had strongly urged the view which had been frequently expressed before that it was absolutely necessary that 120,000 American infantry and machine-gunners should arrive in France monthly during May, June and July, whereas Pershing had agreed to only half

[1] Baker, Vol. VIII, p. 126.

that number, and this view in the form of a paper was duly conveyed
to President Wilson by the French Ambassador in Washington.

Lord Reading to Prime Minister[1]

Washington. May 12, 1918. I have seen Secretary Baker. . . . He told
me of his conversation with French Ambassador and expressed opinion
that no course was open to United States Administration save that of
General Foch approaching General Pershing. Secretary Baker impressed upon me that President could not intervene in face of decision
of Supreme War Council after memorandum of General Foch or
substance of it had been presented to Council. Inclination here is
undoubtedly towards original plan contained in document arrived at
between Mr Baker and me.

I pressed him to send as many infantry men and machine-gun units
as possible at least during this month in view of shipping we had
originally placed at his disposal originally intended for this purpose
only. If all shipping were used for May, 200,000 infantry men could be
sent forward and I suggested this should be done and that other troops
might at least be postponed till next month after final consideration of
Supreme War Council. He was I think sympathetic to view but felt
bound to send considerable number of artillery and other arms in
view of latest arrangement. . . .

I said it appeared lamentable that in most critical moment we should
be carrying troops to the number of some 150,000 in these two months
who could not be made use of for at least some time. His attitude was
that it was effect of agreement passed by Supreme War Council to
which he must give effect although perhaps not too literally.

I am following your view that I should not raise this question with
the President at present and I entirely agree with you. Net result of
all discussions both of French Ambassador and myself with Secretary
Baker and of French Ambassador's interview with the President is
that change must come from Europe and not from here although it
may be assisted from this side.

House, whom Reading saw two days later, commented on the
Ambassador's problems in his diary:

We went through all matters pending, such as the transportation of
troops, the relations between Pershing and the other Allied commanders and the conduct of the War. Reading complained again that
he could not get anywhere with Lansing. He seems thoroughly discouraged, and if it were not for reaching me through Gordon, things
would be at a standstill. He called my attention to the difficulty of

[1] Lloyd George Papers.

keeping Gordon as well informed as he would like because of the secrecy with which it has to be done. He wished most earnestly for the return of Sir William Wiseman, for with him here I am kept in as perfect touch with British affairs as I am with American.

Meanwhile Reading, in accordance with his instructions, continued to press for increased American contingents, and he advised the War Cabinet that if matters had not righted themselves by the end of the month with the use of extra tonnage provided by Britain then another meeting of the Supreme War Council should be convened forthwith. 'I am sure a decision affirming Foch's view would be endorsed by the President,' cabled Reading. 'To put it plainly, it seems to be necessary for the President to have a recorded decision of the Supreme War Council before he could place himself in disagreement with General Pershing.'

'We are adopting your suggestion,' the Prime Minister cabled in reply, 'and are trying to arrange for a meeting of Supreme War Council beginning June. War Cabinet wishes me to say that your assistance in this vital matter has been invaluable. I do not know how we should get on without you.'[1]

4

At the height of the controversy over American military reinforcements, a most unfortunate incident occurred which greatly embarrassed Reading and indeed the whole Washington Embassy. On May 11, Sir Robert Borden, the Prime Minister of Canada, received the usual weekly telegram from the Ministry of Information in London on the progress of the War compiled from material provided by different departments. Neither the Prime Minister nor his staff seem to have noticed anything unusual about it and being a routine communication it was duly released to the Press. However, this particular telegram did contain a most astonishing statement purporting to emanate from the War Cabinet in Downing Street. It was to the effect that the Allies 'are so confident that, having been given the choice of a small immediate American army for defence or

[1] Lonergan, pp. 165, 167, 178–81. Cp. General Pershing's opinion of Reading in his war memoirs. 'It is probable that Lord Reading, skilled advocate that he was, did more while Ambassador in Washington to influence the Administration to grant Allied requests than any other individual.' John J. Pershing: *My Experiences in the World War* (1931), p. 361.

waiting until they are reinforced by a complete, powerful, self-supporting American army, they have chosen the latter'. The news that American troops were not to be used in the fighting line until the United States had built up a complete, self-supporting army naturally caused an immense sensation throughout America and Canada, besides greatly perturbing the British Ambassador. It only required the briefest reflection to convince Reading that the report was quite untrue, and without waiting to clear the matter with London he immediately issued a denial, in which he pointed out that the statement was 'diametrically opposed' to all the information received by him from the War Cabinet and to all the requests which he had been asked by them to make to the United States Administration. 'I am quite in the dark as to the origin of the statement at present,' he went on. 'All I can say is that I am convinced that the document has not been issued with the knowledge of the Prime Minister or the British War Cabinet.'

Lord Reading to Foreign Office[1]

British Embassy,
Washington.
May 13, 1918

In view of official telegrams I have had from London and personal messages from Prime Minister, it is inconceivable to me that the statement should have been issued with any authority. If it had been so issued, I could not remain British Representative here.

It is obvious a glaring blunder has been committed and I trust recurrence will be prevented by strong measures. It is a most unfortunate mistake, more particularly because, even when corrected, it sets the public mind working in direction of complete American army instead of acquiescing in present position.

The explanation came from Colonel Murray, the former assistant Military Attaché in Washington who had been seconded for special duty with the Foreign Office. The offending paragraph, he wired back, was based upon a memorandum supplied by the War Office, but the compiler of the telegram had misunderstood and misinterpreted the purport of the memorandum. Apparently the statement became attributed to the War Cabinet owing to the corruption of the words 'War Aims Committee appointed by the British Cabinet' into 'War Committee of the British Cabinet'. The Press Bureau had overlooked the statement as it formed part of a routine telegram issued

[1] Reading Papers; Reading, Vol. II, p. 101.

by a Government Department. Murray added that 'Beaverbrook [Minister of Information] has accepted responsibility for blunder which was due to an error on the part of one of his subordinates.'[1]

After he had paid a flying visit to Ottawa to get the Canadian version of how the offending telegram came to be released, Reading reinforced his previous public statement by formally declaring that 'the telegram sent through Ottawa did not emanate from the British War Cabinet and is totally at variance with their views'. Although a few American newspapers tried to make capital out of the affair, generally speaking public opinion was behind the President in furnishing prompt aid to the Allies in whatever form it might be required.

At this time, Prince Arthur of Connaught, King George V's cousin, then aged thirty-four, passed through the United States on his way to Japan on a special mission. He carried with him a personal letter in the King's hand to the American President, which referred to the excellent impression created by the arrival of the first contingents of American troops in Britain and which greatly pleased the President when he read it.

Reading brought the Prince to the White House where he handed over the King's letter and had a long conversation with the President. Later he visited Congress. 'H[is] R[oyal] H[ighness] made an excellent impression upon all with whom he came in contact, and there is general regret that he could not stay longer,' Reading cabled the Foreign Office after his departure next day. 'The United States Government took every means to welcome H.R.H. and show him the greatest courtesy for which I am expressing the appreciation of His Majesty's Government.'[2]

Meanwhile the Supreme War Council had been summoned to meet on June 1. Expecting a 'show down' with Pershing, the British Prime Minister cabled Reading with the suggestion that perhaps President Wilson would send over Colonel House or some other emissary to represent the United States on the political side, since 'it is really not fair to General Pershing to expect him to decide these questions. In this case it means practically asking a General who is not trained to estimate political considerations to hand part of his army to another General. This is a responsibility that ought to be taken by a civilian authority.'

[1] Reading Papers.
[2] Reading Papers.

Colonel House to President Wilson[1]

New York,
May 20, 1918

Lord Reading took breakfast with me this morning. He is just back from Ottawa. He had a cable from the Prime Minister, instructing him to see you and request that you send me or someone else to represent the civil end of our Government at the next meeting of the Supreme War Council.[2]

This meeting is scheduled to meet Saturday [week] but he thinks it could be postponed for a few days if I could leave the next day or two. . . . What Lloyd George wants is some one to overrule Pershing. They probably intend to bring up the same old question. . . .

We both believe that whatever is contemplated at this next meeting can rest long enough to get a cable directly from you in the event it is necessary to decide any difference which may arise between them and Pershing. Please be assured that I am perfectly willing to go now or at any time in your judgment I should go. We think, however, it would be much better for me to go later, probably in September or October, if you think it wise for me to go at all. . . .

Both Reading and House felt that the disadvantages of Lloyd George's proposal outweighed its advantages. For if the President's representative sided with Pershing, the President would be gravely embarrassed; on the other hand, if he differed from the American Commander it would openly proclaim a serious difference among the Americans at the Supreme Council. However, Reading put aside his personal feelings and went to see the President two days later. The outcome of this interview was as he anticipated. The President turned down Lloyd George's suggestion. Reading, who was with Wilson on this and against Lloyd George, subsequently told Gordon Auchincloss that it was the most satisfactory interview he had had with the President since he had been in America.

On this occasion the President told the Ambassador that the ultimate question for him to decide was, what was Foch's opinion? 'And neither House nor any political representative could assist him [the President] in ascertaining the answer.' At the same time Wilson

---

[1] House, Vol. III, p. 459.
[2] House noted in his diary the same day: 'Reading said the cable was of such a peremptory nature that it would be necessary for him to ask for an immediate interview with the President so as to present it to him. I asked him not to argue the matter with the President but merely to present it. It is my purpose to write to the President and "beat Reading to it" by a lap or two.'

made it clear that he felt a special responsibility as regards Foch's advice, 'as he has from the first been in favour of unity of command'. In fact, it had already been intimated to Foch by War Secretary Baker through the French Ambassador, with the President's approval, that 'if General Foch felt that the agreement made did not meet the exigencies of the military situation, the best course would be for General Foch spontaneously to send for General Pershing, go over the military situation with him, and get General Pershing to agree to whatever modification is proper'. In that event, there could be 'no possible holdback on General Pershing's part due to a feeling that his Government was not relying upon his judgment'.[1]

Something like this solution appears to have been applied in practice. At all events, the Supreme Council agreed at its June meeting, with Pershing's express concurrence, on future troop transports, namely that absolute priority should be given to 170,000 infantry and machine-gunners for June and a similar priority to 140,000 for July. The surplus provided by the additional tonnage was to be used to complete American divisions. Thus was American manpower transferred to the battle front and at the same time the sinews of a great national army built up. In the event, close on a million American troops were safely sent across to France by the end of July instead of the 480,000 demanded by the Supreme War Council, and many of them fought with the greatest gallantry. 'The news is fine and it is splendid that the Americans are doing so well,' Reading wrote jubilantly to Wiseman on July 21. 'It is a great stimulus to them and also to the Allies.'[2]

5

Besides the question of American reinforcements for Europe, there was another military problem with strong political overtones with which Reading had to struggle at the same time. This was the plan to open up a second Front in the Far East with the object of diverting German troops from the West and at the same time denying to Germany access to the food and raw materials of Russia and Eastern Siberia. Since Japan was one of the Allies and was ready to land an expedition at Vladivostok with the object of rallying the Cossacks

---

[1] Baker, Vol. VIII, p. 135.
[2] Wiseman Papers.

and other anti-German elements (and incidentally anti-Bolshevik) to
the Allied cause, the War Cabinet agreed to support Japanese intervention in spite of the risks involved of annoying the newly established
Soviet Government in Moscow and possibly driving the Russian
people into the hands of Germany, as indeed Mr Robert Bruce
Lockhart, Britain's diplomatic Agent accredited to the Bolsheviks,
had warned might happen. But the President disliked the idea from
the beginning, arguing that interference in the affairs of a foreign
country was contrary to American principles and would be resented
by the American people, who wanted the Russians to work out
their own destiny – also that Japan was unpopular in the United
States who suspected her designs of imperialism in Asia and the
Pacific.

After the Bolsheviks had concluded peace with the Germans,
which they did at Brest-Litovsk in March, 1918, and the Germans
began to transfer divisions from the Eastern Front, the French
demanded immediate action in the Supreme War Council, and Reading was instructed to renew his efforts to win American co-operation.
But the President continued to stall. 'I have not changed my mind,'
Wilson told the British Ambassador. The utmost he would concede
was that he would not object to the Anglo-French request to Japan
to intervene.

Early in April the Japanese landed a small force of marines at
Vladivostok ostensibly to protect their nationals, and the British
promptly sent a similar contingent to insure that any subsequent
intervention should be an Allied as distinct from an exclusively
Japanese one. Reading was thereupon instructed to put two questions
to the President – first, whether the American Government would
co-operate with the British in offering assistance to the Bolsheviks in
the event of renewed German aggression, and second, whether the
Americans would send an expedition to the Far East. Once again the
President hesitated.

Lord Reading to Foreign Secretary[1]

Washington.
May 5, 1918

There is a steady influence upon the President which makes him
decline to commit himself. It is partly that the reports he receives make
him very apprehensive of the effect upon the Russian people and partly
that he thinks the military advantage will not be worth the risk. In

[1] Balfour Papers.

addition there is a decided anti-Japanese feeling in California and among the Republicans and Democrats.

I have been in communication with Colonel House about the matter and told him I was ready to wait patiently provided consideration was being given to it for an answer to your questions, but that if the President had really decided against your proposals and did not mean to consider them further it would be better to let us know.

The Colonel is more favourable to the proposals than hitherto, but no one here wishes to take a decision. I met Senator Lodge today and had some conversation with him upon intervention – he is distinctly in favour of it. I cannot, however, conceal from myself that all the latest reports seem to confirm the American apprehensions of the effect in Russia and moreover suggest that the Bolsheviki are very definitely adverse to Allied assistance. . . .

> Washington.
> May 22, 1918

At my interview with the President yesterday, I again represented your views on intervention in Russia. As I expected, I found the President quite decided that the moment was inopportune, in other words that he did not think the circumstances sufficiently warranted the proposed action. . . .

I asked the President whether in the present circumstances he was of opinion that no action should be taken or whether he proposes any other operation. His answer was that he much regretted it but saw no alternative at the moment other than an anxious watching of the situation. . . .

A day or two before this last meeting with Reading, the President had received a dispatch from Mr Paul Reinsch, the U.S. Minister in China, drawing attention to the chaotic conditions in Siberia and pointing out that the situation there was 'more favourable than ever for effective joint action of Allies and American initiative'. He suggested the dispatch of a relief commission which he thought would be able to reconstruct Siberia as an Allied factor economically. Secretary of State Lansing was not enthusiastic when Wilson first asked his opinion, and seems only to have come round to the idea when House's son-in-law, Gordon Auchincloss, suggested that Herbert Hoover should lead it. (Hoover's name was well known for his Belgian refugee work.) When Wiseman saw the President shortly afterwards, the President had more or less adopted the idea as his own.

May 30, 1918

The President sent for me yesterday, and I had an hour's conversation with him. As to Japanese intervention, he asked what was the genesis of the movement. I told him the idea was two-fold: first of all to re-create a Russian front, and secondly, to help the Russian people. . . .

He said that no military man with whom he had talked had been able to convince him that there was any practical scheme which would recreate a Russian front. . . . If we could have put a large British-American force into Vladivostok and advanced along the Siberian Railroad, we might, he thought, have rallied the Russian people to assist in defence of their country. But if we relied mainly on Japanese military assistance, we should rally the Russians against us, excepting for a small reactionary body who would join anybody to destroy the Bolsheviki. . . .

His own idea was to send a Civil Commission of British, French and Americans to Russia to help organize the railroads and food supplies, and, since currency is worthless, organize a system of barter. . . .

June 14

The President is still firmly opposed to intervention by the Japanese alone. He is also opposed to Allied-cum-Japanese intervention on the ground that this amounts to practically the same thing, because the Japanese would supply the greater part of any military force. . . .

A week later, the British Ambassador took the opportunity of a visit to Harvard, where he received an honorary degree, to spend a day with Colonel House, who had a seaside place on the Boston north shore near by. They mostly discussed the Russian situation. After his visitor had left, House wrote to the President (June 21): 'I believe something must be done immediately about Russia, otherwise it will become the prey of Germany. It has become now a question of days rather than months.' He recommended the President to inform Congress that he was sending out a Russian relief mission under Hoover and had asked for similar assistance from England, France, Italy and Japan. 'This programme will place the Russian and Eastern situation in your hands and will satisfy the Allies and perhaps reconcile the greater part of Russia towards this kind of intervention.' He added that Reading was 'enthusiastic over this plan' and that he

[1] Wiseman Papers; Willert, pp. 147, 148.

had asked him to discuss it with the President when he next received the Ambassador.[1] In point of fact, Reading was not much attracted by the plan, but he thought it was better than nothing.

Meanwhile Reading had received a curious piece of news from London which slightly alarmed him. Alexander Kerensky, the leader of the Russian Socialist Revolutionary Party and former head of the Provincial Government in Petrograd, who was ousted from power when the Bolsheviks took over under Lenin's leadership in October, 1917, and then went underground, had managed to escape from the country disguised as a Serbian army officer and had made his way to England, thanks to a visa granted by Bruce Lockhart in Moscow on his own responsibility. Indeed Kerensky owed his life to Bruce Lockhart, since he was in imminent danger of falling into the hands of the Bolsheviks at this time and, had he done so, he would un-doubtedly have been shot. On June 24, 1918, a few days after his arrival in London, Kerensky called on Lloyd George in Downing Street with a view to securing the support of the Allies for his Pro-visional Government which he claimed to be the rightful one deriving its authority from the Constituent Assembly which the Bolsheviks had dissolved. In fact, he wanted the Allies to guarantee to put him in the saddle again and for this reason he strongly approved of the proposed Allied intervention through Siberia. The Allies must look for their friends among the Liberal and Socialist Parties for whom he spoke. 'They would get no real support from the Bolsheviks or the reactionaries. The only real policy was to continue on the lines of the old alliance.'

Lloyd George listened patiently to what Kerensky had to say, but he could get no clear assurance from him that he represented any organized force, 'apart from resolutions passed in secret by dis-gruntled Socialists'. The Prime Minister's immediate conclusion was that Kerensky was underestimating the strength of the Bolsheviks. On the other hand, he seems to have thought that there would be no harm in his visitor seeing other Allied leaders, and telegrams were ac-cordingly dispatched from the Foreign Office to Paris and Washing-ton to this effect. 'We only let him come here because we understood he was flying for his life,' Balfour telegraphed Reading, 'and are anxious for him to proceed to America as soon as possible where he will be much less embarrassing to the Allied cause generally and would be more useful in enlightening American opinion.'

[1] House, Vol. III, pp. 424–26.

Lord Reading to Foreign Secretary[1]

Washington.
June 24, 1918

It would be most unfortunate if M. Kerensky came here at present. There is a distinct movement here in favour of some steps being taken as regards intervention in Russia. President is now considering matter and will probably in a short time consult you as to his proposals before making an announcement in public. If he made it soon after M. Kerensky's arrival, it would be most unfortunate.

Colonel House whom I have seen and to whom I have mentioned your telegram feels very strongly upon advisability of Kerensky's arrival at present. I trust M. Kerensky's arrival may be postponed. . . .

This view was endorsed by Lansing, who informed the other Allies that he considered such a visit 'undesirable'. Accordingly Balfour was able to reassure Reading that it would not take place 'for some little time', if indeed it took place at all. Nor was the unfortunate Kerensky able to return to Russia. The truth was that his political influence was virtually at an end, and he quickly faded from the scene except as an interesting historical relic of the brief hectic transitional period between Tsarist and Bolshevik rule.

Still the President made no move. On June 27, Marshal Foch cabled him strongly urging a joint military expedition to Siberia 'as a very important factor for victory provided action be immediate on account of the season being already advanced'. Finally, on July 3, Reading called at the White House and presented a document initiated by the British, French and Italian Prime Ministers and approved by the Supreme War Council to the effect that 'since its last meeting a complete change has come over the situation in Russia and Siberia, which makes Allied intervention in these countries an imperative necessity.'

An important factor in the situation was provided by the Czechs of whom 300,000 had deserted from the Austrian forces and after the downfall of the Tsarist régime in March, 1917, had with the consent of Kerensky's Russian Provisional Government been formed into an army known as the Czech Legion by Dr Thomas Masaryk, the Czech political leader and subsequently first President of Czechoslovakia, to fight against the Central Powers on the faith of an Allied guarantee of the eventual deliverance of their country from Austrian rule. After the Bolsheviks took over and made peace at

[1] Balfour Papers.

Brest-Litovsk with the Germans, the Czechs were convinced that the Soviet authorities had decided under German pressure to intern them and so prevent their transference to the Western Front. As a result, they headed for the east and with marked courage fought their way across Asia, in conflict at various times with Germans, Hungarians, Bolsheviks and other Russian elements, seizing large sections of the Trans-Siberian Railway and disarming the local garrisons of the Red Army. Thus they occupied considerable tracts of territory between the Urals and Lake Baikal. On June 29 a contingent of them reached Vladivostok, which they captured after a three-hour battle with the Bolsheviks, and from which they hoped to proceed by sea to France. A pro-Ally Coalition Government was then set up under Czech protection. Twelve days later the British War Cabinet decided to send a battalion of troops from Hong Kong to Vladivostok to support the Czechs there. Their courageous behaviour had excited widespread admiration and there was a growing feeling that neither they nor their comrades west of Lake Baikal should be allowed to be exterminated by the Red Army.

The President felt he could not delay a decision any longer. 'I have been sweating blood over the question what is right and feasible to do in Russia,' he wrote to House on July 8. 'It goes to pieces like quicksilver under my touch, but I hope I see and can report some progress presently along the double line of economic assistance and aid to the Czechoslovaks.' Wiseman, with his usual acute perception, had already grasped the point. 'The Czechoslovak position has, in my opinion, materially altered the situation and will be, I think, the determining factor,' he wrote to Murray at this time. 'The President recognizes that both the Allies and the United States are responsible for the Czechs, and if possible must render them assistance. You may be sure that Reading is acting with great tact and firmness, and we are being helped by the much fuller information which we now receive from the F.O. cables.'

Lord Reading to Prime Minister

Washington.
July 12, 1918

The overthrow of the Czar and establishment of a republic was welcomed with the utmost enthusiasm in America. The sympathy and hope for the new republic was, I believe, far stronger and more genuine here than in Europe. Ever since the question of intervention was first discussed, Americans have feared that the interventionist movement would be controlled by friends of the old Imperial régime, and, however disguised, intervention would eventually prove to be a reactionary weapon and an anti-republican influence. Further, the President is apprehensive lest any intervention should be converted into an anti-Soviet movement and an interference with the right of Russians to choose their own form of government. . . .

We should take care to reassure opinion here in order to carry the President with us in any further movement that may become necessary. At present his intention is to help the Czechoslovaks, but nevertheless as I read his mind, it is still opposed to intervention and somewhat apprehensive lest the step he is now willing to take should lead him into a much more extended policy. It is for this reason that I think it is important to give a liberal turn to our assistance to Russia. . . .

With this last point in mind, Reading suggested, in addition to the military contingent, 'a Labour or Socialist delegation headed by some prominent Labour leader'.

Lt.-Colonel Arthur Murray, M.P. to Sir William Wiseman.

London.
July 16, 1918

I have conveyed to you in my cables the very great stress laid by the Government on the importance of Allied intervention in Russia. Unquestionably, you and Reading have had a very hard task to bring the President round to his present way of thinking. Personally I felt with you that the chief thing was to make a start, and that once American troops were landed at Vladivostok, matters might develop in a way that would be satisfactory to all concerned. I am inclined to think on the whole that in the end the cautious policy of the President may turn out to be the wisest and best. History alone can decide whether a large force composed chiefly of Japanese as was suggested would not have had the effect that the President forecasted. In any case, it seems to me that a bridge now having been built, we can only hope that Allied assistance will take a favourable course. . . .

I have telegraphed you regarding my conversation with Milner [War Minister]. . . . He is very anxious indeed that no time should be lost in conveying the expedition to Vladivostok, in order that its initial preparations in Siberia may be completed before the winter sets in. No one, of course has any formed idea as to what particular course events in those regions may take. All that is hoped at present is that assistance to the Czechs will enable the railway line to be firmly held, and will rally anti-Bolshevist elements in Russia to the allied standards.

Lockhart has lately been insisting in his telegrams that the delay in sending an allied expedition has thrown many elements in Russia that might have been with us into the arms of Germany. He instances especially the case of Miliukov, who, he says, was quite ready to work with us, but in despair has now gone over to the enemy. Personally I never had very much faith in the argument that it would be possible to recreate an eastern front. It is quite true that there may be many Russians who are anti-German, and who would like, if possible, to oust Germans from their country, but on the other hand I cannot really believe that any sufficient number are anxious to recreate such an army as would alone achieve the objects that some of our inter-ventionists have in view. These, however, are speculations, and the main thing at the moment is to get on with the policy that has recently been agreed upon. . . .

A telegram came through last night from Reading to the Prime Minister in which the former suggested that a Labour or Socialist delegation headed by some prominent Labour leader should be sent with the Allied forces. I discussed this question with Philip Kerr [Lloyd George's Private Secretary]. The idea seems to me to be a very good one *au fond*, but a very delicate one to handle and carry out. . . . The real difficulty that I see in the idea is the selection of the delega-tion, and more particularly of its leader. . . . It may be that the best way out would be to leave it to the executive of the British Labour Party to make the choice. . . .

The Prime Minister agreed with the principle of Reading's sugges-tion. 'If the President proposes to send powerful political delegation, representative of the Allies, but in which United States should take leading part,' he cabled in reply, 'we should certainly send Liberal or Labour representatives to accompany it.'

By this time the President had already summoned the key members of his Cabinet and the Army Chief of Staff to the White House and informed them confidentially what he had decided. The Supreme War Council's idea of mounting a second front in Siberia was unrealistic and out of the question. The situation of the Czechs, on the other hand, he said, warranted an Allied effort 'to aid those at Vladivostok in forming a junction with their compatriots in Western Siberia'. If Japan was willing to co-operate, he went on, the U.S. Government would be prepared to join in getting immediate supplies of arms and ammunition to the Czechs at Vladivostok and in making available a military force to guard their line of communication as they moved westward. A force of 7,000 Americans and the same number of Japanese was suggested, with possible smaller contributions from the other Allies, the Japanese to send their troops at once and the

Americans as soon as possible. The President added that the Government would also send a small military expedition to north Russia in co-operation with the British and French. He afterwards told Newton Baker, the Secretary of War, who particularly disliked the latter expedition, that he was 'obliged to do it anyhow because the French and British were pressing it upon his attention so hard and he had refused so many of their requests that they were beginning to feel that he was not a good associate, much less a good ally'.

Nor did the Vladivostok plan command the unanimous approval of the President's advisers. Seeing General Peyton C. March shaking his head vigorously while he was speaking, President Wilson turned to him and asked with some asperity, 'Why are you shaking your head?' Then, without pausing for a reply, he went on, 'You are opposed to this because you do not think Japan will limit herself to 7,000 men, and that this decision will further her schemes for territorial aggrandizement.'

'Just that, Mr President,' said the General who was no 'yes man', 'and for other military reasons which I have told you.'

'Well,' said Wilson, 'we will have to take that chance.'[1]

On July 17 the President's decision was conveyed to Reading and the other Allied Ambassadors in Washington by Secretary of State Lansing in the form of an *aide-memoire*, the original text of which had been composed by the President on his own typewriter. While rejecting any sizeable military intervention in Russia as being 'of no advantage in the prosecution of our main design, to win the War against Germany', President Wilson agreed to the dispatch of a small expedition to Vladivostok and also one to Murmansk.

> For helping the Czechoslovaks there is immediate necessity and sufficient justification. Recent developments have made it evident that that is in the interest of what the Russian people themselves desire, and the Government of the United States is glad to contribute the small force at its disposal for that purpose. It yields, also, to the judgment of the Supreme Command in the matter of establishing a small base at Murmansk, to guard the military stores at Kola, and to make it safe for Russian forces to come together in organized bodies in the north. But it . . . can go no further. It is not in a position . . . to take part in organized intervention in adequate force from either Vladivostok or Murmansk and Archangel. . . .

[1] Baker, Vol. VIII, pp. 256, 284 note. See also the excellent account of the interventions given by George F. Kennan in Chapters 5-8 of his *Russia and the West under Lenin and Stalin* (1961).

It hopes to carry out the plans for safeguarding the rear of the Czechoslovaks operating from Vladivostok in a way that will place it and keep it in close co-operation with a small military force like its own from Japan, and if necessary from the other Allies. . . .

It was also hoped to send an economic relief mission to Siberia. At the same time the President expressed the intention of asking all associated in the proposed course of action either in Siberia or north Russia to unite in assuring the Russian people that there was no intention of interfering with Russia's political sovereignty or intervening in her internal affairs or impairing her territorial integrity in any way 'either now or hereafter'.[1]

When Colonel House had read the *aide-memoire*, he said to Wiseman that he thought it set forth the position quite clearly and was a very earnest endeavour to express the President's considered judgment. 'My own view,' Wiseman told Reading, 'is that this document will annoy London and Paris considerably. In truth the President gives every excuse except the real one, which is that he believes the interventionists are reactionaries under another name.'[2]

Wiseman's prediction was correct. But Balfour tactfully disguised his annoyance in a telegram which he sent Reading in response to the Ambassador's request for an appropriate acknowledgment of the Wilson *aide-memoire*.

Foreign Secretary to Lord Reading[3]

London. July 22, 1918. Your personal and secret telegram of July 19. For obvious reasons it is not very easy to devise a satisfactory message to the President.

On the one hand, we view with great satisfaction his resolve to send an American-Japanese force to Siberia. This will, we hope, be a great encouragement to the Czechs, and will give them much-needed reinforcements. Moreover it admits the principle of giving external aid to Russia and we gladly welcome his acceptance of a policy which we know he regards with much misgiving.

On the other hand, we cannot pretend to ourselves, nor ought we to convey to him, that we regard the size of the American-Japanese force as in any way adequate to the necessities of the case. To us it seems almost certain that either the Allied expedition will fail or that it will have to be largely reinforced: we hope the latter. But these are hopes

[1] Baker, Vol. VIII, p. 283.
[2] Reading Papers; Willert, p. 149.
[3] Balfour Papers.

which you can hardly convey to the President. In any case we trust that what the President is prepared to do will be done quickly.

As regards the President's fears that, through British or French action, America will be dragged into a policy of interference with Russia's domestic affairs, you may express to him in the most emphatic terms that such interference would be quite contrary to our wishes. It is, of course, perfectly true that, with the best will in the world, military intervention is certain to have an effect on Russian Parties. Indirectly it will strengthen any Party which is prepared to fight the Germans, and injure any Party which turns to Germany for assistance. We can only do our best to keep aloof from internal controversies.

Such parts of this telegram as it was felt desirable for the President to know were communicated to him in what was to be the last call which Reading was to make at the White House for some months. At the same time Reading told the President that he expected to depart for England within the next week for a period of leave and consultation.

Reading left the White House with the uncomfortable feeling that the President was far from enthusiastic about what his military advisers regarded as an unnecessary 'side-show', to which he had given his consent reluctantly as the result of continued Allied pressure. Nor did he seem to the Ambassador to be aware of the urgency of the situation in the Far East. Reading's anxiety increased during the next few days as the result of information received from that quarter, which he conveyed to the State Department on the day he left Washington to embark in New York. 'My reports from Siberia and Russia strongly emphasize the need for immediate action,' he wrote on July 29. 'I confess the delay is rather on my mind, as I am sure it is on yours, so I hope the Japanese will hurry. It would be a dreadful reflection if the Czechoslovaks met with a disaster which could have been avoided by prompter assistance.'[1]

6

Several other matters with which Reading was concerned during his Embassy may be briefly mentioned. In particular, there was the perennial question of Ireland; there was the proposal to establish a

[1] Reading Papers; Reading, Vol. II, p. 121.

national home for the Jews in Palestine; and there was the problem of his own personal plans for the future and how long he could remain Ambassador to the United States while continuing to hold the great office of Lord Chief Justice of England.

When the United States entered the War, Lloyd George was pressed by Page, the American Ambassador in London, to settle the Irish question once and for all. The Prime Minister accordingly approached John Redmond, the veteran Irish Nationalist leader, with a proposal for a convention of Irishmen of all parties to work out a scheme of self-government. Under the chairmanship of Sir Horace Plunkett, a well-intentioned idealist, who had devoted most of his sixty-seven years to experiments in co-operative agriculture in Ireland, the Irish Convention sat in secret session throughout the summer and winter, unfortunately without reaching any agreed recommendations, while the extreme elements on either side stood aloof from the proceedings. However, Plunkett kept the White House informed of what was happening, and his secret reports enabled Wilson to resist pressure from the Irish-Americans to sponsor protests against British policy in Ireland. After his arrival in Washington, Reading constantly asked Murray, whom he fed with the latest information on the subject from Washington, to urge upon the Prime Minister to persuade the Cabinet to make an immediate grant of Home Rule to Ireland on as generous lines as possible.

Lord Reading to Lt.-Colonel Arthur Murray, M.P.
(Telegram)

Washington. April 15, 1918. To carry opinion here, and particularly Irish opinion of moderate tendencies, it would be necessary for the British Government to declare its intention not only to stake its existence on the passing of a Home Rule measure but also its intention to put the Act into operation at once. The fundamental trouble is that unfortunately the Irish and their friends have lost confidence in the passing of an Act. What they require is to see an Act put into operation by a Government that will not shrink from it if serious opposition is raised. If the Government is pledged to Home Rule and strives without delay to pass it, the President will, I think, find satisfactory answers to any representations made.

Murray placed the substance of this telegram before the Prime Minister who read it to the Cabinet. After Murray had cabled in reply that 'it had decisive effect on collective opinion of Cabinet regarding policy to be adopted with regard to Home Rule and conscription', the Cabinet decided first to conscript the Irish for military service and then to announce Home Rule for the whole country as a bait for the South to come in. This seemed to Americans of moderate opinion, and indeed to Reading as well, to be putting the cart before the horse. There was the danger too that the Unionists in the North would resist any attempt to coerce Ulster. As the Ambassador told Murray, 'the tendency is for Americans and moderate Irishmen rather to resent happenings in Ireland with regard to conscription which are alienating the sympathy of many who have been good friends of Ireland in the past. If only a generous measure of Home Rule could be given, I think it would satisfy all but the extremists who would never be satisfied. . . . The intelligent American understands that of course Ulster cannot be sacrificed, but he fails to understand why it cannot be safeguarded. Generally my impression is that America would welcome a fair and generous treatment of Ulster, provided that it forms part of the Government of Ireland.'

Lord Reading to Prime Minister[1]

Washington.
May 5, 1918

Everything I sent to Murray about Ireland is daily confirmed by all I see and hear. . . .

If only you can get a good Home Rule Bill into operation, the effect here will be very marked and will remove almost the chief cause of anti-British feeling. It is easy to understand that a people 3,000 miles away, who have resorted to conscription and are sending their men to France, cannot have sympathy with the Irish anti-conscriptionist movement, but the subject at present gets confused with the wrongs of Ireland because the principle of self-determination upon which they lay such stress is not applied.

One Irishman in the United States who did more perhaps than any other to keep Irish-American opinion on moderate lines was Shane Leslie, the eccentric and picturesque Irish Nationalist son of a Unionist baronet and, incidentally, first cousin to Winston Churchill. Leslie was a convert to the Roman Catholic faith and before coming to the United States had served bravely with the American Motor Ambulance Corps in France. After Reading's appointment in Washington, Horace Plunkett asked the Foreign Office to let the new Ambassador know of the excellent work Leslie was doing. 'He hopes that you will find it possible to keep in touch with him,' Drummond

[1] Lloyd George Papers.

K

cabled, 'and turn a friendly ear to what he has to say. As you know he was on excellent terms with Cecil Spring Rice.'

Reading invited Leslie to dine with him privately and 'put him wise' on certain points. Leslie went and talked afterwards for over an hour on the Irish-American-Catholic situations. 'I talked too much,' Leslie recalled afterwards, 'but Reading stayed wide awake and watchful. He realized the difficulties but he seemed courageous and ready. On a delicate point he said Casement was magnificently defended by Serjeant Sullivan. I told him the Irish in America had no grudge against him as the condemning judge. England would have had a magnificent chance of thrilling the world by a royal pardon.'

Leslie thought it would be an excellent idea if the new Ambassador could meet Cardinal Gibbons, the Archbishop of Baltimore, in preference to the latter joining with the other American Archbishops in a public protest about British policy towards Ireland. There had never been any personal contact between the Catholic hierarchy and the Embassy. Since the outbreak of the War the prelates could not afford to go to the Embassy and Spring Rice had not liked to meet them on neutral ground. Leslie enlisted Arthur Willert's help in an effort to put the matter right. Reading agreed to meet Gibbons, and the Cardinal invited him to lunch at Baltimore along with Leslie and Willert. The Cardinal turned out to be a man of humour as well as much wisdom. There was a bottle of Rhine wine on the table which his guests noticed as they went into the dining-room. 'Here,' said the Cardinal, 'is a protest against two tendencies of the age, prohibition and the idea that we should not take advantage of anything good the enemy may produce!' A return visit was arranged at the Rectory of St Aloysius Church in Washington. 'We thought this was a good compromise,' said Willert later, 'as the Cardinal went to Washington and the Ambassador met him on Church territory.'

Willert accompanied the Ambassador to the Rectory, where they found Leslie waiting for them in the street outside. Leslie immediately took them into the entrance hall and opened a door on the right. Inside they saw the Cardinal gleaming in his robes. 'Your Eminence,' said Leslie with mock solemnity, 'I introduce the Old Testament to the New!' (Willert described this as the best epigram in a lifetime.)

Recalling the scene afterwards, Leslie remarked, 'The Cardinal and the Ambassador conferred charmingly for twenty-five minutes. Their profiles made a splendid picture. Given full powers they could have settled the troubles of Dublin and Jerusalem.' Shortly afterwards

Leslie wrote to Willert: 'His Eminence was more than pleased by Lord Reading's courtesy in paying his call. I think it was well worth while. Since the Civil War the British Embassy has restricted its sympathetic attention to the party successful in that war and to the philo-British coterie.'

House noted in his diary at this time (February 24, 1918):

> I dined with Lord Reading. . . . He told me of an interesting conversation he had with Cardinal Gibbons, pledging me to secrecy. It seems the Pope wishes to sit at the Peace Conference. Reading thought it was to reinforce the temporal power, Gibbons denied this. Reading then thought it was to help Austria, and Gibbons only half-way denied this.

When Leslie received an advance statement of Lloyd George's latest Home Rule plan which was to follow conscription, he took it to the President's Irish-American secretary Joe Tumulty in the White House. Tumulty promised to show it to the President that night. Leslie then went on to the Embassy where he saw Reading and asked him about the timing of the plan. 'The Prime Minister has given his word for Home Rule,' the Ambassador told Leslie.

'May I tell Tumulty the Prime Minister will keep his word?'

'Yes,' answered Reading.

When they next met, Tumulty told Leslie that the President had described the Irish situation to him as 'a millstone round his neck'. Leslie asked if he might pass this remark on to Reading in order to strengthen Plunkett's hand at the Irish Convention. Tumulty at first refused, but eventually a compromise was reached by which Leslie was allowed to write a letter to Reading on White House writing-paper reporting the President's remark but without specifying who had made it. The Ambassador understood and acted.

'That was our highest watermark,' said Leslie afterwards. Thereafter the tide of Anglo-Irish-American understanding began to recede. While conscription quickly became a dead letter in Ireland and no attempt was made by the British authorities to enforce it, in the face of combined Nationalist and Sinn Fein opposition, Home Rule was once more shelved. The official excuse was that the Sinn Fein leaders were in treasonable correspondence with Germany. Leslie was greatly disillusioned. He wrote to Reading that he would be 'compelled in honour to enter the American service and disappear'. (This course was facilitated by the fact that his mother was American and he had many American relatives.)

Soon Reading, who shared Leslie's misgivings, was reporting to London the tendency of enlightened American opinion to regard the British Government as having lost the psychological moment for the introduction and passing of Home Rule. In this context his considered opinion of Shane Leslie's efforts, which he later put on record officially, is of interest:

> His own views are those of a strong, I might say vehement, supporter of Home Rule, and he has undoubtedly acquired a position of influence with the Irish and the Roman Catholics in the United States. During the War he has laboured strenuously to prevent outbreaks in the Press of discontent and grievance on the part of sympathizers with the Irish, and he has been instrumental in quieting some of the chief persons in the United States who are interested in Irish affairs by causing them to believe that a measure of Home Rule, in the main based upon the Irish Convention Report, would not only be passed but would be brought into operation at an early date.
> He made representations to this effect only after the announcement was made here of the intention of His Majesty's Government to stand or fall by Home Rule. This announcement helped us very considerably in the United States and rekindled hope among those who had abandoned it.
> . . . I can understand his disgust for the reason that assuredly he has pledged himself that His Majesty's Government would follow the course above indicated, and he now finds himself confronted with this assurance which has not yet resulted in action.[1]

Shane Leslie did carry out his intention of registering for overseas service with the United States forces, but the Armistice came before he could be called up. He was probably the nearest approach which Britain had to a secret and unpaid propaganda agent, and in this respect he proved most useful to Reading, for he was careful never to put a foot wrong. It was not his fault, or Reading's for that matter, that his Irish-Catholic friends thought they had been let down.

To pass from Dublin to Jerusalem. The anti-British feelings of the American-Irish for what the British had failed to do for Ireland were offset by the pro-British feelings of the American Jews for what Britain had publicly expressed her intention of doing for Jewry. The pledge of official British support for a Jewish national home in Palestine was a decision of the Cabinet, but since it was conveyed in the form of a letter to Lord Rothschild, the President of the English

[1] Reading to Walter Long, October 22, 1918: Reading Papers (F.O. 800/222).

Zionist Federation, in November, 1917, and signed by Balfour as
Foreign Secretary, it came to be known as the Balfour Declaration.
Jerusalem had already fallen to General Allenby's forces and the
Turks were in full retreat from the country which now came under
British military occupation. The Jews in America were naturally
enthusiastic, and Reading found himself inundated on his arrival with
invitations to speak at Zionist and Jewish community functions from
Boston to Atlanta. He found it difficult to refuse these invitations,
particularly as his friend Mr Justice Brandeis, later a Supreme Court
Judge, was a prominent American Zionist leader. But he had to do so,
since his job was in Washington. It was the same with requests for
articles and messages to Jewish journals on such themes as 'What
should the American Jew do for Palestine?' On the other hand, he
had no wish to offend American Jewry, particularly when it became
known that Jewish contingents were being recruited for service overseas and one was on the point of embarkation. He was advised by
Willert and the Press section of the Embassy that he should issue a
message to American Jewry for publication in the light of the Balfour
Declaration.

The statement, which appeared over his name throughout the
country on March 27, 1918, gave general satisfaction. One journal
ran it in Yiddish beside his portrait. He paid a warm tribute to the
American Zionists and to the Jewish people of America for their
contribution to the War effort and also praised the Jewish military
recruits. 'It would be magnificent,' he said, 'if some of them could
strike a blow for the freedom of the world in the land of our ancestors.'
He further expressed his satisfaction that Palestine was being re-
habilitated, even while the War continued, by Jewish money and
Jewish energy, so much of which was being provided by American
Jewry. 'My good wishes are with the Zionists in the United States
in the great work that is before them in giving effect to the Declaration
of the British Government,' he concluded, 'and I shall esteem anything that I may be called upon to do in connection with that work
as not the least important or the least satisfactory part of my duties
as British Ambassador in Washington.'

While this was a useful official statement, it must be pointed out
that it did not reflect Reading's personal opinion. When Willert came
to him with the suggestion for the timeliness of something on Zionism
seeing that it was in the forefront of the peace programme and
backed by the best of American Jewry, the *Times* correspondent was

considerably surprised when the Ambassador hung back and instead of having ready what he wanted to say asked Willert to draft something. 'You see,' he explained in effect, 'I have no great personal sympathy with Zionism. Why should I have? Here I am Ambassador, Lord Chief Justice, Peer, and I started from nothing. I owe it all to England. I am English. How can I help it if I do not feel strongly about a national home for the Jews?'[1]

Finally there was the problem of the Ambassador's personal position and future plans. On May 30, he cabled both Lloyd George and Balfour asking to be allowed to come home some time after July, at the latest by October when the Courts resumed, anyhow for discussion if he had to stay on in America.

Foreign Secretary to Lord Reading[2]
(Telegram)

London. June 5, 1918. I cannot express to you how much Prime Minister and I appreciate the work you are doing in U.S. From every quarter, whether Democratic or Republican, testimony arrived of great value of your services in your present position. We feel that it is of highest national interest that you should prolong your period of appointment beyond that originally stipulated though we fully understand greatness of sacrifice we ask you to make.

We cannot think in the circumstances the judiciary would insist on your early return to your high office, as, however great their deprivation may be, it is after all domestic, while duties you are now executing are essential to effective prosecution of the War and cannot be performed by another.

We therefore sincerely trust that you will consent to continue your Ambassadorship. . . .

It seems probable that Reading was always a little unsure of himself in his Embassy post and never felt as close to the centre of things as he felt he ought to be. This was true of his relations with House, with whom his communications, as we have seen, were not so close when Wiseman was away. It applied even more to his relations with the President with whom he was never on anything like such an intimate footing as Wiseman was, and he was disappointed that the President had not taken him more into his confidence. Of course, Wiseman himself was well aware of this; he thought it was a great mistake from the President's own point of view, although he always

[1] Willert, p. 123.
[2] Reading Papers (F.O. 800/223/U.S./56).

did his best to reassure Reading of the President's regard for him. Shortly before the Ambassador sailed for England at the end of July, Wiseman with his usual acumen made an interesting assessment of Reading's position in the light of his special abilities and qualifications.[1]

Reading feels that he came out here not as an ordinary Ambassador, or High Commissioner, but because he thought, owing to his close connection with the Cabinet at home and his friendship on this side with members of the Administration, that he would be able to gain the President's confidence to such an extent that he would be able to discuss with him and consult with him on important questions affecting the War. He has now come to the conclusion that it is quite impossible to break down the barrier between the President and the foreign representatives and that he is unable to do more than any ordinary Ambassador could accomplish. In this I think he is quite wrong, and I have told him so.

In the first place, the President does trust him and values his opinion very highly, but it is simply not the President's nature to be communicative or to discuss affairs of state with anyone. In this respect Reading achieves far more than anyone else I can think of whom the Government could send out. Furthermore, Reading does not realize that the many problems (almost daily problems) which arise regarding finance, shipping, food, supplies, etc., which he negotiates and settles with comparative ease, would present real difficulties to anyone else, and furthermore would probably lead to friction. He has a particular gift for putting his case in a way that will appeal to the American officials and a very nice sense of how far he can go without causing trouble.

He is worried, too, about the question of the Chief Justiceship. He feels more and more that if he stays out here any longer he must resign his position, and, of course, that would be a terrible wrench for him, and in my humble opinion a sacrifice he ought not to be called upon to make. His present plan is to go home and put this position to the Prime Minister, and agree to come back for a short time, say a month or six weeks, in order to clear up here and hand over to somebody else; but I am afraid that his mind is very much against coming back here permanently.

I have discussed the whole situation frankly with House, and more cautiously with the State Department. The opinion is unanimous that it would be a disaster to the Allied Cause if Reading did not remain here until the War is over. I must say, however, that I think it is a pity

[1] Murray, p. 29.

for him to stay here too long without going home. He soon begins to feel out of touch (much more out of touch than he really is) and becomes restless and very anxious to have a full discussion of problems with the Cabinet at home.

'In all respects he has been an unqualified success,' Wiseman told Drummond.[1] 'The French and Italian representatives just follow after him. He has raised our influence and prestige right throughout the country. Among all the people of both political parties he is a great favourite, and has made friends and no enemies wherever he goes.'

Sir Arthur Willert, the London *Times* correspondent in Washington, endorsed this view in a cable to his editor, urging that Reading deserved the best reception the English Press could give him:

> His prompt realization of the danger and his masterly handling of the American officials involved had as much to do with the saving of the food crisis as Hoover's organization. To him more than anybody else belongs the credit for the American troop movements. I am convinced that but for his diplomacy and the success of his personal contact with the President, the Russian issue, the delicacy of which cannot be exaggerated, would have never been pushed to a successful conclusion. He has made himself a commanding position in Washington and in a few months has effectively rescued the Embassy from the slough into which it had fallen. He has been untiring in his work and has never hesitated to spend himself in the making of speeches which have helped us greatly with public opinion. It is essential that he should return here shortly.[2]

7

Reading and his wife made the homeward voyage in the *Mauretania*, which had been fitted out as a troop transport and was 'filled with fine stalwart specimens of American manhood', as he described his fellow passengers in a statement he made to *The Times* on his arrival in England. 'Their conduct was remarkably good, and earned the greatest praise of the British generals and other officers on board. One could not see those American soldiers without realizing they were earnest, thoughtful men, intent upon acquitting themselves well

---

[1] July 19, 1918: Balfour Papers.
[2] Willert to Geoffrey Dawson, July 30, 1918: Wiseman Papers.

for the sake of their country and inspired by the great ideals so well expressed by the President.'[1]

An office was put at Reading's disposal in the War Cabinet offices in Whitehall Gardens, so that he could be available for consultation on American affairs and for any *ad hoc* job which Lloyd George or the Cabinet might give him. A few days after his arrival, he went to Windsor to report to the King. Amongst other topics they discussed was the Allied expedition to Siberia, and Reading found His Majesty extremely anxious about the situation of the Czechs and the urgency of mobilizing an adequate force to relieve them. As Reading noted at the time, the King's observations apart from their own value reflected the opinion of the public.

Lt.-Colonel Arthur Murray, M.P., to Sir William Wiseman
London.
August 20, 1918

Reading has today sent a telegram to you on the subject of the situation in Siberia. He has given very careful thought to its composition with a view to impressing upon you the serious aspect in which the situation is viewed over here. The serious thing, of course, is that the autumn is drawing on, and every week adds to the difficulties with which the relieving forces will be beset owing to the severe winter conditions in that part of the world. . . .

Reading is still very busy, in my opinion much too busy as he is getting no rest at all. He attends all the meetings of the War Cabinet. This in itself is, of course, a good thing because it helps to take him out of and put him on a higher plane than the ordinary run of Ambassadors. He spends the rest of his time seeing various members of the Cabinet individually and many other people, British and American, on important affairs. In addition, he has had unloaded on to him (unfairly in my opinion) an inquiry into the whole problem of shipping and tonnage. This is not his legitimate work and it should not have been put upon him. . . . In the meantime he is looking and feeling somewhat tired, and I am pressing him hard to take his week-ends off and to go out of town. . . .

After again underlining in his telegram the dangers facing the Czechs, Reading asked Wiseman to see whether Colonel House had any suggestion to make. 'In reality it is intended to explain to him how strong is the feeling here and the outcry that would ensue if disaster overtook the Czechs,' Reading wrote the same day to Lord Stamfordham, enclosing a copy of the telegram for His Majesty's

[1] *The Times*, August 14, 1918

information. 'Please inform the King that after much consideration I have adopted this form of communication and hope that it will produce the result desired. It would not do to put the case more bluntly – the President is already inclined to think we are pressing him too far.' To this Stamfordham replied: 'His Majesty thinks you are the best judge as to how much you can say to Colonel House, but the King feels that the situation in Siberia is really very serious.'

At the Prime Minister's suggestion, Reading went over to Paris for a week to see the French Ministers and Allied Generals and to visit the front. He was accompanied by Colonel Murray and they stayed with the Ambassador Lord Derby in the British Embassy. Unfortunately, through no fault of his own, Reading got off to a poor start. Lloyd George had asked Reading to take up two particular questions with Clemenceau, future supplies of British manpower and an independent air offensive, notably long-range bombing operations, designed to destroy military and industrial objectives and also to undermine civilian morale by means of an Inter-Allied Independent Force to be under the command of General Trenchard.[1] Apparently unknown to Lloyd George, Derby had already discussed the latter subject with the French authorities on several occasions. Consequently when a telegram arrived on the morning after Reading's arrival from Lord Weir, the Air Minister, addressed to Reading through the Embassy Chancery and giving him further directions for handling the matter, Derby was extremely annoyed and talked to Reading of resignation. It required all Reading's tact and charm to placate the Ambassador's injured pride. 'I explained how hurriedly this question had arisen,' Reading reported the same day to Lloyd George, 'how pressed you were by other matters, and that you had had no time to discuss it with me. I told him that I should not handle the air offensive matter and that I had no doubt you would wish him to deal with it.' Reading accordingly suggested that the Prime Minister should telegraph the Ambassador in this sense, and the Prime Minister immediately did so, informing Derby that he was unaware that he had the negotiations in hand. It was the kind of incident not uncommon with Lloyd George.

Full accounts of their visit were sent to Wiseman by both Murray and Reading. 'I saw Clemenceau yesterday and handed him your letter,' Reading cabled Lloyd George on September 3. 'He expressed

[1] Weir to Reading, August 3, 1918; Reading Papers (F.O. 800/222/Fr.6).

greatest desire to arrive at satisfactory conclusion and agreement
with you. His tone and spirit could not have been better in reference
to yourself.' Murray wrote on their return to London:

Reading saw everyone of importance whom it was necessary for
him to see. Clemenceau he saw twice, in order to discuss with him the
question of British manpower for next year's campaign. The French
have for some time past hinted that our manpower was not being
made available up to its maximum limit. Memoranda on the question
were therefore prepared and submitted for the consideration of the
French Government. The situation was rapidly, it seems to me,
developing into one in which France would dictate to us how our
manpower should be used. Reading was commissioned by the Prime
Minister to discuss the whole matter with Clemenceau.

Previous to seeing Clemenceau, he talked with Tardieu, who is more
and more becoming one of Clemenceau's right-hand men and a
growing power in official Government circles in Paris. Tardieu
suggested to Reading that the latter and himself should be appointed
by their respective Governments to go into the whole question of
British manpower and decide what should be done. Reading headed
this off by saying that if this course were adopted, a very difficult
situation might develop. He thought it much better, therefore, that the
two Governments should agree that Great Britain, realizing the
seriousness of the situation, would do all that she possibly could to put
the maximum number of men into the field by April 1st next year.
Tardieu expressed himself in agreement with this view.

Subsequently Reading had a conversation with Clemenceau and
took the same line as in his talk with Tardieu. Clemenceau agreed that
on the whole the course suggested by Reading would be the best
course to adopt, although he said that he might still have to make an
official request in the matter. Unquestionably Reading succeeded in
thus ending satisfactorily a very unsatisfactory situation, and credit is
due to him for the manner in which he handled it. At the same time I
would observe that the situation ought never to have been allowed to
develop in the way that it did. Seeing that we have been and are keeping
France's head above water in so many different ways, it is difficult to
see why the proposition that we should in any way allow her to dictate
to us on the manpower question should have been countenanced for a
single moment.

I did not myself see Clemenceau, but Reading told me that he found
him in good fettle and in high spirits. Derby told me that Clemenceau
took him out a couple of weeks ago at half-past five in the morning to
visit the battle front. They spent the whole day driving about, coming
back to Paris at eight o'clock in the evening. 'By that time,' said

Derby, 'I was dog tired, but the old man stepped out of the car as fresh as a daisy, and after having something to eat proceeded to work until close on midnight.'

Reading also met Pershing and Foch, the former in Paris and the latter at his Command Headquarters. On his interview with Pershing, he telegraphed Wiseman:

I saw Pershing and found him just as we anticipated, full of idea that national sentiment demands that all American troops should fight as part of National Army. All questions of brigading troops with the French or ourselves have completely disappeared. He even dislikes divisions fighting with British or French troops and Foch is somewhat nervous in giving orders lest Pershing should fall out with him.

Clemenceau asked me whether the President would support Foch if Pershing would not carry out instructions of Foch. I answered that the President, who had always advocated unity of command, would in my judgment insist on Pershing acting in accordance with it. I doubt whether controversy will eventuate between Foch and Pershing, but it might, and House and probably the President should know situation.

All accounts of fighting powers and achievements of American troops are excellent, but the anxiety is as to the administration of the army in the field during a sustained and heavy American offensive.

The discussion with Pershing was largely taken up with the shipping question. As the American Commander-in-Chief somewhat wryly observed afterwards, 'the increase of British tonnage for our use seemed to hinge on the allotment of a greater proportion of our troops for service with their armies. He [Reading] advocated leaving the American Army near theirs, especially maintaining that our supply and equipment would really be facilitated, all of which was a repetition of arguments other British officials had advanced. But the question as to the employment of our troops was settled.' According to the notes which he made of this interview at the time, Reading urged that 'an Army Corps next to us would still be an American army'. But Pershing declined to commit himself beyond stating that in the present quickly changing circumstances it was 'not possible to say what might become necessary or desirable'.

The question of manpower and how it should best be apportioned as between infantry, on the one hand, and aircraft and tanks on the other, came up at Reading's meeting with Foch. The Generalissimo inclined to the more conservative view that the latter were auxiliary weapons only and that so far as personnel was concerned, they should be subordinate entirely to the requirements of the infantry.

Of this interview Reading wrote as follows:

He thought we were in great danger of over-production of tanks and aeroplanes which required large personnel which could otherwise be made available for infantry. Tanks were auxiliaries which required infantry to make effective advance. Aeroplanes intended for independent offensive could be better employed certainly when required to assist military attack. He begged the Prime Minister to take these matters into consideration and to keep up the number of divisions.

I said I had delivered detailed particulars to M. Clemenceau which showed that it was quite impossible for us to provide necessary requirements and also keep up number of divisions. I said of course more divisions could be kept if not maintained at full strength. He answered, 'by all means reduce strength in winter' provided we had divisions fully completed by April 1st next year.

Advantage must be taken of disorganized condition of German Army. The High Command was straining to save stores and supply, which would otherwise be booty, and was thus fighting comparatively small actions which were costing them dear. He thought they should have retired a long way straight off to enable them to reform. Policy now and to be continued as long as weather lasted must be to give them no rest – here, there and everywhere. No one could say where they would halt as the present retreat was continuing. He said we should keep at it as long as we could and prepare to throw everything in for next year.

He again and again reverted to this which he was obviously most anxious to impress upon me and thus upon the Prime Minister. . . .

I said Germany's hope must rest now more than ever upon disagreements between the Allies which of course would not happen. He agreed and said, 'They must not happen.'

I suggested that good will and confidence in each other were better than exchanges of documents.

His view was that we were preparing for too long ahead instead of the immediate future. . . .

Foch referred also to point made by M. Clemenceau that France and England, having held the fort for four years, should put their full fighting strength into the year of victory and not leave it to America, whose troops although splendid had not the training of those long in the field. . . .

Before meeting Foch, Reading lunched in the château which served as the headquarters of the British Liaison Mission with the Generalissimo. Besides General Sir John Du Cane, who was in charge of the Mission, and his staff, he met Colonel Repington, the lively military correspondent of *The Times*, who had just come from Foch. 'Pleasant as always', was Repington's verdict upon Reading in his diary for that day (September 3). 'We talked about America. They were all out for the War, but got tired of some things soon. He [Reading] had read in some novel the advice of a sage lady to her son, that when he had made a good impression in a house he should firmly leave. He felt that about himself and America. But he expressed his intention to return. He went off to see Foch, who had told me that he would talk effectives to him as he had to me.'[1]

When Reading returned to the château, Repington was still there, and Reading gave him and Du Cane an account of what had passed between him and Foch. 'Though Foch told me he would tell Reading exactly the same thing about effectives that he told me,' Repington noted afterwards, 'he did *not* tell him that if we did not keep up our strengths he might have to refuse to be responsible for our Armies. Reading was looking for it, but Foch never came near it, so Reading says. If this is correct, it shows the difference between Foch and Pétain, for the latter would have told him in set terms. *O! faiblesse humaine!*' This is more or less borne out by Reading's own account. 'General Du Cane was well aware of Marshal Foch's views but evidently thought these would have been expressed in more peremptory and compelling terms,' was how Reading put it. 'In fact this never obtained: Foch's tone was in every respect that of one who wished to induce by reason based largely on change of conditions.' Conditions were indeed changed. Peace through victory, instead of a negotiated peace, was now a practical possibility.

The following day Reading went to Juvigny where the Americans were holding a section of the front line. Here in the semi-darkness of a deep dugout he spoke with such feeling to the troops that the American High Command ordered his speech to be printed and distributed under the title *In Our Hour of Need* throughout the American Expeditionary Force. This was his peroration:

> We will achieve victory by our joint sacrifice, by our combined efforts and by the desire we all have to do the best that is within us. I will say to you, if I may, as a message from America, for I have come from

[1] C. A. Repington: *The First World War* (1920), Vol. II, p. 378.

America far more recently than any of you, and I speak from my own knowledge, that the people of America are watching you with great pride and with great satisfaction. They realize all the hardships and the many sacrifices you are undergoing for the great cause. They are ready to stand behind you. I shall take back to them a message from you, as I feel sure I rightly interpret your feelings. I shall tell them to be of good cheer, that America is here, that the Star Spangled Banner is waving, and that you are taking a noble part in this great struggle, and will continue to do so till the end, till the victory is ours. Good luck to you and God bless you all!

On his way back to the coast he was able to see his son Gerald, who was serving with a Divisional Headquarters Staff near Montreuil. The return journey was made in a destroyer in the company of Lloyd George, Lord Riddell and Edwin Montagu, who had all come over for a day's visit.

Meanwhile Wiseman, who had been staying with House at Magnolia, the Colonel's seaside home on the Boston north shore, where the President was also spending some weeks, fed Reading with all the latest news in telegrams and letters, conveying the President's views on a variety of topics from the proposed League of Nations to the economic policy of the Allies towards Germany after the War to the situation in Siberia. On September 15 Wiseman had cabled that the Czechs in Samara and Ekaterinburg were in grave danger of being cut to pieces. What the Czechs were doing there was anybody's guess. Perhaps Lansing in the State Department got nearest to it when he told Wiseman, 'The Czech forces are moving west when they ought to be going east.' On the other hand, Dr Masaryk, who was in Washington at this time, did not take such a serious view of the situation and seemed to think that his compatriots were reasonably secure. No wonder Wiseman found it all rather puzzling. By this time the Japanese and Americans had landed at Vladivostok, in addition to some more British, all of which had thrown the Bolsheviks into something of a panic and had incidentally led to the arrest of the British Agent, Bruce Lockhart. 'As far as the President's position is concerned,' wrote Wiseman, 'he has lost faith and curiously enough practically lost interest in the Bolsheviks and is, I think, much more inclined to fall in with our programme than he was a few months ago.'

However, to anticipate events a little, the Central Powers collapsed just as the Allied expeditions in Siberia and north Russia were getting under way, and the War came to an end. The Americans withdrew, but the British and French stayed on to become involved in the civil war between the Reds and the Whites on the side of the latter. Meanwhile the Czechs, for whom so much anxiety was expressed, were brought safely home to help President Masaryk set the new Czechoslovak State on its foundations.

Then there was the proposed League of Nations, in which President Wilson was now taking an active interest. Before leaving America, Reading had discussed the project with Colonel House, who had submitted a draft Covenant to the President. 'I desired to get Reading's legal mind to bear upon the different points,' noted House at the time. 'He expressed himself as pleased with the document as a whole. His feeling, however, was that unless Germany changed her form of government and its personnel, it would be useless to include her in the League.'[1] This was broadly speaking the President's view. 'Germany should be invited to join the family of nations,' he told Wiseman, 'provided she will behave according to the rules of the Society.' For the main force which might be invoked against potential law breakers, Wilson looked to economic sanctions. On the question of Allied economic policy towards Germany, the President also held very definite views. He was disturbed by a speech of Lloyd George to the National Union of Manufacturers in Great Britain which seemed to recommend the crushing of German trade after the War. As Wiseman told Reading at this time, Wilson was convinced that it was a great mistake to threaten Germany with any kind of punitive post-war measures against her trade. 'In his view this threat is one of the strongest levers with which the German militarists suppress the growth of any Liberal movement in Germany. . . . The President thinks that we ought to adopt the line that we have no desire to deny to Germany her fair share of the world's commerce, and that it is her

---

[1] In a note of the conversation which he made at the time (July 28, 1918), Reading wrote: 'How to enforce rulings or decrees is the inevitable puzzle which must be solved if the League is to be fully effective. The financial, economic and commercial alliance of the various contracting parties is the only means yet suggested. Whilst this affords on paper a better guarantee to my mind than an international military police, it has within it the possibility of ineffectiveness at the critical moment and consequently there can be no security to nations that they may not be attacked by a combination which has made up its mind at the critical moment not to carry out its treaty obligations. With Germany a party to the Convention and with her past history and avowed policy the only security would be that, when the favourable moment came, Germany would refuse to be bound, and she would probably carry with her certain other States.' Reading Papers (F.O. 800/222/LON10).

own militarists who are ruining her trade by prolonging the war and obliging us to maintain a blockade.'[1]

8

The German armies were now in full retreat. During the first days of October, 1918, General Hindenburg urged the new Chancellor, Prince Max of Baden, to bring the struggle to an end in order to spare the German people and their allies useless sacrifice. ('Every day's delay costs the lives of thousands of brave soldiers.') The Chancellor yielded and on October 5 sent a Note to President Wilson through the Swiss Government, exhorting him to invite the belligerents to enter peace negotiations on the basis of the Fourteen Points and to conclude an armistice at once. The Austro-Hungarian Government associated itself with the German plea.

Reading now wondered whether he should not send a private telegram to Wiseman, expressing the hope that the President would make no reply to the German Peace Note until after consultation with the Allies. But after talking it over with Balfour it was decided that no telegram should be sent in this sense and that they should await events. Reading had now been away from the Washington Embassy for two months, and both he and Lloyd George felt that he should return to his post, although House seemed to think that he should stay on in England for a while longer. On October 8, Murray wrote from the Foreign Office to Wiseman:

> You said to me in your letter under reply that House thought it likely that German peace proposals might be sprung on us at any time, and that he would like to discuss them with the President and then come over to Europe. It seems to me that the moment may be drawing very near, when his presence in Europe would be invaluable. But if he and you are over here, it likewise seems essential that Reading should be in Washington in order to be able to discuss matters with the President.

He turned over very carefully in his mind House's suggestion that he should stay on this side of the water, but came to the conclusion (and I feel that he was right in doing so) that now that he had fully expounded his reading of the American view to the Prime Minister, A.J.B[alfour] and to the War Cabinet generally, it would be much

[1] Wiseman to Reading, August 20, 1918: Reading Papers (F.O. 800/222/ Ger.12.).

better were he to return in order to talk over with the President various outstanding questions, and to bring the British Government atmosphere to Washington. He is now very much better, and the rest during the sea voyage will put him quite on his feet again.

'You must be feeling very happy at the march of events,' Reading told the Prime Minister at this time. 'I think so often of the views you have expressed at various times to me and particularly when I was leaving last time for the United States. One day they will make interesting reading.' The following week-end was spent at Danny Park, Lord Riddell's summer retreat, with Lloyd George and Philip Kerr. 'It is important that you, Reading, should get back to America to look after our interests there,' said the Prime Minister after dinner. Talk then turned on the pending peace negotiations and what the President might propose. 'I have been picturing to myself my first interview with President Wilson,' Lloyd George remarked.

'Clemenceau says that after a few hours only feathers would be left to tell the tale,' said Reading. 'Both would have disappeared!'

The Prime Minister laughed. 'I should like Clemenceau to see him first with me behind the curtain,' he went on. 'That would be an amusing interview. However, he has placed his Allies in a very difficult position. . . . I am not quite sure that it would not be a good thing for Clemenceau or me to make a speech indicating the position in an inoffensive way. The American public would soon understand and would speedily make it clear to Wilson that they must act in accord with the French and British, who have borne the heat of the day.'

Lloyd George then turned to Reading. 'Before you go, you must get the facts about Pershing. It is a pity you cannot get them from the French. Pershing is most difficult. . . . Pershing says that America did not enter the War with the same objects as France and Great Britain, but for independent objects, and therefore wants an independent army. Had the brigading system been carried out, we should have defeated the Germans before this. But it is most important that Pershing should act under Foch's instructions and take advice from those who know more about the job than he can possibly do. Wilson should know the facts, which are being withheld from him.'

Reading agreed. 'Pershing spoke to me in the same way,' he said. 'He was full of that sort of thing.'

After the Prime Minister had gone to bed – unlike Churchill in the Second World War, George was usually in bed shortly after nine o'clock – the news of President Wilson's reply to the German Peace Note was telephoned from Downing Street. Philip Kerr took down the details, which were embodied in a formal letter from the U.S. Secretary of State to the German Chancellor, and brought them up to the Prime Minister's bedroom. First, the President made it clear that the Germans must accept the Fourteen Points as a basis for peace discussions. The letter continued:

> The President feels bound to say, with regard to an armistice, that he would not feel at liberty to propose a cessation of arms to the Governments with which the Government of the United States is associated against the Central Powers so long as the armies of those Powers are upon their soil. The good faith of any discussion would manifestly depend upon the consent of the Central Powers immediately to withdraw their forces everywhere from invaded territory.
>
> The President also feels that he is justified in asking whether the Imperial Chancellor is speaking merely for the constituted authorities of the Empire who have so far conducted the War. . . .

Shortly afterwards Kerr returned to the others whom he had left in the sitting-room. 'There is awful trouble upstairs, I can tell you!' he said. 'He thinks that the Allies are now in a horrible mess. Wilson has promised them an armistice.'

Reading and Riddell studied the text of the letter. 'It does not say that,' observed Riddell. 'It says, "I will not propose a cessation of hostilities while German armies are on the soil of the Allies."' Thereupon Reading pointed out that the next sentence referred to the good faith of the discussion depending upon the consent of the Central Powers to evacuate. 'Does not that mean an armistice to enable them to do so?' he asked.

Riddell did not agree. 'Wilson may well say, "Get out as best you can, and when you are out I will make proposals."'

'He can't mean that,' said Kerr. But Riddell insisted that most people would read the Note in the sense he had indicated.

'It is badly drafted,' was Reading's lawyer-like comment. Meanwhile the Germans had accepted the President's terms. But as to the process of evacuation they suggested that there should be preliminary negotiations which ought to be handled by a mixed commission. This was, of course, an obvious ruse designed to enable Ludendorff to withdraw his armies while hostilities were suspended and so escape from the devastating pressure of Foch's armies.

Next morning, Sunday (October 13), the discussion was continued with Lloyd George on a walk taken with Reading and Riddell to the top of near-by Wolstonbury Hill. According to Riddell, the Prime Minister declaimed all the time against the American President's action in replying to the terms of the Note without consultation with the Allies, and also in regard to the terms of the Note itself.

'The Germans have accepted the terms, as I prophesied they would,' said Lloyd George. 'We are in a serious difficulty. Wilson has put us in the cart and he will have to get us out.'

'The Note says that Wilson will not recommend a cessation of hostilities while the Germans are in possession of Allied territory,' Riddell repeated his argument. 'It is true that the next sentence says that the goodwill of any conversations must depend upon their consent to evacuate, but it is quite open to Wilson to say that there can be no armistice while the Germans remain in possession.'

Neither Lloyd George nor Reading would agree with this construction. 'If any lawyer had written such a letter,' said Lloyd George, 'he would be regarded as guilty of sharp practice if he afterwards claimed that he had predicated for evacuation as a condition precedent.' He added: 'The time is coming when we shall have to speak out. We have borne the heat and burden of the day and we are entitled to be consulted. What do the Fourteen Points mean? They are very nebulous.'

The Prime Minister had invited the members of the War Cabinet to lunch, together with Maurice Hankey the Cabinet Secretary, and the service chiefs. After the meal was over, a conference took place in the course of which Balfour, Reading, Hankey and Kerr were all asked to draft a suitable telegram asking the American President, in Hankey's words, 'to disillusion the Germans even before he consults us about an armistice', and each was put in a separate room for the purpose. Eventually Balfour's draft was adopted, as might indeed be expected from the most experienced draftsman of the party. Afterwards the visitors left on what Riddell described as 'a cloud of motor-cars', Sir Henry Wilson, the Chief of the Imperial General Staff, 'driving his, which had been built for the Tsar of Russia, and the speedometer of which is marked for versts instead of miles'. (Presumably the Revolution had prevented the vehicle's delivery in Petrograd.)

Although President Wilson's next Note to Germany was also sent without prior communication with the Allies, its stiff character showed that the telegram drafted at Danny Park had not been without

Oct 13th 1918

A. J. Balfour

A. Bonar Law

Milner

Winston S. Churchill

R. E. Wemyss: Admiral

Henry Wilson. C.I.G.S.

Reading

M. P. A. Hankey

D. Lloyd George

Philip Kerr

Joseph Richmond

PAGE FROM VISITORS' BOOK AT DANNY, DATED
OCTOBER 13TH, 1918, WHEN REPLY TO PRESIDENT
WILSON'S PEACE NOTE WAS DRAFTED.

its effect. The President made it clear that there could be no mixed commission to negotiate the terms of evacuation. 'It must be clearly understood,' the Germans were sternly told, 'that the process of evacuation and the conditions of armistice are matters which must be left to the judgment and advice of the military advisers of the United States and Allied Governments, and the President feels it his duty to say that no arrangement can be accepted by the United States Government which does not provide absolutely satisfactory safeguards and guarantees of the maintenance of the present military supremacy of the Armies of the United States and the Allies in the field.'

This stern communication speedily brought the Germans to heel. After debating it for a week, their leaders gave in, and on October 20 they replied accepting all the President's conditions. It now only remained to turn the matter over to the Supreme War Council, which was summoned to meet at the end of the month. Meanwhile Colonel House had set off as the American Government's Special Representative. 'I have not given you any instructions because I feel you will know what to do,' the President had said as he bade him good-bye. Wiseman accompanied him on the voyage, breaking his journey for a few days in England and bringing himself up to date with the news there before following House to Paris. In the meantime, at Lloyd George's request Reading had cancelled his passage in the reverse direction so that he could join the British Ministers in Paris.

Wiseman did not lose a moment in seeing House as soon as he reached Paris. Next day (October 28), House made the following entry in his diary:

> Sir William Wiseman came around last night as I was going to bed. He had just arrived from London with Lord Reading and came to tell me of what had happened in England during the past few days. The Cabinet have been having some stormy sessions over the President's peace terms. They rebel against the 'Freedom of the Seas' and they wish to include reparations for losses at sea.
>
> I told Wiseman, and later today told Reading, that if the British were not careful they would bring upon themselves the dislike of the world. The British Navy seemed to me to be analogous to the German Army, except the German Army is under the direction of an autocracy while the English Navy is under the direction of a democracy. I did not believe the United States and other countries would willingly submit to Great Britain's complete domination of the seas any more than to Germany's domination of the land, and the sooner the

English recognized this fact, the better it would be for them; further-more, that our people, if challenged, would build an army and main-tain a navy greater than theirs. We had more money, we had more men, and our natural resources were greater. Such a programme would be popular in America and, should England give the incentive, the people would demand the rest.

The principle of the 'Freedom of the Seas' on which House insisted and which nearly wrecked the pre-Armistice Conference, was em-bodied in the second of President Wilson's Fourteen Points, and it had to be read in connection with the proposed creation of a League of Nations (Point XIV). Point II provided for the following:

> Absolute freedom of navigation upon the seas, outside Territorial waters, alike in peace and war, except as the seas may be closed in whole or in part by international action for the enforcement of international covenants.

Lloyd George, who had been coached by Reading, voiced his objections at the first informal meeting of the Allied representatives. 'This point we cannot accept under any conditions,' he argued. 'It means that the power of blockade goes, and Germany has been broken almost as much by the blockade as by military methods. . . . This power has prevented Germany from getting rubber, cotton, and food through Holland and the Scandinavian countries. Therefore my view is that I should like to see this League of Nations established before I let this power go. If the League of Nations is a reality, I am willing to discuss the matter.'

What House objected to was not the right of blockade, which he was quite prepared to concede, but the British naval practice of contraband control by means of stopping and searching neutral vessels on the high seas in time of war. The United States must have their maritime rights adequately safeguarded, he told Lloyd George bluntly, and they did not intend to have their commerce regulated by Great Britain whenever she was at war. Lengthy discussions followed between House and the British Prime Minister, Reading and Wise-man; once the two latter argued with House for two hours and, in House's words, 'got nowhere'. Next time Reading tackled House alone, taking his stand on the concept of international law. 'I told Reading he was wasting his breath,' House noted afterwards, 'that in no circumstances would we yield the point about the Freedom of the Seas being a matter for discussion between our two Governments,

I insisted that sooner or later we would come to a clash, if an under-standing was not reached as to laws governing the seas. I let him know that it was not my intention to budge and that I had the backing of the President.'

It was the ingenious Premier who broke the deadlock. He proposed that the matter should be left for future discussion to the Peace Conference where, as he told House, 'I don't despair of coming to an agreement.' House accepted this procrastinating formula, and on November 4 the Supreme War Council formally approved an Allied memorandum to President Wilson endorsing his Fourteen Points with the reservation of Point II. Next day the President forwarded it to the Germans with a note referring them to Marshal Foch for the armistice terms which the Allies were prepared to accept. Meanwhile, Bulgaria, Turkey and Austria had sued for peace separately and were now out of the War. 'We have detached Germany's allies one by one and now she is alone,' said Lloyd George on his return to England with Reading on November 5, 'and we have sent her some hot pepper in the shape of our armistice terms.'

The German delegates left Berlin next day and were duly passed through the French lines to be received by Marshal Foch, represent-ing the Allied armies, and the British First Sea Lord, Admiral Sir Rosslyn Wemyss, on behalf of the Allied navies, in a railway carriage in the forest of Compiègne. While the German delegates were considering the armistice terms, the Kaiser fled to Holland where he abdicated and a republic was proclaimed in Berlin. The delegates were plainly in no position to bargain. In the early hours of Novem-ber 11, they signed the armistice agreement, which came into force at 11 a.m. the same day. The Great War was over. 'Autocracy is dead,' House jubilantly cabled his President. 'Long live democracy and its immortal leader. In this great hour my heart goes out to you in pride, admiration and love.'

An important matter was brought forward by Lord Curzon at the first meeting of the War Cabinet after the Armistice, which took place in Downing Street on November 20. It was simply that the ex-Kaiser should be tried as the principal war criminal. 'In my view the Kaiser is the arch-criminal of the world,' said Curzon, 'and just as in any other sphere of life when you get hold of a criminal you bring him to justice, so I do not see, because he is an Emperor and living in exile and in another country, why he should be saved from the punishment which is his due.' Curzon's proposal, strongly supported by Lloyd George, had apparently resulted from a recent conversation between Curzon and Clemenceau in Paris at which the Prime Minister was not present. When asked for his view, Reading with characteristic caution declined to commit himself and moved that the matter should be referred to the Law Officers of the Crown, their terms of reference being to examine the whole question of framing charges against the ex-Kaiser, both (i) for the crime against humanity of having caused the War; and (ii) for offences . . . against international law during the War. The Law Officers were also to take up with the Foreign Office the practicability of inducing the Dutch Government to hand over the ex-Kaiser to an appropriate tribunal for trial. For this purpose the Law Officers (Sir F. E. Smith and Sir Gordon Hewart) were empowered to consult with a committee of juristical experts, which included Sir Frederick Pollock and Professor J. H. Morgan.

'I think the Lord Chief Justice will agree,' said the Attorney-General when he reported to the Cabinet nine days afterwards, 'that it would not be possible in this country to form a stronger Committee for the purpose of arriving at a sound conclusion upon such matters. It is a source of satisfaction to the Law Officers that this Committee has unanimously and independently of them reached the conclusion that the ex-Kaiser ought to be punished, either by way of trial or as Napoleon was punished. The Committee inclines to the first of those courses, namely that he should be tried. . . . As chief Law Officer of the Crown, I say quite plainly that I should feel the greatest difficulty in being responsible in any way for the trial of subordinate criminals if the ex-Kaiser is allowed to escape.'

The feeling of the Cabinet was reflected by the Supreme War Council when it met in London on December 2 to arrange the procedure of the Peace Conference and recommended that the former German Emperor and his 'principal accomplices' should be brought to trial before an international court. At the General Election which took place in England later the same month, 'Hang the Kaiser' was a popular slogan in the speeches of Lloyd George and his Coalition candidates. But it is one thing to recommend and another to implement the recommendation. As the Italian representative Baron Sonnino correctly predicted, Holland would refuse to surrender ex-Kaiser Wilhelm 'and we would be imprudent to make her'. In the event the ex-Kaiser was allowed to live out the remainder of his days in the woods at Doorn and, unlike the aftermath of the Second World War, there were no international war crimes trials.

The same Cabinet which resolved to bring the ex-Kaiser to justice also passed a resolution adding the control and co-ordination of food policy to Reading's ancillary work in the field of shipping. Consequently, when the Supreme War Council met a few days later, it was natural that Reading should become the chief British representative on the Inter-Allied Committee appointed to examine and report on the 'question of victualling and supplying enemy, Allied and neutral countries in all its aspects, including the use of enemy merchant vessels'. This committee was the genesis of the Allied Supreme Council of Supply and Relief. The principal American representative on the committee, as later on the Council, was the U.S. Food Administrator, Herbert Hoover.

In the circumstances it was a grave mistake for Reading to take on this work, as indeed he himself was soon to realize. That he was impelled to do so seems to have been due to a desire partly to oblige Lloyd George and also to participate in some substantial and conspicuous way in the Peace Conference. It was unfortunate that his American opposite number should have been Herbert Hoover, who made it quite clear that he intended to act independently. Their initial meeting was inauspicious and sowed the seeds of future friction between them.

'Hoover seems to have the idea of withdrawing from the relations existing between the various Inter-Allied Councils in which America has taken part,' Reading told Wiseman after this meeting. 'His view seems to be: we will confer and co-operate where necessary, but now the War is over we should be free from any Allied Councils. I am not clear in my mind as to the reason for these views. I think it may indicate the desire of the President to be absolutely free so that he can pursue his course independently of Allies when it suits him. . . . I think this would be most unfortunate for future Anglo-American relations.'[1]

9

Things now began to go wrong for the American President. Unlike Lloyd George, who gained an overwhelming victory at the polls for his Coalition Government, Wilson lost the Congressional Elections. This was largely due to his miscalculated appeal to the voters to

[1] November 26: Reading Papers (F.O. 800/225).

return a Democratic Congress on the ground that a Republican Congress would embarrass him in the peace negotiations. To make matters worse, he omitted the Republican leaders from the American Delegation to the Peace Conference; he also snubbed the Senate by ignoring its members, Democratic as well as Republican, in the composition of the Delegation, in spite of the Senate's constitutional share in the treaty-making power. Finally he insisted on attending the Conference in person and matching his wits against such seasoned parliamentarians and political bargainers as Lloyd George, Clemenceau and Orlando. All this he did against the earnest advice of his friend Edward House. A sense of megalomania drove him on to see his Fourteen Points being put into effect through the Peace Treaty. In Wiseman's words, he was attracted to Paris 'as a debutante is entranced by the prospect of her first ball'.

After a magnificent reception in France, the President and his wife paid a State Visit to England. French destroyers escorted them half-way across the Channel and then the British Navy took over. It was the first time in history that an American President had landed on British soil. As he stepped ashore at Dover to the strains of 'The Star Spangled Banner', he was welcomed officially by the Duke of Connaught on behalf of the King, and by Lord Reading on behalf of the Government. After receiving the freedom of the town, he walked along the station platform to the waiting train, while a party of little girls strewed roses in his path. This gesture seemed to please him as he looked at them and smiled. Otherwise he seldom unbent throughout the four-day visit. Most unfortunately House was confined to bed in Paris with an attack of influenza. Had he come to London with the President, it is just possible that things would have gone better.

At Buckingham Palace, in response to the shouts of the crowd, 'We want Wilson', he came on to the balcony with his wife, looking glum, although Mrs Wilson produced loud cheers when she raised a Union Jack above her head and waved it vigorously. 'I disliked his attitude of academic superiority in words and manner,' Queen Mary's lady-in-waiting, Lady Airlie, observed. 'It seemed to me both officially and unofficially he was determined to undermine the prestige of the British Monarchy. He boasted incessantly.' The unfavourable impression was confirmed the same evening at the State Banquet in the Palace when he responded to the toast of his health which had been most felicitously proposed by the King. 'Wilson replied,' noted Lloyd George, 'with the perfect enunciation, measured emphasis and cold tones with which I was to become so familiar in the coming months. There was no glow of friendship or of gladness at meeting men who had been partners in a common enterprise and had so narrowly escaped a common danger. There was one particular blot on this deliverance which attracted general attention, and which caused many sincere friends of the President real distress at the time. It made no reference to the part played by the British Empire in the tremendous struggle just brought to a close and to the appalling sacrifices which had been sustained by the youth of that Empire in the cause of international right. . . . Not a word of appreciation, let alone gratitude, came from his lips.' Although half the total numbers of American troops carried across the Atlantic had been transported in British ships, the only allusion he made to this fact was when he boasted of the numbers, adding that 'no lives were lost on the crossing except on one ship, and that was a British ship'.

Small wonder that President Wilson sat down to the most tepid applause which has ever greeted a speech from a visiting Head of State at Buckingham Palace. Lloyd George and Reading were both present on this occasion with their wives. The Prime Minister said nothing to the Ambassador at the time, but as soon as he got back to Downing Street he sent Reading a note calling his attention to the blunder and to the mischief which might ensue to Anglo-American relations through popular resentment being aroused. Lloyd George hoped that the President would rectify the omission in the speech which he was due to make at the Guildhall the following day when he was to receive the freedom of the City of London. Reading assured the Prime Minister that it was an oversight on the President's part and he was convinced the mistake would be put right at the Guildhall. Both men were present at the Guildhall luncheon and both 'listened in vain for one word of generous allusion to Britain's sacrifices for or achievements on behalf of the common cause'. Before the visit ended, Lloyd George gave an all-male luncheon for the President in Downing Street, while Lady Reading entertained Mrs Wilson in her home in Curzon Street. By contrast with her husband, everyone found the 'First Lady' charming. To quote Lady Airlie, she 'knew far better the effect of under-emphasis' than the President. On the other hand, Lloyd George was bound to admit that in the first private conversation they had together Wilson was genial and friendly. ('He was a clear and concise talker and an attentive and receptive listener.')

When the Prime Minister accompanied by the Foreign Secretary

called at Buckingham Palace and saw the President in his suite, they
discussed the projected League of Nations. On this occasion Wilson
gave his visitors the impression that the League was 'the only thing
that he really cared much about'. Incidentally it should be understood
that the League was not forced on the Allies by President Wilson. The
idea of a society of nations to insure world peace had long been
advocated by Sir Edward Grey and Lord Robert Cecil in England.
In fact a Committee of jurists and historians presided over by a most
learned High Court judge, Lord Phillimore, had been appointed two
years previously and had worked out a draft scheme which had been
laid before the Cabinet. But at President Wilson's request, transmitted
through Reading, the Cabinet had withheld publication of the Phillimore Report, since the President was most anxious that the League
should only be constituted at the Peace Conference. 'I am expecting
that Cecil will be annoyed by this view,' Reading had warned Lloyd
George at the time, 'but it is imperative that he should know how
seriously our relations with the United States might be embarrassed
by premature public discussion based upon the Report of a Committee
appointed by the Government.'[1]

It had been arranged that the Peace Conference was to be formally
opened in Paris in January, 1919. The advance party of the British
Delegation, which was led by the Prime Minister, in which Reading
was included, arrived on January 11 and most of its members settled
themselves in the Hotel Majestic. Reading's former assistant in
Washington, Maynard Keynes, who travelled over at the same time,
was the principal representative of the British Treasury and had to
work closely with Reading who was the principal British representative on the Supreme Council of Supply and Relief. The Paris scene
was as Keynes had expected and he was later to recapture it in a
brilliant essay. 'No one yet knew what the Conference was doing or
whether it had started,' wrote Keynes. 'But the peculiar atmosphere
and routine of the Majestic were already compounded and established,
the typists drank their tea in the lounge, the dining-room diners had
distinguished themselves from the restaurant diners, the security
officers from Scotland Yard burnt such of the waste paper as the
French charwomen had no use for, much factitious work circulated
in red boxes, and the feverish, persistent and boring gossip of that

---

[1] August 19, 1918: Lloyd George Papers. Asked by Wiseman what he thought
of the Phillimore Report, Wilson replied: 'It has no teeth.' See Wiseman's
telegram to Reading, quoted by Willert, at p. 152.

hellish place had already developed in full measure the peculiar mixture of smallness, cynicism, self-importance and bored excitement that it was never to lose.'[1]

The questions of supply and relief depended upon the continuance of the blockade. The Armistice had expressly provided for its continuance, but with the qualification that 'the Allies contemplated the provisioning of Germany to the extent that shall be deemed necessary'. Hence followed the decision of the Allies early in December as to the victualling of enemy countries that were short of food and the setting-up of the Inter-Allied Committee to which Reading was appointed as British representative. The preliminary debates in London showed that opinion was sharply divided. France and Belgium in particular were against removing or even relaxing the blockade, and these powers had negotiated a separate and supplementary armistice with Germany by which she was prohibited from disposing of her gold and other liquid assets. This consequently made it impossible for her to buy food and her people faced starvation if they were not aided by some form of relief. Herbert Hoover, for the United States, thought that this policy was wrong and opposed it partly for humanitarian reasons and partly for fear of the chaotic conditions which he felt might result in the occupied countries if the blockade should be rigorously maintained.

'I hardly know why we, the English, decided to promote its continuance,' Keynes afterwards wrote in a slightly cruel sketch of the man he considered to some extent responsible. 'I attribute it in part to the irresolution of Lord Reading, who was in charge of the business on our side; for he was intriguing at that time day and night to be one of the party for Paris and was terrified of identifying himself with anything controversial. I recall him picking at the nail of his left thumb for minutes together in his room in the War Cabinet offices in Whitehall Gardens in an agony of doubt which way the cat was jumping; his top hat perfect; his whole face and person so chiselled and polished, reflecting pin-points of light from so many angles that one longed to wear him as a tie-pin; tie-pin on tie-pin, till one hardly knew which was Earl and which was jewel: poor Earl!'[2]

It can be argued in Reading's favour that what Keynes took for irresolution was a sense of judicial impartiality. After all, Reading was not a policy maker in this context; policy was the task of higher

[1] J. M. Keynes: *Two Memoirs* (1949), p. 7.
[2] Keynes, p. 23.

authority. The real reason for continuing the blockade, as Keynes himself admitted, was that it was Britain's one instrument for imposing peace terms on Germany and, once suspended, it could hardly be reimposed.

The pros and cons were weighed by Reading in a memorandum which he sent Lloyd George at the beginning of February, when the Supply and Relief Council was about to be transformed into the Supreme Economic Council with somewhat enlarged powers and responsibilities in the fields of finance, shipping, food and raw materials, etc.[1]

> On the one hand, there is pressure to relax or remove the blockade for economic or industrial reasons; on the other, there is military objection to any substantial relaxation of the blockade, based upon the necessity to maintain pressure notably on Germany by means other than the resumption of hostilities to accept the terms of Peace submitted by the Allied Powers.
>
> It will be for the highest authorities to weigh in the balance the advantages of providing food and to some extent employment in Germany and other enemy countries by the blockade restrictions.
>
> ... Without attempting to prejudge the matter, it will be found that the British Representatives and probably those of other Governments on the Supreme Council will recommend that it is essential to keep the blockade machinery in existence and in operation so that pressure could always be exercised on Germany if necessary.

Reading took the chair at the few meetings of the Supply and Relief Council which he attended. The other British representative was Sir John Beale, solicitor to the Midland Railway, while Keynes looked in from time to time and kept a watchful eye on behalf of the Treasury. A week of meetings in hot and stuffy rooms, as well as clashes with Hoover and the Americans, determined Reading to throw in his hand at a task he should never have undertaken in the first place. He wrote to Lloyd George on January 21:

> After four and a half years' activities in war problems, I have come to the conclusion that I should return to my judicial duties. As you will remember, I came here to help in the formation of the Relief Council and to assist in its first deliberations. The Council is now all on its feet and is working very satisfactorily. I propose therefore to retire from the position of British Representative upon this Council and am returning to London on Friday.

[1] Reading Papers (F.O. 800/222).

At the same time he wrote to Balfour saying that he would return to Washington for six weeks or so for the purpose of winding up his mission there and taking leave.

While his resignation was accepted, Reading was somewhat reluctantly persuaded to stay on in Paris for a few weeks longer, until his successor had been appointed and until the transformation of the Relief Council into the Supreme Economic Council had been completed and approved by the Council of the Big Four (Clemenceau, Lloyd George, Orlando and Wilson). He suggested Lord Robert Cecil as his successor on the Economic Council. Cecil was a man of considerable experience, having served for two years as Minister of Blockade, as the minister responsible for economic warfare was known in the First World War. He had also acted as Balfour's deputy at the Foreign Office, and was already in Paris to negotiate the establishment of the League of Nations from the British side. He agreed to take on Reading's job on the Economic Council if he could continue with his other particular interest. This he was allowed to do; at the same time he was elected into the chair of the Economic Council. Unfortunately, in spite of Cecil's humanitarian approach, the Economic Council failed immediately to relieve the necessitous Germans, largely owing to deliberate obstruction on the part of the French. It was not until a month later, after Lloyd George had made a passionate plea at the Council of Four, and the British Army of Occupation was thoroughly disgusted with the distressing spectacle of half-starved children roaming the streets of Germany, that the French relented and lifted the gold embargo, thereby enabling the Germans to buy food, in return for handing over their merchant fleet.

For Reading, harassed as he was by uncongenial work, the Conference had its lighter and more relaxed moments. With Riddell, who was officially representing the British Press, he was much amused by President Wilson's habit of asking for his typewriter. On the first occasion they conjured up visions of a beautiful American stenographer, but instead a messenger appeared bringing with him a battered typewriting machine on a tray, on which the all-powerful President of the United States proceeded to tap out a memorandum on the League of Nations or some similar subject in a corner of the Conference Room after the other delegates had left. As Riddell put it, 'it was a strange sight to see one of the greatest rulers in the world working away in this fashion'.

Reading's son, who spent a few days with his father in the Hotel Majestic at this time, tells another story. One day they went for a stroll in the adjacent Bois and ran into F. E. Smith and Gordon Hewart. 'F.E.' had just been appointed Lord Chancellor and was about to be raised to the peerage as Lord Birkenhead; at forty-six he was the youngest occupant of the Woolsack since the notorious 'Judge' Jeffreys. At the same time his former post as Attorney-General had gone to Hewart, who was stepped up from Solicitor.

They continued their walk together, and 'F.E.' on being warmly congratulated by Reading began to bemoan the fact that he would never again conduct a case in court. Suddenly Reading interrupted him light-heartedly. 'Look here, F.E., you and I are far too young to be stuck for the rest of our lives as judges. Let us go back to the Bar!'

F.E. was enchanted with the idea and proceeded to explore its possibilities. The three lawyers were so engrossed in their discussion as to whether there was any objection to the plan apart from the absence of precedent that they stepped off the kerb without noticing a large car which came round the near-by corner and narrowly missed running them down. 'Good God!' exclaimed F.E. at his narrow escape, 'the Lord Chancellor, the Lord Chief Justice and the Attorney-General – What a bag! And how grieved the Bar would have been!'[1]

One night, just before he left Paris, Reading and Riddell dined with Lloyd George in the elegantly furnished flat which the French Government had put at his disposal in the Rue Nitot. The conversation turned on the American President, and Lloyd George said he found him much nicer and had got on with him much better than he expected. 'That is a great satisfaction to me,' Reading remarked. 'Nothing is more important than that you two should get on well together.' This remark intrigued Riddell who recorded it with an apt comment in his diary. 'In saying this he was obviously sincere, but gave me the impression that though glad to see the birth of a strong and lusty friendship he regretted that the services of the midwife had been so soon dispensed with by the parents.'

Reading returned to London with the Prime Minister and his party on February 8, the day after the Council of Four meeting. Riddell, who went too, noted that the Lord Chief Justice looked ill and was suffering from gout. Reading hoped to attend the opening of Parlia-

[1] Reading, Vol. II, p. 149.

SIR WILLIAM WISEMAN

WITH THE EMBASSY STAFF IN WASHINGTON

ment, but on reaching his home in Curzon Street, retired to bed, where he continued to be laid up for most of the time until he and his wife sailed again for New York. They left on February 21 to spend rather more than six weeks in a round of farewell functions and speeches. This was none too soon, since his long absence had already been commented upon adversely in a leading article in *The Times*, which pointed to the 'abundant evidence of dissatisfaction there that during the last six critical months the Embassy in Washington should have been left without a head'. But it was not really his fault, and certainly his tenure of the Embassy was to receive the highest praise from both British and American authorities when he finally relinquished it.

One matter, which was virtually completed when Reading wound up his mission, was the final liquidation of the Demand Loan. Before he left Washington in the previous July, he had persuaded the U.S. Treasury to agree to the sale of British-owned collateral securities, and this process took place gradually so as not to disturb the market. The result was that the whole loan was paid off by the middle of 1919. Morgan's of New York sent their congratulations to Reading through their London office of Morgan, Grenfell. 'It is a wonderful achievement to have it all paid without recourse to our Government.'

It was getting on for the middle of May when the Readings got back to England. The Prime Minister and Foreign Secretary were in Paris for the concluding stages of the Peace Conference. After he had cleaned out his desk in Whitehall Gardens, the Lord Chief Justice hastened across the Channel. 'I shall be in Paris on Thursday evening [May 17] for a very short visit to you and Balfour, and to bid good-bye to the President and House,' he wrote giving advance notice to Lloyd George and adding a tribute to the Prime Minister. 'It is a great joy to me to see your wonderful success in spite of the overwhelming complications. Through it all I see you subtle and supple, holding our flag in the many difficult conferences you have had.'

Lloyd George responded with a flattering letter of thanks to the returning Ambassador, which was given out to the Press and widely publicized. 'When the time comes for the history of those most critical years to be written,' he wrote, 'the leading part which you played in co-ordinating the war effort of the United States and the other Allies, and above all, in helping to bring about that dramatic movement of the American Army to Europe in the spring and

L

summer of 1918, which contributed so strikingly to the Allied victory
in the later autumn, will be understood in its true perspective.'

The Prime Minister's encomium was echoed by the Foreign Secretary. 'After your brief but momentous excursion into the realms of
war and diplomacy,' wrote Balfour, 'you now return with added fame
to the calmer labours of the Bench. Perhaps as time goes on, your
recollection of what you did through those strenuous months may
gradually grow somewhat dim. Should this be so, you may easily
refresh your memory, for the record of your achievements will
assuredly find its place in every history of the Great War.'

None of these laudatory communications mentioned one to whom
Reading felt that he owed a large measure of his success, namely his
wife. He had intended to mention her to Lloyd George when they
met in Paris, but the Prime Minister seemed so pressed that Reading
deferred it until he got back to London. He then formally wrote to
Lloyd George recommending that the work she had done in Washington should likewise receive some public recognition.

Lloyd George, who was never ungenerous in the matter of honours,
particularly where his friends were concerned, responded nobly to
this appeal. In the next Honours List it was announced that the
Countess of Reading had been created a Dame Grand Cross in the
Order of the British Empire (G.B.E.), the nearest equivalent to a
knighthood which a woman could hold.

The final word lay with Reading. He had resumed his place on the
Bench when the Peace Treaty was signed in the historic Hall of
Mirrors at Versailles. But he felt he must send the Prime Minister a
few lines of congratulation to mark the occasion. 'It is a splendid
achievement of yours and I rejoice in the fine part you have played
in the stupendous work of the Conference,' he wrote from Curzon
Street. 'Apart altogether from my natural pride that it is you who
have done the great work, I am sincerely and earnestly grateful to
you for the grand upholding of the old country's interests.'

Viceroy

1

In March, 1920, ten months after he had returned to the Law Courts, Reading told Colonel House, with whom he continued to keep in touch, 'I spend my days in the calm and serene atmosphere of the judicial bench, but very often think of the important days that have passed. . . .' Shortly afterwards, the Lord Chief Justice played a round of golf with Lloyd George and Lord Riddell at Walton Heath. Both thought Reading looked older. 'He seems to have lost some of his wonderful spring and vitality,' noted Riddell. The truth was that he had become excessively bored with his judicial work. He chafed at the physical inactivity involved in long hours of sitting on the Bench, and he complained to his son, who had become his private secretary, that it made him feel as if he were only fit to be wheeled up and down the sea-front at Brighton in a Bath chair. The cases he had to try, more often than not 'running down' actions, exhausted his patience and several times he remarked that he could not be expected to go on trying such cases for the rest of his life. He was irked, too, by the indifferent advocacy, with which he sometimes had to bear.

As Gordon Hewart, the Attorney-General remarked at this time, Reading 'had learned to enjoy the glitter of diplomacy', and he yearned to get back to it. Indeed he wrote to Lloyd George and offered to return to Washington for the Long Vacation in 1919 as Ambassador if required. But Lloyd George had already made up his mind to offer the post to Grey, who had become Viscount Grey of Falloden. After Grey's arrival in Washington, Reading asked Lloyd George if he might be given copies of all important communications which passed between his successor and the Government. To this unusual request the Prime Minister assented, and Reading accordingly received copies of all the principal telegrams which passed between the Embassy and the Foreign Office.

By this time, Wilson had quarrelled with House and was in failing health, indeed almost wholly incapacitated as the result of a stroke, and he would not or could not even see Grey, who wished to persuade him to compromise with the Senate so as to bring the United States into the League of Nations. House wrote twice to the President at this time offering help in getting the Senate to ratify the Treaty of Versailles and urging him to accept the amendments to the Covenant of the League proposed by the Republican Senator Lodge. Neither letter was answered. The result was that the Treaty failed to secure the necessary two-thirds vote of the Senate, though only by the narrow margin of seven votes. Thus the political baby so dear to the President's heart was abandoned on Europe's doorstep. Nor did the United States ever join the League.

Reading's diplomatic longings were reflected in rumours which now gained some currency. When, in the earlier part of 1920, it became known that Derby would soon be giving up the Paris Embassy, Reading was tipped in some quarters as a likely successor. This Embassy was traditionally regarded as the highest post in the British Diplomatic Service and was certainly a plum which Reading would not have refused had it been offered to him. But Curzon, who had succeeded Balfour as Foreign Secretary, was anxious that it should revert to a career member of the service, and so Lord Hardinge of Penshurst, then Permanent Under-Secretary of State at the Foreign Office, was appointed. Apparently the same consideration applied in Washington whither it was rumoured that Reading might return after Grey's brief mission ended later the same year. Nevertheless he continued to watch events in the United States as closely as he could. 'My interest will not fade,' he told House, 'and my enthusiasm for the cause of good understanding between our two countries remains as ardent as ever.' He made friends with Page's successor as American Ambassador in London, John W. Davis, an outstanding lawyer, who had previously been Solicitor-General in the Wilson Cabinet, and he sang his praises to House. ('Your Ambassador has done splendidly here; he has made an excellent impression and is part of our public life, always making good speeches, never losing sight of American interests and yet understanding us and our point of view.')

It had been arranged that the twenty-five-year-old Prince of Wales should visit Canada in the autumn of 1919 as the first instalment of an Empire tour. The Prince thought it rather absurd when he was there not to extend his journey to the United States, and he cabled home for his father's permission. The request produced some hesitation in Buckingham Palace, largely owing to the acrimonious debates which were going on in the Senate in Washington over the Peace Treaty. Reading, who was consulted, was strongly in favour of the extension of the Prince's visit, and he told the King that he was certain that a friendly reception awaited the heir to the throne in America. And so the Prince went on to Washington, where unlike Lord Grey he was admitted to the stricken President's bedroom in the White House. He found Wilson lying in Lincoln's bed. They conversed for only a few moments, the Prince remarking afterwards that he thought that his was the most disappointed face that he had ever looked upon. 'If this was the condition in which the cares of high office left a man,' he reflected, 'then as a Prince I was happy to be spared the ravages of party politics.'[1]

The spontaneous enthusiasm of the Prince's reception surpassed Reading's expectations. He wrote about it to Lord Stamfordham, the King's Private Secretary:

> It shows, as I always insist, that at heart the Americans are with us in spite of their extreme sensitiveness lest Britain should be patronizing them. At this present moment nothing could have been happier than this visit. The reception shows our people another side of American opinion and serves to calm the exacerbation of those who might be disposed to say bitter things and thus not help but mar future prospects.
>
> The Prince has proved a better Ambassador than all of us rolled into one. He has caught the American spirit, so difficult to understand quickly, and has done more in America to make their people comprehend the strength of the democratic support to our monarchy than all books and articles and propaganda.
>
> I trust I may be permitted to tell Their Majesties how much I rejoice at this success.

Reading was able to do this at the railway station where the Prince was officially welcomed home by the Royal Family and members of the Government. 'It is most satisfactory to read your views as to the good effect upon the mutual relations of the two countries from His Royal Highness's presence and personal influence,' wrote Stamfordham in conveying the King's invitation to Reading to be present, 'for no one better than you can gauge the public feeling on the other side.'[2]

Both the King and Queen were naturally delighted with their son's

[1] H.R.H. the Duke of Windsor: *A King's Story* (1951), p. 145.
[2] Reading to Stamfordham; Stamfordham to Reading. November 25, 1919: Royal Archives.

success and plied him with all kinds of questions. Neither of them
had ever been in the United States, and the King in particular was
interested in such mundane topics as the height of New York's
skyscrapers, the number of motor vehicles in the streets, the size of
the staff in the White House, and above all what life was like under
Prohibition, for America had recently 'gone dry'. What seems to
have lingered longest in the Prince's memory were not the grand
things that had happened to him but a haunting tune he had heard at
the Ziegfeld Follies, 'A Pretty Girl is like a Melody'.

Such occasions as these served to keep the Lord Chief Justice in
the public eye. Shortly afterwards he attended another function
which gave him much pleasure. He travelled down to Reading to
receive the Freedom of the Borough. Although he had spent many
happy times there in the past, the territorial as well as parliamentary
link with the place from which he took his title had gone. During the
War he had sub-let Fox Hill to Sir Hugo Hirst, afterwards Lord
Hirst, and in 1918 Hirst had bought the remainder of the lease from
him.[1] This meant that he no longer had a country house in which to
relax at week-ends and during the law vacations. In the circumstances of his wife's indifferent and gradually failing health, the house
in Curzon Street was enough for her to manage.

The beginning of the Michaelmas Law Term in 1920 coincided with
Reading's sixtieth birthday. He had sat on the Bench, intermittently,
it is true, for the past seven years, and in the ordinary course of
things he could expect to remain there for at least another nine years
before retiring on a pension. Now that the two biggest diplomatic
plums had eluded his reach, he seemed for the moment resigned to
following this course in spite of his increasing sense of boredom and
weariness. Yet within little more than two months he was to be taken
right out of his judicial rut by being offered and accepting the most
dazzling and splendid public appointment which it was within the
power of the Prime Minister to bestow, namely that of Governor-
General or, to use the then commonly accepted but strictly speaking
incorrect designation, Viceroy of India.[2]

---

[1] Fox Hill is now a hall of residence belonging to the University of Reading.
[2] The style 'Viceroy' was not legally adopted until 1937 as a result of the
Government of India Act, but it had long been commonly used owing to the
fact that the Governor-General exercised viceregal as well as administrative
functions. It is so used in the context of this book. For a detailed survey of the
office at this period, see Dr A. B. Rudra's *The Viceroy and Governor-General of
India* (1940).

How this came about is an extraordinary story. Reading's eventual occupation of the Viceregal Lodge in Delhi was the result of a combination of fortuitous circumstances in the shape of his mother-in-law's death, Austen Chamberlain's prior refusal of the office, and finally Gordon Hewart's willingness to stand aside and waive his traditional right as Attorney-General to the immediate reversion of the Lord Chief Justiceship in the event of the post falling vacant.

Mrs Cohen, Alice Reading's mother, died in the middle of October, 1920, at the age of eighty-one. She and her semi-invalid daughter, whom she used to visit almost every afternoon were the closest companions and quite inseparable. Had Mrs Cohen survived a few months or even weeks longer, it is highly unlikely that Lady Reading would have agreed to accompany her husband as far afield as India, and his devotion to his wife would certainly have impelled him to fall in with her wishes. It so happened that Lloyd George had invited Reading to spend the week-end following Mrs Cohen's death at Chequers, the mansion and estate in Buckinghamshire which its owners, Lord and Lady Lee of Fareham, were about to hand over with its contents to a trust for the use of successive Prime Ministers of Britain in perpetuity. Had not his wife's bereavement prevented him from accepting the invitation, it is possible that Lloyd George would have mentioned the question of the Viceroyalty to him, since he had been considering it for some time.

The incumbent Viceroy, Lord Chelmsford, was due to leave India on the completion of his five-year term of office in the following April, and it was becoming imperative to nominate a successor without further delay. Edwin Montagu, the Secretary of State, wanted a totally different type of Viceroy from that cast in the conventional mould. 'It is borne in on me every moment of the day, every hour, but it is no use because nobody will believe me – the sort of man we seek to make a Viceroy is wholly wrong,' he had written after his first meeting with Chelmsford. 'They approach the problem from the wrong side: they do the work they are called upon to do; they wade through files; they think of their regulations; and then as to the social side precedence, precedence, precedence. . . . Informal discussion, informal conversation, they do not know. Political instinct they have none.'[1]

Early in 1920, Montagu had suggested that he should go out himself for three years to pave the way for the appointment of one of the

[1] Waley, p. 144.

King's sons. But Lloyd George had brushed aside this proposal. The Secretary of State then suggested that the Prince of Wales, who was expected to visit India anyhow in 1921, should become Viceroy for a few months and that then Sir Harcourt Butler, Governor of the United Provinces, should act in the Prince's name for two or three years.[1] This suggestion was also rejected by the Prime Minister. Their correspondence on the subject continued at intervals throughout the summer and autumn. Finally, on December 7, Montagu wrote: 'Austen [Chamberlain] would not accept. After him Reading is probably the best, then Winston [Churchill], then Lytton and then Willingdon or Willingdon and then Lytton.' Incidentally, Montagu's opinion of Churchill as a possible Viceroy is worth quoting. 'It might result in a great failure. It might be a great success. Whichever it was, it would be great.'

According to Hewart, who made a record of what happened at the time, Lloyd George buttonholed Sir Edward Carson one day towards the end of November or beginning of December in the Members' dining-room of the House of Commons.[2] He immediately confided in Carson that Reading was 'very anxious' to be Viceroy of India, but that there was 'a difficulty about money'. The Lord Chief Justice had lived expensively, the Prime Minister went on, and had not made sufficient provision for the future. He had sold his place at Reading, but he had not nearly earned his judicial pension, and the Viceroyalty carried no pension. 'Now what do you say to this plan?' asked Lloyd George. 'Why should he not go to India as Viceroy for five years, and we can put in an elderly judge as stop-gap for that time, and then Rufus can come back and resume the Chief Justiceship and earn his pension?' There was conceivably a hint that Carson himself might care to become Lord Chief Justice *ad interim*.

The veteran Irish lawyer was very much taken aback by this suggestion. 'I told him that it was a shocking and impossible plan,' Carson informed Hewart some time afterwards, 'that it would be an affront to the Bench, and that it would be grossly unfair to you, the best Attorney there had ever been.' He added that he was going to see Bonar Law, then the Conservative Party Leader, to protest against any arrangement which would prevent Hewart be-

[1] Father of Lord ('Rab') Butler, Master of Trinity College, Cambridge.
[2] I am indebted to Hewart's biographer, Mr Robert Jackson, for kindly allowing me to quote from the remarkable account of the affair of the Lord Chief Justiceship which Hewart wrote at the time and which Mr Jackson subsequently used in his biography, *The Chief*.

coming Lord Chief Justice at once in the event of Reading becoming Viceroy.

If Hewart's account of Lloyd George's conversation with Carson is accurate, then the statement by the Prime Minister that Reading was 'very anxious' to become Viceroy of India was an exaggeration, to say the least. Reading's correspondence with Lloyd George proves conclusively that Reading had some hesitation in accepting the offer made to him by the Prime Minister, since he was apprehensive of the possible effect of the Indian climate on his wife's health. 'Think of her feelings if she thought you had refused it because of her,' Lloyd George said to him when the issue was still doubtful. It was only after Reading had been assured on the best medical authority he could summon that 'all would be as here' that he decided to accept.[1]

Meanwhile, undeterred by Carson's rebuff, the Prime Minister proceeded to tackle Hewart. Overtaking him in the Division Lobby of the House one afternoon in mid-December, he linked arms in a friendly fashion and said he would like a talk with him after the division. Ten minutes later Hewart saw the Prime Minister in his room behind the Speaker's Chair.

Lloyd George began by asking the Attorney-General whether his ambitions were legal or political. Hewart had no hesitation in plumping for the former. 'Well, now, I want to tell you this,' said the Prime Minister in his most genial manner. 'The Government cannot do without you here. You are absolutely essential to us.' He went on to say that the appointment of a new Viceroy of India was imminent and that Reading was interested in it. In many ways it would not be a bad appointment, Lloyd George continued. But there was one snag. 'If Rufus cannot become Viceroy without your claiming at once to become Lord Chief Justice, then it is certain that he cannot become Viceroy.'

'It is not fair to say that I am standing in the way of Rufus,' Hewart protested. 'It is a strange thing to penalize me for my merits, whether actual or supposed.'

'On the contrary,' rejoined Lloyd George, still in the best of humour. 'I have no wish to penalize you at all and in fact have thought out a plan which will get over the difficulty.' The remainder of the interview was subsequently recorded by Hewart in these words:

[1] Reading to Lloyd George, February 9, 1921: Lloyd George Papers. Reading to H. A. L. Fisher, January 22, 1921: Fisher Papers.

The plan which he immediately proceeded to unfold was as follows: that Rufus should go to India, that the office of Lord Chief Justice should then be offered to me, that I should for the moment decline it, and that then it should be offered to and accepted by one of the more elderly judges, who had earned or almost earned his pension, upon the terms that he should give it up at any time when requested by the Prime Minister, which request might be made in a few months' time and certainly would be made before he (Lloyd George) ceased to be head of this Administration or before the next General Election, whichever event should first happen, and that thereupon I should be appointed Lord Chief Justice.

The Prime Minister told me that he had thought over this plan with great care, and wanted to know what I thought of it. I said at once that there seemed to me to be grave objections to it, but that it was too serious a matter to dispose of in a moment, and that I should like to think it over for a few hours. He answered that that was most reasonable, and asked me to see him again on the following afternoon.

Hewart went to see the Prime Minister next day as arranged and developed his objections. For one thing, it would be difficult to find a judge of the requisite standing to co-operate. More important, argued Hewart, if he agreed to Lloyd George's plan, the public being necessarily unaware of their private understanding would not unnaturally suspect that Hewart had been deliberately passed over for Lord Chief Justice. 'Neither personally nor as trustee of the great office of Attorney-General,' said Hewart bluntly, 'can I assent to that suspicion.'

The Prime Minister looked disappointed. 'The Government simply cannot do without you,' he repeated. 'I am very sorry. I thought my little plan would have worked. But now I have your decision – a very reasonable decision, no doubt – there is an end of the matter. Our friend Rufus must stay where he is.'

Hewart, too, thought it was the end of the matter. But he was wrong.

2

A few days after Hewart's meeting with Lloyd George Parliament rose for the Christmas recess. Hewart went out of London for a day or two immediately after Christmas. He returned home on Friday, December 31, to find that Reading had telephoned the previous day and finding that he was out of town had asked where he had gone so that he could write to him. Hewart immediately rang up Reading's house in Curzon Street only to find that the Lord Chief Justice and his wife had gone off to Bournemouth for the week-end.

No letter came from Reading on New Year's Day, but at breakfast that morning Hewart's eye fell on a paragraph in the *Daily Mail* which greatly surprised him. It was to the effect that the office of Viceroy of India had been offered to the Lord Chief Justice, and that Lord Reading was considering it. Remembering how definite the Prime Minister had been at their meeting barely a fortnight before, Hewart dismissed the paragraph as an unsubstantiated piece of newspaper gossip. What the Attorney-General did not know, and was not to discover until after the whole matter had been settled, was that the substance of the paragraph had actually been given out to the parliamentary lobby correspondents from No. 10 Downing Street. 'I have been told myself,' one of these lobby correspondents subsequently informed Hewart, 'that you prefer a political career and that you are not to be appointed to the Chief Justiceship.'

Nor was there any news from Reading on the Monday. But on Tuesday morning (January 4) a telephone message reached Hewart in his room in the Law Courts that the Lord Chief Justice wished to see him and would be obliged if the Attorney-General could make it convenient to call at 32 Curzon Street, at four-thirty that afternoon. 'I arranged to do so,' Hewart recalled afterwards, 'and at that time and place I saw him. He had that look of pallor and that earnest demeanour which I had so often noticed in him on occasions of importance. He told me, without much preface, that the Prime Minister was very anxious for him to take the Viceroyalty, and that upon the whole he was inclined to take it.' But would Hewart be prepared to waive his claim to the Chief Justiceship for a little time?

Before answering this question, Hewart inquired whether the Prime Minister knew that Reading was seeing him. 'Yes,' said Reading. Hewart then recapitulated the objections he had made to Lloyd George. Reading countered these by saying that he thought the plan was quite a feasible one. At the same time, he strongly sympathized with Hewart's objection that he should not be passed over, adding that he did not think that the request should be made of him and that he (Reading) certainly would not press it.

'I want you to be very definite,' Reading said. 'I understand that you do not think it right to stand aside.'

'I do not,' Hewart agreed.

According to Hewart's account, Reading said he was not surprised. The Government would just have to reconcile themselves to the appointment of a new Attorney-General which they would not like. 'I am having breakfast with the Prime Minister tomorrow morning,' Reading added, bringing the interview to an end. 'Can you come and see me here at eleven, and I will tell you what has happened? I think everything is going to be satisfactory.'

Hewart was at a loss to understand the reason for this new development. He concluded that Lloyd George had now accepted the inevitable and that he would be appointed Lord Chief Justice as soon as Reading had resigned to become Viceroy. This was confirmed by Reading's parting words as they said good-bye on the doorstep. He told him that he had always been convinced that he would reach the top like 'F.E.'. 'Later on you must give me two or three hours,' he added, 'and I will tell you about the duties of the Chief Justice.'

Hewart called again next morning as arranged. On this occasion Reading seemed to his visitor a different being. He looked to Hewart like a man who had just seen a ghost. Hewart was momentarily taken aback, since the first leader in *The Times* that morning welcomed the prospect of the appointment of Reading as Viceroy, which the newspaper's political correspondent had stated was now 'increasingly probable'.

Reading began by saying that he had seen the Prime Minister and Bonar Law together and that it was all off. 'We have been over all the ground again, and they are as adamant as ever,' he went on. 'They will not part with you at the present time, and I am not going to India. I have just left them, and they are in the act of arranging another appointment to the office as Viceroy.'

To this Hewart replied that he was being put in a cruel and dreadful position. 'It is cruel,' Reading agreed. 'They ought not to do it. But they consider nothing else as important in comparison with the House of Commons.' Reading added that he had no grievance against Hewart. 'None whatever. I do not see how you could have been expected as Attorney to act differently.'

Pacing up and down the room, Hewart protested that the position was intolerable. 'It will be very unpleasant to think about afterwards,' he said. 'I must go at once to the Prime Minister and see if something cannot be done.'

Reading did not think it would be much use. However, Hewart

persisted and it was agreed that he should go off to Downing Street and return to Reading's house as soon as he had seen the Prime Minister again.

Lloyd George received the Attorney-General at noon and told him that it was useless to discuss the matter further, as all idea of appointing Reading to the Viceroyalty was at an end. Hewart's account continued:

I expostulated. I called his attention to the very painful position in which I was being placed, but his answer was that, where the public interest was concerned, he was bound to be ruthless.

I pointed out that I was being penalized for my merits. He said, 'That may be so, but I cannot for the life of me understand why you are not willing to fall in with my plan. It is a plan which would make it quite certain that, perhaps in a few months, and certainly within a couple of years, you would succeed to the position of Lord Chief Justice. *As it is, you may never succeed to it at all.*'

These last words particularly shook the Attorney-General, as indeed they were designed to do. Pressing home his advantage, Lloyd George said he was just off for a couple of days' golf and would be at Sir Philip Sassoon's house at Lympne in Kent. Would not the Attorney join him there for a round and a further talk? But Hewart had urgent appointments next morning which he felt he must keep. But after some further conversation he agreed to go down in the afternoon and spend the night at Lympne.

'In the circumstances,' said the Prime Minister magnanimously, 'I will withhold for forty-eight hours the appointment of another man to be Viceroy.'

The short interview ended with Hewart asking Lloyd George whether he had any objection to his seeing Bonar Law. Hewart was still suspicious. He did not trust Lloyd George, but he had implicit faith in Bonar Law who he felt would never consent to anything savouring of double dealing. The Prime Minister agreed instantly, saying that Bonar Law's views were his views and 'my undertaking would also be his undertaking should anything happen to me'.

Bonar Law confirmed Lloyd George's statement without qualification. 'There are thousands of men who can be Viceroy of India,' he remarked reassuringly, 'but we have only one Attorney.' There was some talk as to whether Carson who had previously held the office of Attorney-General might not after all be persuaded to step into the breach so that Hewart might become Chief Justice immediately. 'If

not,' Bonar Law added, 'I think you ought to give way on terms which
would make it certain that you would be Lord Chief Justice in a very
short time.'

When Hewart went back to Curzon Street to report his conversations with Lloyd George and Bonar Law, Reading welcomed the
suggestion that Carson might become Attorney-General as 'hopeful'.
At the same time, he expressed some concern at the delay involved in
Hewart's visit to Lympne, which meant that he would have to wait
for forty-eight hours to know whether he was going to be Viceroy.
'The delay is not consistent with my position,' he remarked somewhat
peevishly, according to Hewart. 'Everybody is expecting a definite
announcement in the newspapers one way or the other today, or at
the latest tomorrow.' He then suggested that Hewart should go away,
and when he had made up his mind whether or not to accept Lloyd
George's proposal he should return to Curzon Street at six o'clock
the same evening. They could then telephone his decision to the Prime
Minister.

So for the third time that day Hewart rang the door bell of Reading's house in Curzon Street. He announced his decision. He would
give way conditionally.

> Rufus was, as before, alone. I told him that I was prepared, if need
> be, to give way provided that the Prime Minister would assent to two
> further conditions. One was that when Rufus resigned the post of Lord
> Chief Justice and the vacancy actually occurred, the post should be
> definitely offered to me, and that I should be given a real opportunity
> of declining it, and that the offer and the refusal if made should be
> officially announced.
> The other condition was that the plan now proposed should not in
> any degree prejudice my claim to the Lord Chancellorship if and when
> it became vacant.
> Rufus thought that there would be no difficulty about either
> condition.

Reading looked greatly relieved, although he had been expecting a
decision along these lines. A few minutes later, Edwin Montagu
appeared, evidently by prearrangement with Reading. When he was
told of Hewart's decision, the Secretary of State for India warmly
congratulated the Attorney-General on the unselfish course he had
taken. They all three then went to Downing Street to telephone the
news to Lloyd George at Lympne on the Prime Minister's private
line. Hewart did the talking, while the other two looked on and

listened. Lloyd George was delighted at the news and readily agreed to Hewart's two conditions. 'You are a very good fellow, Hewart, as I have always known,' he told him, adding that he looked forward to seeing him next day along with Reading.

The following afternoon Reading and Hewart travelled down together by train to Folkestone, where they were met by the Prime Minister's chauffeur and driven to Sassoon's luxurious mansion. Lloyd George was out walking when they arrived, and came back to join them at tea. He displayed all his customary charm. He repeated his thanks to Hewart for doing the Government a great service – 'not for the first time'. He was sure Hewart would fill the office of Lord Chief Justice with the greatest ability, distinction and success. 'It is your due, and it is quite evident that the Bench, the Bar, and the Press desire your appointment. You are called to it with unanimity, and all we are asking you to do is to wait just a little time. You will not be troubled to fight another election.'

Hewart murmured something about the possibility of Carson being willing to become Attorney-General. But Lloyd George quickly brushed this idea aside; it was quite obvious that he did not like it, notwithstanding the fact that he did in some measure owe his tenure of No. 10 Downing Street to Carson's support in the crisis which brought down the Asquith Coalition. Instead the Prime Minister showed much more interest in finding a judge who would be willing to keep the Lord Chief Justice's position warm for Hewart. 'Of course we must have the terms set out in writing,' he added, mentioning the name of an elderly judge (probably Lord Finlay) with what appeared to Hewart to be the triumphant look of a conjurer who has pulled a rabbit out of his hat.

'I shall send for the judge we select,' the Prime Minister continued confidently. 'I shall not suggest that I am conferring something on him. I shall say that we want him to do the Government a service. I shall tell him that we cannot at present spare the Attorney from the House of Commons, and I want somebody to take the post of Lord Chief Justice for a little time upon the terms that he gives it up when I ask him to do so. It may be within a few months, but at latest when I am about to cease to be head of the Government or a General Election is imminent, whichever event may happen first.'

The subject was brought up again at dinner. There was another thing, said Lloyd George, which he felt Hewart should know and ought to know. The previous day, before leaving London, he had seen the King, whom he had informed of the proposed arrangement. 'I am prepared to assent to that arrangement if the Attorney is prepared to assent to it,' the King had said, 'but my assent is conditional upon his assent.' The Prime Minister added that he was sure Hewart would be glad to know that the King himself was taking such a close and friendly interest in the matter.

When they were having coffee in the drawing-room after dinner, Hewart began to wonder whether he had been prudent to give way. Perhaps Lloyd George and Reading might be bluffing, and he would have automatically followed Reading as Chief Justice whichever way his decision had gone. But he was immediately reassured when the Prime Minister took him aside and showed him two draft telegrams which he produced from his pocket. 'I think you ought to see these drafts,' he said. 'They will show you how far we had gone. In a few more hours, if you had not taken the course you did, this other man would have been appointed Viceroy.' The telegrams, which were not sent, offered the Viceroyalty to someone other than Reading.[1]

The evening's discussion was continued over the breakfast table next morning. Reading remarked that he would really not become Viceroy until he arrived in India and that there was no reason why he should resign for some weeks, certainly not before Birkenhead, the Lord Chancellor, who had gone abroad for the Christmas recess, returned for the opening of Parliament in February. This was an important consideration, since Birkenhead would have to be consulted on any consequential appointments to the High Court Bench. Meanwhile, Reading proposed to sit from time to time in the Lord Chief Justice's Court. According to Hewart, 'the Prime Minister heartily agreed with what he described as a very good plan'. After breakfast Reading and Hewart left for the train in which they travelled back to London together. During the journey, Hewart later recalled, Reading 'remarked to me that the postponement of his resignation might be of great assistance to me, especially in relation to the suggestion about Carson'.

The Prime Minister had arranged a house-warming party for the week-end at Chequers, when the trust deeds of the property were to be handed over by Lord and Lady Lee. Besides Reading, the guests who arrived on the Friday evening included Lords Riddell and Milner, Sir Hamar and Lady Greenwood, Sir Robert Horne, Sir

[1] Probably Lord Lytton, then Parliamentary Under-Secretary for India, later Governor of Bengal and Acting Viceroy.

Bertrand Dawson (afterwards Lord Dawson of Penn), and the American Ambassador and his wife, Mr and Mrs Davis, in addition to the Prime Minister, his wife and daughter Megan. Everyone naturally congratulated Reading on his new appointment, which was to be officially announced from Chequers next morning. To that acute observer Lord Riddell he appeared a new man. 'For some time past he has been on the gloomy side. Now he is like a schoolboy let out for a holiday.' At the same time Riddell recorded his opinion of him as an individual: 'He is a charming person – always the same and equally courteous to all classes. He is an adventurous sort of man and must have a wonderful nervous system.'

At dinner there were some interesting biographical reminiscences, to which Reading contributed his share. The last time he was in India he was the ship's boy on a sailing ship, he said; now he was returning as Viceroy.

During the evening Riddell asked the Viceroy-designate whether he would be able to keep up his law while he was in India by reading the Law Reports.

Reading took the questioner by the arm and whispered in his ear, 'I will never look at a law report again if I can help it! I never want to see another one!'

3

On the whole the appointment was received well in the Press and also in the Temple. Only the *Morning Post* attacked it on the ground that the new Viceroy was a Jew. Some Indian newspapers, on the other hand, pointed out that far from being a hindrance, his Jewish origin was an advantage as enabling him the better and more easily to understand the minds and ways of Eastern peoples.

At the first sitting of the Lord Chief Justice's Court after the appointment had been announced, Hewart offered his congratulations on behalf of the English Bar. Reading replied in rather more formal language than he had used in speaking to Lord Riddell at Chequers, but no doubt just as sincere.

To be the representative of the King-Emperor in India is to be the representative of Justice. I leave this seat, the judicial Bench, not forsaking or abandoning the pursuit of justice but rather pursuing it in larger fields, and where I feel the road is not so certain or well laid. . . .

I trust those in India, who may be reading of my appointment, who are now at the outset of great progressive reforms introduced into their country by the King's Government, may recognize that in selecting the representative of Justice from this country to take the supreme place as the King's representative in India, it is the desire of His Majesty and of His Majesty's servants to make manifest in India that justice will remain the supreme guiding factor in the destinies of India, so long as it is possible for human beings to hold the scales even.

The idea of himself as the supreme dispenser of the principles of English justice and equity among the millions of politically immature Indians was one which made a strong appeal to Reading's romantic nature. He saw himself as a kind of twentieth-century Haroun-Al-Raschid. 'Although I will admit to you that I am under no delusions as to the anxieties and difficulties before me,' he told H. A. L. Fisher, the historian and Education Minister in Lloyd George's Cabinet, who had written to congratulate him, 'I think with you that my position of former L.C.J. may be a real help and that in the many and varied questions that will arise it will not be out of place to have an English lawyer at the head. Above all the appeal to me is in the initiation of the Liberal reforms among a people who as yet have the scantiest political knowledge.'[1]

These reforms, foreshadowed by the official declaration of August 20, 1917, which expressed the Government's intention 'to provide for the increasing association of Indians in every branch of Indian administration, and for gradual development of self-governing institutions, with a view to the progressive realization of responsible government in British India as an integral part of the Empire', were largely the outcome of the Liberal Secretary of State's industry, although the words just quoted were somewhat surprisingly written by the Conservative ex-Viceroy Lord Curzon. Known as the Montagu-Chelmsford Reforms and embodied in the Government of India Act of 1919, they were an experiment in devolution designed to give the Indians executive responsibility for a limited number of subjects and thus to train them for further responsibility. At the Centre a two-Chamber legislature took the place of the old Imperial Council and consisted of a Central Legislative Assembly and a Council of State, both part elected and part nominated. The Provincial Governments on the other hand were entrusted with responsibility for certain 'transferred' subjects such as Local Government, Excise, Health and

[1] H. A. L. Fisher Papers.

Education, while such subjects as Justice, Police, Land Administration, Defence and Foreign Affairs were 'reserved' for the Centre.[1] Both the Viceroy and the Provincial Governors had a power of veto. This system, officially known as 'dyarchy', had many critics, among both the diehard supporters of the British Raj and the Indian nationalist members of the Congress Party. But at least it was an honest attempt at the creation of a half-way house along the road to complete self-government. Of course, like most compromises it was unpopular and much of the odium for its initiation fell upon the head of the single-minded Secretary of State. Yet, shortly before the reforms were due to be implemented at the beginning of 1921, Montagu began to have second thoughts. In a letter to Lord Willingdon, the Governor of Madras, written on September 9, 1920, Montagu gave a clear impression of the atmosphere with which the next Viceroy would be faced.[2]

> As soon as the Indians were told that we agreed with them that they were to become partners with us, it instilled into their minds an increased feeling of existing subordination and a realization of everything by which this subordination was expressed. Similarly, when the Europeans were told that, after driving the Indians for so many years, that régime was to be over and they might find themselves forced to co-operation with the Indians, or even forced to allow Indians to rule India, their race consciousness sprang up afresh.
>
> I am convinced in my own mind that that has been the fatal mistake of our policy in India. We ought to have let Indians run their own show, with all its inefficiency and imperfections. Development would have been much slower, but the inevitable transition would have been less difficult. I am, however, satisfied that the temper of democratic countries such as ours is increasingly against remaining in a country where we are not wanted, and we have either got to make our peace with the Indians, or, as the educated classes grow, we shall find a strenuous desire in this country to get rid of India and all its bother.

Although he was not due to leave England until the middle of March, so as to enable Chelmsford to hand over personally to him in Bombay at the beginning of April, Reading did not sit again as Lord Chief Justice, since he was fully occupied in the intervening period preparing himself for his new sphere. He had not been on a horse

[1] There were nine Provincial Governments, viz, Assam, Bengal, Bihar and Orissa, Bombay, the Central Provinces, Madras, the North-West Frontier Province, the Punjab, and the United Provinces of Agra and Oudh.
[2] Waley, p. 235.

since his marriage. Now he took early morning rides in Hyde Park, since he had been told that there were ceremonial occasions when the Viceroy was expected to appear on horseback. He shot clay pigeons so as to get in practice for the great shoots in the Native States to which the Viceroy was invariably invited, and he even found time for dancing lessons. He went to see Lord Curzon, who had succeeded Balfour as Foreign Secretary. The interview did not take place in the Foreign Secretary's magnificent room in the Foreign Office, but in the Minister's austerely furnished bedroom in Carlton House Terrace, where Reading found him suffering from some minor indisposition and lying on a plain brass bedstead. Reading was surprised at the contrast between Curzon's public and private habits, since he was aware that nothing had ever exceeded the pomp and magnificence of Curzon's own Viceroyalty. As Birkenhead once told Reading, 'he looks upon the Viceroyalty as one of the greatest offices in the world, partly because it is, and partly because he has held it'. Reading asked Curzon about the Indian climate, for he was still a little uneasy about the effect it might have on his wife's precarious health, particularly the altitude of Simla which was the headquarters of the Government of India for half the year. 'Climate?' Curzon queried in his character-istically grand manner. 'The Viceroy has not to concern himself with climate. He goes where he wishes.' During the ensuing weeks – indeed right down to the moment of Reading's departure from Victoria Station – Curzon heaped friendly advice upon him, writing him long and characteristically detailed letters, going into each item of equipment necessary for his tour as Viceroy, even to the number of black and grey tall hats he would require.

Reading spent several hours every day in the India Office, talking to the Secretary of State and reading a vast quantity of dispatches and reports, so doing his utmost, as he told Lloyd George, 'to inform myself as to the causes of the condition of unrest in India in order that I might arrive at my own judgment'. Besides both being Jews, Read-ing and Montagu were old friends, and there was a stronger bond of sympathy between them than in the case of any of the other three Ministers who were to head the India Office during the term of Reading's Viceroyalty. 'I am delighted with Rufus,' Montagu told Willingdon at this time. 'We spend much of the day together. No one can say who is going to make a good Viceroy, but one can confidently predict that Rufus ought to make a good one.'[1]

[1] Waley, p. 253.

A younger son of the first Lord Swaythling, Edwin Samuel Montagu was a brilliant, wayward, and, as his career worked out, tragic figure. Under-Secretary for India at thirty-one, Cabinet Minister at thirty-six, he seemed destined in the natural course of things to become Liberal Premier if nothing went wrong. His wife Venetia was the daughter of Lord Stanley of Alderley and one of the most beautiful, gifted and attractive women of her time. Edwin, on the contrary, was anything but handsome, being ungainly and nearly bald: he habitually wore a monocle, which added a touch of incongruity to his earnest, student-like face. Politics for him were an all-consuming interest and eventually were to prove his undoing. 'That he was an Oriental,' the economist Maynard Keynes wrote of him on his death at forty-five, 'equipped, nevertheless, with the intellectual technique and atmosphere of the West, drew him naturally to the political problems of India, and allowed an instinctive, mutual sympathy between him and its peoples. But he was interested in all political problems and not least in the personal side of politics and was most intensely a politician. Almost everything else bored him. . . . Mr Lloyd George was, of course, the undoing of his political career, as, indeed, Montagu always said that he would be. He could not keep away from that bright candle, but he knew, poor moth, that he would burn his wings.'

For some time Montagu had been worried by the harsh terms which the Allies had imposed upon Turkey by the Treaty of Sèvres in 1920 and the effect upon the great Moslem community in India, which naturally had great sympathy for the plight of their co-religionists in Constantinople. Besides being practically expelled from Europe, the Turks had been fighting the Greeks who had invaded Asia Minor and seized Smyrna. Unfortunately Lloyd George was strongly pro-Greek and as bitterly anti-Turk, whom he called 'the curse of every land on which he has laid his hand'. Reading's study of the question convinced him of the weight of Mohammedan objections to the Treaty, as evidenced by the strength of the so-called Khilafat movement in India, and he expressed his uneasiness in a confidential letter to the Prime Minister before he set off:

> That these objections form one of the main causes of the unrest is, of course, well-known to you. I know you will bear them in mind when considering the position as it now is. It is a great opportunity if it can be taken by you.
>
> I know you are surrounded with difficulties. I do not want to add to

them and am writing only for the purpose of telling you how important it is, in my judgment, to make concessions to Mohammedan opinion if you think they can safely be made. After all that has happened in India in relation to the Treaty, there will be the greatest disappointment if no revision is made, particularly now that our own newspapers are asserting that it is England and you that oppose and that France, etc. are willing.[1]

The recent downfall of the Government of M. Venizelos in Athens and the restoration of the monarchy under the pro-German King Constantine had doomed Lloyd George's pro-Greek policy in Asia Minor and made some modifications of the Treaty of Sèvres inevitable in Turkey's favour. At an Inter-Allied Conference held in London in February, 1921, Lloyd George put forward some proposals in this sense, but they failed to satisfy either the Greeks or the Turks, who both rejected them. Montagu was equally disappointed. 'Unless the Allies can do more than this,' he told the Prime Minister, shortly before Reading sailed, 'peace is impossible in Turkey, in the whole of the Middle East, in Afghanistan and in India. . . . As regards India, Lord Reading would convince you, if I cannot, that now that the Reforms are working, if the Turkish Treaty could be satisfactorily settled, *there is every prospect of profound peace and the cessation of all of our troubles.*'

Montagu was not the only discontented Minister who wrote to the Prime Minister at this time. Birkenhead was furious when he returned from his holiday to learn that Lloyd George proposed to appoint a temporary Lord Chief Justice who would consent to give up his post when Hewart could be released from the House of Commons. He told the Prime Minister quite bluntly that the plan was illegal under the Judicature Act, which provided that all High Court judges held their offices for life and were removable only for serious misbehaviour at the instance of Parliament. An acrimonious correspondence developed between the two in which they addressed each other as 'My dear Lord Chancellor' and 'My dear Prime Minister' instead of the informal 'Dear F.E.' and 'Dear Ll.G.', ending 'Yours sincerely' instead of the usual 'Yours ever'. Birkenhead wrote with dignity:

> The proposal under contemplation would make the Lord Chief Justice a transient figure subject to removal at the will of the Government of the day and the creature of political exigency. I do not think that, if such an arrangement were publicly discussed, it would be capable of reasoned defence.

[1] February 21, 1921: Lloyd George Papers.

But Lloyd George replied in offensive terms:

If it is contrary to the Judicature Act that high legal functionaries should not cling to their posts into years of decrepitude, then it is high time that these Acts were amended.

Of course, Birkenhead was only too well aware that, unlike the other judges, the appointment of Lord Chief Justice lay with the Prime Minister. All he could say, therefore, was that, if Lloyd George appointed the ex-Lord Chancellor, Lord Finlay, which was then his intention, he would do so 'without any condition, relying upon his age to terminate his tenure of office within a reasonable time'. As will be seen, the Prime Minister declined to act upon this advice. The incident made for bad feeling between the two for a time, although their former intimate relations were later resumed.

Meanwhile, Hewart was becoming increasingly concerned that the Lord Chief Justiceship was not offered to him in accordance with his understanding with Lloyd George. Nor was he any less worried as the result of the newspaper stories that he had consented to be passed over. After Reading's valedictory appearance in Court, Hewart had written to him to thank him for the pleasant things he had said about him in his speech and added that he had been a little troubled by the Press statements about him. The letter was not answered, and Hewart began to wonder whether he had not been tricked after all. Two things now appeared to him on reflection to be significant. He described them thus:

The first was that, from the beginning to end of these conversations I had not received a scrap of paper – not even a letter from the Prime Minister or from Rufus for the purpose of making an appointment.

The second was that, up to the time of the official announcement, my name had been completely suppressed in the newspapers' accounts of the various comings and goings. No word had appeared, for example, about my visit to Lympne; the whole delay had been imputed to questions concerning the health of Lady Reading; and it had been falsely though officially stated that the decision had been taken at Chequers, where Rufus was with the Prime Minister.[1]

[1] The fact that the announcement of the appointment was made from Chequers seems to have implied that the decision was also taken there. The explanation of the delay, which evidently originated in Lloyd George's press office, was stated by *The Times* (January 10, 1921) to be as follows: '*Apart from some technical considerations which remained to be cleared up*, Lord Reading's hesitation was inspired by anxiety as to the effect of a prolonged residence in India upon his wife's health' (Author's italics).

I perceived further that the whole matter had been transacted during the absence of the Lord Chancellor from England.

Eventually on January 17, Reading invited Hewart to lunch. At this meeting, according to Hewart, Reading dismissed the newspaper paragraphs as unimportant. When he said that the date of his departure had been set for March 17, Hewart remarked, 'Very near Easter.' Hewart added that he did not see why he should not succeed Reading on the Bench after the Easter Vacation. On this Reading is stated to have assured Hewart that he would give him any help he could and would not formally resign until after Birkenhead had returned to London.

Nearly a month passed, and when Hewart had heard nothing further from the Prime Minister, he addressed him a stinging letter accusing him of breaking faith. ('The position is to me most painful and distressing.') Lloyd George read it with 'pained disappointment'. He then showed the letter to Reading who gave it as his opinion that the two men were now 'as free as if no discussion had taken place'. At the same time Reading did stress that Hewart was 'a fit person to appoint' to his (Reading's) judicial office.[1] In his reply Lloyd George denied that Hewart's interpretation of their understanding was complete. But, he added, showing his annoyance as clearly as he had done with Birkenhead, 'it is hardly worth entering into a discussion on that point, as you assume that whatever the arrangement it must now be treated as impracticable and therefore terminated. Had you expressed that opinion to me at the time, no vacancy would have arisen in the Lord Chief Justiceship, and this unhappy episode would not have occurred. However, I accept your statement that whatever the understanding you feel yourself no longer bound by it. That also involves my release from any undertaking given by me.'

There were many farewell functions to attend. On March 15, Reading and his wife were received in audience by the King, when he kissed hands on his appointment and was invested with the insignia of a Knight Grand Cross of the Order of the Star of India and of the Order of the Indian Empire, of both of which Orders the Viceroy was *ex officio* Grand Master during his term of office. At the same time his wife had the Order of the Crown of India conferred upon her. Next day, a farewell dinner was given for him in the historic Middle Temple Hall by the Bench and Bar, at which the Lord Chancellor

[1] Reading to Lloyd George, February 27, 1921: Lloyd George Papers.

presided. In the speech proposing his health, Birkenhead singled out the three qualities which he felt were specially illustrative of the new Viceroy's career – exquisite courtesy, inexhaustible patience, and a vehement and passionate desire to do justice.

The following morning the Readings left their house in Curzon Street on the first stage of their journey by train. They were accompanied by a staff of six, consisting of Colonel Craufurd-Stuart, the Military Secretary who had been with them in Washington, two A.D.C.s, and Lady Reading's private secretary, nurse and maid. This entourage was to be augmented on their arrival in India by the Viceroy's Private Secretary and Assistant Private Secretary, a Comptroller, a Surgeon and six more A.D.C.s, of whom two were Indians. Lady Reading's secretary, Miss Yvonne Fitzroy, was the twenty-nine-year-old daughter of Sir Almeric Fitzroy, the Clerk to the Privy Council, and returning visitors from India were to testify to the great value of her tact and judgment in the viceregal household. The maid was the faithful old family retainer Squires, who had originally been the Viceroy's 'nanny'. Since she was getting on in years and suffering from rheumatism, his Lordship intended to pension her off. 'Squires,' he said, having sent for her in Curzon Street to break the news, 'her Ladyship and I feel obliged to tell you that we have decided to go to India.' 'Oh, have you, my Lord?' Squires interrupted before her master could get to the point. 'That will be very nice. I have always wanted to see India.' Reading had not the heart to go on. So Squires went to India with her master and mistress – and returned with them five years later.[1]

Among those who went to Victoria Station to see them off was Lord Curzon. The ex-Viceroy was the last person to whom Reading spoke before boarding the train, and although neither of them knew it at the time, it was the last time they saw each other. Edwin Montagu and the Readings' son Gerald went with them as far as Dover, where they had arranged to spend the night in the Lord Warden Hotel, so that Lady Reading might have an undisturbed rest before crossing the Channel and continuing the overland journey to Marseilles to catch the P. & O. steamship *Kaiser-i-Hind* for Bombay. From the hotel Reading addressed a farewell note to Lloyd George, begging him to appoint Hewart Lord Chief Justice, 'if you can possibly do it'. Bonar Law had just resigned as Chancellor of the Exchequer on medical advice and was retiring temporarily from

[1] Sir Almeric Fitzroy: *Memoirs* (1925), Vol. II, p. 763; Reading, Vol. II, p. 153.

public life; if there was a consequent reshuffle of Government offices, Reading suggested this might facilitate Hewart's succession.

Next morning they caught the ferry boat to Calais. The Secretary of State, who had also stayed the night in the hotel walked with them to the Admiralty Pier and shook hands – like Curzon, as it was to turn out, for the last time.

When they embarked at Marseilles, the Readings found that their friend Lord Inchcape, the Chairman of the P. & O. Line, had made the most extensive alterations to one of the decks for their comfort. Several staterooms had been thrown into a suite, so that they could have a commodious bedroom, two bathrooms and private sitting-rooms. Particular pains had been taken to make Lady Reading comfortable, and even a cow had been taken on board so that she could have supplies of fresh milk.

The voyage was uneventful and from Alice Reading's point of view gratifyingly calm. They went ashore at Port Said and on to Cairo where they spent the night in the Residency, having arranged to pick up the *Kaiser-i-Hind* next day after the ship had gone through the Suez Canal. That night Field-Marshal Lord Allenby, the High Commissioner, gave a glittering dinner-party at the Residency. An official conference on Near and Middle East affairs was taking place in Cairo, so that there was a distinguished gathering of guests on this occasion, including the High Commissioners of Palestine and Mesopotamia, the Governors of Cyprus and Somaliland, the Resident of Aden and the Colonial Secretary in the Imperial Government who at this time was Winston Churchill. Much of the talk at dinner turned on the Greco-Turkish War which had flared up again, and Churchill's denunciation of Lloyd George's pro-Greek policy, which he had conveyed to the Prime Minister before leaving England, won general agreement. 'We shall everywhere be represented as the chief enemy of Islam,' he said.

Churchill's words were to prove a remarkably accurate prophecy, as indeed Reading was to appreciate when Viceroy.

4

The skies were clear and sunny on the morning of April 2, 1921, as the Viceroy and Vicereine walked down the gangway of the *Kaiser-i-Hind* and took their places in the waiting launch to the strains of 'For He's a Jolly Good Fellow', sung by the ship's company and passengers. A few minutes later this air gave way to the more solemn music of 'God Save the King', when the Readings disembarked at the Apollo Bunder and walked up the flight of steps leading from the water to the 'Gateway of India', the massive grey archway built to commemorate the landing of King George V and Queen Mary ten years before. After a formal greeting from Sir George Lloyd, the Governor of Bombay, they were conducted to a red and gold pavilion beside the archway and took their places on two thrones set on a dais at one end of the pavilion. Then the President of the Bombay Municipal Corporation, Sir David Sassoon, who belonged to a wealthy Parsee family, delivered an address in which he welcomed the new Viceroy in the name of one great oriental civilization to the member of another.

Reading's reply, as befitted his first speech on Indian soil, ranged from the working of the Montagu-Chelmsford Reforms to the Bombay municipality's plans for the improvement of local housing, water-supply and drainage. But he did not forget the personal touch.

> I note especially your sympathetic reference to the ancient race to which I belong, [he said] and I observe with pleasure that you state that your pride in welcoming me is enhanced by this circumstance. It is my only connection with the East until the present moment and this leads me to wonder whether perhaps, by some fortunate almost indefinably subtle sub-consciousness, it may quicken and facilitate my understanding of the aims and aspirations, the trials and tribulations, the joys and sorrows of the Indian people, and assist me to catch the almost inarticulate cries and inaudible whispers of those multitudes who sometimes suffer most and yet find it most difficult, if not impossible, to express their needs. . . . I know that the task that awaits me is as you say 'arduous indeed' – I was aware of it when I gave up my place of serene dignity to accept a place of perhaps greater dignity but certainly of less serenity. But I shall set out, cheered and encouraged by your welcome, with hopefulness in my heart, and mainly because all my experience of human beings and human affairs has convinced me that justice and sympathy never fail to evoke responsive chords in the hearts of men, of whatever race, creed or class.

It was only a few minutes' drive from the 'Gateway of India' to the Bombay University Convocation Hall for the swearing-in ceremony. Then came the beautiful drive along the shore of Back Bay to Malabar Hill and Government House on the point, with its pleasing view of the city across the bay. Here they received a polite but somewhat frigid welcome from the departing Viceroy, Lord Chelmsford, and his wife. Chelmsford seemed depressed and withdrawn. His successor soon learned the reason. Chelmsford had only been given a viscountcy as a reward for his five years of service, whereas he, and particularly his wife, thought that he merited an earldom.

Two strenuous days followed with more addresses of welcome, a large dinner-party given by the Lloyds, two luncheon-parties and a garden-party, in the course of which Reading met all the leading people in Bombay. He had long talks with Lloyd and all the members of the Governor's Executive Council, except one who was ill and could not come to Government House, besides the Commander-in-Chief, Lord Rawlinson, and the Admiral, also the Vice-President of the Council of State Sir William Vincent who had come down from Delhi to meet him. Another caller at Government House whom the Viceroy received was the collaborator of Mahatma Gandhi and former President of the Indian National Congress, seventy-four-year-old Mrs Annie Besant, who arrived from her theosophist headquarters near Madras and, in Reading's words, 'expressed her earnest desire to co-operate with me and my Government'. Gandhi, on the other hand, who had recently persuaded the Congress Party to adopt his technique of passive resistance or 'non-cooperation', as he called it, as its policy, with the *hartal*, or strike during which people were supposed to devote themselves to prayer and fasting, as the conspicuous feature, did not call on the new Viceroy. However, he told his followers not to make any trouble for the new Viceroy on his arrival but to await events.

At the end of the second day the Viceroy and Vicereine left Bombay for Delhi in the magnificent viceregal train with sitting-rooms, bedrooms and bathrooms and the royal arms emblazoned on every coach. 'In the evening we dined with the Admiral,' Reading cabled Montagu from the train, 'and I was greatly struck on the journey, both from Government House to the Admiral's house and from the latter to the railway station, by the large cheering crowds which lined the streets in spite of the lateness of the hour. I feel sure from the warmth of the welcome accorded to me by all classes in Bombay, which exceeded greatly my expectations, that India is going to give me a fair chance. Press notices are uniformly favourable, sometimes fulsome. Even the *Bombay Chronicle* [the Congress Party organ] has found itself able to bless me and my coming. . . . It is very hot, but we are both standing the heat and the strain very well so far.'

The 845-mile train journey to Delhi took three days and three nights, and the line was guarded the whole way by men standing at twenty-yard intervals, their flickering torches at night being visible for miles around. Passing through places like Surat, Ahmadabad and Ajmer gave the viceregal party fleeting glimpses of the old India, while brief stops at Baroda, Jodhpur, Jaipur and Alwar drew attention to the existence of the powerful Native Princes of those territories. Outside the central station in Delhi the Viceroy's Bodyguard, magnificent warrior types in their red and blue uniforms, were drawn up in readiness to escort the Viceroy and Vicereine to the Viceregal Lodge on the Ridge to the north of the Old City, with its memories of the Mutiny. They drove past the famous Red Fort of the Moghul Emperors, past the mutiny hero John Nicolson's grave by the Kashmir Gate, and past Maiden's Hotel, beloved of English travellers, through the Civil Lines and the Cantonments and a miscellaneous agglomeration of official buildings.

Viceregal Lodge was barely twenty years old, having been built for the Coronation Durbar of Edward VII, and only became the Viceroy's winter headquarters after the transfer of the capital from Calcutta to Delhi in 1911. It was a long, low white building with a high white-pillared porch and a colonnade of rounded arches, but it had not been constructed on anything like the grand scale of the viceregal residence in Calcutta, being really intended as a temporary establishment until the building of New Delhi had been completed. 'I do not complain of this,' said Reading, 'for I like the present house at Delhi and think I should prefer it infinitely to the far more imposing and palatial abode which will some day be occupied by the Viceroy.' Although it could become well nigh unbearable in the hot weather, it had pleasant, shady gardens with water courses which dated from Moghul times. It was now uncomfortably warm and the move by the staff to the Government's summer quarters at Simla had already begun.

From Delhi Reading cabled Montagu about the reason for the departing Viceroy's discontent:

My impression was that Chelmsford was embittered with ingratitude shown him in India, particularly in the Indian Press. On top of this and on the day he sailed came the announcement regarding the Viscountcy. I do not think that he had or has any specific quarrel with you personally or with His Majesty's Government but I gather that the feeling was that, as his predecessors had received an Earldom or the

Garter, he could not accept less for his services to India and the Empire without loss of self-respect. He considered that his services were not inferior to theirs, and when only a Viscountcy came to him at the moment he was embittered by the Indian Press, his cup was full. In this instance the adage '*Cherchez la femme*' is, I think, pertinent.

Later, after Montagu had described Chelmsford in a three-hour talk, which he had with him immediately on his arrival in London, as 'just rather sloppy ice', Reading admitted that he was not surprised by this description. On the other hand, he was careful not to do Chelmsford any injustice.

For my own part, although I found him singularly lacking in charm and geniality, which may perhaps account for some of the difficulties in his path, he was actuated by high purpose and strove his utmost for India. I have an impression, though I do not wish to state it more emphatically, that he was too disposed to tread conventional lines and was apparently apprehensive of any action for which there was no precedent, and moreover, although I express this with great diffidence, I think he was rather easily inclined to adopt a negative attitude. However, it is very easy to criticize looking back over his five strenuous years, and in any event, as it struck me when I dictated the above, he joined with you in initiating the greatest reforms India has ever known. Certainly I shall never be able to strike so epoch-making a note.

It used to take something like three weeks to change the viceregal residence from Delhi to Simla, and as a rule the Viceroy would stop on the way at the pleasantly situated station of Dehra Dun in the United Provinces. 'It seems rather absurd,' was how it struck Reading at the time, 'that there should be all this trouble and expense of moving the paraphernalia of a big household and carrying glass and plate and all the various impedimenta of a household from one place to another. I must see whether I cannot change this system. I cannot conceive that it is in the interests of economy or efficiency.'

The Viceroy and Secretary of State customarily wrote to each other once a week, this correspondence supplementing the daily stream of official and private telegrams which they also exchanged.[1] Reading's first letter to Montagu was written as he was about to set out on a short visit to the Punjab, where there had recently been disturbing reports of renewed unrest among the Sikhs.

[1] The Reading-Montagu correspondence forms part of the Montagu Papers in the India Office Library. The telegrams are separately preserved in the volumes of 'Private Telegrams between the Secretary of State and the Viceroy'.

Viceroy to Secretary of State

Viceroy's Camp.
April 13, 1921

I am writing from Dehra Dun which we like immensely. This is a real bungalow and very prettily situate and the temperature so far has not been excessively hot. . . .

As I telegraphed to you, everything went very well on our reception at Bombay, and so far as I can gather from all I have read, seen and heard, the reception was what may I think be properly described as enthusiastic. Of course it meant nothing more than a hearty welcome to the new Viceroy – perhaps with the addition of the Lord Chief Justice thrown in. Lady Reading and I both liked Sir George and Lady Lloyd very much. I was struck by their capacity; he is full of drive and energy; she is very attractive and has dignity and presence and manner. . . .

I find the situation much as you and I expected. There has so far been no overt act against me by Gandhi; on the contrary, he issued a notice to his non-cooperators to be neutral. But we shall see a little more as time progresses what his plans are. The interview I had with Mrs Besant, of which I cabled to you, was very interesting and her statements were borne out by events. I will not pursue this at the moment save to confirm that his movement is far away the most serious factor in the present situation. . . .

It was an easy overnight train journey to Lahore, the Punjab capital, where the Governor, Sir Eric Maclagan, and the leading officers of the Government were waiting to greet the Viceroy. Afterwards beneath the high portico of Government House the Governor enlarged upon the Sikh troubles. These centred on the struggle for the possession of the Sikh holy places, many of which had passed into the possession of people not even nominally Sikhs, whose prime interest was to milk the pilgrims. The agitation for the reform of the Sikh shrines was carried on by religious warriors known as Akalis, who wished to restore Sikh political independence. To finance their campaign their eyes turned to the shrines, and they began to take the law into their own hands, plundering some of the smaller shrines without any interference on the part of the British authorities. The climax had come in February, 1921, when the Akalis attempted to gain possession of the famous shrine of Nankana Sahib, the birthplace of Guru Nanak, the founder of the Sikh religion, in the western Punjab, alleging that the Mahunt, or abbot in charge, was an evilliver and kept a Moslem mistress. But the tables were turned on them with a vengeance. Once they were inside the shrine, the Mahunt closed the gates, and he and his priests opened fire on the invaders killing 131 of them. This naturally provoked reprisals from the Akalis, who proceeded to terrorize the surrounding countryside.

The Akalis, who were by this date allied politically with the Indian Congress Party, also strove to keep alive the bitter anti-British feelings engendered by the unhappy affair of General Dyer. In April, 1919, a mob in Amritsar, without provocation, had killed five Englishmen, looted two banks, and beaten up a woman missionary, leaving her for dead in the street. Brigadier-General R. E. H. Dyer, the area military commander, who was a native of the Punjab and knew the province well, issued a proclamation forbidding public meetings under martial law. In defiance of his order a dense crowd of several thousands assembled in a confined grassy space in the city known as the Jallianwala Bagh. Thereupon Dyer marched fifty of his riflemen to the spot and opened fire on the crowd without warning. The crowd took fright, rushing the exits which were inadequate, and many jumped into a large open well where they were suffocated. Meanwhile, Dyer, thinking the people were massing to attack him and his men, did not give the order to cease fire until 1,650 rounds had been expended. The casualties were officially stated to have been 379 killed, with about three times that number wounded, but they were undoubtedly much higher. A few days later, Dyer issued an order that no Indian should be permitted to pass along the street where the missionary had been assaulted except in a crawling posture. He also caused six persons, whom he believed to have been responsible for the assault, to be publicly whipped in the same street, although they were not actually convicted of the crime until some time later.

General Dyer restored law and order to the district and even the guardians of the Golden Temple, the central Sikh shrine, who feared pillage at the hands of the mob, thanked him and made him an honorary Sikh. But some of his actions, such as the crawling order, unfortunately emulated elsewhere by some of his subordinates, were indefensible, and promptly disowned by higher authority. A committee of inquiry, which was appointed by Montagu to investigate the disturbances and the measures taken to cope with them, censured Dyer severely and he was forced to resign from the service. Many of the more senior supporters of the British Raj protested that Dyer had been unjustly 'broken' for doing no more than his duty. This was not,

EDWIN MONTAGU AND
LLOYD GEORGE

WITH THE PRINCE OF
WALES IN DELHI

At the unveiling of the
All-India Memorial to
King Edward VII in 1922

LEAVING CALCUTTA FOR THE LAST TIME (*Radio Times Hulton Picture Library*)

WELCOME HOME.' Scene at Victoria Station, showing *(from the left)* Sir W. Joynson-Hicks, Lady Reading, Lord Reading, Lord Birkenhead (Secretary of State for India), Sir Alfred Mond, Lady Birkenhead. *(Radio Times Hulton Picture Library)*

of course, the Liberal progressive view held by Montagu, nor for that matter by the new Viceroy. 'The more I read of these occurrences,' Montagu had written immediately after the Amritsar disturbances, 'the more I am struck by the fact that there is every reason to believe that they are the inevitable consequences of that easiest of all forms of government – firm and strong government.'

To the Viceroy, Montagu cabled at the time of his visit to the Punjab:

> I do not in the least wish to influence your judgment at this stage about what it is best to do with regard to the Punjab. We have discussed it so often and we are fully aware of the difficulties. I hope, however, you will not take it amiss if I suggest to you that I have no doubt you will be careful, in expressing the repugnance of Englishmen to the humiliation orders, not to let it be inferred that there is not the same horror of the doctrine of preventive murder enunciated by Dyer. If you could see your way to saying that you hope you have taken steps to prevent a recurrence of humiliation orders and that anybody issuing them will in future be at once dismissed from India without pension, I think it will have a good effect.

Reading was anxious to go to Amritsar and get something of the atmosphere of the historic Sikh city. At first both the Governor and Sir William Vincent, who had accompanied Reading to Lahore, were strongly opposed to the visit, as they feared it might imply, or be taken to imply, an intention to reopen the Dyer matter and would certainly cause Press criticism. But the Viceroy insisted and eventually had his way.

> I expressed my view that to visit Lahore without going to Amritsar would occasion more comment, and might be taken as implying callousness. My proposal was to pay an informal visit, necessarily hurried by my limitation of time, and in the end both the Governor and Sir William Vincent agreed that it was advisable I should pay the informal visit.
>
> Accordingly the Governor and I and staff went yesterday morning early to Amritsar, where reception was quite friendly and no untoward incident happened. We drove through the streets and visited the Jallianwala Bagh and then saw the Golden Temple, but we had no time to enter it, and indeed I thought perhaps it was inadvisable. Everybody seemed very satisfied with the visit and were very glad we had gone, and so far as one can gather the visit seems to have given satisfaction. I have not yet seen Press comments, but of course am prepared for criticism. . . .

M

Apparently the fact that I had visited Lahore and Amritsar, notwithstanding the great heat, made some impression.

Although the Viceroy's visit to Amritsar was improvised and unannounced, he was quickly recognized as his carriage made its way through the ancient, narrow streets and on the whole his visit was welcomed not merely in the Punjab but throughout India as being an imaginative gesture of goodwill at the outset of his viceroyalty, except by the most extreme political elements. Back in Lahore he received a deputation of the Punjab leaders or 'Chiefs', who presented him with an address of welcome. In his reply, which was in effect the first political speech he made as Viceroy, Reading made a plea for racial co-operation, incidentally stressing the Government's undertaking to bring the scale of monetary compensation to Indians who had suffered 'by the events of Jallianwala Bagh and elsewhere in the Punjab' into line with the payments to British sufferers. 'Can we not now do our utmost to banish suspicion,' he pleaded, 'to cease imputing evil motives, to believe again in the sympathetic justice of the Government, to concentrate in united effort to reach by peaceful and constitutional means the end which is promised under your new Reforms and which indeed is already in course of fulfilment? Let us, you Indians in your hundreds of millions, and we British in our small numbers, join hands and determine to work together for the realization of this great aim and ideal.' Unfortunately this truly noble end was not destined to be accomplished without a great deal of bloodshed.

While he was in Lahore, Reading learned the news of the appointment of his successor as Lord Chief Justice. It was the seventy-seven-year-old Mr Justice A. T. Lawrence, a veteran King's Bench judge who had been called to the Bar over half-a-century previously, in fact in the year in which public executions were abolished in England. 'My dear A.T.,' Reading telegraphed Lawrence, 'heartiest congratulations and good wishes!', while to Montagu he wrote: 'I noticed that Gordon Hewart has apparently fallen into line and the P.M. has had his way.' According to report, before the appointment was made Lawrence wrote out his letter of resignation, leaving the date blank, which document he gave the Prime Minister. It was as well that Lloyd George took this precaution and did not rely on advancing years to bring about Lawrence's retirement. Less than one year later, the new 'Lord Chief', who had in the meantime been created Lord Trevethin, was coming up to London in the train in order to finish a case which had been adjourned from the previous day when he read of his resignation in the morning newspapers. He was succeeded by Hewart, so that on this occasion Lloyd George kept his word. Incidentally Trevethin lived on for many years in happy retirement, dying at the age of ninety-three in 1936 – the year after Reading – the result of falling into the River Wye while trying to catch a salmon and being carried away by the stream.

5

The journey from Dehra Dun to Simla occupied the best part of three days. At Kalka, near the foot of the Simla hills, the grand viceregal train was exchanged for a smaller petrol-driven locomotive with open coaches adapted to the narrow gauge railway. The line was an impressive example of mountain engineering, since it had to pass through more than a hundred tunnels in the course of the tortuous sixty-mile journey to the 8,000 feet high Indian summer capital. At Summer Hill Station, just below Simla, most of the staff got out to be pulled up the last stage of their journey to Viceregal Lodge in rickshaws, while their Excellencies continued the final mile by themselves to the Simla terminus, thence to make their entry in a state carriage escorted by the men of the Viceroy's Bodyguard. On the Mall, the ridge which forms Simla's main thoroughfare, the only vehicles allowed at any time, besides the Viceroy's, were those of the Commander-in-Chief and the Governor of the Punjab, who also made Simla their headquarters for the six hot weather months of the year. Lesser mortals had to proceed on foot.

Viceregal Lodge, which lay beyond the Mall on Observatory Hill, was an immense and ugly building, Scotch baronial in style with a tower from which the Viceroy's flag fluttered in the breeze. It had been constructed of blue and grey stone in Lord Dufferin's time in the 'eighties and commanded the most superb views of the Himalayas with their majestic ranges on the one side, and the plains with the winding river Sutlej on the other. It also had pleasant gardens, which at the moment of the Readings' arrival were filled with seven hundred or so of Simla's inhabitants waiting to pay their respects to their new rulers, whose first duty it was to shake hands with them all. There they were, the men in uniform or grey tropical suits and pith helmets, the women with their print dresses and floppy hats and long white gloves, chattering away as they sipped tea and ate ices in the shade of a *shamiana*, while a military band played the current dance tunes at a discreet distance. If Simla no longer had the proportion of grass widows and idle hill captains that it did when Kipling wrote his *Plain Tales from the Hills*, there was still plenty of gossip and intrigue and petty jealousies in this most celebrated of Indian hill stations, and the spectre of Mrs Hawksbee still haunted the Mall.

It must be admitted that many of the service people who appeared on this occasion and afterwards signed their names in 'the book' did so with mixed feelings. With one exception, every Viceroy and Governor-General of India since the time of Warren Hastings had belonged to an aristocratic and ennobled British family. And here was a Viceroy whose father had been a Jewish merchant and ship broker in the City of London, so different in every way, even though he had been made an earl, from the patrician Lord Chelmsford and his long line of predecessors from Lord Cornwallis to Lord Hardinge of Penshurst. That Welshman Lloyd George was to blame, of course Had he not made another Jew Secretary of State? And wasn't 'that damned fellow Montagu' determined to give away the brightest jewel in the Imperial Crown to the natives, aided and abetted no doubt by this new Viceroy? So went some of the talk in the clubs and messes and bungalows over the whisky *pegs* and teacups, not to mention the palaces of the Native Princes. Some references which Reading was supposed to have made to the circumstances of his earlier visit to the sub-continent were likewise taken amiss in some quarters. 'It is not his having come to India as a common seaman that matters,' a certain lady was to remark to the Prince of Wales during his visit later in the year, 'but why did he have to remind us of it?'

Yet both the Viceroy and Vicereine were immediately to succeed in endearing themselves to the local community, both British and Indian; they were liked, too, by the staff to whom they were always considerate, which is more than can be said for some royal representatives. 'I hear great accounts of you,' Montagu wrote to Reading soon after his arrival. 'Everyone seems delighted with you, and, according to one letter that I have seen, with your cook, who is described as being much better than any of his predecessors as you are than yours. An extremist writes to me that you have not yet made a mistake. After two months' experience, that is to my mind absolutely marvellous, coming from such a source.' Official entertaining – and it was virtually all official – was on a truly regal scale, for which the rooms in Viceregal Lodge were well adapted in spite of the building's some-what bizarre external appearance. Perhaps the most impressive of the rooms was the State dining-room, where sixty or seventy covers were not uncommonly laid. This room was entirely panelled in teak, the upper part supporting shields charged with the armorial bearings, illuminated with the proper heraldic colours, of all the Governors-General and Viceroys since the beginning of the Raj with Clive. Portraits of these former pro-Consuls looked down from the walls of the staircase and long gallery to remind the visitors of more than one hundred and fifty years of British rule. The hundred or so ser-vants on the domestic establishment anticipated the Viceroy's and Vicereine's slightest wish. They were posted at every doorway and along every corridor, salaaming and bowing low in their *pugris* whenever their Excellencies approached.

Certainly the requirements of viceregal protocol were not as dis-tasteful to Lady Reading as they were to her successor Lady Irwin. At large dinner-parties guests would be brought up by an A.D.C. in the state drawing-room for a few minutes' talk with the Viceroy and Vicereine individually in the manner of royalty, for after all they were the official representatives of the King-Emperor and the Queen. But it was a boring and often trying procedure, which the Irwins were later able to drop without apparent loss of 'face'. Neither Viceroy nor Vicereine could, of course, leave the grounds even for the shortest walk without a considerable escort. Lady Reading's shopping expedi-tions to the Simla bazaars were remarkable. Preceded by two members of the Viceroy's Bodyguard, a victoria and pair – with two servants dressed in scarlet and gold on the box in front and two more standing behind – conveyed Her Excellency where she wished to go, being followed by the A.D.C.-in-waiting in a buggy, while the rear of this impressive cavalcade was brought up by two more members of the Bodyguard.

The Readings had certainly come a long way since those early days in Broadhurst Gardens. Once, when on a visit to Simla, their son Gerald had occasion to remind his mother of this, while taking her in to dinner on his arm. 'Yes, but those years were good too,' she answered. 'All this would have meant so much less without them.' Fortunately for the Readings they were both endowed with a strong sense of humour as well as a sense of proportion, and although they enjoyed the pomp and ceremonial of the Viceroy's position, just as Curzon had done, they never succumbed to any pronounced *folie de grandeur*. An oft-told incident deserves to be repeated here. One evening, during a dance at Viceregal Lodge, Lady Reading turned to the A.D.C.-in-waiting, whose first night on duty it happened to be, and asked what was the name of the tune the band was playing. Just at that precise moment the music stopped, and in the minute's silence which followed the voice of the A.D.C. could be clearly heard across the ball-room replying, '"I shall remember your Kisses", your Excellency, "When you have forgotten my Name".' The effect of this announcement on the assembled company, it need hardly be added, was sensational. On another occasion the famous American advocate of Prohibition, Mr 'Pussyfoot' Johnson, who was touring India in an endeavour to win converts to his cause – not with any marked success amongst the British officials – was invited to luncheon. There were several other guests, all women, and he was the only man. Naturally the ladies all did a little 'bob' on being presented to Their Excellencies, and the renowned 'Pussyfoot', anxious not to be out-done in paying his respects, also essayed a curtsy, to the barely concealed amusement of his hosts and their staff.

For administrative purposes the Central Government was divided into seven departments, each of which was represented by a political Member on the Viceroy's Executive Council. Each department had a permanent Secretary, who was directly responsible to his Member of Council. The Council met once a week with the Viceroy as President in the chair, or in his absence the Vice-President. When Reading assumed office, the Members, who included three Indians, were: Sir William Vincent (Vice-President and Home Affairs), Sir Malcolm Hailey, later Lord Hailey (Finance), Sir Thomas Holland (Industries and Munitions), Sir T. B. Sapru (Law), Sir B. N. Sarma (Agriculture and Public Works), and Sir Mahommed Shafi (Education). The remaining two portfolios (Foreign Relations and Political) the Viceroy retained in his own hands. The Members were also expected to sit and answer for the Government in both Houses of the Indian Parliament, where they were heavily outnumbered by the non-official members. Meanwhile the Viceroy remained the supreme executive power. 'With the Members of his Council,' he jocularly remarked on one occasion, 'he constitutes the body known as the Governor-General in Council, perhaps the most abused body I have ever known. But the duties of both Viceroy and Governor-General are discharged by one man, and I cannot tell you how often as Viceroy I have longed to take off my silken gloves and to enter the lists to defend my action and that of my Council instead of being compelled to sit in a high chair, on a throne, on a pinnacle, to receive reports of Proceedings in the Legislature, and to read that this or that Minister has been attacked and had defended himself well and routed his assailants.'[1] In the last resort the Viceroy could overrule his Council, and he could also 'certify' any legislation which Parliament refused to pass, that is he could enact it himself by issuing an Ordinance, which had the force of law.

Immediately on his arrival in Simla, the Viceroy got down to work. 'I am as hard pressed as I can be for time,' he wrote at the end of his first week. 'I find that I already want forty-eight hours in every day, but I am standing it well and am deeply interested in the work.' Montagu was delighted with the initial results. 'Rufus, you are wonderful!' he wrote after a few weeks had passed. 'Every time I say anything in a letter, back comes a letter from you showing how patiently, how cheerfully, how energetically, you go into everything I say.'

At the same time, Reading was naturally anxious to get as much information as he could from sources outside the Indian Civil Service. He wrote to Montagu from Simla on May 12:

> I have not lost sight of my wish to get greater non-official light on affairs; indeed every day that I am here emphasizes the necessity for it. The Members of Department, the Secretaries and all concerned work loyally and devotedly, but they are perforce constrained to give their attention to the official papers that come before them, and their range of vision – except the Members of Council – is necessarily limited and concentrated upon their own departments. I have been much impressed by this in my intercourse with them. It is but natural and indeed it would be remarkable if it were otherwise.
>
> With the Members of Council of course it is different, but yet you must remember that their views are formed in India and they have had little if any intercourse with the affairs of other countries. I don't mean to criticize them because they do excellent service, but I do feel the need of getting away on to the hilltops, so that my vision may soar above departmental matters.

It was impossible in the nature of things for the Viceroy to divest himself of very much of his office work. In this he was hampered by departmental staff difficulties. After he had gone back to Delhi, he wrote again to Montagu (January 12, 1922):

[1] *Speeches by the Earl of Reading* (1926), Vol. II, p. 598.

I have tried the various chief people in my entourage, particularly Vincent and Hailey, to find good men to recommend for possible posts in future, but they both tell me that it is a very unfortunate time. Hailey goes near the mark when he says that the older men are too impregnated with the former notions, and the younger men have not had time to make their capacities felt and known.

The work is very heavy but I get along, helped by my early morning ride, but I very rarely get out again and am at it from 9.30 a.m. till 8 at night. I can stand it, but it tries my people, more particularly those who have had a long course of years in India.

Most immediately affected by the long hours of work were the two members of his staff with whom the Viceroy's relations were closest, his Private Secretary and his Military Secretary. His first Private Secretary was Mr S. R. Hignell, who belonged to the Indian Civil Service. 'The strain is very heavy on my Private Secretary,' Reading remarked at the end of his first nine months, 'and I see signs, quite unmistakable, that Hignell, who is a devoted and loyal I.C.S. man, who served Chelmsford for a year or so before I came, is getting more and more tired, and if he should break down I shall be hard put to it.' Mr Hignell did in fact come near to a breakdown and a few months later was replaced by Sir Geoffrey de Montmorency, later Governor of the Punjab. Later on Colonel Craufurd-Stuart, the Military Secretary, also had to be relieved. His successor Colonel R. B. Worgan, a dashing cavalry officer, who might have galloped straight out of the pages of Kipling, was evidently able to stand the pace, as he lasted into the succeeding Irwin régime.

At the same time Reading often felt extremely lonely. With the possible exception of the Commander-in-Chief, there was no one with whom he could discuss problems on anything approaching a basis of equality. As he wrote to Lloyd George, 'I was never so conscious of the loneliness of my position, particularly after the life of companionship I had led at home. It is not only that the position shuts out the possibility of intimacy – it is also that those one sees are strangers to that life.'

Within a week of his arrival in Simla, Reading was confronted with the problem of what to do with two Moslem extremists, the brothers Mahomed and Shaukat Ali, who were publicly urging their followers that, in the event of the Afghans invading India, it was their duty to join with their fellow Moslems in overthrowing the Government of India. Not only were these exhortations embarrassing to the Government, but they also embarrassed the Hindu leaders such as Gandhi and Motilal Nehru, who did not relish a Moslem invasion from beyond the Khyber Pass.

Viceroy to Secretary of State

Viceregal Lodge,
Simla.
April 28, 1921

I have had a very interesting meeting with my Executive Council this morning, which was called for the purpose of considering the prosecution of Mahomed and Shaukat Ali in the United Provinces. . . .

We adjourned not because we had any doubt about the prosecution but in order that Sir Harcourt Butler might visit me and thus enable us to confer on the political situation in the United Provinces which may be caused, not only there but elsewhere, by these prosecutions.

All of us felt that it was an unfortunate moment at which to prosecute, but equally it was impossible to allow the present state of things to continue. Sapru, Shafi and Sarma seemed to be of opinion that there was just a possibility that Gandhi is wishful to come to some arrangement. As you will have gathered from my telegrams, I am not at all sanguine about this; indeed, everything impels me against my will to the opposite view. But at the same time it was obviously desirable to wait a few days to give the opportunity if there was any foundation for the suggestions made of a desire to arrive at some compromise of the present position.

In fact, the three Indian Members of the Viceroy's Council were right in their surmise. The Viceroy and the leader of the Swaraj (Home Rule) movement were brought together through the intermediary of Pandit Madan Mohan Malaviya, a prominent orthodox Brahmin and intellectual, who called on the Viceroy at the beginning of May.

A more subtle brain I think than Gandhi's, but I doubt whether he has the same capacity for action. I was deeply interested in my conversations with him: they were the forerunners of Gandhi's visit. I liked him also, although they tell me here that he is unreliable. He was most careful never to go one step beyond the legitimate.

Malaviya suggested that the Viceroy should command Gandhi to his presence; but Reading insisted that the first move must come from Gandhi. Malaviya said he supposed the Viceroy wanted Gandhi to write his name in 'the book' and then ask for an interview. Reading replied that he cared nothing about this and never thought of it – it was an act of courtesy to the King-Emperor and Gandhi must do as he thought right, as Malaviya had. In the result Gandhi did sign his name immediately on his arrival. The enthusiastic shouts which greeted his appearance in the streets were clearly heard by Reading through the windows of Viceregal Lodge.

Two days later, on May 14, the Mahatma had the first of six interviews with the Viceroy, which Reading described in his next weekly letter to Montagu.

There is nothing striking about his appearance. He came to visit me in a white dhoti and cap, woven on a spinning-wheel, with bare feet and legs, and my first impression on seeing him ushered into my room was that there was nothing to arrest attention in his appearance and that I should have passed him by in the street without a second look at him. When he talks the impression is different. He is direct and expresses himself well in excellent English with a fine appreciation of the words he uses. There is no hesitation about him and there is a ring of sincerity in all that he utters, save when discussing some political questions.

His religious views are, I believe, genuinely held and he is convinced to a point almost bordering on fanaticism that non-violence and love will give India its independence and enable it to withstand the British Government. His religious and moral views are admirable and indeed are on a remarkably high altitude, but I must confess that I find it difficult to understand his practice of them in politics. To put it quite briefly, he is like the rest of us; when engaged in a political movement he wishes to gather all under his umbrella and to reform them and bring them to his views. He has consequently to accept many with whom he is not in accord, and has to do his best to keep the combination together. This is particularly true of the Hindu-Moslem combination which I think rests upon insecure foundations. . . .

In the course of six interviews – the first of four hours and a half, the second of three hours, the third of an hour and a half, the fourth of an hour and a half, the fifth of an hour and a half and the sixth of three-quarters of an hour – I have had many opportunites of judging him. A critical point came towards the end of the second interview, when I, for the first time, adopted a firm and rather severe attitude. He seemed surprised and I think his attitude changed from that moment.

Our conversations were of the frankest; he was supremely courteous with manner of distinction. A slight incident at our first interview reveals a pleasant Oriental courtesy. I wanted tea and I pressed him to have some. He would take nothing. He then asked for hot water, which was immediately brought whilst I waited for tea. I was concerned lest his hot water should get cold, and when my tea was brought said he was letting his hot water get cold. He replied: 'I could not think of tasting it until you had had your tea.'

He held in every way to his word in the various discussions we had. He explained in public that he had applied for interviews and gave quite an accurate account of the events leading to his letter to my Private Secretary. Altogether you will judge that I liked him and that I believe there are possibilities in the future. Upon leaving he seemed quite affected and earnestly assured me he would come whenever I wanted him.

Details of the talks were telegraphed daily to the India Office. On the subject of the activities of the Ali brothers, Gandhi was emphatic that they had never strongly approved of violence in any form. In reply the Viceroy quoted some of Mahomed Ali's public utterances. Gandhi made no comment.

Discussion then led to the meaning attributed to Swaraj and frankly I am as much at a loss now to explain it as when he came into the room, although I have tried hard to get a definite meaning from him. All I could gather was that, when the Indians had regained their self-respect and had pursued a policy of non-cooperation with the Government and had refrained from violence, they would have gained Swaraj. I asked the question point blank: 'What is it in the actions of the Government that makes you pursue the policy of non-cooperation with the Government?'

The answer, repeated more than once during our interviews, was that he was filled with distrust of the Government and that all their actions, even though apparently good, made him suspect their motives. I pressed him to be more precise, and eventually he stated that he had some time ago arrived at the conclusion that every action of the Government which appeared good, and indeed was good, was actuated by the sinister motive of trying to fasten British dominion on India. This was his answer to all the arguments about the new reformed Councils, and in my judgment is the root cause of his present attitude to the Government.

So far as the Ali brothers were concerned, Gandhi promised to see them and endeavour to extract from them an undertaking to refrain from further incitements to violence in future and to express regret for their previous offence, in return for which the Viceroy agreed to use his influence with his Council to drop the intended prosecution on sedition charges. 'I hope you will agree with the policy I have been pursuing,' Reading told Montagu. 'I have no manner of doubt that it is right and that prevention by agreement and expressions of regret, etc., in this case is far better than arrest and prosecutions. ... Further, it should be remembered, and will be understood by the Indians, that if Gandhi does succeed in saving the Ali brothers from prosecution, it will have been as the result of his application to the Viceroy for interviews and of the terms imposed, to which he had to submit and which he has been compelled to force upon the Ali brothers. It cannot be doubted, as all my advisers familiar with India and Indian opinion tell me, that this will have an important political effect throughout the country and will tend to lower his influence and authority.'

In fact, Gandhi had been outmanœuvred. If he declined to secure the Ali brothers' acquiescence and they were convicted of sedition, it would probably be a disastrous blow to the Hindu-Moslem alliance, which Gandhi had assiduously fostered. On the other hand, if he prevailed upon the two brothers to apologize and if the prosecution was called off on the Viceroy's terms, this must result in a loss of 'face' for the Mahatma, particularly with his more extreme supporters. Gandhi chose the latter course, as the lesser of two evils from his point of view. 'We are all delighted with your skilful treatment of Gandhi,' Montagu congratulated the Viceroy. 'You gained a great victory.'

6

A club had been founded in Simla, inspired by the Montagu-Chelmsford Reforms and called the Chelmsford Reform Club, to which – unlike many other clubs in British India at this period – Indians were admitted on an equal footing with Europeans. Shortly after the meetings with Gandhi, the Viceroy accepted an invitation to dine with the members and he chose the occasion to emphasize, in replying to the toast of his health, that there must be no trace of racial inequality in British-Indian relations. 'Whatever may be thought by our Indian friends not present in this room,' he said, 'I do not refer to those present because they are conscious of the contrary – I say we do not for a moment indulge in any notions of racial superiority or predominance. . . . And as a corollary . . . I say that there cannot be and must never be humiliation under the British Rule of any Indian because he is an Indian. And . . . further . . . we British people in India and those also in our own country must realize that we have much suspicion to disperse, many misunderstandings to banish from amongst us, and in truth the essence to my mind of co-operation between us and Indians is that we should convince them by our actions, which will accord with our thoughts and intentions, that we honestly and sincerely mean what we have said with regard to India.'

Reading was warmly applauded by the club members present for these fine sentiments. Unfortunately they were by no means invariably borne out in practice.

Viceroy to Secretary of State

Simla.
July 7, 1921

Almost immediately after my pronouncements against racial inequality at the Chelmsford Club there was a trial of a European in Bengal for shooting at and wounding an Indian whose daughter it was said the European had coveted. I won't go into a long story of it, for of course it is in a sense a purely local matter; but the result of the trial was an acquittal of the European – an Englishman – although there was no doubt that he had actually fired at and wounded the Indian coolie. The defence was that he was after barking deer and fired with a revolver which he had in his pocket and thus accidentally shot the coolie. The case was tried by an English Judge – Mr Justice Buckland – and a jury of nine, of whom eight were Europeans. The verdict was given by a majority of eight to one – a clean racial division. No fault could be found with the summing-up as I gather from the Press, but there has been very considerable criticism of the result. Some of our English papers – notably *The Pioneer* – have had leading articles showing how unsatisfactory such a trial is.[1] It undoubtedly creates the impression that there is one law for the Englishman and another for the Indian.

There was also another case tried by an English Magistrate or Judge of a young British soldier who committed an assault upon an Indian woman obviously with the purpose of outraging her. He was however only charged with assault and was convicted by the Magistrate and the sentence was a fine of Rs.50. Moreover, observations were made by the Magistrate for the purpose of finding extenuating circumstances. The trial and these observations have also formed the subject of angry comment and of course, as you can well imagine, the cry is repeated everywhere – what would have happened in each of these cases if the culprit had been an Indian and the offence had been against a European?

I cannot of course express any opinion upon the trials, but I must confess that I am very seriously perturbed by the results of both these

---

[1] *The Pioneer*, on which Kipling formerly worked, was published in Allahabad.

cases, and more particularly by the indignation caused among Indians. I am having the law examined for the purpose of arriving at some solution, but I know that there are grave obstacles in the path of any alteration of the system, and yet I am convinced that we must take steps to put the law on an equal footing. I am only expressing a very hasty view, as I have not yet been able to give full consideration to the subject, but I believe the mischief is in the jury of a majority of Europeans. It is easy to understand the mentality of those who sit on these trials, but sober-minded and justice-loving Englishmen do not like the impression created. My hasty view is that if the trials were by Judges alone there would be no cause for complaint. English Judges would act with justice, but to attempt to abolish juries is a very thorny path to pursue. Equally I fear that to give a corresponding right to Indians of trial by a jury of a majority of Indians presents grave difficulties in the administration of the law. But the problem is there and must be solved. . . .

Again complaints come forward of unequal treatment of Indians at railway stations and in the railway trains. You are familiar with the problem – equally it presents troublesome and difficult questions and I am going to devote attention to them.

I am convinced that we shall never persuade the Indian of the justice of our rule until we have overcome racial difficulties of the character above-mentioned. As you and I agreed when we discussed these questions at home the root of most difficulties is the racial problem. However desirous we may be of removing inequalities, I fear that we shall for a long time have before us the social problem even if we manage to solve the legal one. I could go on for a long time discussing this subject, but you are as well aware of it as I and you have known it longer. It is the cause of most of the bitterness.

Do not think from my observations that instances of inequality or unjust treatment have become more frequent; indeed I gather from all my inquiries that they have become less frequent; but unfortunately one bad instance lingers long in the memory and reverberates throughout India and causes recurrences of the indignation of the Indian at the humiliation he has to suffer. I believe our people really try to act well and I suspect that sometimes the Indian is oversensitive as is so often the case when humiliation is expected; and that sometimes he resents as an affront conduct which one Englishman might easily display towards another Englishman without offence being taken and without there being the faintest intention of giving it. But that does not dispose of all cases and even in my short period examples have been brought to me which display arrogance and an assertion of dominant racial superiority.

Sooner or later Reading was bound to come into touch with the Native States and their rulers, who were under British protection. These amounted to over four hundred in number, varying from huge territories larger than England such as Hyderabad and Kashmir, to tiny states of no more than a few acres. The first of the Native Princes whom the Viceroy met was perhaps the most deplorable, the Maharaja of Alwar, a sadist and a pervert, who claimed descent from the Sun God. 'Alwar is at present staying with me and I have had much conversation with him,' Reading wrote to Montagu on July 21. 'He is undoubtedly clever and attractive but rather baffling. I usually arrive at rapid conclusions with regard to any individual with whom I am brought into personal contact, and yet I confess that I am not able to arrive at a complete estimate of Alwar. That he is a most interesting individual and full of ideas and intelligent reasoning there is of course no doubt. . . . His visit was in consequence of a letter to me informing me that he wished to see me on several matters and was coming to Simla. I then of course invited him to stay. He is spending four days here.' The Maharaja was concerned about two matters in particular. The first was that the Viceroy alone as the King-Emperor's representative rather than the Viceroy and his Council should deal with the Ruling Princes. The second was that he had heard that the statute which made it a criminal offence 'to cause disaffection or hatred of the Government of a Ruling Prince' was to be repealed. Reading was able to satisfy him on both matters, pointing out as to the first that only in exceptional circumstances, such as where the succession to the throne of a Native State was involved, did he consult the Council; and, as to the second, that he considered that serious cases would still be governed by the general Indian Penal Code.

Reading, who seems to have had a premonition of the Maharaja's evil ways, apparently did not know that he terrorized his subjects and had murdered at least one man who had stood in his way; he was also supposed to have tethered a recalcitrant polo pony to a hillside in hot weather, coming each day to see it dying of thirst. Eventually his subjects were to revolt and he was forced to leave his state and go to Europe where he died miserably a few years later in Paris. He repaid Reading's hospitality by running him down to mutual acquaintances. 'Reading is a very weak Viceroy,' he told Lord Curzon. 'He never reads a file or studies a subject but has people in who state a case to him orally, just as though he were a lawyer in chambers and then decides.' Alwar went on to say that 'Lady Reading loves the Viceroyalty, which her health has been good enough to enable her to enjoy, so much so that she was enabled to accompany her husband on a tiger shoot where she had the satisfaction of seeing him miss three tigers running.'[1]

The first Native State to be visited by the Viceroy and Vicereine was the remote and romantically situated Kashmir bounded by the huge mountain ranges of the Himalayas and the Hindu Kush, with the snow-capped peak of Nanga Parbat towering over all. They travelled from Simla in the viceregal train to Rawalpindi and thence by road to Murree, the Punjab hill station, where they were the guests of General Sir William (later Lord) Birdwood, at that time in command of the Northern Army in India. From Murree they followed the course of the river Jhelum to Srinagar, the capital, being met about half-way by the Maharaja, Sir Pratab Singh. The last twenty miles or so through the Valley of Kashmir were covered by water. 'It was a wonderful journey here,' wrote Reading on his arrival in Srinagar, 'and culminated in a kind of triumphal procession on the Jhelum in the State barge, in which my wife and I were seated with the Maharaja in State, and his and our suites around us. It was over an hour's procession to the Residency where we are staying, and simply crowded on either side of the river to the tops of the roofs. It was a wonderful show and extraordinarily interesting.' Both Reading and his wife were much amused by a banner which bore the friendly but ambiguous words of welcome: 'God Bless the Viceroy. God Help Lady Reading.'

There had recently been a sharp rise in the price of *shali*, the un-husked rice which formed the staple diet of the Kashmiris, largely due to profiteering by the local grain dealers and money lenders, who exploited both the small farmer and the consumer without the least compunction. The laws passed against profiteering seemed quite ineffective. Reading reported on the situation generally to Montagu:

> The Resident, Colonel Windham, had already told me of the serious condition and it was partly for this reason that he was urging me to come to Kashmir. I have consulted with him and other English people living here who have been doing their utmost to alleviate the trouble, and according to them all sorts of intrigues are carried on and there is unfortunately bribery and corruption which make it very difficult to be sure that a law will be obeyed however stringent it may be. The

[1] Marchioness Curzon of Kedleston. *Reminiscences* (1955), p. 182.

Maharaja himself is full of suspicions, and particularly of Sir Hari Singh – the heir-presumptive. He appears to me to have been under the impression that there was some intrigue to get me to depose him and place Hari Singh at the head of affairs. I have however, I think, completely reassured him upon this point, although I doubt whether I have removed from his mind the anxieties about Hari Singh and all who seem to favour him. It is the usual story of the occupant of the seat of power glancing askance at his successor and feeling anxiety lest his successor should be too eager to get the place and not be willing to wait for the natural course of events. I have seen Hari Singh several times and am bound to say from my own impressions, and from all that I hear, there is not the faintest ground for these suspicions. . . .

The visit to Kashmir set the pattern for the Viceroy's State visits to other Native States, of which he paid upwards of twenty during his term of office. Besides the change of scene, they provided him with some sport, so that his clay-pigeon shooting practice in London was worthwhile. He got his first tiger when staying with the Maharaja Scindia of Gwalior, a source of much satisfaction to him, and in Mysore he took part in a thrilling *keddah*, or wild elephant hunt. Besides the Maharaja Scindia, his particular friends among the Native Princes were Bikaner, Patiala, and the Jam Singh of Nawanagar, best known for his cricketing prowess as 'Ranji'. In two days of grouse shooting in Bikaner, which he visited for the first time immediately after Christmas, 1921, Reading brought down a hundred birds in two days, and he also shot a few *chinkaras* (buck gazelle). As he told Montagu, 'it was great fun there, although there was a huge party but it didn't really interfere with us. My wife also enjoyed it very much. . . .' Their host, Sir Ganga Singh, Maharaja of Bikaner, was perhaps the most distinguished of the Princes both in personal appearance and achievements. It was mainly at his instigation that the annual conference of native rulers developed into the Chamber of Princes, of which he became the first Chancellor in the year of Reading's arrival in India. But even this amiable Maharaja was not free from the taint of snobbery, as was evident from his behaviour when he entertained the Readings' successors. On this occasion he told Lady Irwin 'how nice it had been that Lady Reading had enjoyed India so much. She had positively radiated happiness, but it was perhaps a pity that she had eaten cheese on her knife.'[1]

The Viceroy was also expected to keep in close personal touch with

[1] Earl of Birkenhead: *Halifax* (1965), p. 186.

the various provincial Governors. During his first summer he paid Sir Harcourt Butler, the Governor of the United Provinces, a visit at his summer headquarters in Naini Tal. This picturesque hill station with an attractive lake for sailing was two thousand feet lower than Simla, and it seemed to agree better with Lady Reading than Simla. Unfortunately their stay there came to an abrupt conclusion after only a week with the news of serious rioting and violence on the part of the Moplahs, a fanatical Moslem sect, in the Malabar region of Madras. Lady Reading insisted on returning to Simla with her husband, whose first inclination was to go on to Madras. But when he realized that his absence was likely to have the effect of paralysing the Government at the centre, he reluctantly decided to remain in Simla until the crisis was over. In fact the crisis quickly assumed the proportions of a rebellion, which was only terminated by the equally reluctant decision on the part of the Governor-General and Council to impose martial law in the area. As Reading told Montagu, 'This was an organized rebellion of a whole countryside which was populated by Moslem tribes of a peculiarly backward and ignorant character, whose fanaticism the Khilafat leaders had by their speeches and writings deliberately excited.' Hundreds of Hindus were murdered, thousands were plundered, others were forcibly converted to Islam, and many Hindu temples were desecrated. That the rising was stimulated by the renewed seditious activities of the Ali brothers there appeared to be little doubt. When the two brothers finally attempted to seduce the troops and police from their duty, they were arrested. After a civil trial, they were convicted and sentenced to terms of imprisonment.[1]

Shortly after the Government's return to Delhi from Simla towards the end of October, 1921, Reading received a call from Mahomed Ali Jinnah, the President of the Moslem League and the leader of the moderate Indian Moslems, who favoured the policy of Hindu-Moslem unity. This elegant barrister in his middle forties, who had studied law at Lincoln's Inn, presented a complete contrast in appearance and manner to Gandhi. The impression he made on Reading was also very different from that left by the Mahatma.

[1] Full particulars of the Moplah rising and its aftermath were given in a lengthy series of telegrams between the Viceroy and the Secretary of State and published in two Government White Papers, *Telegraphic Information, etc. regarding the Moplah Rebellion 24 August–6 December 1921* (Cmd. 1552) and *Telegraphic Correspondence regarding the Situation in India 8 February–11 March 1922* (Cmd. 1586).

Viceroy to Secretary of State
(Telegram)

Delhi. November 2, 1921. Jinnah came to me yesterday and had long interview. I found him distinctly able, rather extremist, not a non-cooperationist, but somewhere between moderate and extremist. I think he stands politically where Malaviya does, i.e. he holds strong views about acceleration of Swaraj, redress of Punjab wrongs, in favour of Khilafat agitation, but has not joined Gandhi, whose policy he regards as destructive and not constructive. . . . Punjab grievances, were capable, he thought, of settlement on basis of expressions of regret, and perhaps more emphasized statement that humiliation orders must be made impossible for future, and that some officers inculpated should be dismissed. On Swaraj he realized the difficulty of making any definite statement at moment, but thought it would not be difficult to agree upon some formula. . . .

I definitely declined to commit myself in any shape or form, save in expressions of sympathy with Moslem Indian opinion which I had already publicly made. On Punjab grievances I reiterated the various steps we had taken, and added that I could not countenance even discussion of dismissal of subordinate officers who had merely obeyed superior orders. . . . I pointed out the injury that would be done to India and to obtaining of Swaraj if any insult or affront was offered to the Prince of Wales. . . . He agreed, but thought that it was very difficult for the general public to take this view. . . . I was impressed by his evident desire to use the present moment for settlement, which is on the eve of the All India Congress Committee Meeting on the 4th.

He left me on the understanding that if better conditions prevail with regard to Greece and Turkey, and I find that I can give greater hope, I should let him know and he would come again at any minute I called him. I am left under the impression that there is a real desire to arrive at a settlement, particularly as he told me he had seen both Gandhi and Malaviya before he left [Bombay] for Delhi. I have no solid ground for this impression, and therefore give it with caution. I was not particularly desirous of encouraging him in his role of broker, as he termed it, for I see little if any prospect of agreement between Gandhi and myself. Moreover, anxious as I am to banish illegal and substitute constitutional agitation, I am not at present prepared to make substantial sacrifices to arrive at it.

Jinnah's personality, as distinguished from intellect, did not favourably impress me. I thought I discerned strong anti-British feeling, although masked at the moment, and some want of scruple. He has acute sensibility and subtlety of mind, and yet I think he lacks perception of impression he is creating. I prefer Malaviya.

Although they came politically very close at this time, the Moslems and the Hindus were never to fuse in India. Indeed they were to draw further and further apart, while under Jinnah's leadership the parts of the country with Moslem majorities were eventually to achieve independence as Pakistan.

7

The Prince of Wales arrived, according to programme, in H.M.S. *Renown*, which dropped anchor off Bombay on November 17, 1921. With him, as one of his naval A.D.C.s was Sub-Lieutenant Lord Louis Mountbatten, who was to return a quarter of a century later as India's last Viceroy to engage in what the Prince as Duke of Windsor has described in his autobiography as 'the process of liquidating the immeasurable Imperial trust he and I, each in our own way, had endeavoured to defend in our youth'. As yet there was no hint of the coming of political independence in the foreseeable future. Only Gandhi promised Swaraj in a matter of months, and to those engaged in governing India his pronouncements appeared completely unrealistic. At the same time Gandhi urged his followers to boycott the celebrations planned to welcome the Prince, a *hartal* was proclaimed, and a monster Congress Party meeting on the outskirts of the city was timed to coincide with the morning of the Prince's arrival. 'To have attempted to stop it or prohibit it would have been a serious blunder,' Reading reported at the time, 'as it would have meant taking police away from the processional route and the city generally and driving non-cooperationists into places where they could have done most mischief. The meeting was designed to attract the crowds and thus give a deserted appearance when the Prince drove through. It most signally failed in this respect. . . .'

Standing on the steps of the Apollo Bunder to welcome the Prince to Indian soil was the Viceroy dressed 'in a white sun helmet and a grey morning coat, with the Star of India pinned to his breast, presenting a grave study in Imperial protocol'. Behind him was Sir George Lloyd, Governor of Bombay, and near by were seven of the leading Indian Princes. After the Prince had listened to the usual addresses and had delivered a suitable message from the King-Emperor ('I want to know you and I want you to know me'), he drove in an open horse-drawn carriage to Government House, with a *kitmatgar* holding a gold-embroidered umbrella over his head. There were large crowds lining the streets on the drive to Malabar Point, in spite of the *hartal* and the rival attraction of the Mahatma's oratory. There was an audible murmur of approval and sustained hand-clapping as the royal carriage went by, and on his arrival at Government House the Prince sent Reading a message to say how very pleased he was by his reception. Unfortunately this excellent initial impression was spoiled by a collision between Gandhi's supporters who had been attending his meeting and the spectators of the Prince's procession who clashed when some hooligans tried to stop the trams. In the ensuing disturbance three police were killed and several more civilians. No Europeans were injured, although several fled to the protection of a police station and others took refuge in the Byculla Club. Next day further disturbances broke out and developed into communal strife, with Hindus attacking Moslems and both setting about Parsees. Altogether fifty-three people were killed, including several Europeans, and approximately 400 were injured.

On leaving the India Office on the night of the Prince's arrival, Montagu was alarmed by a news poster which met his eyes: 'PRINCE LANDS IN BOMBAY. NATIVE RIOTS.' This was the result of the news agencies cabling home the news of the disturbances at the same time as the details of the Prince's welcome in Bombay, and it created a misleading impression in the public mind which not un-naturally tended to connect the two and in some instances gave the impression that the Prince had to fight his way through molesting crowds.

In fairness to Gandhi, it must be admitted that he tried to stop the disturbances by personal appeals to his followers, as indeed the Prince himself realized. But he was too late. In Reading's words, 'Gandhi has again called forth a spirit which he could not control, as he now admits. I am told that in several quarters in which he appeared to quell the trouble, he was powerless. He admits that his emissaries came back having been badly assaulted, and he is so disappointed that he expresses himself now against civil disobedience for the moment.' At the same time Gandhi pointed out in a public statement that the pledge of non-violence by non-cooperationists to protect the Prince of Wales from harm had been broken, since Europeans and others who participated in the procession had been insulted and assaulted, and as a penance he proposed to observe a weekly fourteen-hour fast. Reading told Montagu:

> I understand how distressed the King and you are, as are we also by these disturbances, but serious as they are we must view them in their proper proportion. Gandhi and non-cooperation Press and agitators put forward their utmost strength to make people abstain from attending the procession, and the only result has been the triumphant success of the Prince and that so-called non-violence and non-cooperation have caused violent disturbances. Every item in the Prince's programme has been carried out and always with complete success. The reception at Government House was attended by over 3,000 persons and the Prince shook hands with them all. It was his own wish and caused the greatest satisfaction.

The climax of the Prince's three-month tour had been planned to take place towards the end in Delhi, where a bungalow was specially built for His Royal Highness and his staff in the grounds of Viceregal Lodge. Meanwhile, attended by a staff of a hundred human beings and a stable of twenty-five polo ponies specially lent by the Native Princes, the King-Emperor's heir made his way across the sub-continent to the accompaniment of galloping hooves on the polo fields and half empty and deserted streets, mute testimony of the success of the *hartals* proclaimed by Gandhi. By the time he reached Calcutta six weeks after leaving Bombay, the Prince was thoroughly disillusioned and felt ashamed that so much should have been spent – '£25,000 of English money and goodness knows how many lakhs of rupees' – on a tour which so far could not be described as successful.

He was irked too by what he considered the excessive security precautions with the police lining the processional routes with their backs to the Prince's carriage so that they could better keep watch on the spectators. ('In my opinion such severe police tactics can scarcely be conducive to encouraging even loyal natives to come and see me.') His one delight was the magnificent reception that he had everywhere he went from the British people and native officers and men of the Indian Army. But at the same time these loyal representatives of the British Raj like their colleagues in the Indian Civil Service made it quite clear to the Prince that they would not recommend their sons or for that matter anyone else's sons to join these services. 'The reason for this is,' as the Prince bluntly told Montagu, 'that India is no longer a place for a white man to live in.'[1]

[1] Montagu Papers; Waley, p. 261–66.

Since the time of the transfer of the capital from Calcutta to Delhi ten years previously, the Viceroy had been accustomed to spend the month of December in the old capital of British India, his visit culminating at Calcutta Races on Boxing Day when he presented the Viceroy's Cup to the winner. On this occasion Reading curtailed his visit to the first three weeks of December, so that his presence would not interfere with the entertainment of the Prince of Wales by the Governor of Bengal, at this time Lord Ronaldshay, whose term of office was nearing completion. Consequently Reading returned with his wife to Delhi before the Prince reached Calcutta on Christmas Eve, and it fell to the Prince to present the Viceroy's Cup at the races. This was a ceremony which gave the Prince 'great pleasure', so he afterwards told the Viceroy.

Since 1911, when the magnificent Government House became the official residence of the Governors of Bengal, the Viceroy on his visits to Calcutta usually occupied Belvedere, near the race-course, which had been the official home of Warren Hastings and other Governors-General in the eighteenth century before Government House was built on the model, considerably enlarged, of Kedleston Hall in Derbyshire. It appealed to the Readings much more than the formal grandeur of Government House. It was steeped in the history of the early days of the East India Company, and Reading learned with some interest that close by the entrance to its grounds Warren Hastings had fought his famous duel with Philip Francis.[1]

After the migration of the Viceroy and the Central Government to Delhi with the transfer of the capital there were complaints from the powerful Anglo-Indian commercial community in Calcutta that they had been to some extent neglected by the Government. Reading therefore went out of his way to pay attention to the merchants and financiers and non-official element generally. In the course of his visit he delivered nine major speeches, had an honorary degree at the University conferred upon him in company with the famous Indian poet Rabindranath Tagore, opened the annual exhibition of the Indian Society of Oriental Art, and received a strong delegation of constitutional reformers at Belvedere headed by Pandit Malaviya and Mrs Besant. At a dinner given for him by the Calcutta Press, the chairman in introducing him recalled to his mind, as Reading put it, 'a passage in my life which is somewhat obscure and indeed which, I

[1] Belvedere is now the National Library of India.

thought, was little known, when he referred to my first visit to Calcutta, coupling it up by the mention of this being my second visit'. On
this occasion he resisted the temptation to dilate upon his earlier
visit. ('There is little to be said about this visit of mine in my younger
days – and when I was not invited to a dinner such as this.') However,
a sense of nostalgia did induce him to reminisce when he accepted
an invitation from Sir Clement Hindley, Chairman of the Calcutta
Port Authority, to take a day off from his public engagements and
go for a cruise on the river Hooghly in the Port Commissioners'
sloop *Pansy*.

It was a small party, the only other guests being half a dozen of
the leading business men in Calcutta. The Viceroy was in an expan-
sive mood and at the breakfast table he went back forty-four years
to his first visit to Calcutta and his experiences as ship's boy on
the *Blair Athole*.

A sequel to his reminiscences was later described by the Port
Authority's Chairman and the Viceroy's host for the day:

> A few hours later, steaming downstream, we got into wireless touch
> with H.M.S. *Southampton*, the flagship of the East Indies Squadron,
> then proceeding up the river on an official visit to Calcutta. The
> presence of the Viceroy on board was communicated to H.M.S.
> *Southampton*, and we were able to arrange to pass her in a long open
> stretch of the river, which formed an admirable setting for the dramatic
> scene which then took place.
>
> As H.M.S. *Southampton* came round this wide curve of swiftly
> flowing water in brilliant sunshine, she fired a salute of thirty-one guns,
> and her whole ship's company were paraded on deck, while the Viceroy
> of India stood alone on the upper deck of the *Pansy* to acknowledge
> the salute, his own flag flying from *Pansy*'s main mast. When the two
> ships passed, we heard the National Anthem played by the band, the
> marines drawn up on deck presented arms, and the White Ensign at
> the stern dipped.
>
> Not one of those present aboard the *Pansy* can ever forget the
> impression made by the solitary figure of the Viceroy standing bare-
> headed in the sunlight to acknowledge these royal honours, remember-
> ing as we did the simple words in which he had just been telling us of
> his humble visit and the incident of the pilot, which had taken place
> almost at the same spot so many years before. There can be very few
> Viceroys who have received a Royal Salute from one of His Majesty's
> ships afloat, and certainly no other Viceroy in such circumstances.

Reading was not often given to outbursts of emotion. But on this occasion he was seen to brush away some tears, which had come into his eyes.

On the day of the Viceroy's arrival in Calcutta, a leader had appeared in *The Times of India*, written by the editor, Sir Stanley Reed, criticizing the Viceroy for his alleged timidity in alluding to Indian opinion, both Government and non-official, in his public utterances. On his return to Delhi, Reading learned that his old friend Northcliffe was about to pass through on a world tour and he invited both him and Reed to spend a few days at Viceregal Lodge, so that they could talk over the question of coverage of Indian affairs both domestically and overseas. Reading found Northcliffe 'deeply interested' and wrote to Montagu (January 26, 1922):

I hope his visit will do good. He is proposing to keep one of his best men here for a time in order that the British public may be better acquainted with the difficulties and perplexities you and I have to encounter. Northcliffe is undoubtedly desirous of helping in the present trying state of affairs and will give greater publicity to Indian news and situation. I never read our English newspapers without wishing that they were better informed. Of course I know the difficulties: there are so many other affairs closer at hand although certainly not more important. But to the average Englishman India is a long way off and the picture of it to him is, I fear, antiquated. Indeed events move so fast nowadays that the vast sweeping Reforms initiated at the beginning of last year are already regarded here as old-fashioned.

Although he found Viceregal Lodge 'a most hospitable and friendly house', the great Press lord did not care for India. 'A wearisome country' he called it, and asked: 'What do we want India for? Prestige? Perhaps. Cash? We certainly don't get any from it. The thousands of able men from home could do far better almost any-where else.' He sensed too a pervading anxiety about the future – 'almost as anxious as 1857' – and he was depressed by the half-finished avenues and buildings of the new city. He had been assured that the eighth Delhi would see the end of British rule in India, and 'this vast New Delhi, a wonderful pre-war conception which is unpopular with everyone we meet' was the eighth Delhi. The Vice-reine found Northcliffe 'quite rejuvenated', so different from when she last saw him in London, and 'in excellent spirits'.[1] But his out-ward appearance was deceptive. He was about to enter the shadows of a terrifying mental illness and the Readings never saw him again.

[1] Pound and Harmsworth, p. 821–22.

In less than seven months, the pioneer of popular journalism, the astonishing Alfred Harmsworth, Viscount Northcliffe, lay dead in his London home in Carlton House Gardens.

The Prince of Wales reached Viceregal Lodge in the middle of February on the last leg of his Indian tour. He was in much better spirits than when he had written to the Viceroy from Calcutta. In spite of Gandhi's boycott and the *hartals* and the attempts of the Congress Party leaders to keep the people away from the great shows organized in his honour, the Indian masses followed him about in all his public appearances, for their curiosity got the better of them, however they may have felt about the injustices of British rule. Reading was not too happy at first about the prospects of the Delhi visit, but it turned out to be the most successful of all. 'Throughout the eight days there has never been a shadow of a marring incident,' Reading telegraphed the King. 'Every day has increased the enthusiasm of the public, which culminated in a great demonstration at the Peoples' Fair held in the open air. There were quite 50,000 people present and the Prince rode amongst them and was received with the greatest enthusiasm.'

The Prince of Wales concluded his tour by visiting the Punjab and the North-West Frontier Province in what is now known as West Pakistan. In Peshawar he was the target for a hostile demonstration by the local non-cooperationists, a number of whose leaders were arrested, with the result that a *hartal* was proclaimed. But there were no serious incidents, and next day the Prince continued with his programme as if nothing had happened. Nevertheless, in spite of the activities of Gandhi and Jinnah and their followers, the 'brightest jewel' appeared to its heir to be still firmly set in the Imperial Crown. The Viceroy finally saw the Prince safely aboard the *Renown* at Karachi. 'British dominance in India was the product of two hundred years of war, work and wisdom,' the Duke of Windsor reflected years later on his departure from India. 'Had anybody tried to persuade me as I left Karachi, with a regimental band on the quay crashing out "God Save the King", that all this would be lost in my lifetime, I would have put the man down as a lunatic.'[1]

The last weeks of the Prince's Indian tour coincided with Gandhi's progression from a policy of passive non-cooperation to one of active and aggressive civil disobedience which on his part expressed itself in acts of open and flagrant sedition. At the same time his campaign

[1] Windsor, p. 178.

to boycott imported textiles, particularly cloth from the English mills, and his advocacy of the use of homespun material in its place, developed the mystique of the spinning wheel which became a positive obsession with him, designed as it was to be at the same time a form of manual training, a spiritual exercise and the means of freeing India from 'the stranglehold of foreign capitalist exploitation'. Early in 1922 Reading had reported that there was an opinion strongly held among others by Sir George Lloyd, Governor of Bombay, 'that under the guise of preaching non-violence Gandhi is really preparing for revolution by violence'. He was reluctant to arrest Gandhi, but mounting criticism at home, also directed against Montagu, that constitutional reform in India had gone too far, eventually forced the Viceroy's hand. 'It looks to me as if there was nothing for it but a vigorous attempt to smash the organization against us and to deal with sedition wherever it shows itself,' wrote Montagu to the Viceroy at this time. 'The fact of the matter is, Rufus, that people here are fed up with India, and it is all I can do to keep my colleagues steady on the accepted policy, let alone new instalments of it. The Indians are so unreasonable, so slow to compromise, so raw in their resentments, and the insults to the Prince of Wales have made fierce feeling in this country. . . . If only Indians could be got to realize that they could have everything they wanted for loyalty and that there never was a more unjustified unrest than theirs!'[1]

8

On March 10, 1922, Mahatma Gandhi was arrested on a charge of sedition and in due course convicted and sentenced to six years' imprisonment. By a coincidence the day of Gandhi's arrest in Bombay saw the delivery up by Edwin Montagu, six thousand miles away in London, of his seals of office as Secretary of State for India, following upon his resignation or rather his contemptuous dismissal by Lloyd George. Montagu's abrupt departure from the India Office came as a bombshell to Reading, who was greatly upset, the more so when he realized that his own action was the direct though unintentional cause of it. The same night he went to Agra on his first official visit, but not even the sublime beauty of the Taj Mahal by moonlight, which he saw with his wife immediately on their arrival, could take his mind

[1] Montagu Papers; Waley, p. 269.

off the distressing news. He was impelled to make a public reference to it next morning when he replied to an address of welcome from the Agra Municipality, and spoke of his 'deep sense of personal loss', at the same time contradicting rumours.[1]

> Whatever comments and criticism may be passed here or in England upon the discharge of his duties as Secretary of State for India, his devotion to the cause of India according to his views cannot be doubted. I have been Viceroy nearly twelve months and during that period have been in the most constant and intimate communication with Mr Montagu. Rumours have been circulated that there were differences of opinion between him, representing His Majesty's Government and myself and my Government regarding the policy to be pursued towards non-cooperation and its leaders. There never has been the faintest ground for those rumours.

The 'comments and criticism' to which Reading referred had found vehement expression a few weeks previously in the House of Commons, when a Conservative M.P., Sir William Joynson-Hicks (later Lord Brentford) had moved a vote of censure on Montagu and his Indian policy, accusing the Secretary of State of the 'criminal betrayal of every white man and white woman in India all through 1919, 1920 and 1921' and also of having 'broken the heart of the Civil Service'. Yet, although over ninety M.P.s had signed the petition for Montagu's dismissal, he came through the debate with flying colours and the censure motion was defeated by a substantial majority. 'Of course I hate these attacks as anyone would,' he had told Reading, 'but I don't think they really matter much in the sense of embarrassing you or weakening our position or our policy. . . . At any rate even the die-hards admitted that they did not desire a reversal of policy.'

Secretary of State to Viceroy

India Office.
February 23, 1921

Meanwhile the Conservative Party seems to be getting more and more restive at the existence of the Coalition. The trend of events is by no means closer alliance but rather towards separation, and whatever happens it looks as if Liberalism at the moment is not in a bright position, hopelessly split, more so than ever between the fires of Ultra-Conservatives on the one hand and Labour on the other.

Lloyd George appears imperturbable, but if anything is endeavouring to right himself with the Conservatives. Chamberlain looks anxious

[1] *Speeches by the Earl of Reading* (1924), Vol. I, p. 212.

and worried, torn between loyalty to his party and loyalty to the Prime Minister. F.E. is a strangely isolated figure and very unpopular with the Conservatives. Winston jumps from the diehard to the Liberal camp as he works from Egypt or India to Ireland. That is a pithy summary of the position of the more important Members of the Government.

How do these circumstances affect us? Well, they affect us this way, that if we are not to have a reversal of the policy in India, which to my mind would mean the end of the Indian Empire, we must try and avoid, until things get brighter, presenting to the Government or Parliament proposals that they would reject. . . .

Despite the fact that the Indian debate last week had a bad Press, mainly due, I think, to the swinging of the British public against India for the moment, I am informed that it has had a very good parliamentary effect, and after all, I said nothing which could not be found in other language in the Montagu-Chelmsford Report. But the trouble is that nobody will accept the facts merely because Gandhi has not been actually arrested. No statement seems to convince the public that your Government and the Local Governments have been dealing vigorously and effectively with disorder.

In the light of Montagu's successful performance in this debate, in which he put up a convincing defence of the Government's Indian policy, the news of his sudden resignation was all the more surprising, particularly as it was not the result of any personal difference of opinion in regard to this policy or its practical application.

The reason for Montagu's enforced resignation was the unauthorized publication by him of an official telegram from the Viceroy on the necessity for the revision of the Treaty of Sèvres in conformity with Moslem Indian feelings. The relevant portion of this telegram, which was dispatched from Delhi to London on February 28, read as follows:

The Government of India are fully alive to the complexity of the problem, but India's services in the War, in which Indian Moslem troops so largely participated, and the support which the Indian Moslem cause is receiving throughout India, entitle her to claim the extremest fulfilment of her just and equitable aspirations.

We are conscious that it may be impossible to satisfy India's expectations in their entirety. But we urge upon His Majesty's Government three points which, due provision having been made for safeguarding the neutrality of the Straits and the security of the non-Turkish population, we ourselves regard as essential:

(1) the evacuation of Constantinople;

(2) the Sultan's suzerainty over the Holy Places;

(3) restoration of Ottoman Thrace, including the sacred Moslem city of Adrianople, and the unreserved restoration of Smyrna.

We earnestly trust that His Majesty's Government will give these aspirations all possible weight, for their fulfilment is of the greatest importance to India.

'So important is it,' the telegram concluded, 'for the Government of India to range itself openly on the side of Moslem India, that we press for permission to publish the foregoing . . . forthwith.'

There was nothing new in the contents of the telegram which had not been expressed before by Reading in his replies to various Moslem deputations which he had received from time to time, except perhaps that the telegram was phrased in more formal and succinct terms. 'Of course I know that the Greco-Turkish Treaty [of Sèvres] was one of international complications,' Reading explained afterwards in a confidential message to the Prime Minister. 'I was, however, with my Government definitely of opinion that, having regard to the situation in India, it would be of great value if we as a Government, together with the provincial Governments, could impress upon the Mohammedan population by our action and by publication of the telegram of 28th February that we had done all in our power to present their views as forcibly as possible to His Majesty's Government. Further, we were of opinion if it could be permitted it would be of special importance to publish before the arrest of Gandhi. . . . The simple fact is that, as head of the Government and conscious of the strength of Mohammedan feeling in regard to the Treaty, I was actuated by a desire to press home the views of an important community who were playing so large a part in Indian agitation and unrest.'

Montagu received the telegram on March 1 and sent it out for circulation to the Cabinet in the ordinary way. Its members received their copies on March 4. This was a Saturday, and on the same day Montagu, who had gone off to the country for the week-end, received a further telegram from Delhi pressing for an answer to the original telegram, as Gandhi's arrest was expected within the next few days, and adding that the latest reports from the Provinces showed that the violent disturbances which had broken out there 'had been largely attributed to the turbulent and fanatical element among all the Mohammedans'. Montagu immediately cabled permission to publish without consulting any of his Cabinet colleagues. He afterwards explained that, owing to the Prime Minister's temporary absence through illness, he was not expecting an early meeting of the Cabinet, and in any event he thought permission in the circumstances was unnecessary. On returning to his office on the following Monday, Montagu sent a further telegram amplifying his permission to publish. The Cabinet met the same day, the Conservative leader Austen Chamberlain presiding in Lloyd George's place. The matter of the telegram was not raised at this meeting which Montagu attended, but Curzon mentioned it to him in conversation, remarking that he supposed Montagu would not authorize publication without reference to the Cabinet. 'I have already done so,' replied Montagu, 'on Saturday last.' According to his own account, Curzon was dumbfounded as he was about to attend a conference in Paris on the very issues raised by the offending telegram. Later that day he sent Montagu an angry note. 'Had I, when Viceroy, ventured to make a public pronouncement in India about the foreign policy of the Government in Europe,' he wrote, 'I should certainly have been recalled. . . . That I should be asked to go into Conference at Paris, while a subordinate branch of the British Government 6,000 miles away dictated to the British Government what line it thinks I ought to pursue in Thrace seems to me quite intolerable.' The Foreign Secretary added that he had consulted Chamberlain in the Prime Minister's absence and found that 'he entirely shared my views'.

Three days later, Lloyd George returned to work. He immediately sent for Montagu and demanded his resignation which the luckless Minister had no alternative but to submit. 'That you were actuated in the course you pursued solely by a sense of public duty, I do not for a moment doubt,' the Prime Minister told him sternly. 'Nevertheless the fact remains that, without being urged by any pressing necessity and without consulting the Cabinet or the Foreign Secretary or myself or any one of my colleagues, you caused to be published a telegram from the Viceroy raising questions whose importance extends far beyond the frontiers of India or the responsibilities of your office. Such action is totally incompatible with the collective responsibility of the Cabinet to the Sovereign and to Parliament.'

Montagu's dismissal from office came as a terrible blow which was to cast a deep shadow over the remainder of his brief life. By an unhappy mischance Mrs Montagu was in the Speaker's Gallery of the House of Commons when Chamberlain announced that her husband's resignation had been accepted by the King and she had the mortification of hearing the loud cheers which this piece of news evoked among the die-hards on the Tory benches. As Montagu himself bitterly remarked at the time, 'the great genius who presides over our destinies has done for them what they could not do for themselves and presented them with what they so long desired – my head on a charger'.

Reading conveyed his reactions to the news to the Prime Minister in a confidential telegram. 'I am very distressed by the resignation,' he wired on March 13, 'first, because it arose from the reply of Montagu to my application for leave to publish, and, secondly, because of my close connection with him since I became Viceroy. Ever since I began to understand Indian affairs I have been convinced that the Mohammedan attitude in relation to the Treaty of Sèvres was of cardinal importance. Communications were published by me on instructions from Home Government, setting out substance of modification of Treaty it was hoped to obtain. Since then I have at various times received deputations from Mahommedans and have made replies that I would support their views to the best of my power. . . . There is little if anything in the telegram published that is new and has not already received approval.'

In the circumstances Reading wondered whether he too ought not to resign. That he did not do so was the result of an official message from London inspired by the Prime Minister and confirming that he was not only entitled but perhaps bound to place his views before the Home Government and was entitled to ask for publication; 'but it was for the Cabinet or Ministers principally concerned to decide whether, in view of the general international situation, publication could be permitted at this time'. For the fact of publication Montagu was alone held responsible. 'There is no imputation against you or your Government. Montagu did not suggest that he relied on you or seek in any way to shelter himself behind you.'

On thinking it over, Reading had no doubt where his duty lay. This is how he put it in a letter to Montagu:

> What has particularly troubled me is the course I should take. On the one hand, I had great part in the initiative in the telegram incidents. On the other, I could not conceal from myself that my departure from office simultaneously with you would have a remarkably bad effect in India – not because of my own personality, but because I had become identified in Indian minds with the Liberal policy you had pursued.

The Government at home have made it plain that they find no fault with the Government of India's action. Otherwise, of course, my road was plain before me.

Montagu was succeeded at the India Office by a man ten years his senior and cast in a very different mould, Lord Peel. Bred to public life, the new Secretary of State, whose father had been Speaker of the House of Commons and whose great-grandfather had been Queen Victoria's Prime Minister Sir Robert Peel, was a Conservative who sat in the Upper House, and as such might be expected to regulate the pace of India's progress towards self-government much more slowly than his predecessor had done. Although he possessed little or no knowledge of India, Peel had as a young man been a special correspondent for the *Daily Telegraph* during the Greco-Turkish War of 1897 and this had given him some understanding of the Near-Eastern Question. At all events he seems to have quickly appreciated the feeling of the Indian Moslems and indeed seen eye-to-eye with Reading on Indian policy generally. His only criticism of the Viceroy was repeated in the course of a conversation he had with Sir Almeric Fitzroy, the Clerk to the Privy Council, when he had been at the India Office for about a year. According to Fitzroy, Peel 'expressed himself pleased with the complete accord which prevailed between him and Lord Reading on the great issues of policy and could not wish for happier personal relations, though there were moments when hesitation on the spot, whatever it may be due to, revealed a feature of the situation which is the source of some disquiet. However, Lord Reading's decisions in the end have always carried confidence. The judicial habit of looking all round a problem is perhaps prone to retard executive action, but is none the less emphatic in the character it gives to resolution, when once taken.'[1]

Reading's tardiness in taking drastic executive action was particularly exemplified in the case of Gandhi.

Viceroy to Prime Minister[2]

Simla.
May 4, 1922

I am sure you must have been interested in following the developments of the non-cooperation movement which culminated some two months ago in the arrest of Gandhi. He lives a rigorously ascetic life and is a religious enthusiast who believes he can regenerate human

[1] Fitzroy, Vol. II, p. 796.
[2] Lloyd George Papers.

N

nature and in a brief space of time raise it to a high pinnacle of ethics. He preaches – and I verily believe with all sincerity – non-violence as the most powerful weapon in the hands of man against those who, like Government, exert force and violence. ...

As his influence increased, as it undoubtedly did and very largely in consequence of what Indians regarded as his saintly character and life, he gradually found himself the leader of a political party ready, for a time at any rate, to follow him blindly. Moreover, he had made a bridge between the Hindu and the Mohammedan and from the political side that became of great importance. The Punjab disturbances and Amritsar gave him a great opportunity in 1919, and he seized hold of the Mahommedan discontent for the purpose of making a combined movement in favour of Swaraj. Thus his power grew, but equally he had to meet all the difficulties of a political combination of this character.

I have always thought that he became more the politician than the holy man and in the former capacity had to say and do things which were not strictly compatible with the latter. Although he has shown considerable astuteness at times in his handling of the political situation, yet he never seemed to have a practical plan of government. It may be that he feared that it would cause dissension among his supporters, for some were for complete independence, whilst others – and I believe the majority, speaking only now of non-cooperationists – wanted self-government under the British Empire. As time progressed, it became difficult to know whether he was leading, or attempting to lead, India. As promises made by him, particularly of Swaraj, within one month or three months as the case might be were falsified, so the more sensible began to wonder whether he would achieve anything beyond agitation and disturbance. ...

As you know, I was already ready to arrest him when I thought the proper time had arrived, and, although I have no doubt it seemed to you that we were postponing too long, yet I think results have shown that we had justification for our views and that as his influence waned, so the more moderate and sensible people in India ranged themselves against him. Equally, the more the papers spoke of his impending arrest, the more the people got accustomed to the idea and when it did take place it was no longer a surprise but the happening of the expected. Since then, the internal situation has been quieter than at any period since I have been here. I do not mean to draw too optimistic inferences from it; we have to keep ready and vigilant in case disturbances should arise. Fortunately there is a fine harvest as the result of a good monsoon and this will have its effect.

If only we were fortunate enough to get another good monsoon this year, we should have gone a long way towards peace and tranquillity in India, for the root of the trouble is undoubtedly in the poverty and misery of huge sections of the population. Then, as you know, the vast majority of the people are ignorant and illiterate and easily swayed by sentiment and emotion. And yet, it always seems to me wonderful that in spite of troubles and disturbances British rule has lasted and continues notwithstanding that in a total population of 320 millions, of which 250 millions are in British India, there are less than 200,000 British including all the military. It is a grand tribute to British capacity for administration amidst alien races and creeds.

Fortunately both the monsoon and the harvest were good. On August 14, 1922, Lord Lytton, who had succeeded Lord Ronaldshay as Governor of Bengal, wrote to Montagu: 'It is a real tragedy that you should have left the India Office just at the moment when the atmosphere began to change and the situation to improve. ... The monsoon has been good, crops are promising, agitation has died down, the non-cooperation movement has completely collapsed since the arrest of Gandhi, and the European community is beginning to take heart.'[1]

During the latter part of 1922 and the first half of 1923, Reading's most worrying problem was the Moslem one, and it remained so until a peace treaty was eventually signed between the Greeks and the Turks at Lausanne. By the middle of September, 1922, the Greeks had been driven out of Asia Minor by Mustapha Kemal's forces, who looked as if they might now seize the Dardanelles and cross into Europe, thus coming into armed conflict with the British troops at Chanak who were part of the international force guarding the straits. On September 17, 1922, the British Cabinet, largely at Winston Churchill's instigation, issued a communiqué announcing the intended reinforcement of the British Army of Occupation under General Sir Charles Harington at Chanak who were to act with the British Mediterranean Fleet in opposing any infraction of the neutral zone of the Straits by the Kemalists or any attempt on their part to cross into Europe.

Viceroy to Prime Minister[2]

Simla.
September 20, 1922

For the moment there is a great excitement about the Moslem question, as you can well imagine. There is a wave of enthusiasm sweeping over the Mohammedan population because of the Kemalist

[1] Waley, p. 282.　　　[2] Lloyd George Papers.

victories; of course the more extreme and fanatical Moslems regard these victories as an indication of future domination by the Moslem world, and are inclined to lose their heads accordingly. The moderate Moslems regard the situation more reasonably but equally they insist that the Turk must not be deprived of the legitimate fruits of his victories and that the situation has most materially changed since February and March last.

It is here that we meet the real difficulties. I leave the extremist out of calculation; whether he is Mohammedan or Hindu he is always against us and eager to take advantage of every opportunity that presents itself of embarrassing the Government and of assisting him to his aim which is to drive it out of India. We know him and his views; he is a foe whom we always have to encounter. But the moderate Mohammedan is our friend, and in particular since the publication of the telegram at the end of February which caused so much trouble, he is convinced that the Government of India is trying to do its legitimate best for the Indian Mahommedans and to represent their views, and therefore he wants to work with us and not against us. But he is very troubled by the published news and by the warlike attitude that Britain is adopting. . . .

The extremist propaganda in India is all now directed to showing that it is Britain again who is the true enemy of Islam and the false friend despite all that we may say, and that it is only owing to the action of France and Italy, and because of the strength of the Turkish forces, that Britain does not try to crush Turkey in order to gain advantages for Greece. . . .

Most certainly, in the interests of India, I hope that this Turkish question will be solved. I can imagine how perplexing and troublesome the whole situation must be for you, who have to take into account many sides of the problem that don't confront me. With all my heart I hope that you will get well through these tremendous difficulties.

Despite the fact that the French now decided to withdraw their contingent, not wishing to be drawn into an Anglo-Turkish War, while the Italians assured Kemal of their neutrality in such an event, the British Cabinet was bent on a showdown with the Turks. On September 29, 1922, a telegram was sent to Harington – the notorious 'Chanak telegram' – instructing him to deliver an ultimatum threatening war unless the Kemalists halted their advance and withdrew their forces from the Chanak area. When he heard this news, Reading telegraphed agitatedly from Simla to Peel that events had now become so ominous that he dare not leave India for a meeting which he had secretly planned to have with Lloyd George towards the end of

October at some convenient half-way point such as Suez or Cyprus. 'The excitement among Mahommedans generally is increasing in intensity, and is especially directed against Britain as the only power that is checking the Turkish triumphant march to Thrace. There is much inflammatory propaganda and extremist agitators are using every opportunity to fan the flames.'[1]

Fortunately General Harington, supported by Sir Horace Rumbold, the British High Commissioner in Constantinople, ignored the instructions in the 'Chanak telegram' and did not present the ultimatum to the Turks otherwise war would inevitably have resulted. The crisis was resolved by meetings between Harington and Ismet Pasha at Mudania and Curzon and Poincaré in Paris, as the result of which the Greeks retired behind the line of the Maritza and Allied detachments occupied Eastern Thrace pending its restoration to the Turks. In the long term the peace negotiations, protracted though they were, were facilitated by the fall of the Lloyd George Coalition Government and the return of the Conservatives to power under Bonar Law who did not share Lloyd George's fanatical pro-Greek and anti-Turkish feelings. The peace, which was concluded in Lausanne, considerably modified the harsh provisions of the Treaty of Sèvres and became the territorial basis for the present-day Republic of Turkey. Needless to say, the news came as a tremendous relief to Reading, being received as he put it, 'with unbounded relief and thankfulness by the Moslems of India'.

It is worth recalling that at the time of Reading's appointment as Viceroy of India, the fall of Lloyd George had been foretold by Reading's friend, Sir Alfred Mond (later Lord Melchett), whose daughter Eva had married Reading's son Gerald. 'It means the end of Lloyd George,' Mond had remarked. 'Directly Reading's calming influence is withdrawn from him, his power will decline.'[2]

Peel continued in charge of the India Office under Bonar Law and also under Stanley Baldwin, who succeeded 'the unknown Prime Minister' when the latter was finally obliged to retire by incipient cancer in May, 1923. The advent of the first Labour Government led by Ramsay MacDonald in January, 1924, naturally brought a change in the office of Secretary of State for India, Peel being replaced by

[1] Reading to Peel, October 1, 1922: India Office Papers. On October 5, Stamfordham wrote to Peel: 'His Majesty feels that the decision that Lord Reading should not leave India at present is a wise one.'

[2] Hector Bolitho: *Alfred Mond first Lord Melchett* (1933), p. 250.

Lord Olivier, a distinguished ex-civil servant, Fabian Socialist and friend of Bernard Shaw. However, in spite of their ideological differences, Reading and the new Secretary of State got on remarkably well together, and when the Viceroy was obliged to resuscitate an old statute which empowered the Provincial Governments to detain agitators without trial for indefinite periods, Olivier gave him his wholehearted support.

The situation was complicated by a widespread demand for the release of Gandhi, who underwent an operation for appendicitis early in 1924 and whose supporters felt he should be allowed to convalesce outside the prison walls. Reading and his Executive Council had to balance between the risk of renewed outbreaks of violence if Gandhi was not released and the chances, if he were, that his energies would be fully occupied with his fellow Swarajists in the Congress Party, who had decided to abandon the sterile policy of non-cooperation and participate in the parliamentary government of the country by entering the Central and Provincial legislatures. The decision was taken to release Gandhi and it was fully justified by the result for it was the policy of the two other leading Swarajists, C. R. Das and Pandit Motilal Nehru, which eventually triumphed. 'Gandhi is now attached to the tail of Das and Nehru,' Reading wrote when the Mahatma had been at liberty for about a year, 'although they try their utmost to make him and his supporters think that he is one of the heads, if not *the* head. It is pathetic to observe the rapid decline in the power of Gandhi and the frantic attempts he is now making to cling to his position as leader at the expense of practically every principle he has hitherto advocated.'

For Reading it was still a question of marking time on the issue of further constitutional advances in India. This produced feelings of mistrust among the Swarajists both Hindu and Moslem, and although their elected leaders took part in parliamentary proceedings they refused to attend official Government functions such as the Viceroy's garden-parties. Reading wrote disappointedly to Olivier at this time:

> I am rather surprised at the practical unanimity among Indians of all shades and descriptions, with one or two rare exceptions of no importance. Their attitude is of such doubt of our intentions as to amount also to mistrust. I do not mean that they doubt my intentions to forward the policy of reform. I believe those most opposed to us are convinced of my desire to go forward; but they think I am too slow, too cautious, and have been restrained by public opinion in England.

9

The Labour defeat in England in the General Election of October, 1924, brought the Conservatives back to power under Mr Baldwin. To Reading's surprise and also gratification, his old friend and, in a sense, professional and political rival Lord Birkenhead was appointed to the India Office. Birkenhead had never been to India, but his study of Indian history was extensive and he had absorbed much of the fascinating atmosphere of British India from the early days of Clive and Warren Hastings to the no less colourful age of Kipling and Curzon. He welcomed the opportunity to correspond with Reading, and his weekly letters in particular were always lively and stimulating and often enlivened by a characteristic wit.[1] There was, too, an element of humility in them, unexpected in one of his habitual arrogance. From the outset however, he was convinced that the government of India was a trust which must be firmly administered by Britain and he doubted whether the country with its variety of races and languages and creeds would ever become so politically mature as to enjoy the self-governing status of a Dominion. In this connection he shared the views of the rest of the Baldwin Cabinet that the Montagu-Chelmsford Reforms had already gone too far and had fostered a demand for a further dose of constitutional reform which it would be quite inexpedient to grant for some considerable time, if at all.

Secretary of State to Viceroy

India Office, London.
November 13, 1924

It is a great joy to me to be associated with you and to share your responsibilities in a task new to me, but with which you have already grown so familiar. The knowledge indeed that this Office opened up the prospect of such co-operation largely influenced me in selecting it. I was asked by the P.M. whether I wished to press my claim to the Woolsack. I quite sincerely answered that I did not. I had four years of it, and I had almost reached the end of my patience with an office which, however dignified and important, was so sedentary. I cannot explain to you how much happier I am here, or shall be when I have begun to master this immense and novel subject. I can see that it will

---

[1] I am indebted to the present Lord Birkenhead for putting copies of these letters, largely unpublished, from his father at my disposal, and allowing me to quote extensively from them in the following pages.

take me a long time – though I am, as you know, a fairly rapid worker – to make my opinion of much value. I shall naturally be greatly guided by the experience which you have gained. ...

Since I came here I have made it my business to read many of your speeches and dispatches and I think I am generally, though not of course in detail, aware of your points of view. Like you, I believe strongly that where there is a revolutionary element expressed in action, one must act resolutely. My reading of Indian history has led me to believe that a Government founded so completely as ours is upon prestige can stand almost anything except the suspicion of weakness. You will not suppose that I mean by this that I am advocating any step which goes further than those you have already adopted. I have not the knowledge which would enable me to do so. But I write in this sense in order to make it plain that should events unfortunately, and to me, unexpectedly, so develop that an exhibition of firmness is in your judgment required, you will always meet with the support of this Office as long as I hold the seals.

November 20, 1924

For your secret information I may say that this Cabinet, as is natural, is in my analysis under the influence of a considerable reaction from the Montagu reforms. It has a general impression that under the Coalition, and since, too much has been given away, I will not say through weakness, but through the general malaise which succeeded the War in India, Ireland and Egypt. On any point, therefore, on which you hold a strong view that the line must be firmly drawn, you are unlikely to lack support either from it or from me.

December 4, 1924

I think you know that alone in the Cabinet, I distrusted and, to some extent, opposed the Montagu-Chelmsford Report. To me it is frankly inconceivable that India will ever be fit for Dominion self-government. My present view is that we ought rigidly to adhere to the date proposed in the Act for a re-examination of the situation, and that it is not likely, unless matters greatly change in the interval, that such a re-examination will suggest the slightest extension.

22nd January, 1925

In ultimate analysis, the strength of the British position is that we are in India for the good of India. The most striking illustration of the truth of the position is of course supplied by the infinite variation of nationality, sect and religion in the sub-continent. The more it is made obvious that these antagonisms are profound, and affect immense and irreconcilable sections of the population, the more conspicuously is the fact illustrated that we, and we alone, can play the part of composers.

I, as you know, never liked, or believed in, the Montagu-Chelmsford reforms. I distrusted dyarchy, though I realized that dyarchy was an indispensable experiment in attempting to begin grafting Western parliamentary institutions upon an Oriental population, wholly uneducated for their receipt. But I realize of course that we must give the reforms a fair chance insisting at the same time that those to whom they were offered shall equally give them a fair chance. I detect many signs that in many parts of India the reforms are working more smoothly and more successfully than I had expected, though it seems to me that in some cases at least the success is explained by the innate capacity of Anglo-Saxons to work any constitution; and that, in its attainment in more cases than one, the dyarchial principle has been in fact thrown completely overboard.

Birkenhead's fluent pen, or rather tongue – for like Reading he invariably dictated his weekly letter – illuminated every subject he touched upon, whether it was the expulsion of the Greek Ecumenical Patriarch from Constantinople or the amorous misadventures of the heir to the throne of Kashmir as revealed under the guise of 'Mr A.' in the English Courts.

The problem of the Greek Patriarch was aptly and wittily summarized as follows (February 5, 1925):

... You will have seen that a row is going on in the Near East over the expulsion of the Ecumenical Patriarch; and the Greeks are even talking of war. They talk of it, on the whole, more resolutely than they wage it; but none the less, a situation of some gravity threatens to arise. Personally, I seldom visit Constantinople, and am unlikely, if I journey there again, to stand in need of the services of the Patriarch. But I am none the less trying hard to disinterest Austen [Chamberlain] in the matter, because it seems to me to be so important not to run the slightest unnecessary risk – from the point of view of Moslem opinion – of public controversy or clash with the Turks. To me, the improvement of Moslem sentiment towards us is far the most encouraging symptom at the present moment, and I am deeply concerned that our European policy should not derogate from that improvement.

Technically, I think that the Turks have a good case, and sentimentally, there is nothing, so far as I know, between them and the Greeks which disentitles them from insisting upon their pound of legal flesh. The Treaty of Lausanne specified certain classes of Greek Nationals as 'Exchangeables'. This most reverend gentleman had the misfortune (if it be one) to fall in this class, and thereby to forfeit the privilege (if it be one) of residing in Constantinople. The Greek Electors of this Dignitary, none the less, knowing, it must be presumed, the facts, elected an 'Exchangeable' forbidden by Treaty to reside in Constantinople, to discharge the duties of Patriarch, which apparently can only be rendered in Constantinople. I understand that if anybody in Constantinople really wants a Patriarch badly, the Turks are quite prepared to accept one who does not belong to the 'Exchangeable' class. I am putting the matter rather in this way, though with less levity, to the Foreign Office and the Cabinet, because if anybody is to bell the Turkish cat in the Patriarchal interest, I am extremely anxious that it should not be this country.

A gang of blackmailers, of whom the worst was Sir Hari Singh's own A.D.C., Captain Charles Arthur, had succeeded in extorting £125,000 from the young Prince as the price of their silence on his being discovered in bed in a Paris hotel with the wife of an English bookmaker named Robinson. The matter came to light when Robinson sued the bank in which the money, allegedly unknown to him at the time, had been deposited and subsequently paid out on a forged endorsement upon a cheque drawn by one of the villains. At Reading's request, Birkenhead went to Mr Justice Darling and asked him to keep the Prince's name out of the case, which he succeeded in doing, the Prince being referred to throughout the civil action as 'Mr A'. But when criminal proceedings were set in motion against the blackmailers, it was impossible to conceal the Prince's identity any longer, particularly since it had already been mentioned in the American and European Press. 'It is ironical enough,' as Birkenhead wrote to Reading, 'that the very vastness of the sum which he paid to avoid publicity is the very element in the matter which has produced it.'

Birkenhead shared the indignation of the English newspapers at how such a scoundrel as Arthur could possibly have been appointed A.D.C. to the Prince, since it seemed almost certain that 'he conceived the whole wicked plan to entrap his master at a time when he was being paid and trusted to protect him'. It appeared that Arthur in spite of his unprepossessing military record had been recommended by the English Resident at Kashmir, Sir John Wood, and that the appointment had been approved by the Political Department in Delhi, for which the Viceroy, in theory at least, bore the responsibility. In fact, Reading could offer no defence for those directly responsible in his Government, although he tried to plead in mitigation, at the same time hinting that the much ill-used Prince might soon be paying another visit to England. Birkenhead's comments were caustic:

> Personally, I am extremely sorry for this young fellow. Like another, he fell among thieves and worse, and there was no better Samaritan available than Sir John Wood's protégé, Captain Arthur. Sir Hari paid so much and got so little for it – not even privacy for a squalid amour. I was a little alarmed by a phrase in one of your letters which indicated that the hero – or the victim – of this conspicuous melodrama might come to England within the next year. My most earnest advice to you, in his own as much as in the general interest, is to keep him away for two or three years. If he were to visit this country in the next twelve months, every placard in England – sacrificing for the purpose even a Test Match – would display the simple announcement 'Mr A. arrives', and thereafter the young man would know no privacy from reporters and intruders during the whole of his visit.

The sordid Hari Singh case by no means constituted the sole problem affecting an Indian Native State which confronted Reading during his term as Viceroy. In the name of the King-Emperor, he had to remove two Maharajas from their thrones, Indore and Nabha, for shockingly ill-treating their subjects. He also had to reject the claim put forward by the multi-millionaire Nizam of Hyderabad to the territory of Berar, which had been under direct British rule since 1853. This brought into sharp relief the whole question of the relations between the British Crown and the Native Rulers, and the Nizam was left in no doubt of Britain's right to intervene in the internal affairs of these States besides controlling their foreign relations. Finally, Reading had to determine the complicated issue of the Bhopal succession.

Bhopal was a Moslem state, and the Begum, a formidable old lady, had recently lost her first and second sons and wished the throne to go on her death to her third son, Hamidullah Khan, to whom she was particularly devoted, rather than by strict primogeniture to her senior grandson, who appeared on first sight to have the prior claim in law. The Viceroy was personally sympathetic to the Begum, but he felt that the matter must be decided in accordance with legal precedent – and the precedents in the Political Department, which incidentally did not go further back than the Mutiny, seemed to be against the Begum. Getting wind of this, she decided to go to England, in spite of her age and poor health, and if necessary press her claim before the King-Emperor in person. This she succeeded in doing.

Besides being received at Buckingham Palace, she had a number of meetings with Birkenhead and brought her three favourite grandchildren to tea with Lady Birkenhead, the Secretary of State noting at the time that 'the Begum's tears did not prevent a considerable consumption of hot buttered toast'.

Fortunately for the Begum the records in the India Office Library went back further than those in the Political Department in Delhi, and these showed that from the end of the eighteenth century the practice of the Mohammedan civil law had been followed and this was definitely on the Begum's side. Reading agreed on this with Birkenhead, but it was unfortunate that the delay in announcing the decision from Delhi resulted in a newspaper leak correctly anticipating the decision, which in turn led the Begum to ring up both Buckingham Palace and Lady Birkenhead to inquire whether it was true. It was a relief to both the Secretary of State and the Viceroy to know that at last she was on her way back to India.

The matter was rounded off by Birkenhead in one of his last letters to Reading in India (March 4, 1926):

> I had not any real doubt about the decision in the Bhopal case. My only regret is that her long presence in this country and the many interviews she had had with important people may encourage the idea in India that wherever there is a dispute as to a succession it is necessary for the litigant, if he is to be successful, to make a journey to this country. The point on which my own opinion was really determined was that there was no vestige of evidence that the English system of primogeniture had ever been applied or accepted in Bhopal. In these circumstances, it seemed to me hardly defensible to apply it for the first time in the teeth of many precedents and against the vehemently expressed desires of a popular Ruler. I should imagine that the old lady is in her seventh heaven; but I hope she will spend what remains of it in her own country.

Meanwhile a Committee of both Houses of the Indian Parliament under the chairmanship of Sir Alexander Muddiman, President of the Council of State, had examined and reported upon the working of the 'dyarchy' system. Motilal Nehru refused to represent the Swarajists on the Committee since the inquiry was confined to the 1919 Act, but Jinnah joined as leader of the Independents, and the Liberals were also represented. The Committee, which began work in 1924 when Olivier was Secretary of State, reported in March, 1925, shortly before Reading left for England on short leave. The Committee was unanimously agreed on the defects of dyarchy, such as that the vesting of financial control in the 'reserved' side of the Provincial Governments deprived the native ministers of real power. While the majority thought the Act could be effectively amended to remedy such defects, a minority recommended the scrapping of the Act and the substitution of complete responsible government in the Provinces and at least a measure of responsibility in the Central Government.

Birkenhead's letters in the month the Muddiman Committee's Report appeared reflected Reading's views on the state of the parties in India:

> Your conclusions agree with those of this Office and, for what my own opinion is worth, with my own. I see many signs that the Swarajists are slipping. In my opinion they neither know where they are, nor where they are going. The split between them and the Independents is a new promising and unexpected development. I hope that it will grow. But I have always placed my highest and most permanent hopes upon the eternity of the Communal situation. The greater the political progress made by the Hindus, the greater, in my judgment, will the Moslem distrust and antagonism become. All the conferences in all the world cannot bridge over the unbridgeable, and between these two communities lies a chasm which cannot be crossed by the resources of modern political engineering. Moreover, I have long looked for a revolt against the tactics of the Swarajist Party in obstructing the reforms. It is a gain wherever the Home Rule Party obstructs or defeats a measure which is generally seen to be a public advantage. I look forward, and perhaps in the near future, to a great reaction against a policy of such obvious stupidity. I note with pleasure that in the two most difficult Provinces – Bengal and the United Provinces – you detect favourable indications in this matter.
>
> I agree with you that too high an expectation must not be founded upon a momentary disintegration, but I am nevertheless not without the hope that the events of the next few years will prove that permanent and ineradicable elements in Indian life must work against their continued solidarity. Like yourself, I place considerable hope in the inevitable political education which membership of the deliberative Assemblies in itself produces. The Lobbies and the Smoke Room (if you have a Smoke Room) will do the same kind of work (even if upon a smaller scale) as they have done here within your experience and mine. In the second place, a programme of futility and a more insensate obstructiveness is one with grave weakness and not stronger when tested by experience and by results. In the third place, I see many gratifying evidences of an increase of political responsibility among the

Independents and the Liberals. In the fourth place, the more I study these problems the more convinced do I become that the eternal and immutable distrust between Hindu and Moslem will become more acute in proportion as the Swarajists' strength increases.

10

In taking three months' leave to go home in the summer of 1925, Reading created a precedent, since no previous Viceroy had ever left India during his term of office to go on home leave. Lord Lytton, the Governor of Bengal, acted as Viceroy during his absence. The ostensible purpose of the visit was to enable Reading to discuss the next constitutional moves with the Home Government, but also that he and his wife could get a rest and a change.

Two prominent public figures who had been the last to bid Reading good-bye on his departure from England were absent from the circle of friends to greet him on his return. They were Edwin Montagu and Lord Curzon, the ex-Secretary of State and the ex-Viceroy, who had died within a few months of each other, and whose names, as Reading subsequently told the Indian Legislature, 'will endure conspicuous in the roll of the great English statesmen who have loved India and devotedly served her', although 'they approached Indian problems not always from the same angle of vision'. As might perhaps be expected, Birkenhead was silent on the subject of his controversial predecessor at the India Office; but he spoke feelingly of Curzon. 'He had, as all of us have, his weakness,' the Secretary of State told Reading, 'but we shall lose in him a great and illustrious and indefatigable public servant. His devotion to, his pride and sustained interest in, the Indian Empire and all that it stood for were almost pathetic in their constancy. It seems to me that he will stand very high in the list of Viceroys. I shall certainly miss, as long as I am at this Office, his sane experience and sympathetic advice.'

Reading's visit and particularly his meetings with Birkenhead gave the Secretary of State his first opportunity for delivering a major policy speech on India, which he did in the House of Lords on July 7, 1925. Contrary to general opinion in India, which had expected something reactionary from the Conservative Secretary of State, Birkenhead proved unexpectedly conciliatory, going so far as to invite the Indians to provide their own solution and 'produce a

Constitution which carried behind it a fair measure of general agreement among the great peoples of India', and which far from being resented by the British authorities would be most carefully examined by the Government of India, by himself and by the Statutory Commission 'whenever that body may be assembled'.

A few days later Reading and his wife left again for India. Lady Reading's popular and tactful private secretary, Yvonne Fitzroy, did not return with the Readings to India, her place being taken by Miss Stella Charnaud, who had been introduced to them by a mutual friend while on a visit to India. Miss Charnaud was to play a conspicuous part in the later life of her employer's husband.[1] They reached Bombay on August 6, and made the journey across the burning plains with the temperature in the 120s to Simla, where the Viceroy opened the summer session of the Indian Parliament on the 20th. Reading was agreeably surprised, as also was Birkenhead, when the Legislative Assembly elected Mr V. J. Patel, a leading member of the Congress Party, as President. Patel had previously been a bitter critic of British rule, and it was encouraging that he should accept such an office under the existing constitution.

'Things are quiet here,' wrote Reading to John Simon from Simla after the session had been going for some weeks. 'Indeed, when I see the events and disturbances in Europe and elsewhere, I come to the conclusion that India is the most peaceful of all the countries and we are, I hope and believe, steadily marching forward to prosperity.' The Viceroy's words were echoed by Birkenhead:

> One does not like to be too sanguine, but I cannot help thinking that matters on your side continue to go well and smoothly. Poor Gandhi has indeed perished, as pathetic a figure with his spinning wheel as the last minstrel with his harp, and not able to secure so charming an audience! . . .
>
> I ought to have informed you, when dealing with the documents discovered in the Communist raid, that there was one purporting, I believe, to emanate from Moscow appointing Saklatvala[2] the principal agent for fomenting discontent and risings among the Indian

---

[1] Miss Charnaud, now the Dowager Marchioness of Reading, was a daughter of Charles Charnaud, President of the International Bank of Turkey, who represented Great Britain on the International Public Debt Organization in Turkey.

[2] Ten leading Communists in England had recently been arrested and their papers seized. Shapurji Saklatvala, a wealthy Parsee from Bombay, was Communist M.P. for North Battersea in the British House of Commons at this time.

peasantry. His opportunities for doing full justice to his important appointment must, one imagines, hitherto have been somewhat scanty.

I was delighted with Patel's speech. Indeed, its tone was so admirable that I rejoice now that he was elected; and I am encouraged to hope more than I was that, as they gradually attain desirable appointments, our opponents will abate a great deal of their acerbity. I thought of making a complimentary reference to the tone of his speech when next I have an opportunity. I should be very careful not to do it in a patronizing manner which might embarrass him and defeat my own purpose; but rather in a tone of an old parliamentarian who noted that a remarkable appreciation had been delivered so far away, and one which would have been creditable to any of our own Speakers, of the difficulties and duties of one who presides over a great Assembly. It was specially gratifying that Patel should have referred twice to our English practice and our English traditions.

During this, their last Simla season, the Viceroy and Vicereine entertained King Albert and Queen Elizabeth of the Belgians, who were on an informal tour of India, and at the end of their stay the King invested the Viceroy with the Grand Cordon of the Order of Leopold. After they had seen the royal visitors off at Summer Hill Station, Lady Reading broke the news to her husband that she had been in considerable pain for some days and that her doctor had diagnosed a growth which might or might not be malignant. An immediate operation was necessary and this was successfully performed in Calcutta a week or so later. 'It really is appalling bad fortune that, after all the troubles of the past few years, this domestic trial should have come upon you so near the close of your Viceroyalty,' Birkenhead wrote from London. 'The sympathy with you both here is very great. . . . However well they go, operations are very anxious and disagreeable incidents, particularly when one is no longer young.' This one was to all appearances successful, although unknown to the patient it could only retard and not remove the cancer which was eventually to kill her a few years later. An extremely brave woman, she was urged by the doctors to go home when she was well enough to travel, but she refused and insisted on staying in India for the remaining months of her husband's tour. She appeared in public for the first time at Calcutta Races on Boxing Day for the presentation of the Viceroy's Cup and she got an even bigger cheer than when her husband had invested her with the Kaiser-i-Hind medal, which she had been awarded in the King's Birthday Honours in 1924 for her hospital and welfare work for the women and children of India.

Other house guests at Viceregal Lodge in Delhi at this time included Lord Lee of Fareham and his wife. As they were leaving, Lady Lee made the following entry in her diary, which throws an interesting light on Alice Reading's character and incidentally on that of the lady who was one day to become the second Lady Reading.

I went to lunch by myself with Miss Stella Charnaud, who succeeded Miss Fitzroy as Private Secretary to Lady Reading. She is a nice girl, clever and hardworking, whose job is by no means an easy one looking after anyone so ill and yet imperious as the Vicereine, to whom I went in afterwards to say goodbye. She [Lady Reading] was very sweet to me, as always, and is certainly a remarkable woman. Indeed she must always have been the driving force behind Rufus and but for her passionate ambition for him I do not believe that in spite of his ability he would have risen to any heights at at all. He himself enjoys life so much that he could have enjoyed it equally without a career, and he has a sweetness of nature which would have been satisfied with very much less. They say he consults her on every question and, when he *does* make up his mind, it is often she who has made it up for him.

The question of the nomination of Reading's successor had occupied the attention of the authorities at home for many months before the selection was eventually made in October, 1925. At first there was a rumour that Prince Arthur of Connaught might be the new Viceroy, but this was strongly discounted by Birkenhead when Reading reported it to him. 'The objections in existing circumstances to making any existing Member of the Royal Family Viceroy stare one in the face,' wrote Birkenhead on February 12, 1925. 'The Viceroy at the present time requires an equipment of intellect, character and political sophistication which the warmest admirer of the Prince would not claim for him. When I use the expression "character" in this context I am obviously not dealing with the ethical side of this abstract and complex term. We shall, indeed, have great anxiety when we come to fill your place.' Some months later the King suggested to the Prime Minister, Mr Baldwin, the name of Lord Haig, and when it was pointed out to His Majesty that a civilian would be more suitable, the King put forward the name of Mr Edward Wood, eldest son and heir of Lord Halifax, and one of the younger members of the Baldwin Government; he was Minister of Agriculture. His appointment as Viceroy was accepted by Baldwin and Birkenhead and the rest of the Cabinet. The news was telegraphed to Reading on October 29, 1925. 'He is a man of the highest character, of very considerable ability, great courtesy of manner, and of distinguished appearance,' Birkenhead wrote to Reading the same day. 'He is putting out to sea in calmer waters than those which awaited you. But no one knows better than you do that our anxieties are not over, and I am sure that in the actual situation, and in any way that is foreseeable in the next three or four years, Wood is the best man we could have got.'

In his next letter to Reading, the Secretary of State tempered his praise with a hint of condescension:

The reception of Wood's name in the Press has been extraordinarily favourable, even a little surprisingly so. I have hardly noted a single discordant word. There is an adjective frequently employed in Homer to which the best English rendering is 'blameless'. How much better in life and how much more paying it is to be blameless than to be brilliant; and certainly it pays in such a connection never to have attacked anyone, and therefore never to have antagonized anyone. But, as a matter of fact, as I have already told you, I have a real admiration both for his character and for his quiet but solid qualities. He is really very intelligent; will count no labour excessive, and will not easily be deflected from any course which he has persuaded himself is right. I am really very happy about the whole business, for though I naturally do not know him anything like as well as I know you, I know enough of him to make it certain that my association with him will be harmonious and I hope that it may prove useful and fruitful.

The new Viceroy, by then Lord Irwin, landed with his wife in Bombay on April 1, 1926, to go through the same routine ceremonial that their predecessors had done exactly five years before. At Government House the departing Viceroy and Vicereine were at hand to bid them hail and farewell. Lady Irwin noticed the pallor in Lady Reading's cheeks, and her air of depression at the thought of departure.

Before going on board the P. & O. steamer that night to begin his homeward voyage, Reading was entertained to dinner by the members of the Byculla Club and made his last public speech on Indian soil, when he replied in excellent humour to the toast of his health.[1] 'I have attended many farewell banquets and have had to make many speeches,' he began aptly, 'but I particularly value this opportunity of addressing you tonight with the knowledge that there will be no report in cold print for me to examine in the morning . . . and to realize how much better my speech would have been if I had to make it over again.'

Having surveyed in some detail the outstanding events of his five

[1] *Speeches by the Earl of Reading*, Vol. II, p. 594.

years of office, the departing Viceroy concluded his speech with this peroration, which sounds strange to our ears today but was sincere enough when it was uttered:

> In the end as I leave India, as I wend my way home, I return with a deeper realization of the beneficent outlook of the British Empire, with a wider understanding of its duties and responsibilities, with a larger conception of the influence and power of that great commonwealth of nations. I glory in the high purpose it is our duty as citizens of the Empire to seek to achieve; in the moral standpoint of public service we strive to inculcate, in the endeavour to improve the conditions of the poorer and less fortunate people, in the earnest wish that this country may be the better for our efforts, that we may have contributed to the cause of humanity, and that we may have assisted in promoting the welfare and happiness of India.

He took with him on board the departing vessel a valedictory letter from Birkenhead, which it must have given Reading much pleasure to read:

> You sacrificed much and incurred many risks when you took over the helm in a stormy period. None of us can ever hope, in circumstances comparable to those by which you were confronted, to escape criticism altogether. But I am nevertheless confident that the historian of India, reviewing in cool perspective the resource with which you confronted difficulties so menacing and so novel, will say that England has not often found, at a moment when she specially needed him, a Viceroy more patient, more adroit, more devoted to his charge or better equipped with the indispensable gift of conciliation. . . .
>
> It only remains for me, in laying aside my pen for the last time, to wish you both many years of happiness and prosperity. I cannot doubt that in the tangled skein of the varied memories of your adventurous life, the thread of India will be the most treasured of all; and I hope that its memories will comfort and sustain you in whatever new work you think proper to engage.

Disembarking at Marseilles and taking the overland route for the last lap of their journey, they reached London on April 17, 1926. Their son and daughter-in-law, Lord and Lady Erleigh, met them at Dover, and at Victoria Station there was a sizeable gathering to welcome them home, headed by the Secretary of State. While the Indians garlanded Lady Reading with flowers, newspaper reporters crowded round the returning Viceroy and asked him for a statement. 'It is the end of five great years for me,' he said modestly. 'If it has been of any use, I am very delighted.'

9

Foreign Secretary

1

A few days after they had settled in to their old Curzon Street home, the Earl and Countess of Reading were formally bidden by the King and Queen to dine and sleep at Windsor Castle. The summons was not unexpected, since it was customary for the services of a Viceroy of India to be recognized at the conclusion of his term of office by either being advanced a step in the peerage or else being created a Knight of the Garter. According to Reading's son, the latter, in talking over the matter with his father, expressed the hope that the retiring Viceroy would choose the non-hereditary honour, assuming that he were consulted beforehand. In fact, Reading was given no choice in the matter, for the simple reason that the Garter, which is undoubtedly the premier order of chivalry in the world, has always been confined to Christians.

As soon as Reading had arrived at the Castle, the King sent for him and in the course of an hour's audience expressed his appreciation of his services to the country, culminating in those to India and the Empire. His Majesty then informed him that he had just signed the State paper raising him to the dignity of a marquessate, under the style of 'The Most Honourable the Marquess of Reading', and had sent it to the Prime Minister. The news was given to the Press the same evening. Thus did Rufus Isaacs become the first person since the victor of Waterloo, who did not inherit a peerage, to rise from commoner to marquess in a lifetime.[1]

In spite of this phenomenal rise in the ranks of the nobility, we have it on the authority of his son that Reading found two compensations in his retirement from official life. One was that he could

[1] The Hon. George Nathaniel Curzon likewise became a marquess, but he had already succeeded to his father's barony of Scarsdale.

again have curry made from tinned curry powder, which he much preferred to the exotic curries made by the *kamsama* at Viceregal Lodge. The other was that he could again have money in his pocket to pay for personal shopping purchases, which he could never do as Viceroy. Of course the money had to come from somewhere, and this posed the problem of his financial future. His son tells us that his investments had been too often unsuccessful, his expenses had been too heavy, and he had been able to save nothing during his time in India. Moreover he had no pension from any of his past offices to enjoy, and since the Conservatives were in power and the Liberal Party in disarray if not disintegration, there seemed no opening for him in the political field. It was inevitable in the circumstances that his attention should turn in the direction of the City, where his financial knowledge added to his name and public record would be most likely to secure him a place in any number of board-rooms in which he professed an interest.

Here fortune favoured Reading's endeavours. At the time of his return from India, Sir Alfred Mond, M.P., a Liberal and a Jew like himself, with whom he had formerly sat in the House of Commons, was amalgamating his big industrial chemical interests, principally represented by Brunner, Mond & Co., with various other groups, including that headed by Sir Harry (later Lord) Magowan of Nobel Industries, to form the giant Imperial Chemical Industries, with an authorized capital of £95,000,000. During the process of the amalgamations, Mond declared that he wanted 'men like Reading around him'. Consequently, when I.C.I. came into being, Reading was appointed a director of the new company, whose offices in Millbank, Imperial Chemical House, became his London headquarters. Four years later, on Melchett's premature death, Reading became President of I.C.I. in place of Magowan who succeeded Melchett as Chairman.

The other Boards on which he served included the National Provincial Bank, the London & Lancashire Insurance Co., United Newspapers Ltd., the Palestine Electric Corporation, and finally Carreras Ltd. In the case of the three latter, he was Chairman of the Board. Apart from the fact that it removed any financial worries he may have had, he enjoyed his board-room work, except possibly in the case of United Newspapers. This company published the *Daily Chronicle* and other Liberal journals, and Reading only agreed to accept the Chairmanship at the urgent request of Lloyd George, who had obtained control of the *Daily Chronicle* in order to publicize his own particular brand of Liberalism. But Reading never found the meetings of this Board congenial; he had no specialized knowledge of newspaper production, and he was further embarrassed by the connection between the *Daily Chronicle* and Lloyd George's notorious Political Fund, which was the principal shareholder in United Newspapers.

Reading's marquessate was the prelude to a series of further honours and public marks of distinction, the customary rewards of an elder statesman.

On April 28, 1926, Reading was the guest of honour at a dinner given by The Pilgrims, the celebrated society dedicated to further the cause of Anglo-American understanding. Birkenhead proposed the guest's health with his usual post-prandial eloquence and wit, in which he ranged at some length over the milestones of Reading's career, and he underlined what he felt to be the secret of his achievements.

> It might have seemed, even from the fragmentary sections of the life of our guest that I have selected to comment upon, that his career had been one of unbroken serenity, progress and success. 'Roses, roses, all the way' might have seemed to have been the motto most suited to a career so strangely successful. Yet as one of the oldest of his friends, I shall claim the right to remind you tonight that on at least two occasions in his life when bitter adversity had knocked at his door – and on neither occasion did he bow his head to it, but rather he overcame it – he conquered it, and it is the realization of that strength which enabled him to do so much which made those who knew him certain that he would not weaken before any assault that threatened in India.

In his reply, Reading reminisced cheerfully, and recalled his first glimpse of Calcutta from the deck of the *Blair Athole*. But he also struck a serious note when he forecast the future course of British-Indian relations:

> I believe that as time progresses India will understand better that we do truly mean what we have said, and that we shall not depart from the promises we have made. Five Governments in my time have stood firm, they have never varied one iota from the declarations made or from the proclamations of His Majesty the King. Five Governments have determined, and I have worked with them to do all they can to advance India to the attainment of the goal she seeks and we have destined for her. . . .

A few weeks later the Lord Mayor and Corporation of London conferred the Freedom of the City upon him, an honour which as a native of the City he particularly appreciated. Then the University of Oxford, following the example of Cambridge, Harvard, Yale, Princeton and Toronto, gave him, who had never been an undergraduate, or studied at any higher seat of learning, the honorary degree of Doctor of Laws.

The Readings had not been home long before their thoughts turned towards finding somewhere in the country to which they could get away at weekends. The question was most conveniently and indeed economically solved for them when Lord Allenby resigned the office of Captain of Deal Castle. The office was a sinecure and there were no duties attached to it beyond those of custodian of the fortress, which dated from the time of Henry VIII, when it had been built along with the adjacent castles of Walmer and Sandown so as to protect the anchorage for shipping within the Goodwin Sands, and the Kent coast against foreign invasion. They moved there at Easter, 1927. That this occupant was Reading he owed to Lord Beauchamp, leader of the Liberals in the House of Lords, in whose gift as Lord Warden of the Cinque Ports the Captaincy of Deal Castle lay.

Among the old friends with whom Reading renewed a friendly correspondence on his return from India was Colonel House, the first two volumes of whose *Intimate Papers* appeared in 1926. 'Having studied Grey's book [*Twenty-Five Years*],' he told House, 'I am reading yours with even greater interest, and in some part with a sense of intimacy.' House replied that this represented only half the work, and that Reading would 'take a prominent place on the stage' in the remaining two volumes. Dr Charles Seymour of Harvard, who was editing the papers and writing a connecting narrative, had tried to make his interpretation objective and impartial. 'I want the book to be fair to you and British policy,' House wrote to Reading from New York early in 1927. 'Books are being published over here in increasing numbers by those who have a purpose in distorting the facts. Unless this is controverted, public opinion will become crystallized and it will be increasingly difficult to have the truth accepted.' A few months later, House wrote again:

> You will find that the entire book will be sympathetic to you and your work as, indeed, it will be to Lord Balfour, Lord Cecil and other Englishmen with whom it was my privilege to work.

It was not my original purpose to allow publication of my papers, but circumstances forced me to do so, and now that the first volumes are out it is necessary to finish the story. If I did not allow it done, nevertheless it would be done in any event and in a way that would not be altogether pleasant to many of your countrymen.

Reading was fascinated by the two final volumes, which reached him towards the end of 1927, and he expressed his appreciation in a nostalgic letter to House.[1]

All my available leisure is devoted to reliving those momentous days and especially the periods when I was brought into closest association with you. I cherish the memories of those times when you gave your invaluable assistance to the furtherance of the great Cause.

I am one of those who has always been and always will be glad to give expression to the tremendous service you rendered to it. I suppose Balfour, Northcliffe, Wiseman and I knew most about it from the Allied side, although I did not remain in Paris during the whole of the Peace Conference.

You are very kindly and appreciative in regard to such efforts as I was able to make, and I am particularly glad that Wiseman's activities now stand recorded and take an important place in your chronicles.

Their next communications were on a sad occasion, fourteen months later, when Reading's long and happy domestic partnership was dissolved by his wife's death. For nearly two years, Reading had known from the doctors that she was suffering from incurable cancer, but he kept the knowledge secret from her, telling no one, not even his son, until almost the end. She suffered much pain throughout 1929, and Reading did not leave the house for a single night during that last year of trial. Only towards the end did she realize that she had little longer to live. She died on January 30, 1930, in Curzon Street and was buried in the Jewish Cemetery in Golders Green. 'My every prayer is answered,' she confided in her husband just before the end. 'Thank God, I go before you.'

Reading tried to find consolation in work, but for many months after his wife's death he felt desperately lonely, for she had been, as he put it, 'in the finest sense of the word the best comrade a man could find'. His son and daughter-in-law did their best to comfort him, but he disliked the feeling that they were putting themselves out on his account. The long strain of his wife's illness produced a

[1] Reading to House, April 30, 1926, November 18, 1928; House to Reading, February 23, April 4, 1927, November 30, 1928: House Papers.

reaction which affected his own health. His doctor ordered him to
stay in bed or at any rate indoors for a time, but this enforced confinement only added to his sense of loneliness and depression.

Fortunately he was not to mope and pine away his remaining years.
He found increasing solace and companionship in Miss Charnaud,
who had been his wife's secretary but whom he took over in a similar
capacity on their return from India.

At the beginning of August, 1931, they announced their engagement to a few close friends. 'This step has been in contemplation by
me for some months,' Reading told John Simon. 'It is only within
the last few days, however, that the question was asked and the
decision was taken. I am the luckiest of lucky men.'

At this date Reading was seventy and his fiancée was thirty-seven.
Although the fact that his intended wife was a Gentile did not commend itself to orthodox Jewry, there was no Jewish or other friend
who did not sincerely wish him happiness.

They were married quietly on August 6, 1931, at Prince's Row
Register Office, London. About forty friends and relatives attended
the ceremony, including Sir John Simon, Sir Harcourt Butler and
Mr Alfred Sutro. The King and Queen sent the bride and groom 'our
best congratulations and good wishes' on the occasion.

Ten days after their return from a short honeymoon in Paris an
economic crisis of the first magnitude suddenly burst upon the
country, and recalled Reading to London and a brief and final spell
of public life.

2

Reading naturally continued to take a close interest in Indian affairs,
and as an ex-Viceroy he was consulted from time to time by the
Government. He warmly approved the appointment of his old friend
and colleague John Simon as Chairman of the Statutory Commission
in 1927 to examine the working of the Montagu-Chelmsford Reforms, thus anticipating by two years the latest date for the constitution of the Commission as provided for by the Act of 1919.
The Commission consisted of seven members in proportion to the
existing party political strengths and drawn from both Houses of
Parliament; incidentally one of the two Labour members was
Major C. R. Attlee, who as Labour Prime Minister twenty years

later was to promote the end of British rule in the sub-continent with the establishment of the two independent republics of India and Pakistan within the Commonwealth. The announcement of the composition of the Commission was strongly attacked in India on the ground of the exclusion of Indians, but it was defended by Reading who pointed out, with logic on his side, that it was a British Parliamentary Commission appointed under the terms of a British Act of Parliament, which must in any event legislate for any further step towards Indian self-government. As a matter of tactics, it might have been well to have added two Indians. Lord Sinha, a Hindu, was a Member of the House of Lords, while a prominent Moslem, such as the Aga Khan, could easily have been made a peer in order to balance the Indian representation as well as preserving the Commission's parliamentary content.

The result was that the Congress Party under the inspiration of Gandhi, who had taken on a renewed lease of subversive activity, decided that all good nationalists must boycott the Commission, and its members were met on their arrival at Bombay with placards bearing the legend 'Simon Go Home'. However, Simon and the others persevered and succeeded in collecting a vast amount of material for their purpose, undeterred by insults and more forcible examples of native displeasure, such as the throwing of a bomb into the Legislative Assembly in Delhi when Simon was the guest of honour. After a total of nine months in the country, spread over two visits, the Commission returned to England in 1929 and Simon set about preparing the Commission's Report.

Simon's literary activities were temporarily interrupted by the General Election in May, 1929. On this occasion Baldwin expected to be returned again to power, and he was said to be considering Winston Churchill for the India Office.[1] But the Conservatives were defeated at the polls, and Labour came back, with the Liberals holding the balance between the other two parties in the Commons. As in 1924, the Labour Prime Minister was Ramsay MacDonald, and he chose Mr Wedgwood Benn (later Lord Stansgate), a recent convert to the ranks of Labour from the Liberals, as Secretary of State for India. MacDonald made no secret of his wish to see India's rapid advancement to the status of a Dominion 'which will find self-respect as an equal within the Commonwealth', and in this context he and the rest of the Labour Cabinet determined to anticipate the

[1] G. M. Young: *Stanley Baldwin* (1952), p. 139.

findings of the Simon Commission by the announcement of a Round
Table Conference, in which Indians of all shades of opinion, including
the Native Princes, would meet British leaders as equals round the
conference table, with Dominion status as the ultimate goal of
British policy towards India to be achieved by stages.

Advantage was taken of the Viceroy Lord Irwin's being in England
on leave during the summer of 1929 to discuss the idea and how the
announcement should best be made, which the Labour Government
wished to make as attractive as possible to the Indians. While the
Commission had no objection to the summoning of a Round Table
Conference, its members were inclined to shy away from the proposed
statement about Dominion status, and in these circumstances the
Government decided to make the announcement about Dominion
status separately through the mouth of the Viceroy after he had
returned to Delhi. Baldwin was consulted for the Conservatives and
Reading for the Liberals, and both said they were agreeable on
behalf of their political parties to the announcement provided that
the agreement of the Simon Commission was also obtained. The
agreement of Simon and his colleages was not in fact obtained, and
although Simon seems to have given the impression when he met
Reading and Irwin at Reading's house over lunch that he regarded
the Dominion status part of the announcement as 'academic' and
did not feel very strongly about it, Reading was naturally surprised
when he learned from Wedgwood Benn some time during the latter
part of October that the announcement about Dominion status was
shortly to be made from Delhi. He set out his objections in a strongly
worded letter which he addressed to Wedgwood Benn.

London.
October 27, 1929

The selection of this particular moment immediately after the return
of the Viceroy from consultation with you and His Majesty's Government, and when the Simon Commission is engaged in considering its
Report, will lead Indians to the conclusion that the declaration imports
a change of policy and brings the final stage of constitutional development appreciably nearer in point of time.

I am aware that both you and Lord Irwin maintain that the policy
remains unchanged and that the pronouncement is made merely for
the purpose of setting at rest doubts which have arisen in the minds of
Indian politicians regarding the meaning of 'responsible government'
and the ultimate destiny of India within the Empire. I cannot but

think that Indian politicians will believe that the making of the declaration now and without waiting for the Report of the Simon Commission is evidence of a new policy. . . .

The effect in this country must, I fear, inevitably lead to a serious political controversy which all parties have desired to exclude in relation to the constitutional position of India. The appointment of the Simon Commission and the selection of its members from the three political Parties with the assent of Parliament led to a general understanding that all questions relating to the constitutional development of India should be postponed until the Commission presented its Report.

For the course you are now proposing to take you have failed to obtain the support of the Liberal Party and, I have reason to believe, of the Conservative Party. So far as I am aware the Simon Commission has not given its assent. Nevertheless it is intended, as I gather, to proceed immediately and to make the declaration which must be regarded as of capital importance, otherwise it seems inconceivable that Government should persist in the face of opposition it has met.

Whatever may be the effect of the Government action in India, there can be no doubt that in this country and in Parliament there will be an end of the general understanding above mentioned.

I would beg of you again to consider whether in these circumstances it would not be more to the advantage of India that *no action of the character proposed should be taken until after the Simon Commission has reported and Parliament and the country are in possession of their conclusions and advice.* (Author's italics.)

This letter, and particularly the plea contained in the final paragraph, was brushed aside by Wedgwood Benn. Four days later, on October 31, the statement was officially made by the Viceroy in Delhi to the effect that, in the opinion of His Majesty's Government, 'it is implicit in the Declaration of 1917 that the natural issue of India's constitutional progress as there contemplated is the attainment of Dominion status'.

The immediate result of this announcement, both in India and Britain, was exactly as Reading had foretold. In Delhi the Congress leaders issued a manifesto demanding that their party should have the largest representation at the Round Table Conference, the purpose of which they assumed was not to determine whether or when Dominion status should be introduced but to draft a constitution for the new Dominion forthwith. Otherwise the Viceroy's statement was generally welcomed by native opinion in India as a definite advance. In Britain, however, it provoked strong hostile criticism, especially in Parliament, where the question of India's constitutional future was again thrust into the bitter well of party politics, and Conservatives and Liberals joined in attacking a minority Government which in this matter they thought was proceeding too fast.

In the circumstances of his letter to the Secretary of State, Reading felt bound to raise the matter at the earliest opportunity in the House of Lords, which he did by initiating a debate on November 5, 1929. 'I could wish that those of us who predicted had not turned out to be so correct in our anticipation,' he declared ominously. He quoted the Indian Moslem leader Mr Jinnah as having referred to the Viceroy's statement as a clear, radical change of policy.

> The Government assert that the announcement is no change in policy. Now it cannot mean both. It cannot mean one thing in India and another in this country.

> My great objection to it is that it has conjured up a picture in India which cannot be fulfilled within a very considerable time at least, and that the obstacles remain, as they were before this announcement was made, still confronting India. That they may be surmounted is undoubtedly our hope, but until they are surmounted we cannot give a *status* which would in truth be an abandonment of the principles and responsibilities we have carried for many years, I believe with great advantage and benefit to the people of India.

The Labour Government spokesman in the House of Lords, who replied to Reading, was the seventy-seven-year-old Lord Parmoor, who had previously sat in the Commons as a Conservative. He read so much of his confused and confusing speech that it appeared to Birkenhead, who followed him with a withering castigation, that he was not 'quite aware of what he did or did not suggest'. The one thing which did emerge, encased though this was in a welter of verbiage, was that there was no change in the implications of the Montagu Declaration of 1917. 'Poor old Parmoor,' wrote Lord Stamfordham, who listened to the debate so as to report afterwards to the King. 'He got so mixed, referred to Ramsay MacDonald as "Lord MacDonald", and more than once spoke of "*Her* Majesty's Government", which rather touched me, as I fancied his mind was like mine, often wandering back to the much despised Victorian period!'

During the twelve months which elapsed before the Round Table Conference assembled in London, Gandhi renewed his campaign of civil disobedience and there were fresh outbreaks of violence directed mainly against British officials in India which the Mahatma appeared powerless to control, an unsuccessful attempt being made to blow up the Viceroy's train with His Excellency on board, an experience which never befell Reading. Meanwhile, Sir John Simon and his colleagues on the Commission had put as good a face as they could upon the Dominion status announcement, and went ahead with their Report, which was eventually published in June, 1930. The King, who regarded it as the 'most accurate, faithful picture ever portrayed of that wonderful country', was anxious that the Report should form the basis of discussions at the Conference, a sentiment shared by Reading and his Liberal friends. (Reading described Simon's work as 'really splendid and his achievement monumental'.) Briefly, the Report proposed the abandonment of dyarchy and recommended the introduction of full responsible government in the Provinces but not at the Centre, where the Governor-General and Council would continue in control of defence, the Legislative Assembly being reconstituted on a federal basis. This scheme was designed to apply to British India only, and the Native States were to be left to come in later. In the event the Report proved quite unacceptable to Indian nationalists, who felt that its application in practice must inevitably result in an endless series of disputes between the provincial legislatures and the British Central Government. Consequently the Congress Party decided to boycott the Round Table Conference.

The Conference was formally opened by the King-Emperor in the Royal Gallery of the House of Lords on November 12, 1930. In spite of the Congress boycott there was a very considerable Indian representation, and it was significant that it afforded the first occasion in British-Indian history that the representatives of the two countries had met on the footing of equality at the conference table. Reading headed the Liberal delegation, his colleagues being Lord Lothian and two members of the House of Commons, Sir Robert Hamilton and Mr Isaac Foot. As things turned out, Reading was to play a key part in the conference. At the outset a declaration by the Maharaja of Bikaner that the Princes were in favour of federation transformed the atmosphere, the Simon Commission's Report was quietly shelved, and the delegates got down to the serious business of working out the terms of an early federation. The situation was now completely changed. Hitherto the British Government had doled out successive instalments of self-government; now it was a question of agreeing limitations to the complete transfer of authority. It was to this problem that Reading bent all his attention, and since the Liberals held the balance of the parties in Parliament it was obvious that his views must carry the greatest weight with the Government. Having been assured by his old Indian friends Sir Tej Bahadur Sapru and Sir Mohammed Shafi that, if responsible self-government at the Centre were conceded, then Indians would agree to any reasonable safeguards, Reading delivered the official Liberal Party view, namely a responsible Federal Government, subject to certain safeguards in respect of defence, foreign relations, the protection of minorities, and the maintenance of various legitimate European interests. This was later expressed by Ramsay MacDonald in his final address to the conference before it adjourned in January, 1931. The Indian delegates were delighted with Reading's contribution, coming from the party of Gladstone whose memory they revered. 'Now we shall have a responsible Government at the Centre,' they gleefully proclaimed.

While the conference was in session, Reading gave a large reception for the Indian delegates at his house in Curzon Street, which the Prince of Wales honoured with his presence. On this occasion an amusing incident occurred which showed that there was no ill feeling on the part of a prominent Indian nationalist leader for whose imprisonment for sedition Reading had been directly responsible. This was one of the Ali brothers, whom his host duly presented to the Prince. 'Didn't I meet you when I was in India?' asked the Prince as they shook hands. 'No, sir,' replied Mr Ali, smiling and looking in the direction of the ex-Viceroy. 'I was at that time the guest of your father the King-Emperor!'

In Delhi Lord Irwin now concluded a pact with Gandhi, the civil disobedience campaign was called off, and the Congress leaders even agreed to attend the next session of the Round Table Conference when it was reconvened in the following September.

A responsible Federal Government, with full local provincial autonomy, appeared the solution likely to command most widespread support both in Britain and India; but to Reading's mind such a constitutional experiment could never be equated with Dominion status on the model of Canada and Australia. 'You will forgive me if I use a strong expression,' he told the Indian delegates to the Conference, 'when I say that it is idle to assert at this moment there could be anything like equality of status – that is constitutional status – in India with the Dominions.' In the long term history was to prove him right.

3

Early in 1931, Lord Beauchamp, leader of the Liberal Party in the House of Lords, suddenly resigned all his offices – except, curiously enough, that of Lord Warden of the Cinque Ports – and went to live abroad. As his successor to lead them in the Upper House, the Liberals chose Reading, and in this position it was natural that he should play some part in the negotiations behind the scenes when the existence of Ramsay MacDonald's Labour Government was threatened by the mounting economic and financial crisis which overtook the country in the following summer. Less than a fortnight after he got back to Deal from his honeymoon with his second wife, Reading learned that the Prime Minister was likely to resign consequent upon a split in the Labour Cabinet on the amount of the economy 'cuts' and new taxes necessary to meet the emergency, which had been caused by a current Budget deficit of £170 millions coupled with heavy withdrawals of gold from London by foreign depositors. When he heard that the King was returning from Balmoral, and that Mr Baldwin had left the waters of his favourite French spa, Reading also hastened back to London.

Lloyd George was recovering from a serious operation at this time, and Herbert Samuel had been appointed acting Party Leader in his absence. On the morning of Sunday, August 23, Reading was conferring with Samuel on the situation, when a message arrived from Buckingham Palace summoning Samuel to see the King. In informing the King of his impending resignation, the Prime Minister followed the correct constitutional procedure when he advised His Majesty to send for the leaders of the two other parties. Since the Conservatives had the next largest following in the House of Commons – 261 as compared with 59 Liberals – the King intended to send for Baldwin first, and certainly the general impression in the country was that the Conservative leader would agree to form a Government with Liberal support. By one of those accidents of history which have momentous results, Baldwin was not at home when the message came from the Palace and his whereabouts could not immediately be traced. (According to one account, he had gone for a walk; according to another, he was closeted with Geoffrey Dawson, *The Times* editor.) Samuel, on the other hand, was immediately available, and it was his advice formulated jointly by himself and Reading in favour

THE CABINET OF THE FIRST NATIONAL GOVERNMENT,
AUGUST, 1931

Standing (from left): Sir Philip Cunliffe-Lister, Mr Neville Chamberlain, Mr J. H. Thomas, Marquess of Reading, Sir Samuel Hoare.

Sitting: Mr Philip Snowden, Mr Stanley Baldwin, Mr J. Ramsay MacDonald (Prime Minister), Sir Herbert Samuel, Lord Sankey.

(From a photograph taken in the garden of 10 Downing Street)

" MON DIEU, THE INESTIMABLE VALUE OF EXCHANGING VIEWS WITH MILOR READING!"

CARTOON BY LOW ON LORD READING'S VISIT TO PARIS AS
FOREIGN SECRETARY

(Reproduced by arrangement with the Evening Standard)

of a so-called National Government that the King eventually accepted after Baldwin's support had been secured.[1]

Reading agreed with Samuel that the predominant consideration was the saving of British credit abroad. They also deprecated the holding of an immediate General Election, which would not assist the solution of the financial problem, but would do much to aggravate the crisis. After he had seen the King, Samuel made a note of the form his advice had taken.

> We thought that, in view of the unpalatable character to the masses of the people of many of the economies which were indispensable, it would be to the general interest if a Labour Government were in office during their enactment. If Mr MacDonald, with this or a reconstituted Labour Cabinet, was able to propose economies which were really adequate, that would be the best solution. The proposals hitherto made by the Cabinet were, however, quite insufficient, and I gave some illustrations as to Unemployment.
>
> If that solution proved to be impracticable, then a National Government of members of the three parties would be the best alternative. It would be preferable that Mr MacDonald should be the Premier, unless he found that he could not carry with him a sufficient number of his colleagues.
>
> We deprecated a purely Conservative Government, as we thought it would have great difficulty in securing popular support for the necessary measures. If, however, His Majesty, found that no other solution could be reached, we should of course support the Government of the day in the steps immediately necessary to save the financial situation.
>
> I said nothing as to the possibility of a Conservative-Liberal or Labour-Liberal Administration, and the King did not raise the point.

The immediate result of the audience was that the King became convinced of the necessity for a National Government, since MacDonald was quite unable to carry his Labour Cabinet with him. The same afternoon, the King saw Baldwin and asked him whether in the circumstances of the emergency he would be willing to serve under MacDonald. Baldwin at once said he would. Next morning the King met all three political leaders together in the Indian Room of Buckingham Palace, and they agreed to the formation of a National Government under the Premiership of Ramsay MacDonald so as to enable the necessary emergency legislation to be passed and other steps taken, after which the King would dissolve Parliament

[1] Bowle, pp. 270–71.

o

and there would be a General Election fought on the usual party lines.

When he met his Labour Cabinet colleagues at noon in Downing Street, MacDonald informed them that it had been decided to form a 'Cabinet of individuals' to meet the emergency; he would himself be one of the individuals, he said, and he invited any of them who wished to join him in the new administration. Only three of the assembled Ministers out of a total of nearly twenty accepted his invitation – Lord Sankey, Mr J. H. Thomas and, reluctantly and under pressure, Mr Philip Snowden, the Chancellor of the Exchequer, who was the departmental minister most nearly concerned with the crisis. After lunch, when he had seen the junior Ministers, MacDonald returned to Buckingham Palace and formally tendered his resignation as Prime Minister of the Labour Government which the King accepted. 'I then invited him to form a National Government,' the King recorded in his diary the same evening, 'which he agreed to do.'[1]

Twenty-four hours later, MacDonald was able to announce the names of the principal office holders in the new Government. In the discussions he had with the new Prime Minister and the Conservative leader, Samuel found that both were ready to treat the Liberals generously, having regard to the fact that they had less than a quarter of the seats in the House of Commons held by each of the other parties. First, it was agreed that the Cabinet should be reduced to the minimum of size, and should consist of four Labour, four Conservative and two Liberal Members. The obvious choice for the Liberals was the two parliamentary leaders, Samuel and Reading, and in the share-out they were allocated the portfolios respectively of Home and Foreign Affairs. The Conservatives were Baldwin (Lord President), Neville Chamberlain (Health), Sir Samuel Hoare (India), and Sir Philip Cunliffe-Lister (Board of Trade). In addition to the Prime Minister, Labour was represented by Philip Snowden (Exchequer), J. H. Thomas (Dominions and Colonies) and Sankey (Lord Chancellor). The following morning, August 26, Reading went to the Palace along with the other Ministers to receive their seals of office, and the new Cabinet was sworn in.

Two days later, the new Foreign Secretary presided over a large Liberal Party meeting and informed those present that Lloyd George, whom he had visited on his sick bed in the meantime was in 'complete accord' with what had been done. Nevertheless the ailing Liberal

[1] Nicolson, p. 465.

leader also expressed a firm conviction that the crisis ought never to have arisen and that 'our enormous extraneous wealth ought to have been mobilized', instead of which 'this wealthy country' had been subjected to 'the humiliation of cadging for credits from France and America to save it from insolvency'.

The question of Reading's Parliamentary Under-Secretary had next to be settled. It was of considerable importance, since the Foreign Secretary sat in the Upper House and the Under-Secretary would have to represent the department entirely unaided in the Commons. Austen Chamberlain, the previous Conservative Foreign Secretary, spoke strongly to Reading in recommending a young Conservative back-bencher, who had been his Parliamentary Private Secretary when he was in office. He told Reading he thought the young man had the makings of a future Foreign Secretary and that he should now be given a chance to prove his worth, adding that Baldwin agreed with him. His name was Anthony Eden. The only snag was that Ramsay MacDonald was believed to have earmarked the post for his son Malcolm, who sat on the Labour back benches. However, the matter was speedily settled, the younger MacDonald going to the Dominions Office as Under-Secretary, a post with which he was apparently quite satisfied, while Eden began his ministerial association with a department of which he was to find himself head barely four years later.

As Reading mounted the grand staircase of the Foreign Office and entered the Foreign Secretary's spacious room, with its huge desk and ornate furnishings, overlooking St James's Park, he was conscious of the immensity of the task he had undertaken, particularly for a man within a few weeks of his seventy-first birthday. His first duty was the traditional one of receiving a ceremonial call from all the foreign ambassadors in London, who came to pay their respects and make themselves personally known to the new Foreign Secretary. Protocol required that no serious business should be discussed on this occasion, so that Reading contented himself with asking each of the ambassadors what he thought of the present state of the world. Afterwards Reading recalled that only one, the representative of Turkey, expressed anything like a cheerful view.[1] Certainly the international picture was bleak. Great Britain was not the only country in economic difficulties. Germany was on the verge of bankruptcy as the result of France's war reparations policy. Most of

[1] Simon, p. 175.

Lord Reading

the other European countries, with the notable exception of France, were 'in the red'. Indeed the crisis was so extensive that the American President Herbert Hoover had proposed a moratorium for one year on inter-governmental debts; unfortunately its effects were largely nullified by French intransigence. It is true that there were no war clouds on the European political horizon at this time, but it was otherwise in the Far East where Japan's growing militarism threatened China by a planned intervention in Shanghai and Manchuria. Eden has recorded that he spent the first day in the office reading up the situation in China. 'There are many threads to pick up,' he noted, 'and the task is likely to occupy me fully until the Government goes out.'[1]

The procedure in the office was for all incoming telegrams and dispatches, except those of a routine character, to go first to the Permanent Under-Secretary, at this time Sir Robert Vansittart (later Lord Vansittart), who would pick out those he considered sufficiently interesting or important for the Minister to see for action or information. Appropriate replies would, of course, be drafted by the officials concerned in accordance with ruling policy; drafts were not normally prepared by the Minister, although he sometimes made important changes or additions to them. On the other hand, whenever the Secretary of State saw a foreign diplomatist, and he might see half a dozen or more in the course of a single day when matters of urgency in their respective countries required discussion, he had to make a careful record of what passed at the interview not only for circulation among his own Cabinet colleagues but also for the use of the British diplomatic missions in the countries immediately concerned. In all this work Reading was fortunate in being well served by the permanent Foreign Office staff, to whom he later paid a warm tribute, notably his Private Secretary, Sir Walford Selby. Nevertheless he found the burden of his office terribly heavy. As his successor Sir John Simon was to put it, 'perhaps the plan of issuing official records later on, under classified heads and in different volumes, fails to convey this criss-crossing of matters requiring immediate attention which causes a main strain in a Foreign Secretary's life'.[2]

Reading was also asked by the Prime Minister to take on the duties of Leader of the House of Lords, so that in addition to answering for his own department he was responsible for getting the whole of the

---

[1] Earl of Avon: *The Eden Memoirs: Facing the Dictators* (1962), p. 20.
[2] Simon, p. 177.

Government business through the Upper House. Parliament met on September 8 and an emergency budget and Economy Bill were rushed through in the teeth of strong Labour opposition except from the handful of his party who had thrown in their lot with MacDonald. These measures only halted the drain on gold temporarily. The drain was renewed after the refusal of some naval ratings at Invergordon to obey orders. Foreign investors mistook the Invergordon affair for a full scale mutiny of the Royal Navy heralding a bloody revolution, and the withdrawals of gold were such that after parting with over £30 millions of specie in four days the Governor and Directors of the Bank of England told the Government that they must immediately be relieved of their statutory obligation to sell gold at a fixed price on demand. The Cabinet thereupon decided that the gold standard must be suspended, and legislation to this effect was passed through all its stages in a single day. Had it not been for the fact that this measure was accompanied by the most drastic economies, Britain's action in going off gold would have produced inflation on a vast scale such as overwhelmed post-war Germany. As it was, the consequent devaluation of sterling – the pound dropped from $4.86 to $3.40 – helped the British export trade.

Reading's hand can be seen in the telegram dispatched in his name on the evening of September 20, 1931, to the principal British missions abroad informing them of the Government's decision to leave the gold standard. The circular telegram concluded with these words:

> His Majesty's Government have arrived at their decision with the greatest reluctance. But during the last few days the International financial markets have become demoralized and have been liquidating their sterling assets regardless of their intrinsic worth. In the circumstances there was no alternative but to protect the financial position of this country by the only means at our disposal.
>
> His Majesty's Government are securing a balanced budget and the internal position of the country is sound. This position must be maintained. It is one thing to go off the gold standard with an unbalanced budget and uncontrolled inflation; it is quite another to take this measure, not because of internal financial difficulties, but because of excessive withdrawals of borrowed capital. The ultimate resources of this country are enormous, and there is no doubt that the present exchange difficulties will prove only temporary.

Meanwhile a special appeal had been made to France. Mr (later Sir) Ronald Campbell, the *Chargé d'Affaires* in the British Embassy in Paris – the Ambassador, Lord Tyrrell, having been recalled to London for consultation – was instructed to deliver a most urgent note to the French Prime Minister, M. Pierre Laval, in person and with the utmost dispatch. The English text of the note, stating that the Bank of England had been faced with an unprecedented run on its gold reserves, reached Campbell about one o'clock in the morning of September 19. After hastily translating it into French, he telephoned Laval and asked him for an immediate interview. The French Prime Minister, who was then living in the private quarters of the Ministry of the Interior, obligingly got dressed and received the agitated British Minister in the small hours.

At first Laval proposed to put the matter before the French Cabinet next day, but on Campbell pointing out the danger to British credit if there should be 'the slightest indiscretion on the part of any one of them', Laval assumed full responsibility himself, told Campbell to find out the sum the British Government required, offered to put up half if the Americans would come forward with the other half, and if America was unable or unwilling to do so, then he would make himself responsible for the whole amount. 'I will throw my country's vaults open to you,' he added with an unexpectedly generous Gallic gesture. 'My country will never forget you,' said Campbell, clasping Laval's hands in his own, and rushed back to his Embassy to telephone the news through to the Foreign Office.

The French Premier was as good as his word. Not only did he get his Finance Minister, M. Flandin, to co-operate by agreeing to close the Paris Bourse so as to synchronize with the closing of the London Stock Exchange while the suspension of the gold standard was being debated in Parliament, but on no help being forthcoming from the United States he put through the amount of the loan requested in full – 3,000 million gold francs.[1]

A fortnight later, Reading paid a short visit to Paris in order, as he put it, 'to get into contact with the French Ministers and to lay the basis for future co-operation wherever it was possible'. He was accompanied by Sir Frederick Leith-Ross, one of the senior financial experts at the Treasury, who joined in the conversations with Laval, Flandin and Briand, the Foreign Minister. No decisions were arrived at, but a great many questions were discussed, particularly relating to the future stabilization of the pound and France's attitude to the resumption of reparations after the expiry of the Hoover moratorium,

[1] Hubert Cole: *Laval* (1963), p. 47.

Laval asserting that it was politically impossible for the French 'to wipe the slate completely, but they might do so partially if they could get the necessary advance on other questions'. Laval was about to go to Washington for talks with President Hoover, and it was clear that France would not join in any general scheme of disarmament unless she was given adequate guarantees for her own security. Before leaving Paris, Reading emphasized that in view of the forthcoming General Election in England the British Government 'was only in the position of a caretaker and could not therefore take decisions on a long policy or make any promises'. At the same time he reassured the French Ministers, with some personal warmth as well as diplomatic courtesy, that the British Government was 'very anxious to do everything in their power to keep in close agreement with France'. In due course, Reading was able to report to the British Cabinet that in his view the purpose of the visit to Paris had been achieved. Certainly there is no doubt that Reading's behaviour impressed the French Prime Minister favourably on this the only occasion on which the two met.

A few days after his return to London, Reading set off again, this time to Geneva for a meeting of the League of Nations, to which China had appealed as the result of Japanese military intervention in Manchuria, following an alleged attack by Chinese on Japanese troops in the neighbourhood of Mukden and the occupation of that town by a Japanese force. At this time the League was relatively weak. The United States, in spite of the fact that it had been the late President Wilson's brain child, had never joined, and Soviet Russia still remained outside. America, however, had sponsored an international treaty, the so-called Kellogg Pact, to which the signatories, which included China and Japan, had agreed to renounce war as a method of settling their differences. In these circumstances Reading joined with the Foreign Ministers of France, Italy and Germany in a proposal to the United States to nominate a representative to sit in on the proceedings of the League Council, and despite some resistance on the part of the Japanese delegate this was agreed to. Telegrams were thereupon dispatched in the name of all the Governments concerned to Tokyo and Nanking reminding the Japanese and Chinese authorities of their international obligations under the Kellogg Pact, urging them to refrain from fighting each other and proposing terms for the solution of their differences – the withdrawal of Japan from the territory she had occupied and the guarantee by

China of security conditions within this territory. The Council thereupon adjourned to allow the parties to consider these terms and to await their replies.

By the time the League met again to consider the matter, the National Government had been reconstituted and Reading was no longer Foreign Secretary. He could only bewail in private the ineffectiveness of the League's resolutions, which were unable to prevent a militarily powerful Japan from overrunning Manchuria, bombarding Shanghai and creating the puppet state of Manchukuo.

4

Ramsay MacDonald's decision to ask the King to dissolve Parliament so that a General Election could be held, was taken at a Cabinet meeting on the evening of October 5, 1931, just before Reading left for his meetings with the French Ministers in Paris. Both Reading and Samuel argued strongly in favour of postponing the election, since the National Government's work could hardly be regarded as complete. The Prime Minister and the Labour members seem to have been of the same mind. But the Conservatives were insistent, and rather than face the break-up of the Cabinet caused by the withdrawal of the Conservative element MacDonald yielded to its pressure. Later the same night a formula was found by which the National Government would appeal to the country for a 'doctor's mandate', which was to embrace every kind of cure for the country's economic ills, even if necessary a cautious dose of tariffs, although it was agreed that the word 'tariffs' was not to be stressed in any joint manifesto the Government might address to the electorate. At the same time each of the three parties was left free to issue its individual manifesto, while the Prime Minister came out with a general pronouncement drawn in such vague terms that everyone could assent to it. As one Conservative put it, 'the appeal to the country would be made by a National Government which has adopted a Conservative policy'.

The election returns, which were declared three weeks later, resulted in an overwhelming victory for Ramsay MacDonald and his National Government supporters, who numbered 558 in the new House of Commons. Of these 68 were Liberals, nearly evenly divided on the question of tariffs, Samuel's followers being faithful to their Free

Trade principles and Simon's being converted to Protection, but united in supporting the National Government. The small Labour Opposition, numbering only 52, was augmented by Lloyd George and three followers who had declined to associate themselves with the National Government's election campaign.

The composition of the new Cabinet, which reverted to its normal size, proved of no little difficulty to MacDonald, especially in the face of the Conservative Party's demands for key positions for their men. When the list of the new appointments was completed on November 9, it was seen that Reading's place as Foreign Secretary had been filled by Sir John Simon and that Reading had dropped out of the Government altogether. According to his son, Reading suddenly found himself superseded without any warning from the Prime Minister of his intention to replace him. However, other evidence indicates that Reading's retirement was voluntary and that he put his office at the Prime Minister's disposal, along with other over-seventies in the earlier caretaker administration, such as Austen Chamberlain and Lord Crewe.[1]

Reading admitted afterwards that he was also feeling the strain of the work. 'I liked both the office and the officials with whom I was in closest contact very much indeed,' he told his old war-time friend Arthur Murray. 'I only gave up because I knew I was at breaking point.' The pity was, of course, that Reading was Foreign Secretary for too short a time – barely two-and-a-half months – for him to have made any real impact in the field of policy, beyond establishing friendly personal relations with the principal European ministers and their representatives in London. It is worth noting that Eden, who stayed on as Under-Secretary, was to find Simon a less satisfactory chief to work for in spite or perhaps because of his 'remarkable intellectual gifts'.

As events turned out, Reading got no respite from work, since the Indian Round Table Conference had reassembled in London and Reading was still in charge of the Liberal delegation. The Conference, which naturally tended to be overshadowed by the current economic crisis, proved a sad disappointment. This was due partly to communal differences between the Indian delegates as to the composition of the provincial legislatures under the new constitution and partly to the suspicions of the Native Princes that they might be swamped in the proposed Federal Assembly. The Congress Party

[1] Avon, p. 22.

delegates refused to agree to the withholding of responsibility for defence and foreign affairs even for a transitional period; and when Gandhi, who attended this session, saw that it was impossible to secure general agreement on the structure of an All-Indian Federation, he ceased to make any serious contribution to the discussions. There was a considerable stiffening of the British Government's attitude towards the proposed safeguards for minorities, particularly after the Election, and this was reflected in the general atmosphere of deadlock.

Reading, who realized the inherent danger in the break-up of the Conference without being able to agree upon a federal constitution for India, did his best to impress upon Ramsay MacDonald where his Government's duty lay. He wrote to MacDonald on November 28, 1931:

> I feel bound to state my view that, if serious trouble in India is to be avoided, the Government's essential task is to convince the Indian representatives at the Round Table Conference of the determination of the Government to carry out its promises and of the willingness of Parliament to support it in fulfilling them. . . .
>
> What is the alternative? That the British Indian representatives should return sullen, disappointed and suspicious of Britain's good faith. Civil disobedience may be restarted. Communal troubles may grow worse. Political India will inevitably throw the blame upon the Government. We shall drift into an era of repression and 'strong Government' with no real friends.

At the same time he urged the Prime Minister not to let the Conference die but to keep it in being by reconvening it the following winter so as to work out questions of finance and the details of the new Indian franchise.[1] Eventually the Prime Minister announced that unless Indians themselves could produce a constitutional scheme acceptable to all parties, then the British Government would have no alternative but to apply a provisional one drawn up in London.

Once more Reading's dismal forecast proved correct. Gandhi and his associates were now confronted with a less sympathetic Viceroy than Irwin in the person of Lord Willingdon, who had had some experience of the Mahatma's tactics when he was Governor of Bombay. Within a short time of Gandhi's return to India, civil disobedience started up again, Gandhi was rearrested and imprisoned

[1] Samuel Papers.

and during the next few months 34,000 of his supporters found themselves likewise behind bars.

Reading was now thoroughly exhausted – he had had only one week's rest in an extremely strenuous year – and his doctors insisted that he should take a prolonged holiday. He eventually decided on a voyage with his wife to Palestine and Egypt, neither of which countries he had previously visited, except for travelling from Port Said to Suez with a brief overnight stop in Cairo on his way to India. They went first to Palestine. Although he had never been a Zionist, he had supported the Balfour Declaration, and he was now eager to see what progress had been made by the Jewish settlers under the British Mandate. His name and achievements were enough to secure him a warm welcome from his co-religionists, and he and his wife were cheered when they were recognized by the crowds in the streets of Jerusalem and Tel Aviv. On December 27, at Haifa, he delivered a public address on the first anniversary of Lord Melchett's death, frankly admitting that what he himself had done for the Jewish National Home was very largely the result of Melchett's inspiration.

From Alexandria he followed the usual visitor's route up the Nile. Unfortunately he got no farther than Luxor, where he was stricken with double pneumonia and lay gravely ill for many weeks. However, thanks to the skill of a Swiss doctor and the devoted nursing of his wife and several trained nurses he gradually recovered.

He was back in Curzon Street by the following spring, after a short convalescence in Lord Inchcape's yacht in the Mediterranean, and he resumed his work in the House of Lords and the board-room with little if any noticeable falling away of his powers. In October, 1932, he was able with his wife to accept an invitation, as the official representative of the Bench and Bar of England, to the laying of the foundation stone by President Hoover of the new Supreme Court building in Washington. The Americans appreciated his visit, the last he was to make to their shores.

Reading and his wife returned to England by way of Ottawa, where they were the guests of Lord Bessborough, the Governor-General, at Rideau Hall. As befitted an elder statesman, he accepted an invitation from the Canadian Prime Minister, Mr Bennett, to address members of both Houses of the Canadian Parliament at an informal luncheon in the Parliament Buildings. He ranged widely over such questions as tariffs – the Ottawa Conference agreements had recently been concluded – war debts and disarmament. True to his Free Trade principles, Reading urged that the interpretation of these agreements 'should be guided rather by the spirit of mutual co-operation than by the narrow letter of the actual documents'. He also touched on War debts and disarmament. As to the latter, he remarked, with considerable foresight, that 'the nations of the world must face genuine disarmament or be prepared to face further disastrous conflicts'.

Reading reached London again in time to take part in the third and final session of the Round Table Conference, which was mainly concerned with technical questions of constitutional law. Far fewer delegates attended than in the two previous sessions, and Gandhi's chair was conspicuously empty. The Conference, which eventually broke up for good on Christmas Eve, 1932, gave birth to the project of a Federation of All-India, but there were many incidental matters which remained unresolved, particularly concerning minority safeguards and the terms on which the Native States would come in. The truth was that the Princes' original enthusiasm for Federation had rapidly waned when they realized that, if they joined a Federal system, they must surrender a measure of their sovereignty. Their shortsightedness and mutual jealousies were to spoil the scheme's chances of success.

But first, the federal scheme had to be digested by Parliament and then incorporated in a fresh Government of India Act. As Lord Lothian, the first Under-Secretary for India in the National Government, expressed it, the country was sick to death of committees and inquiries and wanted a decision and action without further delay. However, British democracy is a slow working process, and before Sir Samuel Hoare's Bill could be drafted there were to be many long and weary hours devoted to the discussion of the basic features of this contemplated legislation in a Joint Select Committee of Parliament. The Committee on which Reading served sat almost continuously from April, 1933, until November, 1934, holding 159 meetings in all and examining 120 witnesses. Reading conscientiously attended and participated in all its deliberations, greatly sapping his energies in doing so. When the resulting Government of India Bill, which eventually passed into law in August, 1935, was before the House of Lords, he was equally assiduous in debate, his final speech which he insisted on delivering contrary to his doctor's orders being practically inaudible as a result of an attack of laryngitis. Realistic to the last, it was largely as the result of his insistence that the controversial phrase 'Dominion status' – 'this foolish and deceiving declaration', as Birkenhead had once dubbed it – was omitted from the preamble to Hoare's measure.

On the whole the British people took little interest in the long-drawn-out process by which the measure eventually reached the statute book. Such interest as existed was due not to the intrinsic merits of the measure, but to the unrelenting opposition displayed against it by Mr Winston Churchill and his die-hard Conservative group in the House of Commons. Churchill emerged from the struggle defeated and discredited, estranged from the bulk of his own party and detested by the Labour Members and also by many of his former Liberal colleagues. To Reading and most others at the time he seemed a man with no political future, and surprising as it may appear in the light of hindsight, when Baldwin, who replaced Mac-Donald as Premier in June, 1935, thought of strengthening the Government before the next General Election, it was to Lloyd George who had recently come out with a blueprint for the future ('The Council for Action for Peace and Reconstruction') that his thoughts momentarily turned rather than to Churchill who seemed to be living in the past glories of the British Raj in India.

If Reading was out of sympathy with Churchill over India, he shared his apprehensions over the rise of Adolf Hitler and his National Socialist followers in Germany and the spread of their pernicious anti-Semitic propaganda. He was naturally horrified to learn of Nazi atrocities against the Jews openly encouraged by the man who had now become German Chancellor. He publicly denounced this persecution in the House of Lords, and begged the Government to take some action.

Three years previously Reading had helped to found the Anglo-German Association to promote better understanding between the two countries, and became the Association's President. He now resigned this office as a protest against the conduct of Hitler and his Nazi Brownshirts. He hoped, too, that his gesture in accepting as a prominent British Jew one of the most ancient and venerable public offices in England would not be lost upon the Germans.

Early in 1934, Lord Beauchamp, who had been living abroad for personal reasons, at last resigned the office of Lord Warden and Admiral of the Cinque Ports, and Ramsay MacDonald, who was still Prime Minister, offered it to the man whom he had been unable to reappoint as Foreign Secretary after the General Election. It was a very ancient office dating back to before the Norman Conquest when the original 'Five Ports' (Hastings, Romney, Hythe, Dover and Sandwich) banded themselves into a confederacy through a common interest in fishing, being granted special privileges by Edward the Confessor in return for supplying the King with ships. The two 'ancient towns' (Rye and Winchelsea) were added to the confederacy in the twelfth century, and in the course of time about thirty other places in Kent and Sussex and one in Essex (so-called 'limbs') were attached to the head ports to help with ship service; for instance, Deal was a 'limb' of Sandwich. By the reign of Edward I the office of Lord Warden, which was in the King's gift had become one of permanent authority over the Cinque Ports and their appendages and was usually held for life. To reinforce the coastal defences, Henry VIII built the three fortress castles of Walmer, Deal and Sandown, as has already been noted, and Walmer later became the headquarters of the Lord Warden who was responsible, particularly when an invasion was feared, for raising troops as well as seeing that the Cinque Ports produced their quota of ships. The younger Pitt, who was Lord Warden during the Napoleonic Wars, was very active in this respect and spent long periods at Walmer. So, too, later in the nineteenth century, did the Duke of Wellington, who died there, although by his time the Lord Warden's duties had become almost entirely ceremonial and the £3,000 salary which the office used to carry had been abolished. Besides Pitt and Wellington, Reading's predecessors included five other Prime Ministers (North, Liverpool, Palmerston, Salisbury and Asquith), two Viceroys of India (Dalhousie and Dufferin), and a Foreign Secretary (Granville), who was responsible for the 'Scotch baronial' addition which gave thirteen extra rooms to the living quarters. The attractive gardens, much larger than those of near-by Deal Castle, were laid out by Pitt's eccentric niece and confidante Lady Hester Stanhope, who also commanded the local defence force, both naval and military, when the Lord Warden was away. Reading was said to be the 156th Lord Warden and the first Jew to hold the office.

His installation took place in Dover with all the traditional cere-monial on June 30, 1934, in the presence among others of the Prime Minister, Foreign Secretary, Archbishop of Canterbury, the fourteen Mayors of the Cinque Ports Confederacy and its 'limbs', and the Judge of the Court of Shepway, the Cinque Ports' peculiar Court of Justice. After a service in the Church of St Mary, Dover Castle, where the Archbishop delivered an address, the installation ceremony was concluded in the Court of Shepway, which met in Dover College, once the Priory of St Martin. Here the Lord Warden, wearing the cocked hat and full uniform of his office, solemnly swore 'to maintain the franchises, liberties, customs and usages of the ports', whereupon the Lord Warden's flag was broken at the flag-staff outside and the battery of Dover Castle fired a salute of nineteen guns. More speeches followed at a luncheon in the Town Hall, to which Ramsay MacDonald, John Simon and the new Lord Warden all contributed.

5

Reading thoroughly enjoyed himself at Walmer, which the Duke of Wellington once described as 'the most charming marine residence' he had ever seen. Although it was not so close to the sea as Deal Castle, the living quarters were more commodious, and the large dining-room and drawing-room with their curious coloured window-panes, said to have been put in by Lord Liverpool about the time of Waterloo to spare his wife's eyesight, led on to a large bastion terrace with a splendid view of the sea and the coast of France in the distance. The new Lord Warden was fascinated by the Castle's historical associations, and he liked to invite his friends to visit it and see the historic rooms, Pitt's study with its unusual library chair which the reader bestrode like a horse, resting his arms and the book on the back, and Wellington's simple bed-cum-workroom with its spartan couch and high desk at which he liked to work standing up. Queen Victoria spent a month at Walmer with the Prince Consort when Wellington was Lord Warden. 'The Duke' had a large plate-glass window put in so that she could have a better view of the sea across the ramparts, as well as new furniture including a mahogany four-poster double bed with yellow hangings. This room, with the contents still very much as they were in the Queen's time, Reading appropriated for himself.

Much of the remaining eighteen months of Reading's life was to be spent in these congenial surroundings. At Christmas, 1934 – his first and last at Walmer – he had a large family house-party. 'He was in exuberant spirits and enjoyed every moment, and his examination of the contents of his stocking was as excited as it might have been if stockings had come his way seventy years before. His only trouble was his voice. The hoarseness which had descended upon him some months earlier refused to yield to any treatment and he was difficult to hear, except in an otherwise silent room. This disability worried him greatly for he realized that it might be permanent. . . .'[1] Unfortunately it was a disability of advancing age which proved incurable and virtually put an end to his public speaking. His last appearances in the House of Lords, when he spoke on the Government of India Bill were as pathetic as they were inaudible.

Although he did not fully appreciate it, time was taking its physical toll of him as it was of his contemporaries. Shortly before he went down to Walmer for this last happy Christmas, he was driving through the London streets with his son Gerald. Looking out of the car, Reading's eye lit on a news poster announcing the death of Lord Buckmaster, the former Liberal Lord Chancellor with whom Reading had sat in Parliament for many years, first as M.P. and later as appellate judge in the Lords. 'That is the real tragedy of growing old,' he remarked, 'that your friends drop off one by one. I sometimes look round the House of Lords at my contemporaries, and I notice this one failing in one way and that one in another, and I wonder whether they themselves are conscious of it. And then I wonder whether it is all the time happening to me without my knowing it.'

What he dreaded above all things was losing his faculties and lingering on a hopeless bed-ridden invalid. Fortunately he was spared this experience, for when death claimed his friend Buckmaster he himself had barely twelve months left of life. He got through that winter well enough. He was glad to be able to attend and indeed participate in the Silver Jubilee celebrations of King George and Queen Mary, in May, 1935, the service in St Paul's Cathedral, and the presentation of loyal addresses from both Houses of Parliament in Westminster Hall.

Except for an occasional brief visit to London, he spent the whole of the summer at Walmer, carrying out the Lord Warden's relatively light duties and receiving visits from his friends. One visitor that summer was Sir Herbert Samuel, still the Liberal Party Leader but no longer a member of the National Government from which he had resigned on the issue of protection, although he and Reading continued to support the Government on other matters of policy, such as the need to rearm in the face of Germany's growing air strength. They discussed Lloyd George's 'Council of Action for Peace and

[1] Reading, Vol. II, p. 371.

WITH THE SECOND LADY READING

Outside his London house on the day before their marriage, August, 1931 *(Radio Times Hulton Picture Library)*

LORD WARDEN AND ADMIRAL OF THE CINQUE PORTS

Inspecting the Silver Oar, his official wand of office, on his installation at Dover Castle, August 30, 1934 *(Radio Times Hulton Picture Library)*

Reconstruction' about to be launched by the ex-Premier ostensibly as a 'non-political campaign for peace and prosperity', but in reality as a means of hitting back at Baldwin, who had now succeeded MacDonald at 10 Downing Street and was thought to be contemplating a General Election. Reading advised cautious support and thought the true Liberals distinct from the Liberal Nationals would be in favour of a campaign which was endorsed by such intelligent Conservatives as Lord Robert Cecil and Mr Harold Macmillan as well as by the Labour leader George Lansbury. 'Although it is expressed to be non-political, it is not so, as it makes appeal to all candidates, etc,' he pointed out when he had read Lloyd George's manifesto. 'How can the pursuit of peace and the remedies of unemployment be separated from politics? Of course, what is meant is free from party. It may be taken as an assault upon the present Government.'[1] As an assault it was not undeserved, since there were still a million and a half unemployed, while in Europe the rearming of Europe presaged the coming of another large-scale war. However, in the event the Council of Action proved a flash in the pan.

At the beginning of September, the Lord Warden made what was to be his last public speech, when he opened the Cinque Ports Fête at Hythe. He had hoped, with the aid of a microphone, to make some extended remarks, but he was in such poor voice that all he could do was to mutter in a hoarse whisper: 'This is the most romantic and interesting occasion, and I am very glad to be here and to declare the fête open.' But he enjoyed the inevitable mayoral luncheon and examined with genuine interest the town's charter granted by Edward I in 1278, the only one of the Cinque Ports to possess such a contemporary document. On this occasion some public argument arose as to which of the Ports took precedence over the others; but the Lord Warden refused, as he invariably did, to be drawn into any discussion which might involve him in giving an opinion as to their proper order.

Except for his throat trouble, he felt physically much better than he had for some months, and he decided to take up golf again. Since he was out of practice, he went off to a secluded part of the Royal Cinque Ports links with his regular caddie and proceeded to play off a number of balls in rapid succession as practice shots. He did not realize that this exercise put a mnch greater strain upon his frail physique than a leisurely round in the ordinary way. That night he

[1] Samuel Papers.

P

was seized with a violent attack of cardiac asthma, which nearly finished him off. Doctors were summoned and the remedies which they prescribed alleviated the effect of two subsequent attacks in the following week. The doctors told him he must resign himself to staying in bed for some time under a régime of professional nursing. For weeks he lay in the large four-poster, once occupied by Queen Victoria and the Prince Consort, from which happily for him he could see the passing ships. A Finnish barquentine with square-rigged foremast, which reminded him of the *Blair Athole*, anchored close inshore for ten days and gave him particular pleasure as he watched her swinging at her moorings. Otherwise the Poet Laureate John Masefield's sea stories served to while away the time and he would read them well into the night in spite of the nurses' remonstrances.

While Reading lay ill at Walmer, his old friend and antagonist in the Courts, Edward Carson was slowly dying of leukaemia at Cleve Court, his place near Ramsgate. Each would send the other friendly messages and wishes for recovery. Reading was convalescent when they brought him the news of Carson's death, and he was able to respond to an invitation from the Press for a short appreciation of the great Irishman. 'He never failed to win respect, even if he did not always carry conviction,' said Reading. 'He has left his mark upon history. It was at the Bar that he and I were brought into an affectionate friendship that has lasted through many years of active and often fierce conflict between us in the Courts. Nevertheless, and notwithstanding the acute political differences between us, our personal relations were never for a moment disturbed.'[1]

At this time the newspapers were full of the Italian invasion of Abyssinia, which had begun early in October, and was answered by a moderate policy of sanction on the part of the other member states of the League of Nations, acting at last in support of the principle of collective security, with the French markedly lukewarm. The more fervent champions of the League advocated the imposition of stiffer sanctions, such as the denial of oil supplies to the aggressor and the closing of the Suez Canal. The risk was that such measures might well spread the conflict. Reading longed to get back into the thick of things and find out what was going on, instead of chafing in continued inactivity. He wrote regretfully to the Liberal Party Leader, Sir Herbert Samuel:

[1] *The Times*, October 24, 1935.

Walmer Castle, Kent.
October 18, 1935

I am ever so sorry that I cannot take part in the present important and anxious deliberations. Although I feel great anxiety as to the outcome of the Government's action if unduly pressed, I cannot feel that I know enough of the inner aspects of the situation to express a general view, except that I cannot believe it would be right to close the Suez Canal against Italy as a means of enforcing sanctions.[1]

A few days later, the King dissolved Parliament at Baldwin's request and the writs went out for a General Election. As usual the election was fought largely on domestic issues, such as housing and unemployment; so far as Italy and Mussolini's Abyssinian excursion went, all parties except their more extreme members seemed to be agreed on a policy of 'all sanctions short of war'. The election campaign drew Reading back to London, for he was now tolerably well recovered and the weather at Walmer had broken, which did not dispose him to stay on there. Unfortunately the Liberals went into battle hopelessly disunited. The rift between the official party, still faithful to the Free Trade gospel, and the National Liberals led by Simon, who had swallowed Protection, was complete. As for Lloyd George he took an independent line, as the fancy moved him and his small family group. 'No one really trusts him,' said Lady Oxford, the former Mrs Asquith, at this time, 'and he hasn't a friend in the world.' The result of the election, which was declared on November 15, came as a personal disappointment to Reading. The once-great Liberal Party, which in the 1906 Parliament had mustered 377 Members, was reduced to 21, little more than a handful, including the four members of the Lloyd George family, but exclusive of the National Liberals who were now practically indistinguishable from the Conservatives.

By the beginning of December Reading had progressed sufficiently to be able to hold company board meetings at his house in Curzon Street and to put in an occasional appearance at his office in Imperial Chemical House. He followed the international situation closely in the newspapers and shared the general consternation when the news of the so-called Hoare-Laval Pact for the partitioning of Abysinnia leaked out, since he realized that this cynical piece of diplomacy meant the end of the League of Nations and the principle of collective security in Europe. But he had the satisfaction of seeing Anthony Eden, one of the League's staunchest upholders, whom he greatly

[1] Samuel Papers.

liked and with whom he had worked so pleasantly during his own brief tenure of the Foreign Office, succeeding Sir Samuel Hoare and thus becoming one of the youngest Foreign Secretaries of modern times.

In the middle of December, he suffered another severe attack of cardiac asthma.

On December 20, the newspapers carried an announcement that Lord Reading was confined to his house with a slight chill, but that his condition was 'in no way serious'. By this time it had become necessary to issue a bulletin since the news of his illness had reached the Press, but the statement was so expressed as not unnecessarily to alarm the patient who continued to read the daily newspapers, both morning and evening, with the keenest interest. During the following week his condition progressively deteriorated, so that by December 27 it was decided to send a bulletin to the evening papers to the effect that his condition was now causing anxiety. Both his wife and his son, who were keeping vigil at his bedside, did not think that he could rally sufficiently to read it. But to their surprise, he woke up in the middle of the afternoon and asked for the papers. Laval's Ministry was facing a crucial vote in the French Chamber, as a result of the Right-wing Paul Reynaud having joined forces with the Left-wing Léon Blum, and Reading wished to know the result of the division. A secretary was hurriedly sent off to Fleet Street to get hold of the earlier editions which did not contain the bulletin. Nor, for that matter, did they carry the Paris news. However, Lady Reading and her stepson were able to tell him that they had just telephoned Reuter's to learn that the wily Laval had defeated the Opposition by seventeen votes. This news satisfied his curiosity, even if it failed to give him much pleasure.

He survived three more days and nights, never apparently aware how near the end was. 'These attacks are a horrid bore,' he said to his son. 'I am afraid that, when I am fit again, I shall have to give up some of my work, instead of taking on anything new.' That night he lapsed into unconsciousness from which he never emerged. The end came peacefully the following afternoon as the street lights were being turned on. The date was December 30, 1935.

Next day many messages of sympathy were received in Curzon Street, including one from King George V, whose own death was less than a month away. 'His services to the State will always be remembered by the nation,' said the King simply. Others who paid their tributes were the Prince of Wales, Lloyd George, Herbert Samuel, John Simon, Ramsay MacDonald, Anthony Eden, Lady Oxford and Asquith, Colonel House, Pierre Laval and the Mahatma Gandhi.

On New Year's Day, 1936, in accordance with the wish expressed in his will, his remains were cremated at Golders Green and afterwards his ashes were buried near the remains of his first wife in the Jewish cemetery there. Next day, a Memorial Service was held in the Jewish Synagogue in Upper Berkeley Street, close to Reading's London home. His favourite verses, beginning with the line 'I vow to thee, my country', and composed by his predecessor in the Washington Embassy, were appropriately sung at this service. Four days later, another memorial service took place in the Christian Church of the Redemption in New Delhi.

There was some interested speculation, especially in the Temple, as to how much Reading's personal estate would prove to be worth, since stories were current at the time of his appointment as Viceroy of India that he could ill afford to sacrifice the Lord Chief Justice's pension. There was some surprise, therefore, when the publication of his will revealed that he had left nearly twice the amount left by his most successful contemporary at the Bar, Lord Carson – to be exact £290,487 11s. 9d. Allowing for the fact that he invested his savings shrewdly and with expert financial knowledge, no practising member of the English Bar has left anything approaching this figure. The record is all the more remarkable when it is remembered that Reading began his legal career owing £8,000 to his Stock Exchange creditors as a result of having been 'hammered'.

It was truly said of him when he died that he was 'fundamentally humble' and showed 'no sort of vanity' in his make up. This was the opinion of an acute woman critic, the former Margot Asquith, to whose husband when Prime Minister Reading owed all his official legal preferment. 'What differentiated him for me from other men was his nature,' she said. 'I have had friends of more rigid character and of greater intellect, but I have never known any man of a sweeter, richer nature than Lord Reading. Although very ambitious – and his ambition was always crowned with success – it never affected his character or his nature. . . . He was as considerate with strangers as he was with Kings.'

No doubt the secret of Reading's achievements lay in his unquenchable spirit of determination. This appeared in a revealing incident, trifling in itself, which occurred a few years before his death during a round of golf with his son on an unfamiliar course. After playing some holes, he put his ball on a short distance from the near side of a formidable bunker. His caddie, who knew the course and so far had not formed a noticeably favourable opinion of his master's proficiency as a golfer, gave him a piece of advice. 'You had better not go for the carry, my Lord,' said the caddie, handing him an iron. Reading waved away the proffered club, which he promptly exchanged for a spoon. 'Not go for the carry?' he exclaimed in amazement. 'I have gone for the carry all my life!'

Bibliography

A. UNPUBLISHED SOURCES

Reading's private papers are in the custody of his widow, Stella Marchioness of Reading, and have been made subject by her to the operation of the 'fifty-year rule', so that presumably they will not become available for general public inspection until 1985. Although I have consequently been unable to see them, they have already been used by the second Marquess of Reading in writing the official life of his father. Apart from a few family letters, they would not appear to contain anything of importance which is not duplicated elsewhere. Furthermore, such confidential memoranda as Reading preserved he wrote in a form unintelligible to anyone except himself; he once told Lloyd George that he employed this method to prevent them from being understood should they fall into unauthorized hands. (See above, p. 177 note.) On the other hand, he wrote many letters in his own hand, and did not keep copies. These holographs have come to light in other collections, of which the most important as well as the most voluminous is that of Lloyd George. Most of Reading's official and private correspondence and other papers as Ambassador to the United States of America and Viceroy of India are now accessible to students. These, together with the other collections which I have consulted, are located as follows:

Asquith Papers. Official and private papers of the first Earl of Oxford and Asquith. In the Bodleian Library, Oxford.

Balfour Papers. Official and private papers of the first Earl of Balfour relating to the United States of America. In the British Museum. (Add. MSS 49741)

Birkenhead Letters. Letters from the first Earl of Birkenhead as Secretary of State for India to Lord Reading as Viceroy, 1924–26. In the possession of the second Earl of Birkenhead.

Foreign Office Papers. State papers relating to the Anglo-French Loan Mission, 1915. In the Public Record Office. (F.O. 371/2589–2590)

Grey Papers. Official and private papers of the first Earl Grey of Fallodon relating to the United States of America. In the Public Record Office. (F.O. 800/45)

H. A. L. Fisher Papers. Miscellaneous papers of the Rt. Hon. H. A. L. Fisher. In the Bodleian Library, Oxford.

House Papers. Diaries and Correspondence of Colonel Edward M. House. In Yale University Library.

India Office Papers. Telegrams between the Secretary of State and the Viceroy. In the India Office Library.

Lloyd George Papers. Official and private papers of the first Earl Lloyd George. In the possession of the Beaverbrook Foundation.

Montagu Papers. Correspondence between the Rt. Hon. E. S. Montagu as Secretary of State for India and Lord Reading as Viceroy, 1921–22. In the India Office Library.

Walter Hines Page Papers. Papers of Walter Hines Page, U.S. Ambassador in London. In the Houghton Library, Harvard University.

Reading Papers. Official and private papers of Lord Reading as Ambassador to the United States of America, 1918–19. In the Public Record Office. (F.O. 800/222–225)

Royal Archives. Correspondence between Lord Reading and King George V. In the possession of Her Majesty the Queen at Windsor Castle.

Samuel Papers. Official and private papers of the first Viscount Samuel. In the House of Lords Record Office.

Simon Papers. Official and private papers of the first Viscount Simon. In the possession of the second Viscount Simon.

Wiseman Papers. Miscellaneous papers of Sir William Wiseman, tenth Baronet. In Yale University Library.

B. PUBLISHED SOURCES

The official biography has been written by Reading's son, the second Marquess (*Rufus Isaacs First Marquess of Reading*. 2 vols. London, 1942–45). Other biographies, not directly based on original material, are by Syed Sirdar Ali Khan (*The Earl of Reading*. London, 1924), C. J. C. Street (*Lord Reading*. London, 1928), and Stanley Jackson (*Rufus Isaacs First Marquess of Reading*. London, 1936). Sir Derek Walker-Smith has dealt fully with the legal side of Reading's career in

Lord Reading and his Cases (London, 1933). Short biographical sketches, based on personal knowledge, have been written by the first Earl of Birkenhead in *Contemporary Personalities* (London, 1924) and by Lord Simon in the *Dictionary of National Biography* 1931–40 (London, 1949). Reading's *Speeches* as Viceroy were published by the Government of India in two volumes (Simla, 1926). His official telegraphic correspondence with the India Office on the Moplah rebellion and the events leading up to Gandhi's arrest were published in two British Government White Papers, *Telegraphic Information, etc., regarding the Moplah Rebellion 24 August–6 December 1921* (Cmd. 1552) and *Telegraphic Correspondence regarding the Situation in India 8 February–11 March 1922* (Cmd. 1586).

Other printed sources consulted include the following:

Asquith, Margot. *Autobiography*. 2 vols. London, 1920–22.

Avon, Earl of. *The Eden Memoirs: Facing the Dictators*. London, 1962.

Baker, Ray Stannard. *Woodrow Wilson. Life and Letters*. Vols. VII and VIII. London, 1939.

Beaverbrook, Lord. *Politicians and the War, 1914-1916*. London, 1928–32.

—— *Men and Power, 1917–1918*. London, 1956.

—— *The Decline and Fall of Lloyd George*. London, 1963.

Birkenhead, Earl of. *'F.E.' The Life of F. E. Smith first Earl of Birkenhead*. London, 1959.

—— *Halifax. The Life of Lord Halifax*. London, 1965.

Blake, Robert. *The Unknown Prime Minister*. London, 1955.

Bowle, John. *Viscount Samuel*. London, 1957.

Cecil of Chelwood, Viscount. *All the Way*. London, 1949.

Churchill, Randolph S. *Lord Derby 'King of Lancashire'*. London, 1959.

Cole, Hubert. *Laval*. London, 1963.

Cooper, Duff (Viscount Norwich). *Old Men. Forget*. London, 1953.

Curzon of Kedleston, Marchioness of. *Reminiscences*. London, 1955.

Donaldson, Frances. *The Marconi Scandal*. London, 1962.

Fitzroy, Sir Almeric. *Memoirs*. 2 vols. London, 1925.

George, David Lloyd. *War Memoirs*. 2 vols, London, 1938.

—— *The Truth about the Peace Treaties*. 2 vols. London, 1938.

Grey of Falloden, Viscount. *Twenty-Five Years, 1892–1916*. 2 vols. London, 1925.

Haldane, Viscount. *An Autobiography*. London, 1929.

Hankey, Lord. *The Supreme Command*. 2 vols. London, 1961.

Hardinge of Penshurst, Lord. *The Old Diplomacy*. London, 1947.

Harrod, R. F. *The Life of John Maynard Keynes*. London, 1951.

Heuston, R. F. V. *Lives of the Lord Chancellors, 1885–1940*. Oxford, 1964.

House, Edward M. *The Intimate Papers of Colonel House*. Ed. Charles Seymour. 4 vols. London, 1926–28.

Hyde, H. Montgomery. *Carson. The Life of Sir Edward Carson, Lord Carson of Duncairn*. London, 1953.

Jackson, Robert. *The Chief. The Biography of Gordon Hewart Lord Chief Justice of England*. London, 1959.

Jenkins, Roy. *Asquith*. London, 1964.

Jones, Thomas. *Lloyd George*. London, 1954.

—— *A Diary with Letters*. London, 1954.

Keynes, J. M. *Two Memoirs*. London, 1949.

Lamont, Thomas W. *Henry P. Davidson*. London and New York, 1923.

Leslie, Shane. *Long Shadows*. London, 1966.

Lonergan, Thomas Clement. *It Might Have Been Lost!* London, and New York, 1929.

McAdoo, William G. *Crowded Years*. London, 1932.

McKenna, Stephen. *Reginald McKenna*. London, 1948.

Marjoribanks, Edward. *The Life of Sir Edward Marshall Hall*. London, 1929.

—— and Ian Colvin. *Life of Lord Carson*. 3 vols. London, 1932–36.

Masterman, Lucy. *C. F. G. Masterman*. London, 1939.

Murray, Arthur C. *At Close Quarters*. London, 1946.

Nicolson, Harold. *King George the Fifth*. London, 1952.

Owen, Frank. *Tempestuous Journey. Lloyd George His Life and Times*. London, 1954.

Oxford and Asquith, Earl of. *Memories and Reflections*. 2 vols. London, 1928.

Pershing, J. J. *My Experiences in the World War*, London, 1931.

Pound, Reginald, and Harmsworth, Geoffrey. *Northcliffe*. London, 1959.

Repington, C. A. *The First World War*. 2 vols. London, 1920.

Rice, Sir Cecil Spring. *Letters and Friendships of Sir Cecil Spring Rice*. Ed. Stephen Gwynne. 2 vols, 1929.

Riddell, Lord. *Diaries*. 3 vols. London, 1933–34. I. *More Pages from*

My Diary. II. *War Diary.* III. *Intimate Diary of the Peace Conference and After.*

Samuel, Viscount. *Memoirs.* London, 1945.

Simon, Viscount. *Retrospect.* London, 1952.

Spender J. A. and Asquith, Cyril. *Life of Lord Oxford and Asquith.* 2 vols. London, 1932.

Templewood, Viscount. *Nine Troubled Years.* London, 1954.

Waley, S. D. *Edwin Montagu.* London, 1964.

Willert, Sir Arthur. *The Road to Safety.* London, 1952.

Windsor, H.R.H. Duke of. *A King's Story.* London, 1951.

Woodward, E. L. and Butler, Rohan. *Documents on British Foreign Policy. 1919–1939.* 2nd Series. Vol. II. London, 1947.

Index